KNOWLEDGE-BASED SOFTWARE ENGINEERING

Frontiers in Artificial Intelligence and Applications

Series Editors: J. Breuker, R. López de Mántaras, M. Mohammadian, S. Ohsuga and W. Swartout

Volume 80

Previously published in this series:

Vol. 79, H. Motoda (Ed.), Active Mining
Vol. 78, T. Vidal and P. Liberatore (Eds.), STAIRS 2002
Vol. 77, F. van Harmelen (Ed.), ECAI 2002
Vol. 76, P. Sinčák et al. (Eds.), Intelligent Technologies – Theory and Applications
Vol. 75, I.F. Cruz et al. (Eds), The Emerging Semantic Web
Vol. 74, M. Blay-Fornarino et al. (Eds.), Cooperative Systems Design
Vol. 73, H. Kangassalo et al. (Eds.), Information Modelling and Knowledge Bases XIII
Vol. 72, A. Namatame et al. (Eds.), Agent-Based Approaches in Economic and Social Complex Systems
Vol. 71, J.M. Abe and J.I. da Silva Filho (Eds.), Logic, Artificial Intelligence and Robotics
Vol. 70, B. Verheij et al. (Eds.), Legal Knowledge and Information Systems
Vol. 69, N. Baba et al. (Eds.), Knowledge-Based Intelligent Information Engineering Systems & Allied Technologies
Vol. 68, J.D. Moore et al. (Eds.), Artificial Intelligence in Education
Vol. 67, H. Jaakkola et al. (Eds.), Information Modelling and Knowledge Bases XII
Vol. 66, H.H. Lund et al. (Eds.), Seventh Scandinavian Conference on Artificial Intelligence
Vol. 65, In production
Vol. 64, J. Breuker et al. (Eds.), Legal Knowledge and Information Systems
Vol. 63, I. Gent et al. (Eds.), SAT2000
Vol. 62, T. Hruška and M. Hashimoto (Eds.), Knowledge-Based Software Engineering
Vol. 61, E. Kawaguchi et al. (Eds.), Information Modelling and Knowledge Bases XI
Vol. 60, P. Hoffman and D. Lemke (Eds.), Teaching and Learning in a Network World
Vol. 59, M. Mohammadian (Ed.), Advances in Intelligent Systems: Theory and Applications
Vol. 58, R. Dieng et al. (Eds.), Designing Cooperative Systems
Vol. 57, M. Mohammadian (Ed.), New Frontiers in Computational Intelligence and its Applications
Vol. 56, M.I. Torres and A. Sanfeliu (Eds.), Pattern Recognition and Applications
Vol. 55, G. Cumming et al. (Eds.), Advanced Research in Computers and Communications in Education
Vol. 54, W. Horn (Ed.), ECAI 2000
Vol. 53, E. Motta, Reusable Components for Knowledge Modelling
Vol. 52, In production
Vol. 51, H. Jaakkola et al. (Eds.), Information Modelling and Knowledge Bases X
Vol. 50, S.P. Lajoie and M. Vivet (Eds.), Artificial Intelligence in Education
Vol. 49, P. McNamara and H. Prakken (Eds.), Norms, Logics and Information Systems
Vol. 48, P. Návrat and H. Ueno (Eds.), Knowledge-Based Software Engineering
Vol. 47, M.T. Escrig and F. Toledo, Qualitative Spatial Reasoning: Theory and Practice
Vol. 46, N. Guarino (Ed.), Formal Ontology in Information Systems
Vol. 45, P.-J. Charrel et al. (Eds.), Information Modelling and Knowledge Bases IX
Vol. 44, K. de Koning, Model-Based Reasoning about Learner Behaviour
Vol. 43, M. Gams et al. (Eds.), Mind Versus Computer
Vol. 41, F.C. Morabito (Ed.), Advances in Intelligent Systems

ISSN: 0922-6389

Knowledge-based Software Engineering

Proceedings of the Fifth Joint Conference on Knowledge-based Software Engineering

Edited by

Tatjana Welzer

Faculty of Electrical Engineering and Computer Science, University of Maribor, Maribor, Slovenia

Shuichiro Yamamoto

NTT Data Corporation, Tokyo, Japan

and

Ivan Rozman

Faculty of Electrical Engineering and Computer Science, University of Maribor, Maribor, Slovenia

IOS Press

Ohmsha

Amsterdam • Berlin • Oxford • Tokyo • Washington, DC

ISBN 1 58603 274 7 (IOS Press)
ISBN 4 274 90534 9 C3055 (Ohmsha)
Library of Congress Control Number: 2002110237

Publisher
IOS Press
Nieuwe Hemweg 6B
1013 BG Amsterdam
The Netherlands
fax: +31 20 620 3419
e-mail: order@iospress.nl

Distributor in the UK and Ireland
IOS Press/Lavis Marketing
73 Lime Walk
Headington
Oxford OX3 7AD
England
fax: +44 1865 75 0079

Distributor in the USA and Canada
IOS Press, Inc.
5795-G Burke Centre Parkway
Burke, VA 22015
USA
fax: +1 703 323 3668
e-mail: iosbooks@iospress.com

Distributor in Germany, Austria and Switzerland
IOS Press/LSL.de
Gerichtsweg 28
D-04103 Leipzig
Germany
fax: +49 341 995 4255

Distributor in Japan
Ohmsha, Ltd.
3-1 Kanda Nishiki-cho
Chiyoda-ku, Tokyo 101-8460
Japan
fax: +81 3 3233 2426

PRINTED IN THE NETHERLANDS

Foreword

The present book contains the proceedings of the Joint Conference on Knowledge-Based Software Engineering (JCKBSE) held in Maribor, Slovenia on 11th – 13th September 2002. It was the fifth of the JCKBSE conferences, a series of biannually organized events.

JCKBSE aims to provide a forum for researchers and practitioners to discuss the latest developments in the areas of knowledge engineering and software engineering. Particular emphasis is placed upon applying knowledge-based methods to software engineering problems. The Conference originated in order to provide a forum in which the latest developments in the field of knowledge-based software engineering could be discussed. Although initially targeting scientists from Japan, the CIS countries and countries in Central and Eastern Europe, JCKBSE warmly welcomes participants from all countries. JCKBSE 2002 continued with this tradition and achieved a truly wide international participation. Furthermore, the scope of the conference as indicated by its topics was updated to reflect the recent development in all the three covered areas, i.e. knowledge engineering, software engineering and knowledge-based software engineering.

The JCKBSE 2002 proceedings are a collection of contributions of authors from thirteen different countries. The book covers a wide range of topics related to knowledge-based or automated software engineering. The papers, which were selected after a standard refereeing process (at least 3 reviewers for each paper), address the major open research issues of the field, such as architecture of knowledge; software and information systems; requirements engineering; domain analysis and modeling; formal and semiformal specifications; knowledge engineering for domain modeling; data mining and knowledge discovery; automating software design and synthesis; object-oriented and other programming paradigms; knowledge-based methods and tools for software engineering, including testing, verification and validation; process management, maintenance and evolution; applied semiotics for knowledge-based software engineering; knowledge systems methodology; development tools and environments; practical applications and experience of software and knowledge engineering; information technology in control, design, production, logistics and management; and enterprise modeling, workflow.

For JCKBSE 2002, we initially received 51 submissions that came from 14 countries spread over 4 continents. The Program Committee finally selected 25 submissions to be included in the proceedings as full papers and 10 as short papers. Quality and originality were the main criteria for the selected papers. The Program Committee also wanted to give a chance to the papers that present and discuss an interesting idea, but need an additional work and in-depth evaluation of the results. The Committee selected 6 such submissions that fall into the category of position papers.

The whole volume is structured into the following sections, which reflect the major themes of the JCKBSE 2002 event:

- Software Architecture, Applied Knowledge Engineering,
- Knowledge Modeling and Reasoning,
- Program Understanding, Reuse, Knowledge Discovery,
- Knowledge-Based Methods and Tools for Software Engineering,
- Knowledge Management for Business Processes,
- Position Papers.

At this place, we express our sincerest gratitude to the Program Committee members for the responsible and hard work done by reviewing the contributions. To the authors of the papers we owe a great debt of thanks for contributing their ideas and research results, and for the effort in producing the final versions. We would also like to thank IOS Press for publishing the proceedings.

Many people helped us to make the conference as friendly as possible for the participants. The local organizing committee recruited from the Database Technologies Laboratory of the Faculty of Electrical Engineering and Computer Science at the University of Maribor. We would like to express our sincerest gratefulness to the student members of the Lab, Božidar Drozg, Aida Kamišalič, Aleš Vrabič and Dušan Zarić for their superb work on the conference web system and for being available for other jobs that always needed to be done immediately. Our acknowledgement goes also to Boštjan Brumen who supervised the conference activities.

Tatjana Welzer, Shuichiro Yamamoto and Ivan Rozman
Editors

Conference Organization

Organizers
University of Maribor, Faculty of Electrical Engineering and Computer Science, Institute of Informatics, Slovenia
SIG-KBSE, The Institute of Electronics, Information and Communication Engineers, Japan

Co-operating Institutions
IEEE Tokyo Section Computer Chapter
Japanese Society of Artificial Intelligence
Russian Association for Artificial Intelligence

General Chair
Ivan Rozman, University of Maribor, Slovenia

JCKBSE Steering Committee
Christo Dichev, Bulgaria
Morio Nagata, Japan
Pavol Navrat, Slovakia
Vadim L. Stefanuk, Russia
Haruki Ueno, Japan

Program Committee Chairs
Tatjana Welzer, University of Maribor, Slovenia
Shuichiro Yamamoto, NTT Data, Japan

Program Committee Members
Syed Sibte Raza Abidi, Dalhousie University, Canada
Andras Benczur, Eotvos Lorand University, Hungary
Maria Bieliková, Slovak University of Technology, Slovakia
Peter Brusilovsky, Carnegie Mellon University, USA
Vladan Devedzic, University of Belgrade, Yugoslavia
Christo V. Dichev, Winston-Salem State University, USA
Darina Dicheva, Winston-Salem State University, USA
Tomaž Domajnko, University of Maribor, Slovenia
Marjan Družovec, University of Maribor, Slovenia
Johann Eder, University of Klagenfurt, Austria
Ulrich W. Eisenecker, University of Applied Sciences Kaiserslautern, Germany
Yoshiaki Fukazawa, Waseda University, Japan
Matjaž Gams, Jozef Stefan Institute, Slovenia
Jozsef Györkös, University of Maribor, Slovenia
Masa-aki Hashimoto, Kyushu Institute of Technology, Japan
Jaak Henno, Tallinn Technical University, Estonia
Behrouz Homayoun Far, University of Calgary, Canada
Masahiro Hori, IBM Tokyo Research Laboratory, Japan
Kenji Kaijiri, Shinshu University, Japan
Ahto Kalja, Tallinn Technical University, Estonia

Sponsors
Slovenian Ministry of Information Society

Contents

Program Understanding, Reuse, Knowledge Discovery

Software Architecture, Applied Knowledge Engineering

Knowledge Modeling and Reasoning

Position Papers Panel

Knowledge-based Methods and Tools for Software Engineering

Knowledge-based Software Engineering
T. Welzer et al. (Eds.)
IOS Press, 2002

Applying the MAS-CommonKADS Methodology to the Flights Reservation Problem: Integrating Coordination and Expertise

Alvaro E. ARENAS, Gareth BARRERA-SANABRIA
Laboratorio de Cómputo Especializado, Universidad Autónoma de Bucaramanga
Calle 48 No 39 –234, Bucaramanga, Colombia

Abstract. This paper applies the MAS – CommonKADS methodology to the flights reservation problem. We develop each model included in this methodology, illustrating the complete development of both the coordination and expertise models. We incorporate UML activity diagrams in the task model and use sequence diagrams to model communication between agents (human and software) and to detail the participation of each agent. We illustrate the implementation of the system using AGLETS, an agent building tool, and emphasize its integration with JESS, the Java Expert System Shell.

1 Introduction

The flights reservation problem is a benchmark one in the development of multiagent systems [1, 4]. The problem consists in building a flight-booking system that gives back the cheapest available flights upon consultation. The construction of this kind of systems brings challenges such as the use of distributed information, the definition of trustable criteria for flight selection, learning from the user preferences and getting short response times. Typical examples are Apollo, SABRE, System One AMADEUS and Teleport Travel [5].

This paper describes a solution to this problem using the MAS-CommonKADS methodology for the development of multiagent systems [4]. We make special emphasis on the conversation between agents (the *coordination model*) and the description of the knowledge needed by the agents to achieve their goals (the *expertise model*).

MAS-CommomKADS [4] comprises seven models that cover the main aspects in the development of multiagent systems. The *agent model* specifies agent characteristics such as reasoning capabilities, sensors/effectors, services, agent groups and hierarchies. The *task model* describes the task that the agents can carry out, for instance goals, decomposition, problem-solving methods, etc. The *expertise model* defines the knowledge needed by the agent to achieve their goals. The *organisation model* describes the social organisation of the agent society. The *coordination model* illustrates the conversation between agents. The *communication model* details the human-software agent interactions. The *design model* includes, in addition to the typical action of the design phase [6], the design of relevant aspects of the agent network, selecting the most suitable agent architecture and the agent development platform.

The next section illustrates the application of the methodology to the study problem. Section 3 describes the implementation of the system using AGLETS [10] and JESS [2]. Finally, section 4 gathers some concluding remarks.

2 Applying the Methodology

The models described previously will be developed below.

2.1 Conceptualisation

An initial phase corresponds to the conceptualisation. This phase aims to carry out an elicitation task to obtain a general description of the problem by following a user-centered approach based on use cases [8]. In this approach, an *actor* represents a role played by a person, a piece of hardware or another system that interacts with our system. A *use case* corresponds to a description of the sequence of actions needed to produce an observable result useful for an actor. Table 1 describes the actors and identified use cases.

Actor	Description	Use Cases
Client	Person who wishes to travel	Introduce profile; Request flight availability; Select recommendation; Book; Confirm/Cancel reservation
Travel Agent	Select and recommend flights, given a client profile	Select flights; Determine recommendations; List recommendations
Flights Database	Database system with information about flights, seat availability and prices	Provide information about flights

Table 1: Actors and use cases

The outcome of this phase is a description of the different actors and their use cases. As an example, Table 2 describes the use case *Select flights* for actor *Travel agent*.

Use Case *Select Flights* **Summary.** *Travel Agent* takes the information given by the *Client* and searches for similar information into the different airlines databases, finally giving a set of possible flights that the client may book. **Actors.** *Travel Agent* and *Flights Database*. **Preconditions.** Sufficient information about client profile and have access to the airlines databases. **Exceptions.** Do not find information of flights or erroneous/ incomplete information of client profile.

Table 2: *Select flights* use case for *Travel agent* actor

2.2 Analysis

In this part we apply the first six models of MAS-CommonKADS in order to obtain a specification of the requirements of the multiagent system.

Central to the methodology is the agent model, which specifies the characteristics of an agent, and plays the role of a reference point for the other models. An agent is defined as any entity – human or software – capable of carrying out an activity. The identification of agents was based on the use cases diagrams generated in the conceptualisation. Such an identification could be augmented in the task model. The agents identified in the agent model are:

- **Client agent**: Human agent who interacts with the system by providing basic information such as his/her profile and flight information.
- **Database agent:** Software agent (one for each participating airline) that obtains flight information from the database of its associated airline.
- **Flight selection agent**: Software agent which determines the most suitable flights for a client.
- **Reservation agent:** Software agent that receives the request for a flight reservation and is in charge of either confirming or cancelling the reservations.

The methodology defines textual templates for each constituent in order to describe it. For instance, Table 3 presents the template for the *Flight selection* agent.

Agent *Flight Selection (Class Recommendation)*
Name. Flight Selection **Type**. Software agent. **Role**. Information provider. **Location**. Inside the agent society. **Description**. This agent determines the best alternatives according to the service requested by a client, providing him a list with choices taken. **Objective**. Provides to users, a list of possible flights and their related classes, that match the needs described in a profile. **Exceptions**. Absence of available information about flights and classes that match the profile. **Input parameters**. User profile, and information provided by DataBase Agents. **Output parameters**. Possible flights recommendations. **Services**. Brings information related to recommendations, making the reservation process easier. **Expertise**. This agent must know the profile of the client who requests the service, the flight data and the available classes, in order to apply heuristics to the flights recommendation process. Also, it must store all information about already given recommendations, and about the user profile that has generated those recommendations, so that the learning process may start. **Communication**. Client Agent. **Coordination**. DataBase Agents.

Table 3: *Flight selection* agent textual template

Let us now turn to the task model that describes the tasks that the agents can carry out. Since MAS-CommonKADS does not include a graphic structure for modelling tasks, we use UML *activity diagrams* [8] to represent the activity flows and the textual template to describe the task (name, short description, input and output ingredients, task structure, etc). Figure 1 shows the *activity diagram* for the *Flight selection* agent and (along with) its corresponding textual template.

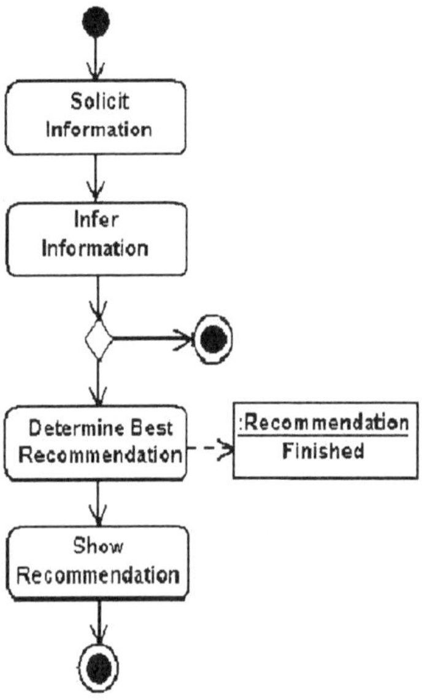

Task *Infer Information*
Objective. Compare the information given by the Client Agent to the information provided by the DataBase Agents.
Description. Getting the flights information from the DataBase agents, flights selection agent could start the inference process to the given information, aiming to determine the flights recommendations.
Ingredients. Information related to flights, classes and user profile.
Constrains. None
Exceptions. Absence of flights or profile information

Task *Determine best recommendations*
Objective. Determine best recommendations related to a given client profile.
Description. Taken the flights selected in the infer information task, flights selection agent organizes and structures this information, looking for the best recommendations.
Ingredients. List of all available flights to reserve.
Constrains. None
Exceptions. None

Figure 1: *Flight selection* agent *activity diagram* and its corresponding textual template for the main activities

As shown in Figure 1, the *Flights selection* agent initiates the process of information request to the *Database* agents; then it infers this information in order to determine all available flights and their corresponding classes. In the absence of available flights, the agent terminates the process; otherwise it proceeds with the selection of the best recommendations, updating this information in the *Recommendation* class. Finally, it provides the user with a list of the best selection results.

In the *organisation model*, we show the static or structural relationships between the agents. Following [4], we use a graphical notation based on OMT [7] to express these relationships, adding a special symbol in order to distinguish between agents and objects.

Figure 2 illustrates the class agent diagram for our agent system. Here, an upper box does not store the defined attributes (as in OMT) but instead the mental and internal attributes of an agent.

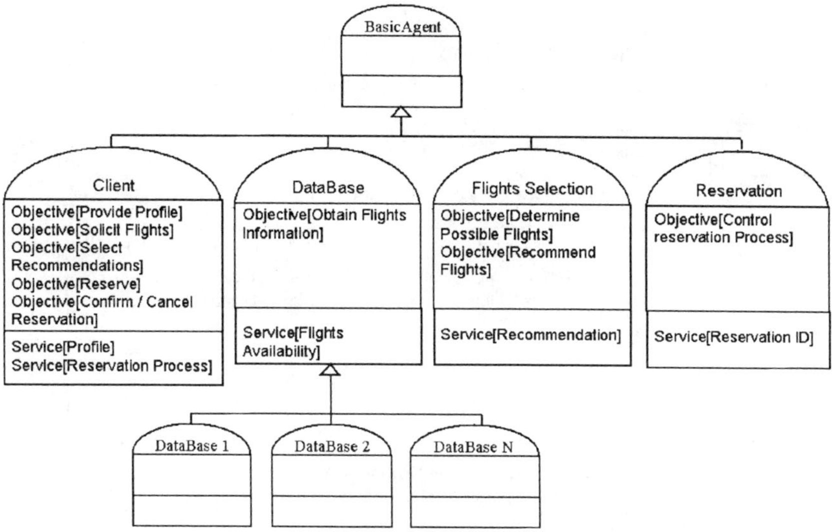

Figure 2: Class agent diagram for the flight reservation system

Unlike the *organisation model*, the *coordination model* shows the dynamic relationships between the agents. In this model we begin with the identification of the conversations between agents, where *use cases* play again an important role. At this level, every conversation consists of just one single interaction and the possible answer, which are described by means of templates as illustrated in Table 4.

Conversation ***Determine Flights***

Type. Getting information.
Objective. Get available flights and classes according to a given profile.
Agents. Flight Selection, Data Base, Client.
Beginner. Flight Selection.
Service. Available flights and classes, according to the described client profile. This is the information about flights that the customer can book.
Description. This agent determines which flights or schedules are available, as well as the existing classes for these flights. in order to do this, the agent keeps in touch with the Data Base Flights and Client agents. The Flight Selection agent has a limited time to get information about other agents. In case there is a timeout, the agent should know it on time, in order to immediately send a message to the Client agent, notifying that it was not possible to finish the recommendation search.
Precondition. Information of available flights.
Postcondition. List of possible flights recommendations to book.
Ending condition. Process aborted by the customer or absence of information about flights and classes that match client profile.

Table 4: Conversation *determine flights* textual template

Next, we model the data exchanged in each interaction by specifying speech acts and the synchronisation type. We collect all this information in the form of *sequence diagrams* and textual templates as shown in Figure 3. A second phase in the *coordination model* consists in analysing the interactions in order to determine their complexity (we do not emphasize this phase due to lack of space).

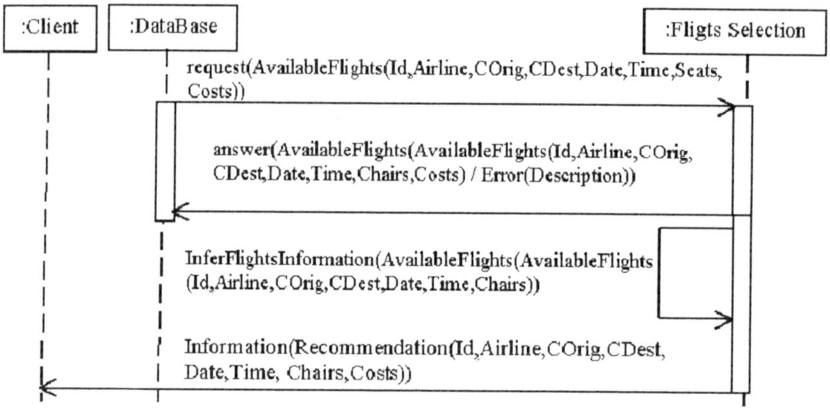

Figure 3: *Flight selection* agent *sequence diagram*

In our case, the *communication model* only includes interactions between the *Client* agent (human agent) and other agents. We use templates similar to those of the *coordination model*, but taking into consideration human factors such as facilities for understanding the recommendations given by the system.

The *expertise model* is split into the development of the application knowledge and the definition of the problem solving method [3]. In order to develop the application knowledge, we determine the domain knowledge, which defines the ontologies and models of the domain; the task knowledge, which specifies the knowledge needed by a task to reach its goals; and the inference knowledge, which represents the inference steps needed to solve a task. In our case study, the domain knowledge consisted of a set of concept definitions. The task knowledge is represented in Table 5.

Agent	Generic Task	Knowledge
Client	None	None
DataBase	None	None
Flights Selection	- Look for similar profiles done previously. - Infer information of flights, classes and profiles.	- Previous Recommendations. - Client profile. - Available flights. - Available Classes.
Reservation	- Make reservation	-Recommendations information. - Available seats.

Table 5: Generic tasks of the flights reservation system

We use an *inference diagram* to model the inference domain. Figure 4 illustrates the case of our most complex task: that of the flight selection.

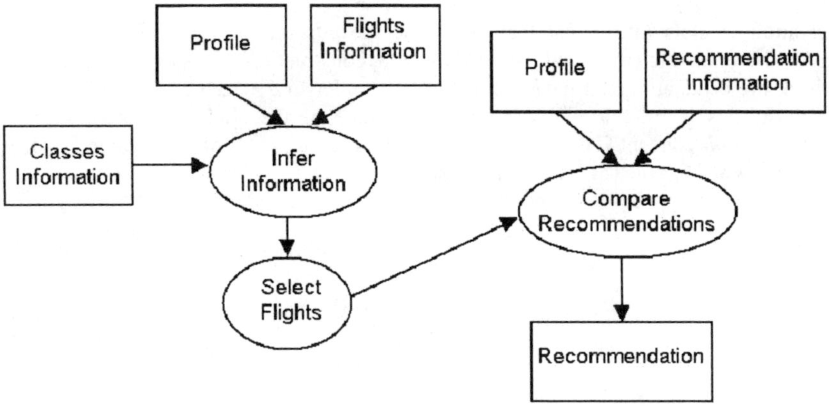

Figure 4: *Flights selection* task *Inferences diagram*

In Figure 4, the boxes represent information sources, the ovals illustrate the inferences made by the *Flights selection* agent and arrows indicate information flows between the information sources and the inferences. In this figure, the *Flights selection* agent takes the information related to flights and the user profile information, in order to determine the existing flights. Following, it combines the existing flights with the previous recommendations, in order to identify user preferences and provide new recommendations.

In the definition of the problem solving method, we use ASSESSMENT as the methodology to generate schemes for organising the knowledge [9]. This methodology includes the representation of the relevant knowledge (i.e. the knowledge that generates special actions in the system, for instance special discounts for senior citizens), the definition of norms that guarantee integrity (for instance, the number of reserved seats cannot be greater than the total number of seats in the flight), and its definition in a representation language. We use the language associated to JESS as the representation language, as illustrated in Table 6.

Client Concept	**Students Discount Rule**
(deftemplate client (slot name) (slot id) (slot IdType) (slot address) (slot age) (slot email) (slot occupation))	(defrule studentdiscount (profile (occupation ?x)) (test (eq ?x "student")) => (recommendation (Cost ?cost)) (recommendation (student ?discount)) (bind ?rate (- ?cost (* ?cost ?discount))) (recommendation (topay ?y)) (recommendation (topay (- ?y ?rate))))

Table 6: Knowledge representation using JESS syntax

Table 6 illustrates the construction of the *Client* concept and the *Students Discount* rule, using JESS as a representation language. The *Client* concept (left-hand side) involves the creation of slots (attributes) that determine the concept structure. Furthermore, the *Students Discount* rule (right-hand side) shows the construction of a simple rule, in which we check the occupation slot of a client profile in order to determine whether he/she is a student. If this is true, it will determine the value of the student discount from the *Recommendation* concept. The new value to be paid is the result of the subtraction of the student discount from the (full) price of a non-student ticket.

2.3 Design

The *design model* consists of the design of the agent network, the agent and the platform. The agent network consists of a set of agents that maintain the network, knowledge and coordination facilities (for example, yellow and white pages services, encryption, ontology servers, protocol servers, etc). In our case study, we do not use any facilitator agent, so that this design is not defined.

As part of the process of agent design, we determine the most suitable architecture for each agent by decomposing each agent in modules for user communication (from the *communication model*), agent communication (from the *coordination model*), deliberation and reaction (from the *agent, expertise* and *task models*). Figure 5 describes the design of *Flight selection* agent.

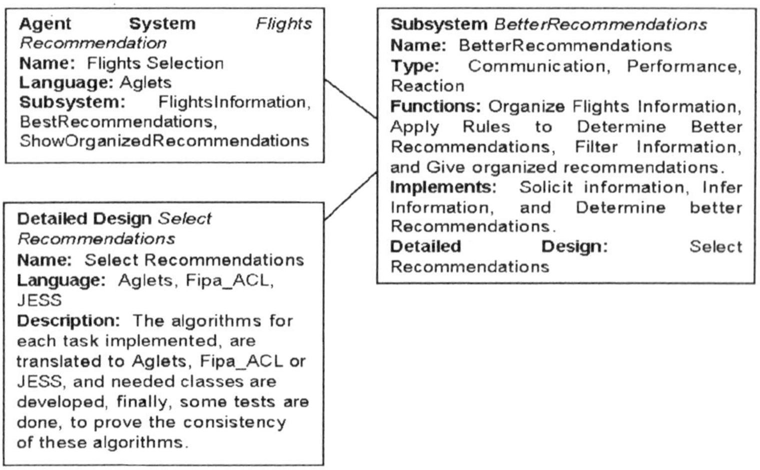

Figure 5: Design of *Flights selection agent* and some of its subsystems

3 Implementation

The implementation and test phases are not part of the methodology, since they depend on the employed platform. The first step in the implementation consisted in the construction of the user interface, based on an interface flow diagram generated from the *communication model*, as shown in Figure 6.

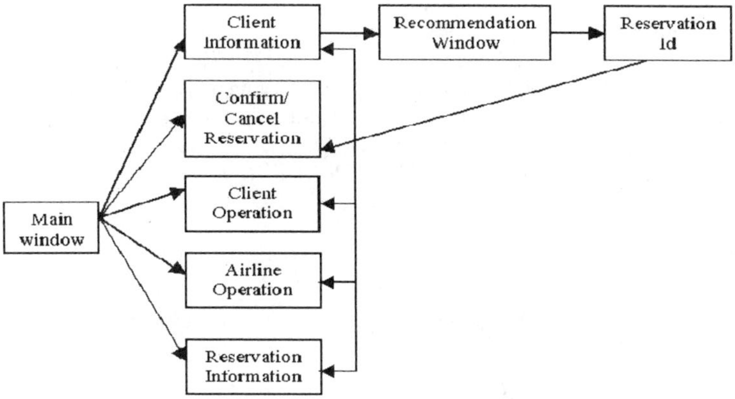

Figure 6: Flights reservation system interface flow diagram

Each interface element activates a process developed by either an agent or a specific class. We employed Java as the programming language for the implementation of the agent and classes, and AGLETS [10] as our agent development platform.

To include the expertise, we use JESS, the Java Expert System Shell tool [2], which consists of a set of Java classes in order to building and operating knowledge databases, following an object-oriented approach. The experience of combining coordination and expertise through AGLETS and JESS was very positive, and the fact that both were based on Java facilitates the whole process.

4 Conclusions

The agent-based approach to system development offers a natural means of conceptualising, designing and building distributed systems. The successful practice of this approach requires robust methodologies for agent-oriented software engineering. This paper applies MAS-CommonKADS, a methodology for agent-based system development, to the solution of the flights reservation problem. We have developed each of the models included in the methodology and illustrated the implementation of the system using AGLETS and JESS.

MAS-CommonKADS has been used previously to solve this problem [4]. However, our solution includes new features such as UML *activity diagrams* in the task model, a complete development of the expertise model, and an illustration of how to integrate aspects of coordination and expertise in the implementation using AGLETS and JESS. Another solution to the problem is presented in [10] using FIPA-OS. It differs from our solution in that it uses a role-centered approach to identify agents, expressing the knowledege by ontologies and emphasizing the communication process by using FIPA-ACL.

The work presented here is part of an ongoing project aiming to compare and extend different methodologies for multiagent system development. MAS-CommonKADS covers all relevant aspects of a software development method. The output of the design model corresponds to a description close to the implementation. It contrasts with other methodologies such as GAIA [11], where the output of the design phase is more abstract.

Acknowledgments

The authors are grateful to Carolina Rodriguez-Buitagro for her contribution to the development of the system prototype. Thanks also go to Jesús Pérez-Alcazar and Juan Carlos García-Ojeda for valuable comments and criticisms. This work was partially funded by the Colombian Research Council (COLCIENCIAS-BID).

References

[1] Foundation of Intelligent Physical Agents – FIPA. Personal Travel Assistance Specification. FIPA architecture board. 2000.

[2] E. Friedman. The Java Expert System Shell, Distributed Computing Systems, Sandia National Laboratories, Canada, 1997.

[3] C. A. Iglesias, Definición de una Metodología para el Desarrollo de Sistemas Multiagentes. Universidad Politécnica de Madrid, España, 1998

[4] C. Iglesias, M. Garijo, J. Centeno-Gonzalez, J. R. Velasco. Analysis and Design of Multiagent Systems Using MAS-CommonKADS. Agent Theories, Architectures, and Languages. Lecture Notes in Artifical Intellegence. Vol. 1365, pages 313-326. Springer-Verlag. 1998.

[5] M. Kantrawitz, Air Travel's Handbook. Available in www-2.cs.cmu.edu/afs/cs.cmu.edu/user/mkant/public/travel/html/online.html

[6] R. Pressman, Software Engineering: A Practitioner's Approach. 5 ed. McGraw – Hill College Div, 2001. p. 387 – 424

[7] J. Rumbaugh, M. Blaha, W. Premerlani , F. Eddy, W. Lorensen. Object-Oriented Modeling and Design. Prentice Hall. 1991.

[8] J. Rumbaugh, I. Jacobson, G. Booch, The Unified Modelling Language Reference Manual. Addison Wesley 1999.

[9] G. Schreiber *et al,* Knowledge Engineering and Management : The CommonKADS Methodology. Cambridge, Massachussets : A Bradford Book, 2000. 455 p.

[10] H. Tai, K. Kosaka. The Aglets Project. Communications of the ACM. Vol 42, number 3, 1999.

[11] M. Wooldridge, N. Jennings, The GAIA Methodology for Agent – Oriented Analysis and Design. Kluwer Academic Publishers, Boston, 2000.

Knowledge-based Software Engineering
T. Welzer et al. (Eds.)
IOS Press, 2002

Flexible Distributed Agent System and Its Application

Hideki HARA[†], Kenji SUGAWARA[†], Tetsuo KINOSHITA[‡] and Takahiro UCHIYA[‡]
† *Faculty of Information and Computer Science,*
Chiba Institute of Technology, Narashino, Japan
‡ *Research Institute of Electrical Communication,*
Tohoku University, Sendai, Japan

Abstract. In this paper, we discuss an agent-based computing framework called DASH Framework which supports the design and implementation of flexible distributed systems. The aim of our research is to establish a new design methodology of the flexible distributed systems based on agent-based computing technology. We also present an intelligent music deliver system as an example system using DASH. This system observes network configration, network band-width, PC configration of a user who wants to listen music to convert a format of music data to a suitable one automatically. So the user can receive a music data suitable for his/her PC environment even if he/she has little knowledge about PC.

keywords: intelligent agents, rule-based language, flexible system, component repository

1 Introduction

Distributed systems that can provide various services are desired by the users living in the networked information spaces. In the real world, the distributed systems confront with various perturbations of their functions which are caused by the changes of both the users' requirements and operational conditions of the system's environment. As a result, the quality of service of such systems is changed and degraded along with these changes of the systems.

Recently, the studies aiming this problem have been started in the fields such as the advanced information networks [1][2][3][4] and the distributed multi-media application systems [5][6][7][8]. In order to provide the user-oriented, intelligent and stable services for users, a distributed system should have a mechanism to maintain the quality of service against various changes observed in the system's operational environment. With this mechanism, a distributed system has a capability to deal with the fluctuating operational environment, and we call such a distributed system a flexible distributed system.

In this paper, we discuss an agent model and its architecture called DASH, and a framework which supports the design and implementation of flexible distributed systems.

2 DASH Agent Model

To realize an agent-based distributed system, the functional components of a distributed system are designed and implemented as the agents which work cooperatively to realize the users' requirements based on knowledge of both the structure and functions (services) of respective agents. To do so, we propose a design model of an Distributed Agent System, named *DASH*.

The features of the DASH model can be summarized as follows;

(1) **Agentification of software components:** The functional components of distributed systems have been designed and implemented as the computational processes called *base processes* in this paper, that run on the platforms of distributed systems. Acquiring knowledge of a design of a base process, the functions to manage and control the base process as an agent are defined and combined with the base process. In the DASH model, this kind of agent is called *primitive agent*. An operation to define a primitive agent is called *agentification* of a base process. The DASH agent architecture provides an agentification mechanism for designers.

(2) **Requirements-driven design:** According to the users' requirements, the primitive agents can be combined each other to make an organization of agents which provides the requested services for users. In an organization of agents, there exists an agent which is responsible to manage and control an organization and its members. This kind of agent is called *organizational agent*. The hierarchical construction of services can easily be designed by defining an organizational agent which holds several organizational agents as its members. Hence, the design of distributed system is reformed into the design of the agents and the organization of agents based on the users' requirements.

(3) **Reuse of assets:** It is useful to provide the existing sets of both organizational agents and primitive agents for designers in advance, because the designers can select suitable agents which have the required services and functions, and also reuse these agents to construct the target distributed system. The reuse-based design is one of effective methods to develop the design object in an efficient and systematic way. Using agentification operation, the existing useful base processes can be defined as the primitive agents. The organizational agents can also be defined to reuse the design cases of services/functions of distributed systems. Accumulating and reusing the assets based on the DASH model, the reuse-based design of distributed system can be promoted.

Under the DASH model, an DASH is designed as an organization of agents which consists of both the primitive agents and the organizational agents. The organization of agents can work as an intelligent software robot which provides the required services for users. Moreover, an DASH can cooperate with the other DASH to deal with the complex tasks. Such an organization of DASH can be considered as a society of intelligent software robots.

3 DASH Agent Architecture

An DASH agent architecture depicted in Fig.1 is introduced to design and implement the primitive and organizational agents. An agentification mechanism consists of three functional modules, i.e., 1) *Communication Module* (CM), 2) *Knowledge Module* (KM), and 3) *Action Module* (AM).

The CM provides the communication functions not only to exchange information between agents but also to construct/reconstruct the organization of agents. The CM

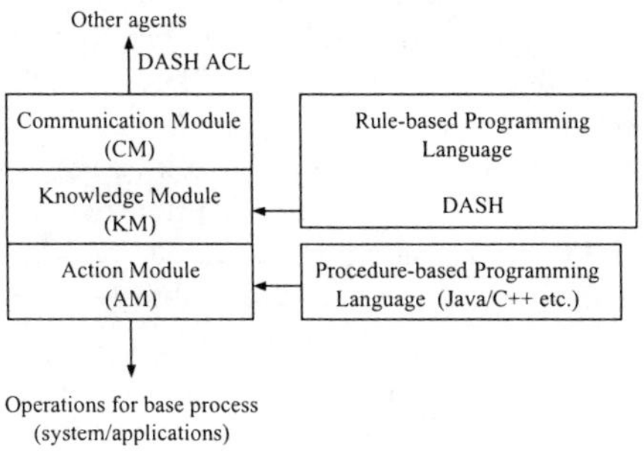

Figure 1: DASH Agent Architecture

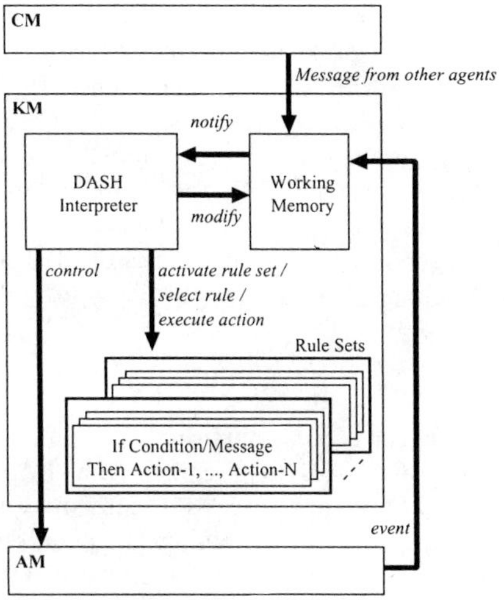

Figure 2: Structure of KM of DASH agent

uses two kinds of communication protocols, i.e., *DASH organization/reorganization protocol* (DORP) and *DASH communication/cooperation protocol* (DCCP). The details of the protocols are explained in the next section.

The AM is responsible to execute and control a task assigned to an agent via the communication between CM and KM. An AM of a primitive agent is responsible to manage the task execution done by its base process. In an organizational agent, an AM is responsible to manage and control the execution of subtasks assigned to the members of its organization.

The KM holds knowledge and knowledge processing mechanisms to control whole behavior of an agent. As shown in Fig.2, a KM is a modified production system consisting of rule interpreter (*DASH Interpreter*), *Working Memory* and *Rule Sets*. A Rule Set holds a set of rules (heuristics) which deal with a task required by a user or other agents. KM can switch sets of rules according to the situations of the agents. For example, when the agents determine to change the structure of the organization it has managed, a rule set for remaking organization is going to be activated. When an agent receives a message from other agent, the message is transformed into a description (a fact form of a production system) and stored in the Working Memory. An event happened in the environment of the agent is also transformed by AK into a description and stored. The message and the event are dealt with by the suitable rule set respectively.

The agents work on the DASH virtual machine installed on the Java virtual machine on a OS. The whole of the modules on a PC/WC is called a *DASH Workplace*. Agents can communicate each other and move to other workplaces.

To realize the essential functions of flexible distributed systems, various knowledge have to be represented and stored in the agents. For instance, the functional specifications of base processes, the heuristic to control the base processes and the organization of agents, the strategies to cooperate with other agents and so on, are acquired and represented as the agent scripts by using a Rule Set. Moreover, many kinds of knowledge processing mechanisms can be defined and utilized as the message processors to make an agent intelligent. Depend upon the capabilities of the KM, the designers can develop various agents from deliberative type to reactive type.

4 DASH Framework

The DASH Framework is an agent-based computing environment to implement and execute the DASHs based on various users' requirements. The DASH framework, which is a practical version of ADIPS Framework[9][10][11], consists of three subsystems as shown in Fig.3. 1) *DASH Workplace* (DW) is an agent operational environment. 2) *DASH Repository* (DR) is a mechanism to manage and utilize the reusable agents. 3) *DASH Design Support* (DDS) provides the facilities for designers to design and implement various agents based on DASH model.

From a viewpoint of implementation of the DASH Framework, the agents are classified into two types of agents, i.e., *class agent* and *instance agent*. An agent stored in the DR is called a class agent that is designed as a primitive/organizational agent and managed as a reusable component of DASH in the functional class hierarchies. On the other hand, an agent run on the DW is called an instance agent that is generated as an instance of a class agent in the DR to realize an executable component of DASH.

An DW is allocated as an agent operational environment on a distributed platform. According to the structure and functions of an DASH to be designed, a lot of DWs can be installed on many platforms.

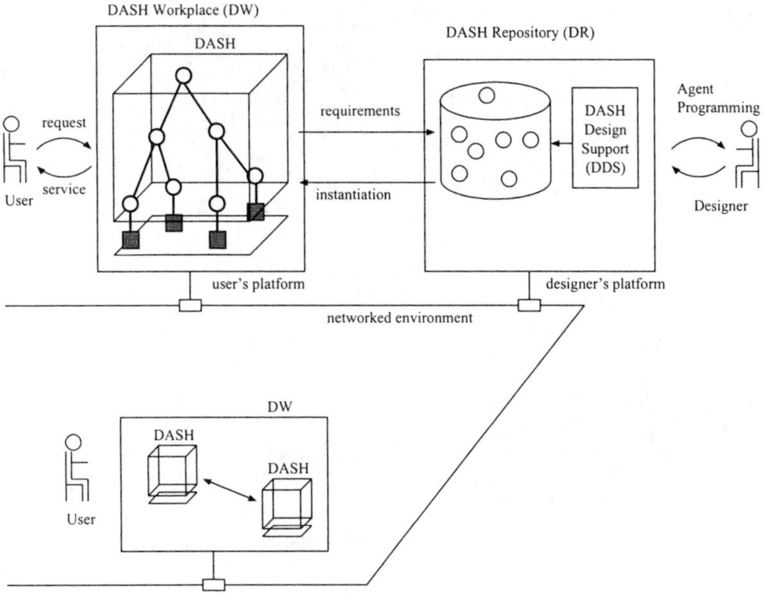

Figure 3: A Framework of DASH

The instance agents of an DASH are created from the class agents stored in DR by using the *DASH organization/reorganization protocol* (DORP). For instance, a user sends a message for requiring a new service to a user agent in DW. The user agent sends a message for creating the requested service into an DR run on the other platform. Responding to the message, the DR creates the suitable instance agents on the designated DW. Activating the instance agents, the requested service is provided for the user. Due to the requests of the instance agents or the users, the DW can also remove the useless instance agents using the DORP.

The instance agents run on the DWs can communicate with each other by using the DASH communication/cooperation protocol (DCCP) which has a set of the customized performatives of the agent communication protocol of KQML.

The DR and DW work together cooperatively based on the DORP. As explained above, the DW sends a message of requesting a service to the DR. In the DR, the received message is sent to the class agents to construct an organization of agents that can provide the requested service. Although this process is basically the same of a task-announcement-bidding process of the contract net protocol, the DORP is defined as a unique inter-agent communication protocol for construction/reconstruction of DASH's agents.

In the DASH Framework, the construction of an organization of agents is regarded as a design task of the required service of the DASH. The DR is responsible not only to determine the whole structure of organization of agents that can provide the required service for users, but also to generate the instance agents of the designed organization in the DW. Moreover, it is required to reconfigure the DASHs to maintain the required services against various changes of both the users' requirements and the system environment, as explained in section 2. In such a case, the DR and the DW work cooperatively

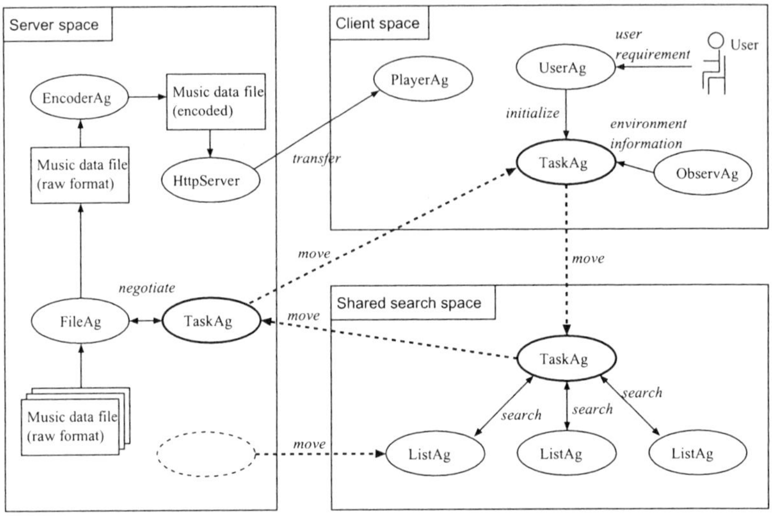

Figure 4: An overview of example system

to reconstruct the organization of instance agents based on the DORP. For example, when an organizational agent in the DW detects the irregular situations and issues a message to replace some of members of its organization, this message is sent to the DR. In the DR, several class agents are selected and instantiated again to reconstruct the corresponding organization of agents based on the DORP.

5 DASH Application

We have developped an example application system to evaluate DASH framework. This application receives users' requests about music. Requests is, for example, a title of music, a time limit to start listening music, and so on. Then some agents working on DASH workplaces start searching music data, encoding music data and transfering encoded music data to the user. In this process, agents observe conditions of user's PC environment, for example, network bandwidth, playable music format, and decide suitable encoding format considering the conditions. Our example system consists of some DASH workplaces and mobile agents as shown in Fig. 4.

Server space is DASH workplace where many music data files are stored. There are some server space. Music data files stored each server spaces are different. *File agent (FileAg)* has information about music data files, such as file size, encoded format, quality and so on. FileAg gives ListAg all information about music data. When TaskAg comes to the server space, FileAg negotiates with TaskAg and select suitable music data file. This file is sent to EncoderAg. *Encoder agent (EncoderAg)* converts raw format music data file to encoded format music data file using an audio CODEC in the server space. Encoding parameters, such as bit rate, file size, are decided by FileAg and TaskAg when these agents negotiate. Encoded music file are transfered to the client space as http contents by HttpServer. In the server space, FileAg, EncoderAg and TaskAg cooperate to encode music data file and transfer it to the client space as shown in Fig.5(a).

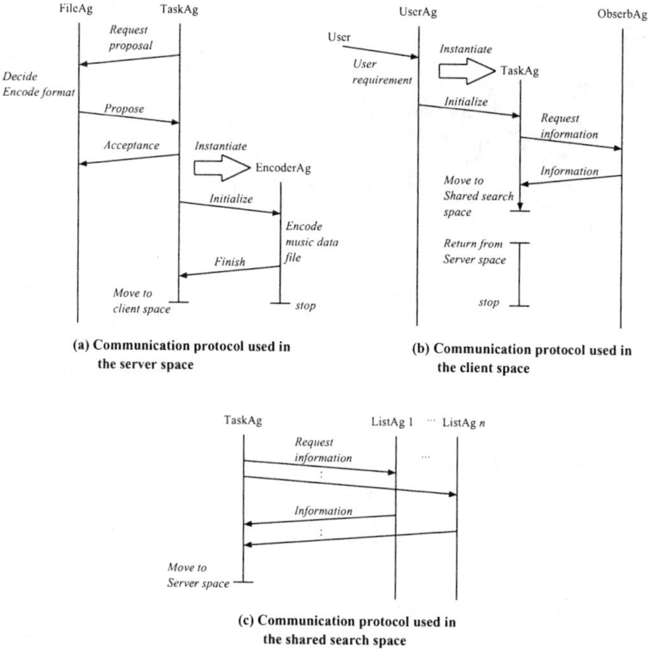

Figure 5: Communication protocol

Client space is a workplace for user. *User agent (UserAg)* receives user requirement in the client space. A users inputs their requirements such as a music title, a limit time to start listening music, and so on. UserAg receives their requirement via user interface and send it to TaskAg. *Observation agent (ObservAg)* keeps staying on the client space to watch user's PC environment such as a name of operating system, amount of memory, network bandwidth, and so on. These information are send to TaskAg. *Player agent (PlayerAg)* residents in the client space. This agent receives encoded music data files sent from the server space and playbacks music for the user. When this system starts, agents in the client space communicate using a protocol as shown in Fig.5(b).

Shared search space is a workplace where TaskAg searches a workspace that stores the music files that matches user's request. In this space, the TaskAg that has moved from the client space communicates with list agents to find a server space where music data file that satisfies user's request is stored. *List agent (ListAg)* receives information about music data files in the server space from FileAg when start up this system. Then, ListAg moves to the shareed search space to communicate with TaskAg that search a server space where suitable music data file is stored. *Task agent (TaskAg)* is a mobile agent. First, TaskAg is instantiated from DASH Repository DR into the client space and initialized to satisfy user requirements. Then it moves to the shared search space, the server space and the client space in turn. After that, TaskAg leaves from the client space and stop its activity. When TaskAg moves to the shared search space, TaskAg asks ListAgs where the music data file is stored that is suitable for user's requirement as shown in Fig.5(c). Then TaskAg moves to the server space that stores the music file.

If the TaskAg find a server space where the music data is stored, it moves to that server space and negotiates to the FileAg to find suitable encoder for user's PC environment. After encoded music file are transfered to client space, the TaskAg moves to the client space and wait for user's request again.

We implement and evaluate the application system described above. It is cleared that our agent application system can

- find an environment where suitable music file are stored, and
- convert music files into other format thar is suitable for both user requirement and users PC envilonment.

6 Conclusion

In order to realize the next generation distributed systems, we propose a design model of flexible distributed systems called DASH and its design support environment called DASH Framework, in this paper. Various agents can be designed and implemented using knowledge embedded in respective agents together with the agentification mechanisms and the agent execution mechanisms of the DASH Framework. At present, many problems remain as our future work, e.g., a ease-of-use knowledge representation and manipulation mechanisms for intelligent agent, the design support functions, an effective design method of agent-based system, and so on. However, we confirm that the DASH Framework is useful to make a conventional distributed system flexible in order to deal with the changes of both the users' requirements and the system environment through the experiment of prototypical applications.

References

[1] Feldhoffer, M., "Model for Flexible Configuration of Application-oriented Communication Services", Comp. Commun, 18(2), (1995) 69-78.

[2] Magedanz T., et al, "Intelligent Agents: An Emerging Technology for Next Generation Telecommunications?", Proc. INFOCOM'96, (1996) 1-9.

[3] Shiratori, N., Sugawara, K., Kinoshita, T., Chakraborty, G., "Flexible Networks: Basic concepts and Architecture", Trans. Comm. E77-B(11), IEICE (1994) 1287-1294.

[4] Sugawara, K., Suganuma, T., Chakraborty, G., Moser, M., Kinoshita, T. and Shiratori, N., "Agent-oriented Architecture for Flexible Networks", Proc. the Second International Symposium on Autonomous Decentralized Systems, (1995) 135-141.

[5] Campbell, A., Coulson, G. and Hutchison, D., "A Quality of Service Architecture", Computer Communication Review 24(2), ACM SIGCOM (1994) 6-27.

[6] Vogel, A., Kerherve, B., Bochmann, G. and Gecsei, J., "Distributed Multimedia and QoS: A Survey", Multimedia Mag. 2(2), IEEE (1995) 10-19.

[7] Nahrstedt, K. and Smith, J.M., "The QoS Broker", Multimedia Mag. 2(1), IEEE (1995) 53-67.

[8] Turletti, T. and Huitema, C., "Videoconferencing on the Internet", IEEE/ACM Trans. on Networking 4(3), IEEE (1996) 340-351.

[9] Fujita, S., Sugawara, K., Kinoshita, T. and Shiratori, N., "Agent-based Architecture of Distributed Information Processing Systems", Trans. IPSJ 37(5), (1996) 840-852.

[10] Fujita S., Sugawara K., Kinoshita T., Shiratori N., "An Approach to Developing Human-Agent Symbiotic Space", Proc. Second Joint Conf. on Knowledge-based Software Engineering, JSAI&RAS, (1996) 11-18.

[11] Kinoshita, T., Sugawara, K., Shiratori, N., "Agent-based Framework for Developing Distributed Systems", Proc. CIKM'95 Workshop on Intelligent Information Agent, ACM-SIGART (1995).

Knowledge-based Software Engineering
T. Welzer et al. (Eds.)
IOS Press, 2002

Sub-optimal Journey Supported by Agents

Aleksandar Takači , Mirjana Ivanović
Institute of Mathematics,
Faculty of Science,
Trg Dositeja Obradovića 4,
21000, Novi Sad, Yugoslavia,
takacsi@eunet.yu, mira@im.ns.ac.yu

Abstract. One of the fields where agent-oriented programming techniques can be successfully applied is the travel ticket reservation problem. This paper presents one travel ticket system and reports the progress made in its implementation in Java. Besides the travel ticket reservations, the system is capable of sub-optimal journey selection. Generally, the system consists of three types of agents: agents located at stations/airports (facility agents), agents performing the parallel search for optimal journey (travel agents), and agents providing geographical information (geographical agents). The agents are geographically distributed all over the world. They communicate with each other and allow user access through the Internet. In this paper, an idea how to implement a travel agent using fuzzy reasoning to accomplish the sub-optimal journey is presented.

1 Introduction

The massive expansion of Internet has led to a broader use of Agent-oriented methodologies. The idea to have a computer program do most of your work and represent your interests as good as possible, or even better than you could, makes agent oriented methodologies an attractive field. Multi-agent systems(MAS) are systems that consist of many agents who either work together to accomplish a common goal or they act in the best interest of their owner/maker. Agent in the MAS should have role which they play in the MAS (buyer, seller, information), and also should communicate with each other using a protocol characteristic for that MAS. The most common applications of MAS are the market (agents buy or sell goods trying to make the best deal), airports(agents that represent planes and the control tower coordinate with each other in order to land the planes) and many other. One of the often mentioned applications of multi-agent systems is the travel ticket reservation problem. In this paper an approved version of MAS to be used in travel agencies will be presented.

Generally, in the proposed MAS there are three types of agents:

- agents located at stations/airports (facility agents),
- agents performing the parallel search for optimal journey (travel agents),
- agents providing geographical information (geographical agents).

The papers focus is on intelligent techniques that agents should use in selecting the sub-optimal journey. Agents use fuzzy reasoning in order to accomplish their tasks.

The paper is structured as follows: in Section 2 a short description of a system is given, in Section 3 the fuzzy reasoning that a travel agent uses for finding the sub-optimal journey is described, in Section 4 an example is shown and Section 5 concludes this paper.

2 Multi-Agent Global Travel Agency

The multi-agent system for sub-optimal journey selection and ticket reservations which will be described in this paper consists of several big-sized agents. Although most of the tourist MAS are intended to work world wide, having agents in every town in the world, the proposed system can be implemented on a smaller area as a prototype.

A great advantage of a multi-agent approach in design, implementation, and maintenance of a large area system over the centralized one is the avoidance of inherent problem complexity. Every agent "knows" only his local information, thus avoiding a system with inherent complexity. As it is common for MAS, agents communicate with each other in order to complete the tasks demanded by a user(passenger).

The prototype multi-agent system for sub-optimal journey selection and ticket reservations contains three types of agents:

- travel agents,
- facility agents,
- geographical agents.

The general structure of the system is based on a proposition that every town in the area has at least one travel agent. User (passenger) communicates with travel agent using World Wide Web (WWW). Depending on the importance of its town, every travel agent has some level of importance for the whole system. On the other hand Every traveling facility (airport, see-port, train-station, bus-station, etc.) has its particular facility agent.

Facility agent 'knows' the timetable of arrivals and departures from the port or station where it is located. It is also able to make or cancel a ticket reservation. Travel agent uses a facility agent, but it can be accessed directly as well, through the WWW.

Every geographical area has been supplied with a geographical agent. For example, every country has its geographical agent. The purpose of a geographical agent is to provide geographical information. A geographical agent informs a travel agent about the nearest more important towns of a given town. It can also obtain the Internet address of a travel agent of any town in the system. Geographical agents cooperate among themselves when necessary.

When a user asks a travel agent for the sub-optimal journey from the place where they are located to any place in the world, the travel agent starts parallel search involving other agents in the system. The journey found in most cases consists of several parts. For every part of the journey the travel agent can make ticket reservation.

One of the good qualities of the system is its scalability and graceful degradation. New agents can be added to the system as time goes by and thus increasing its performance and usefulness.

For the implementation of a prototype system based on proposed Global Travel Agency, Java programming language is used. In the prototype agents of each of the three types are implemented. The implementation is deeply based on the Java package LASSMachine, which is a tool for agent programming.

An agent programmed using the package LASSMachine possesses its beliefs, intentions, services, plans for service executions, behaviors, and meta-capabilities. It is 'aware' of time and it can be accessed via WWW. More detailed description of LASSMachine is given in [1,2,3]

2.1 Travel Agent

Travel agents communicate with users and they have the main role in the parallel search for the sub-optimal journey and in the tickets reservation process.

Some of the travel agent services are:

1. WEBSERVICE - enables users to access a travel-agent through the WWW. A WEBSERVICE asks user to select the destination of their journey, to enter the constrains, and to select the criterion for the optimum value.

There are three types of constrains:
a. avoidance of particular means of transportation (e.g. airplane),
b. avoidance of particular towns,
c. avoidance of particular areas (e.g. due to visa problems).

The criterion for journey optimum value can be:
d. minimal expenses
e. minimal traveling time
f. cost lower(or around) the given sum
g. less(or approximately) time than given.

After obtaining user specification, a WEBSERVICE initiates the search. The search result will be presented to user, which can then ask the agent for travel tickets reservation. The ticket reservation may not succeed, because in the meantime someone else can reserve the ticket that the user wants to reserve, and there are no more tickets available. Then the second best solution is offered to the user, repeating the process.

2. GETJOURNEY - searches for the sub-optimal journey from the town where the agent is located to the given town. The service has the following input parameters:
a. *dest* - the destination town of the journey,
b. *constrain type* - parameter that specifies the type of the constrain,
c. *constraint parameters* - value of parameters characteristic for the constrain type.

GETJOURNEY is the most complex service in the system.

```
IF destination is directly reachable THEN
  select the optimal departure;
ELSE
IF starting town is less important than desti-
nation THEN
  get journeys from every superior town of the
starting town to destination;
  add to each journey the journey from
starting town to the corresponding superior
town;
  select the optimal journey;
ELSE
  obtain superior towns of destination (ask Ge-
ographical agent);
  get journey to all of these towns;
  add to each journey its remaining part to
destination; select the optimal journey;
END
END
```

Listing 1. Pseudo code of GETJOURNEY service

The pseudo code [Listing 1] shows that searching for the sub-optimal journey is a task executed using parallel search. The selection of the optimal journey will now be explained.

First, journeys which do not satisfy a, b, c type constrains will be eliminated, which is a relatively simple programming task. If a constraint which of d and e type is given, the journey with the minimum price/traveling time is picked.

In this paper the focus is on f and g type constrains and how to choose the sub-optimal journey according to them.

3 Choosing the sub-optimal journey

For representing approximately like "approximately 10 hours" and "around 200 euro" fuzzy numbers are used.

Fuzzy numbers are special mappings from $\mathbb{R}$ to [0,1], see [12]. The Gaussian numbers are given by a well known formula

$$G(x) = e^{-(x-a)^2/d}.$$

Transformed Gaussian fuzzy numbers [fig 1, 2] will be used. The transformation

$$f(x) = \begin{cases} 0.5G(x), & 0.5 < x < 1; \\ -0.5G(x) + 1, & 0.5 > x > 0. \end{cases}$$

or $f_1(x) = -f(x) + 1$ is applied on depending on weather values higher or lower than the optimal are preferred.

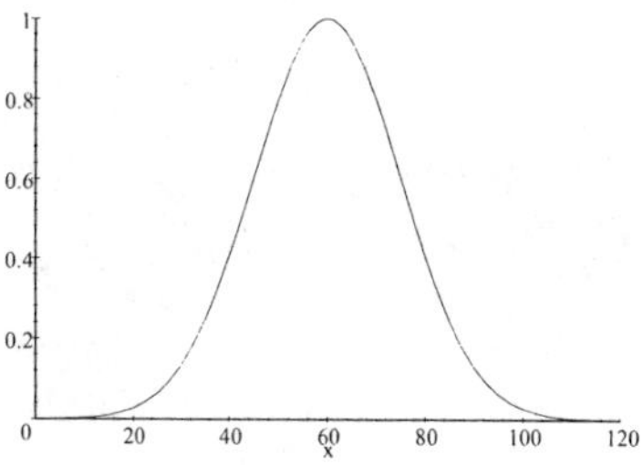

1. The Gaussian fuzzy number

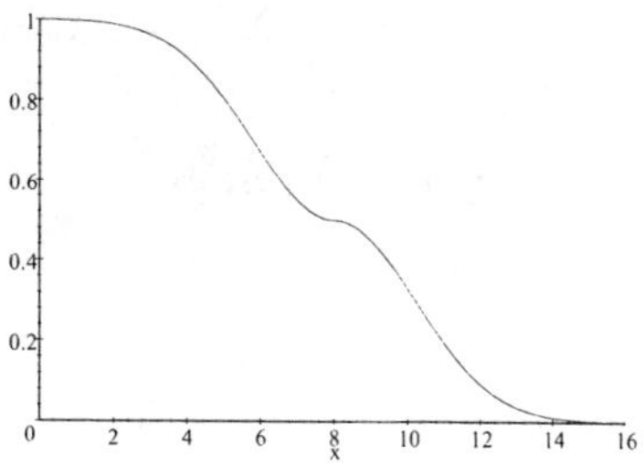

2. The transformed G(x)

The constant a is determined by the parameter of the constrain. The constrain has also an importance parameter i, an integer between 1 and 5. The constant $d = \frac{3}{20}a^2(1 - \frac{i}{10})$, where the formula has been obtained experimentally.

Since two constraints are given (price, traveling time) two values between [0,1] will be acquired from each input. The problem is how to aggregate the previous two values. Since the optimal values have the truth value of 0.5 a uninorm with the unit element 0.5 will be used. A uninorm is a commutative, associative, non-decreasing by components mapping from $[0,1] \times [0,1]$ to $[0,1]$, with a unit element e between 0 and 1. For more information on uninorms one can consult Chapter 9 of [12].

Naturally, the uninorm that suits our needs should be strict, meaning if $x > y$ then $U(x,z) > U(y,z)$, and also should prefer values closer to the optimal meaning for example the trip that costs 90 euros and lasts 11 hours should be aggregate over a trip that costs 80 euros and lasts 12 hours (if the importance factors of the price and journey length constrain are the same and 10 hours and 100 euro are the optimal values). The uninorm generated from this mapping will be used:

$$u(x) = \begin{cases} \ln(1-x), & 0.5 \leq x < 1; \\ -1.5\ln(x), & 0.5 > x > 0. \end{cases}$$

where $U(x,y) = u^{-1}(u(x) + u(y))$.

It is one of the most common uninorms; when $x, y < 0.5$, then it is equal to

$$U(x,y) = 0.5 \cdot T_p(2x, 2y) = 2xy,$$

while when $x, y > 0.5$, then

$$U(x,y) = 0.5 + 0.5 \cdot S_p(2x-1, 2y-1).$$

Here T_p and S_p are one of the common extensions of the conjunction and disjunction respectively to the [0,1] interval, [12]. After aggregating values for every journey, the one that has the maximum value of $U(x,y)$ is chosen.

4 Example

Lets assume that a trip from Novi Sad (Serbia and Montenegro) to Bratislava (Slovakia) is to be taken. The trip should last "around 8 hours" and it should cost "about 60 euro", and money will have a slightly bigger importance than time. This data will be given to the appropriate travel agent and he will start a parallel search. After the search three possible routs are given

- Novi Sad - Belgrade Airport(bus)-Bratislava(plane)
  cost=250 euros, length=4.5 hours;
- Novi Sad - Budapest -Bratislava(train) cost=58 euros; length=9 hours;
- Novi Sad - Bratislava(bus) cost=75 euro; length=8 hours.

Let us assume that the importance (i) parameter for cost equals 3, and for the journey length equals 1. Gaussian fuzzy numbers according to the parameters will be formed. Then the number that represents the cost will have

$$a = 8\ d = 9.6\ h(x) = e^{-(x-8)^2/9.6}$$

and the number that represents journey length

$$a = 60\ d = 442\ g(x) = e^{-(x-60)^2/442}$$

Then h, g are transformed [fig. 3,4].

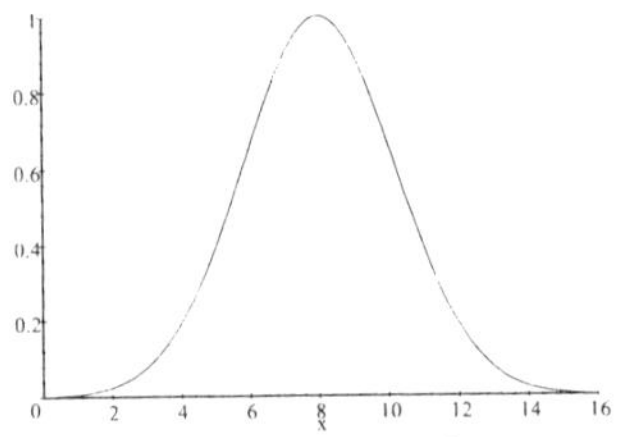

3. $g(x) = e^{-(x-8)^2/9.6}$

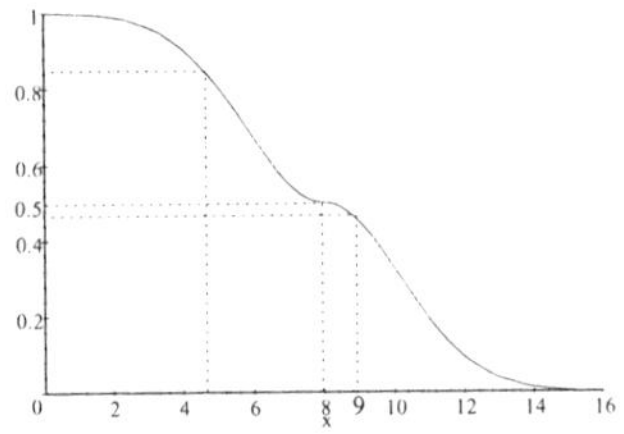

4. The transformed g(x).

When the values for each journey are interpolated and aggregated, the following results will be obtained:

- $U(2.55 \times 10^{-7}, 0.87) = 6.25 \times 10^{-7}$
- $U(0.504, 0.448) = 0.451$
- $U(0.397, 0.5) = 0.397$

$U(x, y)$ calculates the joint values of cost and journey length thus measuring the "value" of each journey. Obviously, the journey with a highest value is chosen. In the example, the journey number 2(train) is selected, because it has the maximum value.

5 Conclusion

This prototype is only a step towards a global travel multi-agent system. The reasoning mechanism applied here is general enough and it can be easily extended to multiple constrains and can be applied on many similar problems. Also, adding fuzzy reasoning to the system allows the system to act more human-like, thus obtaining a certain level of machine intelligence. Since fuzzy reasoning is added as an independent component of the system, it can be used in any part of the system.

The adding of the fuzzy reasoning component to the system, allowed the system to deal with new type of constraints (f and g type). Adding a tool to resolve complex contraints to the system, made the system advance from a information service to an advisor to its user.

If completely implemented, Global Travel Agency MAS based on the proposed prototype will allow traveling anywhere in the world by only pressing a button and showing up for a ride. Thus, the hard job of booking and choosing the optimal journey is left to the travel agent.

References

[1] M. Badjonski, "Implementation of Multi-Agent Systems using Java", Master Thesis, Novi Sad, Yugoslavia, 1998, 156 pages.

[2] M. Badjonski, M. Ivanović, Z., Budimac, "Software Specification Using LASS", Lecture Notes in Computer Science, Vol. 1345, Springer-Verlag, 1997, pp. 375-376.

[3] M. Badjonski, M. Ivanović, Z., Budimac, "Agent Oriented Programming Language LASS", Computer Science and Electronic Eng., Horwood Publishing Ltd., 1999.

[4] M. Badjonski, M. Ivanović, A. Takači, "Agent-Based Travelling", Proc. of 2000 ADBIS - DAS FAA Prague, Eds. Masunaga, Y., Pokorny , J., Stuller J., Thalheim, B., 2000, pp. 11-20, Czech Republic.

[5] A. H. Bond, L., Gaser (Eds.), "Readings in Distributed Artificial Intelligence", Morgan Kaufmann, 1988.

[6] H. D. Burkhard, "Agent-Oriented Programming for Open Systems", Intelligent Agents, Lecture Notes in Artificial Intelligence, Vol. 890, Springer Verlag 1994, pp. 291-306.

[7] N. R. Jennings, "Agent Software", Proceedings of UNICOM Seminar on Agent Software, London, UK, 1995, pp. 12-27.

[8] N. R. Jennings, M. Wooldridge, "Application of Intelligent Agents", Agent Technology: Foundations, Applications, and Markets (eds. N. R. Jennings and M. Wooldridge), 1998, pp. 3-28.

[9] Y. Shoham, "Agent-Oriented Programming", Artificial Intelligence, 60(1):51-92, 1993.

[10] A. Takači, "Multi-agent Systems in Travel Agencies", Diploma Thesis, Novi Sad, 1999, 39 pages (in Serbian).

[11] M. Wooldridge, N. R. Jennings, "Agent Theories, Architectures, and Languages: A Survey", Intelligent Agents, Lecture Notes in Artificial Intelligence, Vol. 890, Springer Verlag 1994, pp. 1-39.

[12] E. Klement, R. Mesiar, E. Pap, "Triangular norms", Kluwer Academic Publishers, Series: Trends in Logic, Vol. 8, 2000.

Knowledge-based Software Engineering
T. Welzer et al. (Eds.)
IOS Press, 2002

Software Agents for Uncertain and Complex Environments

Behrouz HOMAYOUN FAR
Faculty of Engineering, University of Calgary
far@enel.ucalgary.ca

Abstract. Complexity, knowledgeability and uncertainty issues of multi-agent systems (MAS) are discussed. Complexity of MAS is composed of structural and algorithmic complexity. We define metrics to measure the complexity of MAS. The metrics are used for devising a candidate set of agents for MAS design. Knowledgeability of MAS is defined in terms of problem solving and cognitive capabilities and the ability to cope with agents' interactions, such as cooperation, coordination and competition. Uncertainty usually arises when agents are engaged in competitive tasks. We devise models and techniques to cope with uncertainty in competitive situations.

1. Introduction

Nowadays, an increasing number of software projects are being revised and restructured in terms of multi-agent systems (MAS). Software agents are considered as a new experimental embodiment of computer programs and are being advocated as a next generation model for engineering complex, heterogeneous, scalable, open, distributed and networked systems. However, agent system development is currently dominated by informal guidelines, heuristics and inspirations rather than formal principles and well-defined engineering techniques. There are some ongoing initiatives by The Foundation for Intelligent Physical Agents (FIPA) (http://www.fipa.org) and some other institutions to produce software guidelines and standards for heterogeneous, interacting agents and agent-based systems. However, such initiatives fall short to address the quality and complexity issues explicitly.

Quality for software systems can be defines in terms of conformance to requirement [3] or fitness for use [8]. In the former, the requirements should be clearly stated and the product must conform to it. Any deviation from the requirements is regarded as a defect. Therefore, a good quality software product may contain fewer bugs. The latter, puts emphasis on meeting user's needs. Therefore, a good quality product provides better user satisfaction.

Conventional software quality models, such as CUPRIMDA [9], Boehm's [2], McCall's [12], and ISO 9126 address quality in terms of a few quality attributes (or factors) and criteria (or intermediate and primitive constructs) to represent the attributes. The criteria (or primitive constructs) are later mapped to actual metrics. Quality in MAS can be examined from various viewpoints such as:

- *Conformance:* conformance to customers' requirements; conformance to standards;
- *Development process quality:* requirement, design, implementation, test and maintenance quality;
- *End-product quality:* reliability, usability and availability;

- *Relativity:* advantage over similar products;

The two main factors affecting quality of MAS from both the customer and developers' point of view, are *complexity* and *knowledgeability*. Complexity of MAS is either structural or algorithmic. Knowledgeability of MAS can be defined in terms of problem solving and cognitive capabilities and the ability to cope with interactive scenarios, such as cooperation, coordination and competition. Complexity and knowledgeability issues are discussed in the next two sections.

2. Complexity in MAS

In conventional software systems complexity is structural in nature. As the system evolves new components or functions may be added to the system. By doing so, the structure of the software may deteriorate to the extent that major effort is needed to maintain its consistency and conformity with the requirements. Complexity of MAS is both *structural* and *algorithmic*. They both can be defined in either objective or subjective way.

2.1 Structural Complexity

A main complexity component in MAS is structural because new agents may be added to the system or new functions, program modules or packages may be added to the existing agents.

The MAS architecture is the primary artifact for conceptualizing, constructing, managing, and evolving the system under development. It is difficult to draw a sharp line between software design and its architecture. Software architecture is a level of design concerned with issues beyond the computation. Architectural issues include strategic decisions upon:

- Structural issues including gross organization and global control structure.
- Selection among design alternatives.
- Assignment of functionality to constituent agents.
- Composition of constituent agents.
- Protocols for communication, synchronization, etc.
- Physical distribution.
- Scaling and performance.

Hierarchical decomposition is a major method of handling complexity in conventional software analysis and design, assuming that the final product shall have the hierarchical architecture. Unfortunately, hierarchical decomposition cannot be used directly in MAS system development due to the facts that the MAS architecture may not necessarily be hierarchical and MAS analysis and design is not essentially top-down or bottom-up. That is, the participating agents of the MAS cannot be defined at the outset in a hierarchical way. The interactions of the MAS system with the outside world, i.e., *use case models*, usually come first and then the architectural pattern and participating agents may be decided upon. This is equivalent to moving up the hierarchy. Defining detailed design for each agent is equivalent to moving down the hierarchy.

An architectural pattern expresses a fundamental structural organization schema for the MAS systems. It provides a set of predefined agents, specifies their responsibilities, and includes rules and guidelines for organizing the relationships between them. The most popular architectural patterns for MAS are:

- *Layers:* application is decomposed into different levels of abstraction, such as application layer, business specific layer, middleware layer, etc., and each constituent agent may belong to one layer only.
- *Blackboard:* independent specialized agents collaborate to derive a solution, working on a common data structure called blackboard.

The architectural pattern may be extended to devise the internal architecture of each constituent agent. Common internal architectural patterns are:

- *Model-view-controller (M-V-C):* application is divided into three partitions. The *model*, which is the business rules and underlying data; the *view*, which is how information is displayed to the user; and the *controllers*, which process the user input.
- *Reasoning-communication-documentation engine (R-C-D):* the application is composed of three processing engines. The *reasoning engine* to process the basic business logic; the *communication engine* to manage messages to and from the outside world; and the *documentation engine* to manage data internally [4].

In MAS the relationships among the agents are dynamic. Two kinds of dynamic relationships can be devised: *interactions* among subsystems and *intra-actions* within subsystems [5]. Interactions are between an agent and its outer environment and manifested by the messages sent, received (in case of cooperation and coordination) and perceived (in case of competition). Intra-actions are the characteristics of the agent's inner environment. Contemporary software engineering techniques can manage the intra-actions using decomposition and abstraction techniques and interactions using RPC, RMI, etc.

2.2 Algorithmic Complexity

Algorithmic complexity stands for the mechanisms for knowledge processing and knowledge sharing as well as the ability to engage with the other agents in cooperative, coordinative and competitive tasks.

2.3 MAS Complexity Metrics

Subjective complexity accounts for the way that a human user evaluates the complexity of the agent system. A modified version of *Function Point (FP)* [1], that accounts for algorithmic complexity can be used. For each participant agent, the parameters involved in the model are: External inputs (N_i) and external outputs (N_o), external inquiries (N_q), external interfaces (N_{ef}), internal data structures (N_{if}), algorithmic complexity (N_m) and knowledge complexity factor (N_k). The algorithmic complexity (N_m) factor is the sum of three Boolean variables stating whether cooperative, coordinative and competitive mechanisms are implemented or not ($0 \le N_m \le 3$). The knowledge complexity factor (N_k) has a value between 0 and 5 depending whether the agent has a knowledge-base and whether the knowledge-base is sharable or is based on a shared ontology.

$$UF_eC = 4N_i + 5N_o + 4N_q + 7N_{ef} + 7N_{if} + 10N_m + 6N_k$$

The adjusted MAS function point (MAS-FP) is derived by multiplying UF_eC with the subjective assessment of technical complexity, the *TCF* factor [1]. The overall complexity of the MAS will be the mean of the adjusted feature points of its constituent agents.

Objective complexity accounts for complexity as an internal property of the agent-based system. If the MAS system is nearly-decomposable, the cyclomatic complexity [11] metrics can be used. Complexity of the MAS is the sum of cyclomatic complexities of its constituent agents. As a measure for nearly-decomposability, the communicative cohesion metrics can be examined. The communicative cohesion metrics (*CCM*) for an agent g_i is defined in terms of the ratio of internal relationships (interactions) to the total number of relationships (i.e., sum of interactions and intra-actions).

$$CCM(g_i) = \frac{R_{\text{internal}}}{R_{\text{internal}} + R_{\text{external}}}$$

The *CCM* for the MAS is the statistical mean of *CCM* of its constituent agents. Systems with $CCM \geq 0.91$ are usually considered to be nearly-decomposable.

In this research, we identify two types of organizational relationships: *signal level* and *symbol level* relationships. *Signal level* accounts for dynamic message passing. At this level, messages between two communicating agents are interpreted via ascribing the same meaning to the constants used in the messages. In this way, mutual understanding of the domain constants before further message passing is guaranteed. *Symbol level* relationships, on the other hand, account for dynamic knowledge sharing. The internal and external relationships in *CCM* account for signal level relations only.

2.4 Application

The first step in design of a MAS system is to sketch the use cases and then identify constituent agents using the use cases and architectural patterns. The problem is how to devise the constituent agents. The MAS complexity metrics can be used for decomposing the problem based on function/ input/ output into an organization of agents and refining this list. First, the target *CCM* and UF_eC is set and decomposition is performed to devise a tentative set of agents with *CCM* greater than the target value. Then the UF_eC is measured for each agent and those with higher UF_eC value will be the target for further decomposition. These steps are repeated until all the agents have satisfactory *CCM* and UF_eC.

3. Knowledgeability in MAS

Traditional software engineering can handle *data* and *information*. *Data* is defined as a sequence of quantified or quantifiable symbols. *Information* is about taking data and putting it into a meaningful pattern. *Knowledge* is the ability to use that information. Knowledgeability can be defined in terms of:

- *Interactions,* i.e., the ability to directly communicate or collect data on the other agents.
- *Cognitive capabilities*, i.e., the ability to manipulate knowledge and make decisions based on the knowledge and collected data.

The following subsections elaborate this.

3.1 Cognitive Capabilities

Three main capabilities of agents in MAS are *representing*, *using* and *sharing* the knowledge. A modified version of semantic net called *Symbol Structure (SS)* is used to represent individual agent's knowledge structure [5]. Ability to use the knowledge is realized by having the knowledge-base in the form of SS and mechanisms for problem solving using the SS [5]. Finally, ability to share the knowledge depends on ontologies for the domain and task. Mechanisms for using and sharing are presented in [6].

3.2 Interaction in MAS

Basic agents' interactions are cooperation, coordination and competition.

- *Cooperation:* Cooperation is revealing an agent's goal and the knowledge behind it to the other party. In cooperation both agents have a common goals.
- *Coordination:* Coordination is revealing an agent's goals and the knowledge behind it to the other party. In coordination, agents have separate goals.
- *Loose Competition:* Loose competition is revealing only an agent's goals but masking the knowledge behind it to the other party.
- *Strict Competition:* Strict competition is neither revealing an agent's goals nor the knowledge behind it to the other party.

3.3 Decision Making Mechanism in MAS

Figure 1 shows decision making mechanism based on agents' interaction. Agents engaged in cooperative and cordinative tasks usually have precise information about the other agents' goals due to the fact that direct communication between the agents is possible. Therefore the predictive model is usually deterministic. In case of competition, the agent must predict the other agents' goals based on the signals from the opponents rather than direct communication. Thus the predictive model is usually non-deterministic.

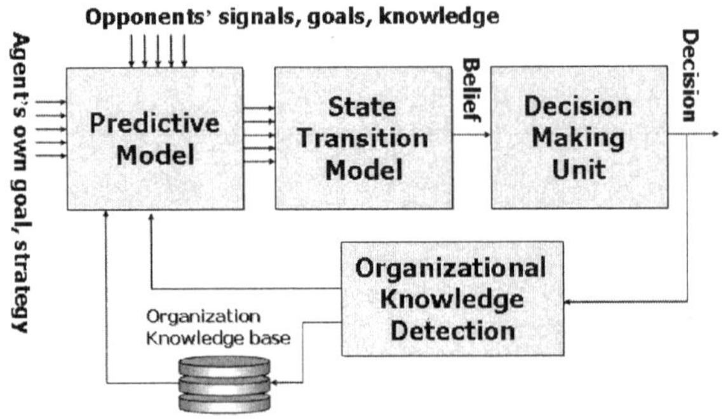

Figure 1. Decision making mechanism

4. Uncertainty in MAS

In this section, we consider multi-agent interaction under competitive and uncertain environments. Information gained through agents' behaviour, i.e., *signals* may be incomplete. Agents in competitive environments, must make decisions under uncertainty, predict environment's parameters, predict other agents' future moves, and successfully explain self and the other agents' actions. The crucial factors are both the amount and specification of the information. Any lack of information and/or noise affects the quality of decisions, the moves to be performed and conclusion to be devised.

4.1 Overview of multi-agent competitive environment

Fig. 2 shows the outline of agent competition. The process for deciding competitive strategy includes following steps. First, each agent tries to predict opponents' strategy. Second, the agent chooses the best response strategy based on previous predictions. And finally, each agent will get a payoff by using a utility function.

Figure 2. Overview of agents' competition

From the decision making viewpoint, since the amount of payoff in extended games is influenced by the opponent's moves, exact predictions of the other agent's strategies is crucial to guarantee a stable payoff. Information about opponents' moves is *uncertain* because they may try to hide their strategies and the knowledge behind it as much as possible. The work presented here suggests modeling an incomplete game theoretical based decision making method for competitive agents.

4.2 Modeling competitive environment

One cannot exactly predict some agent's strategy because of lack of knowledge on opponent's *preference* since strategies are selected based upon each agent's preference relations. In order to model such situation, we divide (opponent) agents into following two kinds:

- Agents whose preference relations are exactly known.
- Agents whose preference relations are not known.

As for first, we treat them based on normal game theoretic approach. As for second, we regard these agents as *natural* objects and their strategies as *state of nature* and treat them by lumping up all of the natural objects as uncertainty. Following this principle, we define a multi-agent competitive environment as:

$$\Gamma = \left\{ A, N, X, \{S_i, \succ_i, P_i\}_{i \in A} \right\}$$

Where A is the set of agents, N is the set of states of nature; X is the outcome of competition and it is defines as: $S_1 \times ... \times S_n \times N \rightarrow X$; where, S_i is the set of strategies of agent i; $\succ_i$ is the preference relation of agent i; and P_i is the information partition over the state of nature of agent i. It is represented by extensive form of a game as shown in Fig. 3. This is a simple but illustrative example of agents' competition model (*agent 1* versus *agent 2*).

In this example, we consider that *agent 1* doesn't know the preference relation of *agent 2* and thus, *agent 1* is uncertain about which strategy *agent 2* might adopt. Here, P_1 is an information partition of *agent 1* and it is not sure which nodes he stays in (left, right or center) within P_1. Under this uncertain environment, *agent 1* must decide which strategy to adopt so as to optimize its utility. In this case, *agent 1* assigns its *belief* over the state of nature and adopts the strategy which maximizes the expected utility. If all the agents decide upon strategy in this way, there is a possibility that it leads to social Bayesian perfect Nash Equilibria [10].

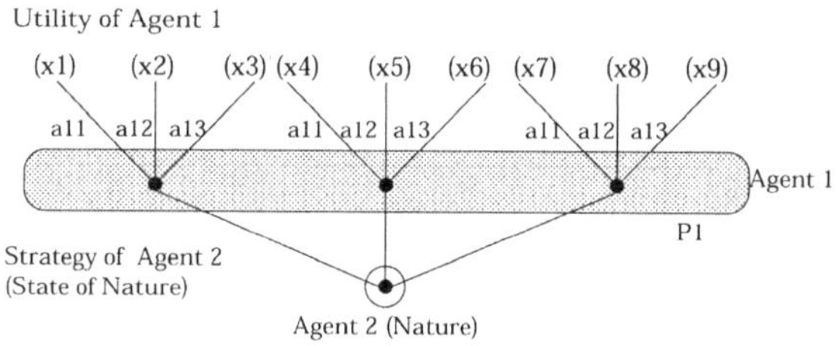

Figure 3. Example of competition model

A question which naturally arises here is how each agent assigns his belief autonomously. The answer can be achieved by dividing uncertainty into levels. Generally, certainty is divided into three levels according to the amount of information about the state of nature or given signal observed before choosing among several strategies [7].

- *Level-1*: Decision making under certainty
  The agent knows exactly what the state of nature will be. In this case, decision making is straightforward. The agent selects the strategy which maximizes its utility using traditional game theorey.
- *Level-2*: Decision making under risk
  It is assumed that the agent is not sure what state of nature will be, but it has a probability distribution over the state of nature. In this case, the agent assigns known probability distribution as its belief and selects the strategy which maximizes expected utility. Below we propose a risk management method in order to reflect each agent's *attitude toward risk*.
- *Level-3*: Decision making under uncertainty
  In this level, we assume that the agent doesn't know anything about the state of nature except for that it is in some set, $N = \{\omega_1, \omega_2, ..., \omega_n\}$. In this case, agent has to

assign his belief without using probability distribution. Below we propose a new decision making and belief assignment which reflects agent's *degree of optimism.*

•

It should be noted that decision making under certainty (*Level-1*) is a special case of decision making under risk (*Level-2*).

4.3 Decision making under risk

In case of decision making under risk, the agent naturally selects a strategy which maximizes its expected utility. Generally, utility function is decided by calculating expected value of cost and/or benefit. If expected values of two strategies are the same, these two strategies always become non-discriminateable. However, one cannot say that this decision rule is rational. This is because, even if the expected values are the same, when variance is large, risk of failure increases. Therefore, it is natural to consider that risk of failure influences decision making. Therefore in order to make decisions under the risk, we must reflect each agent's *attitude towards risk.* Generally, attitude towards risk is categorized into the following three types [7].

- *Risk prone*: In this case, agents prefer high risk-high return strategy rather than low risk-low return strategy.
- *Risk aversion*: In this case, agents prefer low risk low return strategy rather than high risk-high return strategy.
- *Risk neutral*: If expected value is the same, these strategies always become non-discriminateable.

In the field of economics, attitude toward risk is reflected by defining subjective probability strictly. But this is too complicated and computationally expensive to be implemented on artificial agents. Therefore, we use heuristic function that reflects the agent's attitude towards risk. The utility function is defined by:

$$u(x) = E(x) - \eta V(x)$$

Where x is a pure benefit when agent adopt some strategy, $E(x)$ is a expected value when agent adopts some strategy, $V(x)$ is a variance and η is a coefficient of degree of risk aversion taking values between –1 and +1. If η is plus, the function $u(x)$ becomes risk aversion because, the larger variance is (means the larger risk of failure is), the smaller utility becomes. Conversely, if η is minus, function $u(x)$ represents risk prone because, the larger variance is, the larger the utility becomes. And if η is zero, $u(x)$ represents risk neutral because, $u(x)$ is equal to the expected value when the agents adopt some strategy.

Using this method, agents are allowed to select a strategy reflecting attitude toward risk and this simple representation can be easily implemented.

4.4 Decision making under uncertainty

In case that the agent has to decide upon the strategy under uncertainty, it has to assign its belief without using a probability distribution. According to psychologists, when human doesn't know probability distribution over uncertainty (such as state of nature), he/she decides upon action or strategy based on *degree of optimism.* Here we quantify each agent's *degree of optimism.*

In order to quantify degree of optimism, we use Ordered Weighted Averaging (OWA) operator [13]. OWA operator of dimension n is defined as the function F that has associated with a weighting vector **W**,

$$\mathbf{W} = [w_1, w_2, \ldots, w_n]$$

such that, $0 \le w_j \le 1$ and $\sum_j w_j = 1$ and for any set of some value $a_1, \ldots, a_n$

$$F(a_1, a_2, \ldots, a_n) = \sum_j w_j b_j$$

where b_j is the jth largest element in the collection $a_1, \ldots, a_n$.

Various semantics can be associated with the OWA aggregation procedure in this framework of decision making under uncertainty, such as viewing the OWA weights as a pseudo-probability distribution [14]. In particular we can view w_j as a kind of probability that of the jth best thing happening. In this case, weights (pseudo-probability) are assigned not to a particular state of nature, but to a preference order of the utility. Thus, w_1 is the weight assigned to the best utility and w_n is assigned to a worst utility. Here, a question that naturally arises is how the agent assigns the weights it is going to use in solving some problem. At the fundamental level, the answer is that a human expert interacting with the agent subjectively assigns it. But this may be a hard job in autonomous environments. Thus, we propose a method to assign the weight vector automatically reflecting *degree of optimism* of agents. Using OWA operator, the degree of optimism is defined below [13].

$$Opt(W) = \sum_j w_j (n-j)/(n-1)$$

Using this definition, we propose the method to assign weight vector automatically. Users of agents subjectively decide upon their degree of optimism *Opt(W)*. They then input this value into a following linear programming equation

$$\max \ -\sum w_j \log_2 w_j$$

Subject to:

$$Opt(W) = \sum_j w_j (n-j)/(n-1)$$

$$Opt(W) \in [0,1]$$

$$\sum_j w_j = 1$$

$$w_j \ge 0 \quad \text{for} \quad j = 1, 2, \ldots, n$$

This approach is closely related to the maximum entropy method used in probability theory, which is a commonly used rationale for selecting a canonical probability distribution from among a set of relevant ones.

Advantage of this method is that for various cardinalities of OWA, we can consistently provide weights corresponding to given *Opt(W)*. Using this method, we can treat decision making under uncertainty (problem of *Level-3*) within the previously mentioned framework of decision making under risk (problem of *Level-2*) since we can view OWA operator as pseudo-probability distribution.

4.5 Analyzing opponents' moves

Using decision making method mentioned above, the agent can decide upon optimal strategy even under uncertainty. However, in order to get a stable utility, the agent should reduce uncertainty by analyzing opponents' moves and updating its belief. A method for belief update using *dynamic belief network* (DBN) is presented in [6].

5. Conclusion

In this paper, we addressed the complexity, knowledgeability and uncertainty issues of multi-agent systems (MAS) and defined metrics to measure the complexity of MAS. We also defined knowledgeability of MAS in terms of problem solving and cognitive capabilities and the ability to cope with agents' interactions. Finally, we devised models and techniques to cope with uncertainty in competitive situations.

References

[1] Albrecht, A.J. and Gaffney, J.F., Software Function, Source Lines of Code and Development Effort Prediction: A Software Science Validation, IEEE Trans. Software Engineering, vol. 9, no. 6, pp. 639-648, 1983.

[2] Boehm, B., Software Risk Management, IEEE Computer Society Press, CA, 1989.

[3] Crosby, P.B., Quality is Free: The Art of Making Quality Certain, McGraw-Hill, New York, 1988.

[4] Far, B.H. et al, An Integrated Reasoning and Learning Environment for WWW Based Software Agents for Electronic Commerce, Transactions of IEICE, vol. E81-D no. 12, pp. 1374-1386, 1998.

[5] Far, B.H., Agent-SE: A Methodology for Agent Oriented Software Engineering, Enabling Society with Information Technology, Q. Jin et al. eds., pp. 357-366, Springer, 2001.

[6] Onjo, H., and Far, B.H., A Unified View of Heterogeneous Agents' Interaction, Transactions of the IEICE, vol. E84-D, no. 8, pp. 945-956, 2001.

[7] Ichikawa, A., Decision Making Theory, Kouritsu Pub., 1983. (in Japanese).

[8] Juran, J.M., Gryna, F.M. Jr., Bingham, F.M. (eds.), Quality Control Handbook (3rd edition), McGraw Hill, New York, 1979.

[9] Kan, S.H., Metrics and Models in Software Quality Engineering, Addison-Wesley, 1995.

[10] Kajii, A. and Matsui, A., Micro Economics: A Strategic Approach, Nihon-Hyouron Pub., 2000. (in Japanese).

[11] McCabe, T.J., A Complexity Measure, IEEE Transactions on Software Engineering, vol. 2, no. 4, pp. 308-320, 1976.

[12] McCall, J.A., Richards, P.K., Walters, G.F., Factors in Software Quality, RADC TR-77-369, 1977. Vols I,II,III, US Rome Air Development Center Reports NTIS AD/A-049 014, 015, 055, 1977.

[13] Yager, R.R., On Ordered Weighted Averaging Aggregation Operators in Multi-Criteria Decision Making, IEEE Trans. SMC, no. 18, pp. 183-190, 1988.

[14] Yager, R.R., Decision Making Under Dempster-Shafer Uncertainties, International Journals of General Systems, vol. 20, pp. 233-255, 1990.

Knowledge-based Software Engineering
T. Welzer et al. (Eds.)
IOS Press, 2002

The consistency management of scenarios from different viewpoints

Atsushi Ohnishi, Zhang Hong Hui, Hiroshi Fujimoto
Department of Computer Science, Ritsumeikan University
Shiga 525-8577, JAPAN

Abstract. *Scenarios that describe concrete situations of software operation play an important role in software development, and in particular in requirements engineering. Scenario details should vary in content and detail when described from different viewpoints (e.g. types of user or external interface), but this presents a difficulty, because informal scenarios cannot easily be translated from one viewpoint to another with consistency and assurance. This paper describes (1) a language for describing scenarios in which simple action traces are embellished to include typed frames based on a simple case grammar of actions and for describing the sequence among events, and (2) a transformation method of scenarios described from different viewpoints with the scenario description language.*

1 Introduction

Scenarios have important uses in software specification and design synthesis, particularly when used to gain insight into the implications of design decisions and for customer validation and acceptance. However, scenarios are vague and imprecise tools and are therefore difficult to integrate into more formal development processes.

For example, without defining what it means for actions to be included in a scenario, it is impossible to compute differences among scenarios reliably. (Is a difference because of an unimportant omission, or a change in names, or a differently instantiated variable, or is it a genuine inconsistency.) Nor is it possible for the scenarios to guide the refinement of a specification other than by providing insight to the specifier. Detailed, instantiated scenarios of the kind used for customer validation of requirements or the generation of system test cases can't be generated mechanically from scenarios described just in text. Most importantly vulnerabilities of the spec/scenario system are not easily flagged. (E.g. what kinds of things might go wrong in the performance of this action? What previously executed actions does this scenario or scenario fragment depend on?)

We claim that scenarios should be represented in a form that is closer to the application-specific concepts relevant to customer validation and system testing than general-purpose concepts such as "actor", "step", "event", "episode", "obstacle", and etc. But going to the extreme of application-specific representations relies on domain-specialists investing work in the development of application-specific (or still worse, system-specific) languages and tools. An intermediate, semantically rich, but application-neutral set of concepts is what's needed.

Extensions to scenario and action representations have been proposed before. Ohnishi's requirements frame model[7] provides a vocabulary of general-purpose action and information types using structures similar to those of case grammar[3].

The requirements frame model defines the case structure of a concept. For example, the data flow (DFLOW) concept has agent, source, goal, and instrument cases. The agent case corresponds to data that are transferred from the source case object to the goal case object. So, an object assigned to the agent case should be a data type object. An object in the source or goal cases should be either a human or a function type object. If and only if a human type object is assigned to source or goal cases, some instrument should be specified as a device case. The requirements frame enables to detect illegal usages of data and lack of cases[7].

Similarly, Potts and Anton [2] suggest that achievement-oriented goals and their occurrences in scenarios should be categorized into a number of basic types, (MAKE, KNOW, etc.) The KAOS language formalizes some of these differences and others in terms of action pre-conditions and temporal-logic post-conditions.

In other areas of research, there are numerous proposals for specializing action types. Case grammar[3] suggests that a verb organizes the propositions conveyed by natural language, the concepts denoted by other parts of speech occupying well-defined cases.

Research in AI has sought to reduce action descriptions (for planning and understanding applications) into semantic primitives [11] and their assembly into knowledge-rich memory structures and cases.

Speech-act theory[12] proposes a number of basic communicative actions that have different assumptions and consequences in human communication. Speech-act theory is an area of continuing interest in linguistic pragmatics. Speech-act theory was first proposed as a framework for IS analysis by Lyttinen [5], and has also been applied in CSCW[6]. Thus, rather than sending each other generic messages, users of a speech act-based CSCW system promise, request, refuse, etc. In the ESPRIT CREW project, goal modeling and scenario authoring approach is proposed[10].

In this paper, we outline a frame-based approach for structuring the actions in a scenario. We use ideas from previous work[7] and Jackson's problem frames [4] for structuring the content of scenarios and action descriptions in specifications. Thus, there are different case frames for different problem frames, but far fewer case frames than there are systems or problem domains.

2 Scenario Description Language

Scenarios can be regarded as a sequence of events. Each of events has a certain action. We have developed a scenario description language based on this concept.

2.1 Event description

Each of events has just one verb, and each of verbs has its own case structure. Verbs and their own case structures are depend on problem domains, but roles of cases are independent of problem domains. There exist several roles, such as agent, object, recipient, instrument, source, and so on.

An entity doesn't have one of these as a type, but plays these as roles. (Thus a person may be a user with respect to requesting services of the system, but a consumer of its outputs.) There are some constraints. Thus, we expect entities either to be users or phenomena, but not both with respect to different actions. We provide action frames as shown in Table 1.

Just like Ohnishi's Case Frame[7], each of actions has its case structure. For example, action "move" has four cases, such that "agent," "source," "goal," and "instrument." A sentence "Mr. X moves from Tokyo to Slovenia by airplane" can be transformed into an internal representation as shown in Table 2.

We assume that a scenario represents a sequence of events, and each of events can be transformed into internal representation based on the above action frame. Just like Requirements

Table 1: Action frames

action	**cases**
Transform/derive/compute	agent, source, goal, object
Collate/compare	agent, source, object
Report on/ monitor/sense	agent, source, operation, instrument
Query/ask/recruit/appoint	agent, object, goal
Command/control	agent, recipient, operation, instrument
Suggest/request	agent, object, goal
Create/make/edit/arrange/decide	agent, source, goal
Feedback	agent, recipient, operation, instrument
Notify/send/receive/distribute/move	agent, object, source, goal, instrument
Allocate/ schedule/seize/assign	agent, object, goal
Cancel/ relinquish	agent, recipient, operation, instrument
Exist/locate	agent, status
React	agent, operation, instrument

Table 2: Internal representation example

Action	**agent**	**source**	**goal**	**instrument**
move	Mr. X	Tokyo	Slovenia	airplane

Frame, we can detect both lack of cases and illegal usages of noun type[7].

2.2 Sequence description

As previously described, scenarios define a sequence of events. We assume seven kinds of time sequences, such as 1) sequence, 2) selection, 3) iteration, 4) AND-fork, 5) OR-fork, 6) eXclusive OR-fork, 7) AND/OR/XOR-join.

Since most events occur sequentially, the sequence of sequential events need not be apparently described. In other words, ordered events can be regarded as sequential events. For example, the following ordered three events occur sequentially.

1. A PC chair decides a schedule.
2. He sends the schedule to a publishing company.
3. He arranges keynote speakers.

To specify selective events, we provide *"if...then...else..."* syntax just like most of program languages. For example,

> **if** *an author has his own e-mail addresses,* **then** *he sends a notification letter to the author via e-mail* **else** *he sends a notification letter to the author via postal mail.*

To specify iterative events, we provide *"Do...until..."* syntax just like most of program languages. For example, in case of late reviewing,

> **Do** *he urges a review report to a reviewer* **until** *the reviewer sends a report.*

To specify parallel events, we provide *"AND-fork...AND-join, OR-fork...OR-join,"* and *"XOR-fork...XOR-join."* An example is shown below.

AND-fork

a) he distributes CFP to related societies and organizations.
b) he sends e-mails to members of the related societies

AND-join

Since our scenario description language enables to define both the syntax and the semantics of scenarios, we can analyze and validate scenarios written with this language.

3 Scenario Example: Program chair's job

We consider a scenario of program chair's job at an international conference. This scenario is based on a problem provided by Requirements Engineering Working Group (RE WG), Information Processing Society, Japan. Similar job description is provided by ACM[1].

3.1 Scenario from PC chair's viewpoint

The followings are program chair's jobs written with our scenario description language.

1. *A PC chair decides a schedule (of the paper submission deadline, program committee's meeting, acceptance/rejection notification, camera ready paper due).*
2. *He sends the schedule to a publishing company.*
3. *He arranges keynote speakers.*
4. *He makes Call for Paper.*
5. **AND-fork**

    a) He distributes it to related societies and organizations.
    b) he sends e-mails to members of the societies.

    AND-join
6. *He recruits program committee members.*
7. *He makes a list of members (including member's name, address, affiliation, phone number, FAX number, e-mail address, and research area).*
8. *He assigns paper IDs to submitted papers.*
9. *Each of submitted papers has title, author name, address, affiliation, phone number, e-mail address, FAX number, abstract, and key words.*
10. **if** *an author has his own e-mail addresses,* **then** *PC chair sends an acceptance mail to the author via e-mail* **else** *he sends an acceptance mail to the author via postal mail.*
11. *He sends a list of papers to all the PC members.*
12. *PC members select their candidates of papers.*
13. *PC members send their candidates of papers for reviews to the PC chair.*
14. *PC chair makes a final assignment of reviewers.*
15. *He sends reviewer's sheets and submitted papers for review to PC members.*
16. *He receives reviewer's results*

17. ...

The events of the above scenario can be transformed into internal representation below. In the transformation, concrete words will be assigned into pronouns and omitted indispensable cases. Some cases are not indispensable, but optional. In case of optional cases, such as the instrument case of action "inform," a concrete word may not be assigned. The 9th event of the above scenario is not transformed, because data structure cannot be internally represented.

3.2 Scenario from PC member's viewpoint

In this subsection, we will describe how to derive a scenario of the same job description of PC member's viewpoint from the scenario of PC chair's viewpoint.

First, we derive events including PC members or reviewers.

1. He recruits program committee members.
2. He sends a list of papers to all the PC members.
3. PC members send their candidates of papers for reviews.
4. PC chair makes a final assignment of reviewers.
5. He sends reviewer's sheets and ...
6. He receives reviewer's results

Actually, the internal representation is independent of viewpoints. For example, in case of action "send, receive, inform, and so on," the action frame can be represented as "source case object" sends "object case object" to "goal case object" with "instrument case object." The viewpoint of this representation becomes source case object. The action frame can be also represented as "goal case object" receive "object case object" from "source case object" with "instrument case object." The viewpoint of the second representation becomes the goal case object. The action frame can be also represented as "object case object" is sent from "source case object" to "goal case object" with "instrument case object." The viewpoint of the third representation becomes the object case object.

In case of the last event of the above example, this event can be represented as

- PC members send reviewer's results to PC chair.
- PC chair receives reviewer's results from PC members.
- reviewer's results are sent from PC members to PC chair.

from the action frame, we can get a scenario from PC members as below.

1. PC members are recruited by PC chair.
2. All the PC members receive a list of papers from PC chair.
3. PC members send their candidates of papers for reviews to PC chair.
4. Reviewers are assigned by PC chair.
5. PC members receive reviewer's sheets and ... from PC chair.
6. PC members send reviewer's results to PC chair.

By checking the derived scenario by PC members, both lack of events and wrong sequences of events can be easily detected. In this case, the lack of an event that reviewer should receive reviewers' guideline from PC chair is detected.

If another scenario of an exceptional handling is specified from PC chair's viewpoint, we can get a scenario of the same exceptional handling from PC members' viewpoint.

4 Conclusions

We have developed an action frame base scenario description language and transformation rules between scenarios from different viewpoints. With these rules, we can get a new scenario from PC members' viewpoint by transforming a scenario from PC chair's viewpoint. Through our example, we found the scenario transformation with action frame enables to improve several quality of scenario.

1. System developer does not need to describe scenarios from several different viewpoints. If he specifies a scenario from one viewpoint, then he can get a scenario from another viewpoint with transformation rules. This contributes to improve the productivity of scenarios.

2. If system developer specifies two scenarios from different viewpoints, he can check the lack of events and check the consistency of scenarios by comparing a scenario with a transformed scenario that is created by transforming other scenario. This contributes to improve the completeness and the consistency of scenarios.

We have been researching an integration method of scenarios described from different viewpoints[9] and developing a prototype system based on our methods. We have to validate the ideas more thoroughly by applying to several different problem domains and have to estimate our methods with the prototype system.

References

[1] "ACM Conference Committee job description," Conference Manual, Section 6.1.1, http://www.acm.org/sig_volunteer_info/ conference_manual/6-1-1PC.HTM.

[2] Anton, A.I. and Potts, C.: "The use of goals to surface requirements for evolving systems," Proc. 20th ICSE, pp.157-166, IEEE Comput. Soc, 1998.

[3] Fillmore, C.J.: "The Case for Case," in Bach and Harms (Eds.), "Universals in Linguistic Theory,"

[4] Jackson, M.: "Problems and requirement," Proc. 2nd ISRE, pp.2-8, IEEE Comput. Soc., 1995.

[5] Lyttinen, K.J.: "Implications of theories of language for information systems," Manage. Inf. Syst. Q., vol.9, no.1, pp.61-74, 1985.

[6] Medina-Mora, R., Winograd, T., Flores, R., Flores, F.:" The Action Workflow approach to workflow management technology," Proc. CSCW '92, pp.281-288, 1992.

[7] Ohnishi, A.: "Software Requirements Specification Database Based on Requirements Frame Model," Proc. of the IEEE second International Conference on *Requirements Engineering (ICRE'96)*, 1996, pp.221-228.

[8] Ohnishi, A., Potts, C.: "Grounding Scenarios in Frame-Based Action Semantics," Proc. REFSQ 01, pp.177-182, 2001.

[9] Ohnishi, A., Zhang, H.H., Fujimoto, H.:" Transformation and Integration Method of Scenarios," Proc. COMPSAC 2002, 2002.

[10] Rolland, C., Souveyet, C., and Achour C.B.:"Guiding Goal Modeling Using Scenarios," IEEE Trans. Softw, Engnr., Vol.24, No.12, pp.1055-1071, 1998.

[11] Schank, R.: "Representation and Understanding of Text," Machine Intelligence 8, Ellis Horwood Ltd., Cambridge, pp.575-607, 1977.

[12] Searle, J.R.: "An Essay in the Philosophy of Language," Cambridge Univ, Press, 1969.

Knowledge-based Software Engineering
T. Welzer et al. (Eds.)
IOS Press, 2002

A Controlling System of Progress for Users by Using Use Cases

Kyoko YOSHIDA
Faculty of Law, Heisei International University
2000 Mizufukaohtateno Kazo, Saitama, 347-8504, Japan
e-mail: yoshida-shirao@eva.hi-ho.ne.jp

Morio NAGATA
Dept. of Administration Engineering,
Faculty of Science and Technology Keio University
3-14-1 Hiyoshi, Yokohama, 223-8522, Japan
e-mail: nagata@ae.keio.ac.jp

Abstract. Controlling the progress for software development project has been managed from only developers' point of view. Especially in implementation phase, the progress reports of coding and testing have been explained by using modules or classes. However, it is not easy for users to understand those specified notions. In object-oriented methods, it is advocated to keep the consistency of the process by using use cases, which are understandable for users and developers. Nevertheless, in the present stage, use cases have not been used enough to improve the communication between developers and users. We propose a new controlling system of progress by using use cases in implementation phase, which doesn't increase developers' burdens. This system was accomplished by linking classes and methods in both of implementation phase and analysis phase.

Introduction

Project management of software development is known by its failure rather than success. Few projects in Japan can keep the conditions on their cost, schedule, or aim of the projects that are planed at the start of development. Even in U. S. A., it is said that one third or two third of software projects overrun the schedule and the cost, too [1]. When the project falls behind the schedule on the way of development, its cost and schedule are re-estimated, but they don't work as expectedly in many cases. A lot of projects spend more money and manpower than expected.

In many cases, these developments have a tight schedule from the beginning. The schedule is determined by customers, users or software companies. But, there are several different understandings on the term for software development between stakeholders and developers. Usually such misunderstandings are not clear at the starting point of development. Many schedules are determined shorter than developers' expectation, but they don't think it seriously. After the start of software development, developers have to concentrate on problems should be solved at each step. On the other hand, the customers who order software development (users are considered as customers here) cannot know exactly how the development is going. Therefore, it becomes more difficult to understand and to communicate on the present condition of the software development each other, and it exerts a bad influence upon the development.

1. Problems on software developments and our proposal

On software development, there is a problem that users cannot catch the situation of development. Usually, process management has been done from developers' point of view and users' viewpoint is neglected. In actually, developers have the initiative of process control, especially after design phase started. Developers explain for users about a situation of process, using classes in object-oriented methods or modules in structural methods. Unfortunately, users know hardly how the actual development is going. Therefore, we need the system that user can understand easily the situation of progress on the development.

In many cases, where software development falls behind the schedule, developers and users are not able to communicate each other well. Then, the project managers increase numbers and working hours of engineers who engage in the development. But the manager doesn't have enough time to explain the situation to users, and it is usually left on the back burner. In this case, it happens often to change the order of programming, and developers and users should communicate each other at this step. Thus, we need the system that helps the smooth negotiation.

Meanwhile, in the Unified Software Development Process by UML, iterative and incremental developments are advocated [2]. These developments are more complex on progress control than development of waterfall methods. Especially in the way of iterative development, once software development delayed, it is difficult to measure the influences of the delay for subsequent works. Then a high priority tasks or a hidden risk might be forgotten. The dangers of these misses are bigger in iterative and incremental developments than the cases of waterfall methods and the controlling progress becomes more important in the former one [3, 4].

With paying attentions such points, this paper proposes a controlling system of progress that both users and developers can use easily. This system, we tried to use use cases for controlling progress of software development from analysis to test phase. Usually, users and developers specify the function of system by using use cases (scenario). After design phase started, developers use the unit of classes or methods, which are not usually understandable by users. But users can understand use cases. Therefore, to bridge the gap between users and developers, we have to first connect use cases with classes and methods in design phase, and then translate classes and methods into use cases in implemental phase, and indicate them to users. This system also helps the communications between users and developers without increasing developers' burdens.

2. Our system

2.1 Assumption

Let us consider a software development of object-oriented methods. We apply the system which will be obtained in 2.2 to implementation phase and testing phase. These phases cause the delay of development and cost up of the development often. This time, we treat only the process of implementation and test phase in its first cycle, and don't consider the influence on the iterative and incremental development. As the scale of software development we take one which will be made within a few months by several people.

In this system we use the form of use cases proposed by Craig Larman (Figure 1). The top part of this use case is summary information. The main part is "Typical Course of Events" which describes events methodically. The first sentence of description states the preconditions of this use case. Next, "actor action" and "system response" is explained with numbering. It describes in detail the conversation of interaction between actors and a system, and it is the most common or typical story of events. In "Alternative Course of Events", the alternatives or exceptions of events are described. And then, actors are defined in the part of actor in the use case [5].

<table>
<tr><td>Use case:</td><td colspan="2">Name of use case</td></tr>
<tr><td>Actors:</td><td colspan="2">List of actors (external agents),indicating who initiates the use case</td></tr>
<tr><td>Purpose:</td><td colspan="2">Intention of the use case.</td></tr>
<tr><td>Overview:</td><td colspan="2">Repetition of the high-level use case, or some similar summary</td></tr>
<tr><td>Type:</td><td colspan="2">primary, secondary or optional
essential or real</td></tr>
<tr><td>Cross References:</td><td colspan="2">Related use cases and system functions.</td></tr>
<tr><td colspan="3">Typical Course of Events</td></tr>
<tr><td colspan="2">Actor Action
Numbered actions of the actors.</td><td>System Response
Numbered descriptions of the system responses.</td></tr>
<tr><td colspan="3">Alternative Course of Events
line number: Description of exception</td></tr>
</table>

Figure 1. The use case form by Craig Larman

2.2 Flow of the system

The system goes as follows.

(1) Users and developers make use cases
(2) System generates automatically the sequence diagrams from the use cases.
(3) By using the sequence diagrams, users and developers can change the names or the places of classes and messages made of sentences in the use cases.
(4) System generates classes and methods for analysis process.
(5) Developers convert classes or methods into implementation process.
(6) Developers input an estimated manpower for each method.

(7) Developers input the degree of progress for each method

(8) System presents the progress reports for users by using use cases and one for developers by using classes or methods

Use cases in (1) should be described by simple sentence according to their abstraction levels. (2) will be stated in Section 2.3. On the basis of the sequence diagram in (2), developers and users analyze the use cases, and connect the two objects and the message. These objects will be classes, which we call the object here to avoid confusion. The corresponding message between them is connected into one sentence of the use cases. In (4), classes and methods for analysis process are automatically generated. In (5) developers convert these objects for implementation process, considering the computer architecture and coding. (4) and (5) will be shown in Section 2.4. After designing of implementation classes, developers can input an estimated manpower for each method in (6). In (7), they input also the degree of progress of coding and testing for each method at every fixed period. As the degree of progress, they use usually rough percentages (for example, 30%, 70%, 90%, 100%). Sometimes only two data 0% or 100% are used to make clear the finished or not of a task. This time, we use 2 data 0% or 100%. In (8), the system completes the progress reports for users and developers.

2.3 Analysis of use cases

We use the Japanese morphological system called Chasen[6] as a preprocessor of our system. Using the output of Chasen, we arrange the analyzed sentences of "actor action" and "system response" according to the order of the events. The sentences have a certain form. In "Actor Action", the subject is always actor, and "action to system" and "action to another actor" are described. In "System Response", the subject is always system, and "action to another system process" and "action to actor" are also described. Thus, it is possible by using particles the sentences in "Typical Orders of the Events" to classify into the patterns of Figure 2, which is stated in Japanese.

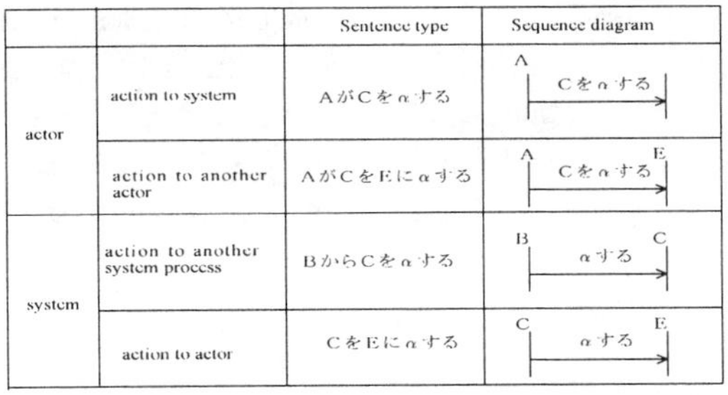

Figure 2. Patterns of sentence in "Typical Course of Events"

For the sentences which are not classified above, we avoid them from our system as meaningless sentences. When these sentences are needed later, then we can add them to the sequence diagram. Thus each sentence corresponds to objects and a message each other. Then users and developers check these objects and message in the sequence diagram and change them if they are not suitable.

2.4 From user classes to implementation classes

Now, let us consider the way to get new classes from the sequence diagram as follows. The message sent to an object indicates methods that the class must define [5]. Also, the message sent from objects to an actor indicates methods that the class must define. By this way, one sentence of use cases corresponds to one method of the class. These classes are called as "user classes" in this paper. They are also called "type" to distinguish from the classes in design process.

Next, we consider following conversion to reconstruct classes in design phase. After these conversions, the classes are called as "implementation classes" in this paper. These conversions are classified as follows (Figure 3).

(1) Uniting several classes to one class
(2) Dividing a class into several classes
(3) Taking a class into several pieces
(4) Making a super class from several classes
(5) Uniting several methods to one method
(6) Moving a method into another class
(7) Dividing a method into several methods
(8) Dividing methods into several methods of another classes

By above works, the method of one user class is recombined into several methods of implementation classes. In case of (4), (7) and (8), one method of one user class is divided into several methods of implementation classes. This dividing ratio of a method of user class is called a "composition ratio" in this paper.

After conversion, developers use implementation classes in implementation phase. When the implementation classes are fixed clearly, it is necessary that developers input the estimated manpower of coding and testing for each method of implementation classes. Then, developers describe codes of those classes and test them. The degree of progress of coding and testing by developers should input in this system weekly or every fixed period of time. In this inputting we use only 2 data, 0% or 100% (0 or 1). The degree of progress of a use case is calculated by the following formulas. We use the first formula to know how much percentage of sentences of a use case is finished and the second one to know how much percentage of manpower of a use case is finished.

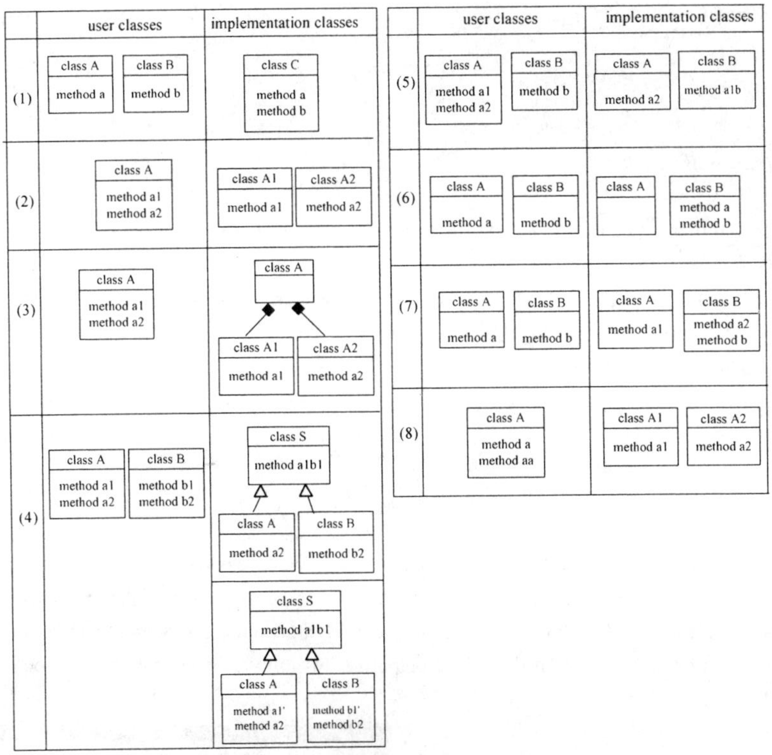

Figure 3. Conversions from user classes to implementation classes

$$\text{the degree of progress of a use case(\%)} = \Sigma\,(\text{the degree of progress} \times \frac{\text{composition ratio}}{\Sigma\,(\text{composition ratio})}) \times 100$$

(based on number of composition ratio)

$$\text{the degree of progress of a use case(\%)} = \Sigma\,(\text{the degree of progress} \times \frac{\text{estimated manpower}}{\Sigma\,(\text{estimated manpower})}) \times 100$$

(based on number of estimated manpower)

For example, we consider one use case which has 2 sentences. First sentence is composed from 2 implementation methods, with composition ratio 40% and 60%. Second sentence is made of one implementation method, and then the composition ratio is 100%. In the case where the first method of the first sentence is finished already but the other methods is not finished yet (the degrees of progress is 1, 0 and 0, respectively), the degree of progress of a use case based on number of composition ratio is calculated as follows.

$$\text{the degree of progress of Use case(\%)} = \left(1\times\frac{40}{40+60+100} + 0\times\frac{60}{40+60+100} + 0\times\frac{100}{40+60+100}\right)\times 100 = 20$$

2.5 Outputs of the system

The outputs from the system are reported to users and developers in the following way.

For users

(1) The state of progress in coding and testing by using sentences of use cases

(2) The graph of progress in coding by using use cases

(3) The graph of progress in testing progress by using use cases

For developers

(1) The state of progress in coding by using class

(2) The state of progress in testing by using class

By these progress reports, users can recognize how the development is going in implementation phase. By these reports, developers can also catch the state of progress in implementation phase. Moreover, it is supposed that developers will not take much time to use this system. And in case the development is felt behind the schedule, these outputs will help to have a communication between user and developers (Figure 4).

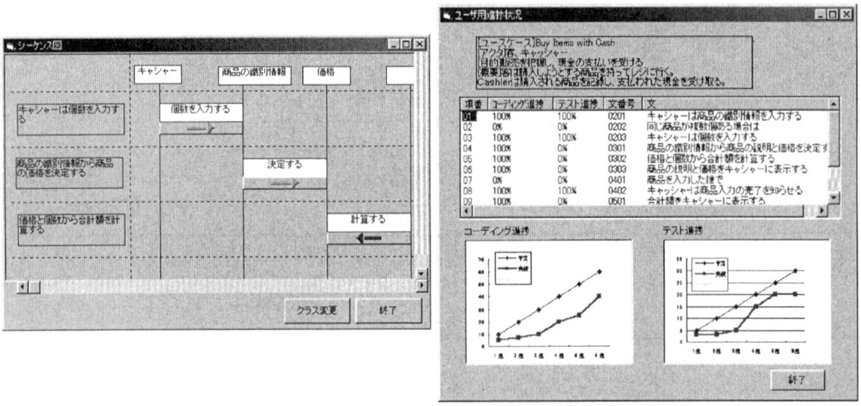

Figure 4. The sequence diagram window and the output window for users

3. Results

As was stated already our system is done as follows, first we classify the type of sentence of use cases that is made by developers and users in analysis phase, and make the sequence diagram from use cases. Then the classes and methods of user class are made from the sequence diagram. After the developers' conversion from user classes to implementation ones, they input the estimated manpower for each method and data of the degree of progress in coding and testing. Thus by using use cases, users can understand the state of the development even in implementation and testing phase easily. Thus, our purpose to make clear the state of the development for users is done through this system.

In this paper, we didn't consider complex changes from user classes to implementation classes. Also, polymorphism is not treated in this paper. To approach more practical level, it is needed to convert classes freely and to use easily with a graphical user interface. On the other hand, several ways of making sequence diagram from use cases are researched already [7, 8]. Using these reports in the first part of our system, it might be possible to make a more suitable sequence diagram. Also, we hope to improve this system to the one that can be applied to iterative and incremental development, which is difficult to control progress.

References

[1] Steve McConnell, Software Project Survival Guide, Microsoft Press, 1998

[2] Ivar Jacobson, Grady Booch, James Rumbaug, The Unified Software Development Process, Addison Wesley Longman Limited,1999

[3] Walker Royce, Software Project Management, A unified Framework, Addison Wesley Longman Limited, 1998

[4] Philippe Kruchten, The Rational Unified Process, Addison Wesley Longman Limited,1999

[5] Craig Larman, Applying UML and Patterns An Introduction to Object-Oriented Analysis and Design, Prentice Hall, 1998

[6] Nara Institute Of Science and Technology, Japanese Morphological Analyzer System "Chasen", http://chasen.aist-nara.ac.jp/index.html.ja

[7] Minoru Harada, Yoshihide Nomura, Kouji Yamamoto, Masasi Ohno, Hiroki Tamura, Sirou Takahashi, An Automatic Generation of Object Modeling Diagrams from Japanese Requirement Statements, journal of IPSJ, Vol.38,No.10, pp.2031-2039 ,(1997.10)(in Japanese)

[8] Tomokazu Yago, Minoru Harada, An Automatic Generation of Object Oriented Dynamic Models from Japanese Requirement Statements, 62th National Convention of IPSJ, special truck4-95-96 (2001.3) (in Japanese)

Knowledge-based Software Engineering
T. Welzer et al. (Eds.)
IOS Press, 2002

Requirements for a Software Process Repository Content

Mikko SANTANEN, Jukka MÄKINEN, Hannu JAAKKOLA
Tampere University of Technology, Information Technology
P.O.Box 300, FIN-28101 Pori, Finland

Abstract. This paper describes requirements for a content of software process repository. Software process repository is aimed to provide software process improvement related knowledge and software engineering related knowledge for software companies and organisational units producing software. Requirements are collected using semi-structured interviewing technique. The results of this study are the requirements for a software process repository content from the user point of view.

1. Introduction

Small software companies and small organisational units developing software often have a lack of knowledge in the area of Software Process Improvement (SPI) and in software engineering (SE). This study describes user requirements for the software process repository (SPORE) content. The user requirements presented in this study are collected interviewing persons working in software producing units (SPUs) in the Satakunta region in Western Finland. These user requirements set the basic content requirements for the SPORE.

A repository providing centralised SPI and SE related knowledge could provide the needed assistance for software production. The project related knowledge could also be an important part of the repository due to project driven development processes. The organisation's standard software process is described at the general level that may not be directly usable by a project [11].

A repository is a shared database of information about engineered artefacts produced or used by an enterprise. Examples of such artefacts include software, documents, maps, information systems, and discrete manufactured components and systems. [2]

The content of the SPORE is knowledge related to SPI and SE activities and is aimed for use of the SPUs. By using this knowledge content SPUs should be able to improve their software processes and SE knowledge areas (KAs). Effectively disseminating process knowledge to process participants is crucial in real-world software engineering settings [8]. The content should include software process database [11] and library [11] of software process related documentation.

A software process is a process a or set of processes used by an organisation or project to plan, manage, execute, monitor, control and improve its software related activities. Process improvement is the action taken to change an organisation's processes so that they meet the organisation's business needs and achieve its business goals more effectively. [6]

The software engineering discipline covers the development of software systems. Software engineers focus on applying systematic, disciplined, and quantifiable approaches to the development, operation, and maintenance of the software. [4]

One of the traditional ways to categorise knowledge is to make distinction between data, information and knowledge [9]. In this study knowledge is defined to be data that (1) *is formal*, and (2) *can be understood*, and (3) *enables systematic actions*. This type of data can be used by the software domain professionals as knowledge – know-how in their work.

In this paper the section 2 explains the background of this study. In section 3 the research method is given. Section 4 lists interviewed roles. Section 5 summarises the results. Section 6 concludes the paper with observations and, future work.

2. Background

This study is related to SPI research in the CoSE (Centre of Software Expertise) – a part of Tampere University of Technology and to the software process improvement network in the Satakunta region (SataSPIN) in Western Finland.

The SataSPIN project started in August 1998 and ended in December 2000. In the first phase of the project ten small (up to 50 employees) software organisations have participated to improve their software processes. The core of the project was to help small and medium sized enterprises (SMEs) in the software business to develop their operations using international software process models. The project used mainly SPICE (ISO/IEC 15504 Technical Report) as the software process assessment and improvement framework. [13]

Seven software producing units in the seven software companies were asked to provide persons for interviewing. These companies have participated in SataSPIN project. The aim of the interviews was to collect user requirements for the SPORE. Interviews were conducted in February and March 2002.

Implemented quality systems and process analysis increases the demand for SPI and SE related knowledge. SPUs that are ready to continue improving their processes could benefit if having access to centralised repository such as SPORE.

Today, the support for SPI initiation is very much depending on competent consultants and trainers, and, especially in the case of small organisations, on external funding. All the supporting resources are limited, and the need to reduce the costs and lower the barriers to start up SPI is obvious. The idea of collecting the tools and methods can be extended to the development of an environment that supports both the SPI work and the related learning process effectively. The environment should include models, methods, tools and information in order to benefit software process improvement. [13]

The knowledge content of SPORE should enable SPUs to improve their process and increase the performance of software production. It is important to find out what kind of SPI and SE related information is really needed in SPUs.

The SPI repository [10] should include at least the following:

- Software process improvement related international standards and models
- Best practices – reference practices (descriptions of the defined and documented processes)
- Forms and templates for software engineering and software process improvement activities
- Examples and instructions of the usage of the repository and the data it includes.

The content requirements listed above are the basis of SPORE knowledge. But there is a need for more detailed information about content requirements from the users' point of view.

3. Research method

The research process consists of a selection of target research group, selection of research method, data collection, analysis and synthesis.

Seven SPUs in seven software companies were asked to provide persons for interview. These companies have participated in a software process improvement network in the Satakunta region (SataSPIN) in Western Finland. These SPUs work in an area of customer related software projects, produce software services, telecommunication software, industrial software, knowledge management software, embedded software and software for logistical systems.

SPUs were asked to provide interviewees that have experience working in software production. Interviews are a traditional means of eliciting requirements [1]. Suitable roles for interview are product a manager, a development manager, a quality manager and a project manager, or other roles related to SPI or SE. All involved SPUs agreed to provide interviewees working with SPI or SE related roles.

The software line and project managers are essential players in a successful process deployment. Shortly stated, they have far more influence on the behaviour of the software projects than process personnel can ever have. The role of process personnel is to provide support in process-related issues for all levels of the line and project organisation. [7]

When interviewing these persons, a semi-structured interview method was used. This method provides flexible means for solving user requirements. Interviewees can state their point of view to the requirements without being restricted to ready made question lists. Interviewing situation contained one interviewee and one interviewer. The length of the interviews was from one to two hours. The number of interviewed person was eleven.

Semi-structured interviews incorporate elements of both quantifiable, fixed-choice responding and the facility to explore, and probe in more depth, certain areas of interest. Thus, this type of interview carries with it the advantages of both approaches as well as the disadvantages. [3]

Data collected from the interviews were analysed and grouped into the main areas of SPI and SE found. In these groupings SPI process models and for SE the KAs [1] was used. The structure of interview topics supports finding of KAs related requirements. There was also other data than content requirements collected from interviewees such as usability requirements and alike. Interviews are available from the author on request.

4. Interviewed roles

In this study the concepts "working role", "organisational role" and "other roles" are used to describe interviewee's roles.

All interviewees had been influenced to a certain degree by SataSPIN project. Interviewees have a Bachelor of Science, a Master of Science or an equivalent education in an area of data processing, software science, software production, information technology, or telecommunications. Educational background of interviewees and the influence of SataSPIN project give a good starting point for interviewees to have enough competence to be interviewed as a source of requirements.

Interviewees' organisational roles are shown in table 1. Here *organisational role* is the role that is written on a person's business card and it states the persons job title. It is not only the organisational role that was important in this study; the interviewed person's have also *other roles* related to their daily work. Here the complete set of roles is called *working roles*. This includes organisational role and the other roles, see Table 1.

Table 1. Organisational roles of interviewed persons.

Group of persons	**Interviewed organisational roles**
Line management	Site Manager and Section Manager
Product management	Director, Product Manager and Feature Manager
Technical	Research and Development manager, Development Manager, Chief Designer and Software Engineer
Quality	2 x Quality Manager

A role is a cluster of defined responsibilities that may be carried by one or more individuals. The one-to-one correspondence between roles and individuals is not required. One person could perform multiple roles, or separate individuals could perform each role. Various individuals are responsible for the workforce activities within an organisation. [5]

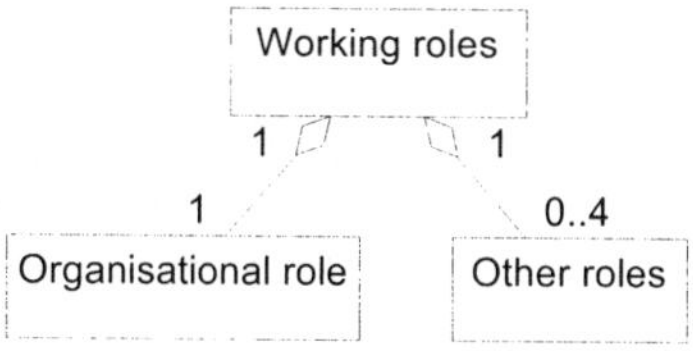

Figure 1. Concept of working roles in this study.

Only one interviewee had one working role and only one interviewee had five working roles. Other interviewees had two or three working roles. The total number of different working roles of the whole interviewed group was 20. Such a distribution of working roles gives multiple views to SPORE content requirements, see Table 2.

Table 2. Different working roles.

Chief Designer	Feature Manager	Production Manager	Research and Development Manager
Customer Manager	Method Developer	Project Manager	Section Manager
Developer	Process Developer	Quality Facilitator	Site Manager
Development Manager	Process Facilitator	Quality Manager	Software Engineer
Director	Product Manager	Requirement Engineer	Team Leader

5. Requirements for the repository content

There are three main improvement areas found by interviewing in this study. These are SPI related knowledge in section 5.1, SE related knowledge in section 5.2, and Project Control related knowledge in section 5.3. The presented findings are summarised in section 5.4.

5.1 SPI Knowledge

The need for SPI related knowledge is focused to the three process models. Interviewed person's rate SPICE [6] as *a most important process improvement model* in their SPUs. SPICE was found suitable for *self-improvement*. Two of the organisations had provisional SPICE assessors trained, which enables self-assessment.

Also the ISO 9001 was seen as an important model for SPI. This is because quality manuals are often based on ISO 9001 documentation. The importance of ISO 9001 certificate is one of the driving forces behind this interest. Two of the SPUs had ISO 9001 internal auditors trained.

There was only a minor interest in SW-CMM [11] (capability maturity model for software). However, there was some evidence that the importance of SW-CMM is going to grow due to customers' requirements. Some customers may require a certain SW-CMM level to be reached at certain time frame as a part of business contract.

Interviewees stated multiple information needs related to SPI. The main SPI topics for SPORE are SPICE, ISO 9001 and SW-CMM. In addition to the SPI reference model and the standard documentation, more specific information needs of the interviewees are listed in Table 3.

Table 3. SPICE, ISO 9001, and SW-CMM information topics.

SPICE	ISO 9001	SW-CMM
– Basic things	– What does it provide	– Basic things
– Current model/coming model	– How to get certificate	– Level 2 and 3
– Question sets and checklists	– Audit of quality system	– Project management
– How to apply	– Internal audits	– How others companies are using
– How others companies are using	– General requirements	– Experiences from other companies
– Assessment and self assessment	– Concepts and terms	– Benefits
– Assessment training and tools	– Quality documentation	– Comparison against SPICE
– Process profiles	– Examples and instructions	– Examples and instructions
– Connections between process groups		
– Comparison against SW-CMM		
– Forms and templates for self assessment		
– Examples and instructions		

SPICE might be the best choice if the SPU is doing maintenance as well as development or the SPU is supplying software to a particular industry where a specific profile of capabilities is important. ISO 9001 might be more appropriate if the SPU have both hardware and software development; it can be applied in both sets of processes and covers the entire organisation. SW-CMM might be more appropriate if the SPU is doing mainly development in projects, or the SPU works with other organisations that are SW-CMM compliant, or the SPU needs to focus mostly on the management of it's software development, not the development process itself. [12]

In this study the definition and the description of the development processes of the SPUs were seen as one of the main improvement areas of SPI related knowledge currently needed. There is a need for formally defined processes in the SPUs. It was seen that an important part of the formality is *process flow charts*. These should define milestones, inputs and outputs, and roles as well as basic concepts and terms.

To be able to handle process flowcharts SPORE should have tools for drawing and defining process flow charts. In SPORE it should also be possible to find out what process means from the *point of view of a given role*. In practise it should be able to explain e.g. what are the responsibilities of a software engineer.

5.2 SE Knowledge

An important part of software engineering is to make a rational choice of development style for a given software project. Another important theme of software engineering is the evaluation of the software products. This includes such diverse activities as peer review of code and test plan, testing, software quality assurance, and measures. [1]

In this study three important SE knowledge topics that should be included to SPORE were found. These topics are *standards and technology*, *development style*, and *evaluation of software products*, see Table 4.

There can also be *construction methods* as an important SE area in the SPORE in addition to the ones mentioned. It is not listed above because the construction methods were seen SPU or product specific, well known inside the SPU, and some of the methods are confidential. This doesn't mean that there couldn't be information e.g. about programming languages such as C/C++ and Java, with styleguides and language specific construction tools.

Table 4. SE related information topics.

Standards and technology	**Development style**	**Evaluation of software products**
– Telecom mainstream	– New techniques	– Measurement of errors
– Internet	– Old techniques	– Examples and instructions
– Wireless technologies	– Modelling methods	– Forms and templates
	– Software lice-cycle models	– Best practices
	– Object based method	
	– Distributed systems	

Ten interviewees were asked to state the need of SE information classified in ten KAs [1] according to the software engineering body of knowledge. Figure 2 shows "yes, information is needed" answers related to these KAs. Interviewees stated that information about requirements, design, construction, testing and engineering processes is the most important to their SPUs. Construction related information is usually acquired by sending persons to training courses or they are trained inside the SPU. Interviewees see that information related to construction is generally acquired elsewhere than from the SPORE.

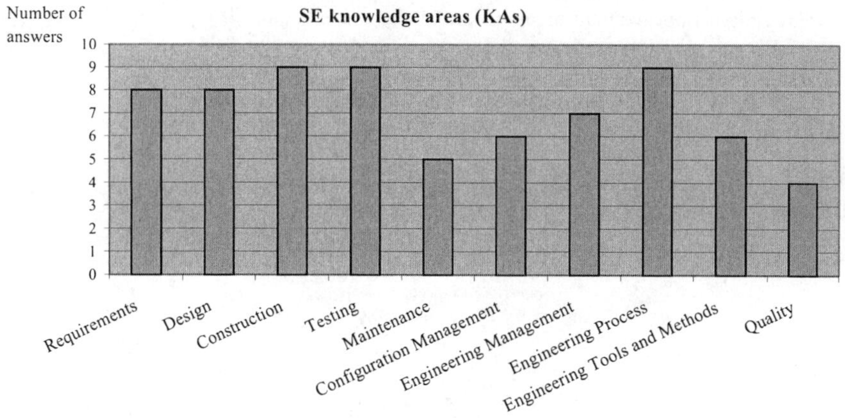

Figure 2. SE information needs by KAs.

5.3 Project control knowledge

At the organisational level, the organisation's standard software process needs to be described, managed, controlled, and improved in a formal manner. At the project level, the emphasis is on the usability of the project's defined software process and the value it adds to the project. [11]

SPUs have adopted project driven development. This emphasises the need for project control. Project control is defined here to be more than just a management of a project by the project manager and the project steering groups. Project control provides all the needed knowledge to complete project successfully. Interviewees stated the need for a *project toolbox* – a collection of basic tools, forms and templates, examples and instructions, best practices and measurement methods to build, manage, and run project successfully. Project toolbox should contain solutions and help for the following topics listed in Table 5.

Table 5. Project toolbox solution and help topics.

– What is the framework of project?	– How to manage project?	– How to measure project?
– How to build project?	– How to follow-through project?	– Benchmarking against other similar projects?

According to the interviewees one of the problematic management issue in the project work is *requirements change management*, which needs well-defined processes and practices.

5.4 Summary of the results

Interviewees in this study stated that repository providing centralised SPI and SE related knowledge could provide the needed assistance to their SPUs software production. Also project related knowledge should be an important part of the repository due to project driven development processes. It was acknowledged that repository providing SPI and SE knowledge would be used as a part of interviewee's work in improvement of their SPUs processes. But this requires relevant information from the SPOREs content.

Three main improvement areas of knowledge were found: SPI, SE and project control knowledge. Information needed in these areas is summarised in Table 6.

Table 6. Information needed in SPI, SE and project control areas.

– Forms and templates	– Best practices	– Benchmarking data between SPUs
– Examples and instructions	– Tools	– Concept and term libraries

The required knowledge content of SPORE is presented in Figure 3 from the user point of view.

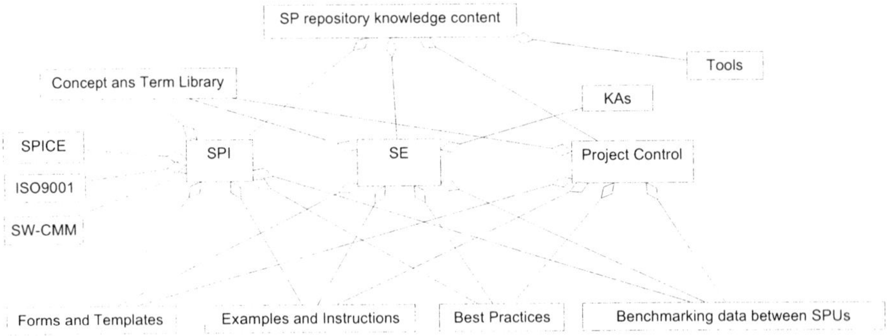

Figure 3. Required knowledge content of SPORE from the user point of view.

6. Conclusions

This study describes the requirements for a software process repository (SPORE) content as found relevant by studying the responses of the interviewee's. Seven software producing units (SPUs) in seven software companies were asked to provide persons for interviewing. Interviewees stated that a repository providing centralised SPI and SE related knowledge could provide the needed assistance to their SPUs software production. Also project related knowledge should be an important part of the repository due to project driven development processes.

The need for SPI knowledge is seen concentrating to three process models. Interviewed persons rate SPICE as *the most important process improvement model* in their SPUs. It was seen that SPICE is suitable for *self-improvement*. Also, ISO 9001 was seen an important model for SPI. This is because quality manuals are often based in ISO 9001 documentation. The importance of ISO 9001 certificate is the one of the driving forces behind the interest. There was only a minor interest in SW-CMM. However, there was some evidence that the importance of SW-CMM is going to grow due to the customers' requirements.

The definition and the description of the development processes of the SPUs were seen as one of the main improvement area of SPI related knowledge currently needed. There is a need for formally defined processes in the SPUs. It was seen that an important part of the formality are the *process flow charts*.

Three important SE knowledge topics that should be included to SPORE are *standards and technology*, *development style*, and *evaluation of software products*.

Interviewees stated the need for *project toolbox* – a collection of basic tools, forms and templates, examples and instructions, best practices and measurement methods to build, manage, and run project successfully.

In the future, more detailed and comprehensive requirement elicitation study is needed to point out what kind of information is really useful to SPUs in the knowledge areas found. Also usability requirements of SPORE should be studied as well as the user roles of SPORE.

References

[1] A. Abrain *et al.*, Guide to the Software Engineering Body of Knowledge SWEBOK, trial version 1.00, IEEE, 2001.

[2] P. Bernstein, An overview of Repository Technology, VLDB'94, Santiago de Chile, 1994.

[3] P. Brewerton and L. Millward, Organizational Research Methods, SAGE Publications Ltd., London, 2001.

[4] CMMI Product Development Team, CMMI for Systems Engineering/Software Engineering, Version 1.02: Continuous Representation, Carnegie Mellon University, Pittsburgh, 2000.

[5] B. Curtis *et al.*, People Capability Maturity (P-CMM) version 2.0, Carnigie Mellon University, Pittsburgh, 2001.

[6] ISO/IEC TR 15504-9:1998 Information Technology – Software Process Assessment – Part 9: Vocabulary, 1998.

[7] T. Kaltio, Software Process Asset Management and Deployment in a Multi-Site Organization, Helsinki, 2001.

[8] M. Kellner *et al.*, Process Guides: Effective Guidance for Process Participants, ICSP 5, Chicago, 1998.

[9] K. Koskinen, Management of Tacit Knowledge in a Project Work Context, Espoo, 2001.

[10] M. Lepasaar *et al.*, SPI repository for small software organisations, EuroSPI, Limerick, 2001.

[11] M. Paulk *et al.*, The Capability Maturity Model: Guidelines for Improving the Software Process, Addison-Wesley, 1999.

[12] The SPIRE Project Team, The SPIRE Handbook - Better, Faster, Cheaper Software Development in Small Organisations, Centre for Software Engineering Ltd., Dublin, 1998

[13] T. Varkoi *et al.*, Requirements For A Software Process Improvement Support And Learning Environment, PICMET'01, Portland, Oregon, 2001.

Knowledge-based Software Engineering
T. Welzer et al. (Eds.)
IOS Press, 2002

The Utilization of BSC Knowledge in SPI – A Case Study

Harri KETO, Hannu JAAKKOLA
Tampere University of Technology,
Information Technology, Pori, Finland, www.pori.tut.fi

Abstract. This paper presents the possibility to utilize Balanced Scorecard knowledge in software process improvement. The research is a case study in a Finnish software company where the author has been working as a quality manager and a product manager. Main focus is to introduce aspects of making visible the business factors of software process improvement steps. The balanced scorecard approach is introduced briefly. Analysis of the case study and derived proposals are introduced. The paper is concluded by an outline of the further work.

1. Introduction

When software process improvement (SPI) [1] assessment report has to be analysed and decisions about SPI plan should be done, there are at least four questions to be answered. How to be convinced of right SPI activities? Do we actually need SPI plan? How to make sure, that chosen SPI activities are proceeding? How to verify, that the SPI activities have positive effect on the business?

The SPI assessment report should include enough explanatory to the first two questions. More information might still be needed to ensure the decision makers. The last two questions are more related to management practices in the organization. There is a possibility the SPI plan will fail to become reality. To offer better knowledge for managers, management systems and software process improvement tools can be used as an integrated toolset.

In this article we are interested about the interface between Balanced Scorecard (BSC) [2] [3] and SPI. BSC offers management level knowledge about improvement objectives and offers information about the status of the SPI plan itself. Balanced scorecard has also potential information, which can be used in SPI assessment. There might still be a gap between the BSC indicators and the phenomenon behind them. That might be, because scorecard's cause-and-effect chain works between those strategic or management indicators and they don't include knowledge about software engineering practices.

Methodologically this is a case study. Ideas of this study are derived from the author's four years experience about working as a quality manager and two years experience about working as a teem leader and a product manager in the case company.

The chapter 2 describes briefly the general principles of BSC. Although strategic issues are the starting point of implementing BSC, profound strategic business issues are not discussed in this article. Detailed discussion about BSC and how to implement strategies can be found in Kaplan's and Norton's book The Strategy Focused Organization [4]. In chapter 3 the definitions of process are. Chapter 4 presents the case company and the utilization of BSC as a measurement system. In chapter 5 some general propositions of the case study are presented. The paper is concluded by an outline of the further work.

2. General principles of Balanced Scorecard (BSC)

2.1. *The four main perspectives of BSC*

Robert Kaplan and David Norton introduced the balanced scorecard approach in 1992 [2]. The basic principles of the model are derived from a study, where a dozen companies from different business area were included. The study was motivated by a belief that existing performance measurement approaches, primarily relying on financial accounting measures, were becoming obsolete [3, p. vii].

The balanced scorecard is a conceptual framework for translating an organization's strategic objectives into a set of performance indicators distributed among four perspectives (Figure 1): 1) Financial, 2) Customer, 3) Internal Business Processes, and 4) Learning and Growth. Through the BSC an organization monitors both its current performance and its ability to learn and improve.

The BSC was first developed to solve a performance measurement problem [4, p. vii]. When companies applied BSC to larger extent, it became a part of the strategic design.

Figure 1: The four perspectives of BSC [2].

The financial perspective is mainly focused on traditional need for financial data. Financial performance measures indicate, whether a company's strategy, implementation, and execution are contributing to bottom-line improvement. Profitability, sales growth and generation of cash flow are examples of financial objectives used in BSC.

The customer perspective is derived from the clear importance of customer focus and customer satisfaction in the business. Good examples of measures are customer satisfaction, customer retention, new customer acquisition, customer profitability, and market and account share of in targeted strategic segments. Poor performance from this perspective is a leading indicator of future decline.

The internal business process perspective reveals on the internal processes that will have an impact on customer satisfaction and achieving organization's financial objectives. Circle time, throughput, quality, productivity and cost are common measures of process view. The concept of process and it's different interpretations is discussed more detailed later in this article.

Learning and growth constitute the essential foundation for success of any organization, where knowledge is the core resource of business. The learning and growth perspective includes employee training and corporate cultural attitudes related to both individual and corporate self-improvement. Knowledge management activities and relating information systems, such intranet, are important factors of this perspective.

2.2. The Cause-and-Effect hypothesis

There is a strong relationship between the four perspectives. Kaplan and Norton proposed a hypothesis about the chain of cause and effect that leads to strategic success [3, p. 30-31].

Management experts agree that learning and growth is the key to strategic success. Effectiveness and high quality in processes is strongly influenced by employees' skills and training. The driver of effectiveness could be the knowledge management activities, which are measured in learning and growth perspective of BSC.

Improved business processes lead to improved products and services. In the customer perspective customer satisfaction is measured, but improved processes produces it. For a company to be profitable, loyal customers are needed, which is known to correlate with product quality. The candidate drivers of customer's loyalty are the quality of products and services, and organization's ability to maintain high product quality.

Improved customer satisfaction leads to loyal customers and increased market share, which directly affects the economy of the company.

The cause-and-effect hypothesis is fundamental to understanding the metrics that the balanced scorecard prescribes.

3. The concept of process and process improvement

Different process definitions are listed in Table 1.

Referrence	The definition of process
IEEE Std 610 [7]	A sequence of steps performed for a given purpose; for example, the software development process [7]
IEEE Std 1220 [8]	A system of operation or series of actions, changes, or functions, that bring about an end or result including the transition criteria for processing from one stage or process step to the next [8]
ISO 12207 [9]	A set of interrelated activities, which transform inputs into outputs [9]
Davenport [5]	A specific ordering of work activities across time and place, with a beginning, an end, and clearly identified inputs and outputs: a structure for action [4]
Hammer & Champy [6]	A collection of activities that takes one or more kinds of input and creates an output that is of value to the customer [5]

Table 1. Definitions of process

According to Davenport [5, p.7], his definition of process can be can be applied to both large and small processes – to the entire set of activities that serves customers, or only to answering a letter of complaint. The approach of Hammer and Champy is business oriented and combines the concepts of quality and process ("...output that is of value to the customer") [6]. Davenport distinguishes the process innovation from process improvement, which seeks a lower level of change. If process innovation means performing a work activity in a radically new way, process improvement involves performing the same business process with slightly increased efficiency or effectiveness [5, p. 10].

The process definitions of IEEE and ISO standards are more theoretical and are used in the theory of SPI models. In the case company of this study, the process concept was used to refer to a business process in a same sense how Davenport [5, p. 7-8] refers to large process. Hammer's and Champy's quality aspect is also implemented. The case company's main business processes are introduced briefly in the next chapter.

4. The Case Company

4.1. Process improvement background

The case company is a Finnish software company with about 90 employees. The main software products are business applications for financial management, personnel management and enterprise resource planning (ERP). From the software engineering point of view the company and the networked partners share a common product policy: the software should be kept as a product, the amount of customer varying code is kept in minimum. This is made by strong version development process where customers' business needs are carefully analysed and developed to a new version of software product. Totally new business ideas might be a start point of another innovation process, development of a new product.

The company was formed in fusion of two small SE companies. Combining two software engineering cultures was the start point to the process improvement activities. The author of this article was transferred from software activities to the quality manager and was closely involved to the implementation of BSC and SPI assessments.

Overall management system was seen to be the first main object of improvement. Business process reengineering, benchmarking, and ISO 9000 quality standard series were the first toolset used in process improvement. A strong focus on business processes and process innovation [4] was emerged. The core business processes of the case company are 1) The Development of a New Product, 2) The Sales and Delivery, 3) The Customer Support Service Process and 4) The Version Development of Existing Products. The case company achieved the ISO 9001 quality certificate after two and half year process improvement work.

The process concept was applied to refer to a business process in a same sense how Hammer and Champy [6, p.35, 50-64] define it and describe the characteristics of a reengineered process. Measurement of business processes took place from the beginning of the process improvement work. It was realized, that there should be an information system behind every indicator and so the number of indicators were limited to those where company's own ERP system offered reliable source of data.

The company was seeking more power to management aspects and BSC approach was chosen. Some modifications to the measurement system was made to fit it into the idea of BSC. New indicators were also introduced. Thus the first implementation of the BSC was purely a measurement system. An example of implemented indicators of version development process is presented in Table 2.

At the time the first BSC was implemented indicator of the product quality showed, that the number of repair delivery was high. There had been both internal and external audits, but ISO 9001 was felt too abstract to give concrete improvement guidelines. The first assessments using ISO/IEC 15504 (SPICE) [10],[11] was done. Careful analysis of the software assessment report and discussions with certain customers and partners lead to an idea to develop a new integration test practice. The SPI plan was implemented as a part of balanced scorecard's learning and growth perspectives.

Table 2. An example of implemented indicators of version development process

BSC perspective	**Indicator categoria**	**Indicator data**
Learning and growth	Process improvement	Activities in process improvement plan
	Training	Product version training New skills training Development process training
Internal busisness process	Process quality	Amount of SE rework Time share between process tasks Quality index of a version development project
	Product quality	Number of component repair delivery
	Internal cooperation	Team cooperation
	Process effectiveness	Version development project schedule Total time share between process tasks
Customer	Customer satisfaction	Customer satisfaction on new versions
Financial	Turnover	Turnover of version agreements

Next is an example, how SPI influenced to some indicators in the internal business process perspective and the customer perspective:

Improved process was implemented before the next product version release. When the first customers started to use the new version, it was soon clear that the process improvement had succeeded. The evidence could be seen from the BSC's indicators: 1) Number of component repair delivery was lowering, 2) amount of SE rework was lowering, and 3) customer satisfaction of the product version was higher than before. In this case the influence of SPI activities on financial perspective was not so clear.

The only financial indicator of version development process, - the turnover of version agreement - gains most of its value in the first quarter of the years, but the version is released in september. So there is a time gap between these two aspects and nothing could be said in the sort term. Because the influence on customer satisfaction was obvious, there should be possitive effects to financial perspective in the long term.

4.2. Analysis of the case utilization of BSC knowledge in the SPI

There can be found three properties, which emphasize the utilization of balanced scorecard knowledge in the case:

1) The SPI plan was implemented to be a part of learning and growth perspective. By representing the state of the SPI plan in every team meeting, general awareness of SPI was growing which further helped on implementing the new practise.
2) The balanced scorecard showed, that there is a deviation in the process, but SPI assessment was needeed to find out proper improvement objectives.
3) The cause-and-chain effect in the BSC worked in the short term only between learning and growth, internal business process and cutomer perspectives.

The real power of the Balanced Scorecard occurs when it is transformed from a measurement system to a management system [3, p. 19]. It is obvious, that when it implemented first as a measurement system, the aspects of control were highlited.

5. Generalization of the case and conclusions

The author worked in the case company as quality manager and product manager. The generalization and conclusion described here are author's perceptions and interpretations. It might be too radical to say that the properties of the previous case can be generalized. More than one case study should be studied before there is enough evidence for generalization.

In a software company the management tools and software process improvement tools can be used as an integrated toolset. BSC offers management knowledge about the improvement objectives and offers information about the status of the SPI plan itself. From the quality managers point of view it was helpful that BSC integrated the earlier measurement practices with quality system's metrics. In the eyes of the employee it concretized the quality system and the SPI work.

The second property seems to refer to the lack of SPI knowledge in balanced scorecard. In BSC the cause-and-effect chain exists between strategic or management indicators and does not include knowledge about software engineering practicies. But if for example customer indicators and internal process indicators are indicating same focus with the outcome of SPI assessment, there should be obvious agreement of the improvement objects at least in the large scale. Also the result and propositions of SPI assessment might include valuable knowledge to explain indicator values in BSC. That means that the explanative relationship functions both ways. The cause-and-effect chain can be extended

The third property of the case seems to be related to properties of chosen financial indicator. The careful analysis of financial indicators in BSC is needed, if they are to serve as indicators of business benefits of SPI.

The generalizations made in this article might be of value in one case, but they still need more evidence and deeper analysis. One interesting subject is the basic concept of SPI, the process maturity, and it's relationship to BSC. The future work will continue with the basic aspects. More evidence will be gathered and a model or approach of utilization of balanced scorecard in SPI is planned to be constructed.

References

[1] Zahran, S., Software Process Improvement: Practical Guidelines for business success, Software Engineering Institute, 2001

[2] Kaplan, Robert S., and Norton, David P., The Balanced Scorecard: Measures that Drive Performance. *Harvard Business Review* 70, no. 1 (January-February 1992): 71-79.

[3] Kaplan, Robert S., and Norton, David P., The Balanced Scorecard. Harward Business School Press. 1996

[4] Kaplan, Robert S., and Norton, David P., The Strategy-Focused Organization. Harward Business School Press. 2001

[5] Davenport, Thomas H., Process Innovation: Reengineering Work through Information Technology. Harvard Business School Press, 1993

[6] Hammer, M. and Champy, J., Reengineering The Corporation. Harper Business. 1993.

[7] IEEE Std 610, IEEE Standard Glossary of Software Engineering Terminology, 1990

[8] IEEE Std 1220, IEEE Standard for Application and Management of System Engineering Process

[9] ISO/IEC TR12207, Information Technology – software lifecycle processes, International Standards Organization, 1995

[10] ISO/IEC TR 15504-2: Information Technology - Software Process Assessment Part2: A Reference Model For Processes And Process Capability, 1998

[11] Jaakkola Hannu, Varkoi Timo, Lepasaar Marion, Mäkinen Timo, Experiences In Software Improvement With Small Organizations. In publication Proceedings of the IASTED International Conference Applied Informatics. The International Association of Science and Technology for Development - IASTED, February 2002.

Knowledge-based Software Engineering
T. Welzer et al. (Eds.)
IOS Press, 2002

A Formalization of the Design Pattern Derivation by Applying Quantum Field Concepts

Mikio OHKI† Yasushi KAMBAYASHI†
Nippon Institute of Technology
4-1 gakuedai miyashiro minami-saitama Japan
E-mail: †ohki@nit.ac.jp, †yasushi@nit.ac.jp

Abstract.
It is widely known that the analysts and the designers of software need to have some criteria applicable for extracting software elements (attributes, methods, and classes) during OOAD. Such criteria should be accurate and easy to understand. Considering such a need in the circumstance of OOAD application, the authors have developed a methodology that derives several criteria for extracting software elements from software characteristics. This methodology is analogous to the quantum field theory. This paper describes the basic concepts of the software field and the derivation of the element-extracting operations and configuration constraints under several hypotheses. In the later part of the paper describes that it is possible to derive typical design patterns by applying those operations to the software field.

1. INTRODUCTION

There has been an urgent request to obtain indicators that forecast the characteristics of software throughout its lifecycle, i.e. the volume of the product, the frequency of requests for changes, the place where the requests for changes occur, and how long each functionality stays alive. Although many research projects have proposed forecasting models to answer such a request, most of them are empirical and lack of enough theoretical bases. Constructing experimental models from measured data may explain some phenomena, but those models tend to miss grasping the essential laws that may dominate the behavior of software. In this paper we will introduce a new approach to explain the behavior of software. Our thesis is that software is a kind of fields in which software elements, such as methods and attributes, interact each other to produce certain behavioral patterns. This idea stems from our previous research result about modeling software development processes [2].

The structure of this paper is as follows. Section 2 proposes the new idea that software can be seen as a field. Section 3 rationalizes this idea by applying this "field" approach to the object-oriented analysis and design. Section 4 demonstrates the applicability to the design pattern derivation. In Section 5, we conclude our discussion that some design patterns may be derived from software field and operations on it.

2. FILED CONCEPT FOR SOFTWARE

2.1 Review of the Basic Characteristics of Software

One of the major characteristics of software is its abstract nature. We cannot see "software." It is abstract and invisible. This fact makes it is difficult to pursue the quantitative measurements on the following characteristics

(1) The "state" of software should include the degree that the software satisfies the corresponding specification, the degree of concreteness of the software and the degree of refinement of the software.
(2) The "elements" of software should include kind and quantity of data., functions, events that the software is supposed to handle.
(3) "Behavioral characteristics" of software should include those parts of software potentially exposed to frequent modification and the degree of association between elements.

In the case of object-oriented software, it may be possible to find corresponding basic mechanisms, i.e. class structure, attributes and methods in classes, and interactions of classes by messages, that dominate objects to the characteristics listed in (2) and (3). In order to discover these basic mechanisms and quantitatively obtain the above characteristics, we have introduced field concepts of quantum physics to object-oriented software. We found that the quantum field concepts can be applicable to object-oriented programming, and they empower the object-oriented concepts to model the real world.

2.2 Analogy of the Field Concepts

"Field" in quantum physics is an abstract concept introduced to explain the behaviors of the elements as an integral system. A field dominates the behavior of each element in it, and each element affects to the field as well. The field represents the state of the entire elements, and it changes the state as time proceeds. A field in quantum physics represents the distribution of probabilities of existence of an electron in a space. The distribution diffuses as time elapses. In a field where multiple sources of force exist such as inside of atom, several eigenstates that are stable against time are known. Each eigenstate corresponds to one of the energy levels of the electron. Even though the field theory of physics has no relation to software, the concepts behind the theory are analogous to the characteristics of software as follows:

(1) Elements that constitute the field themselves are probabilistic. In the case of software, even the same specification may lead to different products. They have different module structures and different data structures depend on characteristics of developers and developing periods.
(2) The state of the field is probabilistically described as the observation is made. In the case of software, attributes and the methods may not be found, even though they potentially exist.
(3) Interactions of multiple forces form an eigenstate. In the case of software, certain requests for functionality and certain constraints lead to a stable state. We consider such a state as a design pattern.
(4) The state of a field diffuses as time elapses. Analysis of software may reveal many implementation possibilities. Software review is a process of selection of such possibilities, therefore it can be considered as an effort to converge such diffusion.

This paper reports the results of our attempt to formalize the analysis and development processes of software by applying the field concepts to characteristics of software elements.

2.3 The Field Concepts

In order to abstract and to model software as a field throughout its lifecycle (we call such a field a software field), we introduced a symbol "F" that represents the entire software. Using "F", we have formulated a process to solidify and to refine software from vague ideas before requirement specification is made. Software field is introduced to explain elements of software and processes of software development. Software field creates elements of software and determines the structure of software. In order to formulate the software field, we introduce the following concepts:

(1) Operations extracting elements from the field

We assume the following. Elements that constitute software such as data and functions are extracted from software field by applying certain operations. The process extracting data and functions from ambiguous specification is explained by this assumption. We will describe the details of the operations later.

(2) Eigenstates of the field

Software field changes its state as time elapses. As the elements of the field and outside constraints (specifications, conditions of development) interact, the field tends to stay in a stable state after a certain period. We call such a state an eigenstate. Repetitions of state transitions such as regressions of software development tend to form an eigenstate. The design patterns can be considered as kinds of eigenstates.

(3) Observation of the field

The observation of the software field can be considered as taking a snapshot of active software. By observing the software field, we can obtain the kinds of the elements (attributes and methods) and instances of objects (combinations of attributes and methods). Observation is the only way to identify instances.

(4) Transition of the field

The field changes its state as time elapses. Software specifications and restrictions do as well. They affect software components, such as function modules and classes. One of the objectives that we introduced the field concepts to the software is to formulate such dynamics of the software.

3. APPLICATION OF THE FIELD CONCEPTS TO THE OBJECT-ORIENTED ANAYISIS AND DESIGN

3.1 Extracting the elements by quantizing the software field

In this section, we derive conceptual rules on the system analysis and design based on the concepts of the software field. These conceptual rules are used to extract the basic elements of software and to determine the structure of software. The motivation to introduce the concepts of the field is our hypothesis that the structure and functionality of software are theoretically derivable by using the concepts of the field.

The complex system theory suggests that complex phenomena may be explainable by repetition or combination of simple rules. We expect that the concepts of the software field may explain the complex phenomena of the object-oriented software analysis and design. We assume a software field that expresses object-oriented software, its coordinate system, and quantizing operations. Upon using these assumptions, it is easy to formulate the extraction of the elements of object-oriented software.

(1) The coordinate system describing the software field

We introduce two axes other than the actual time in the software field as follows:

(a) Trigger time T

The first axis of the coordinate system is trigger time T. T is a discrete time that expresses when the software field changes its state, and is not related to the actual time. It represents when events occur. In the analysis document, it represents when the trigger arrives to invoke a certain function of the software. In the program, it represents when an event occurs.

(b) Identifier I

The second axis of the coordinate system is another discrete value I that corresponding to an identifier (a name of software element). As the analysis and design of software proceeds, the number of identifiers grows and this value I rises. Figure 1 shows the image of the growth of the software field as the actual time t elapses. This picture depicts software changes its state by revision and/or evolution.

(2) Extract operations of elements (quantizing operations)

We introduce two operations that extract software elements.

(a) Method and attribute extraction operation

The operation that extracts methods and attributes is represented as follows:

$$\{ I \mid dF/dT = 0 \}$$

We define the set of identifiers that constitutes the software as the subset of F where the difference of F in terms of T is zero. This operation extracts names of attributes and names of methods in analysis/design phase. This definition means that stable points in the software field F, i.e. not changed the value in terms of T, are interpreted as identifiers in the software. In the object-oriented software analysis and design, the extracted attributes and methods are supposed to be used throughout the entire design phases. We define that identifiers that are unchanged represent attributes and methods.

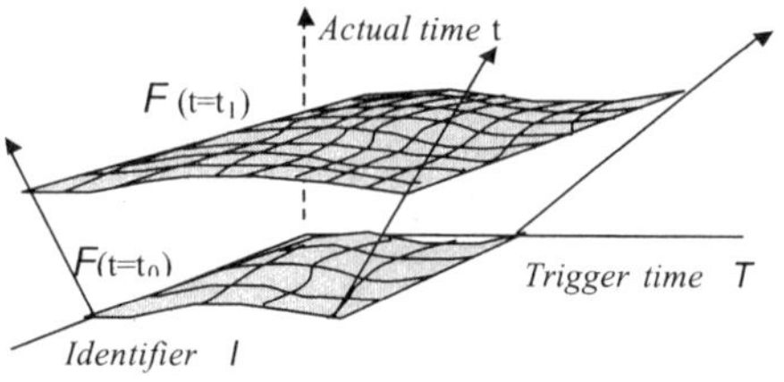

Figure 1. Image of the growth of the software field expressed by three axes

(b) Class extraction operation

The operation that extracts classes is represented as follows:

$\{ I \text{ at } T_0 \mid dF/dT=0 \ \& \ V^{-1}(T,I)=T_0 \}$ where V is the function that determines the instance of I.

The operation defined at (a) extracts the names of attributes and methods. A class is considered as a collection of such attributes and methods that are extracted at the same trigger time T_0, also they are instantiated at the time T_0. Instantiation of an attribute means assignment of a real value. Therefore we consider that a class should contain attributes whose values are determined at the same time.

3.2 Characteristics of the Elements

Collecting elements extracted from the operation described in the previous section does not form a class. In order to construct a class, each element must have some common characteristics. Those characteristics can be considered as meta-attributes for the instances of attributes and methods. In the software field context, each extracted element has the following three meta-attributes.

(1) Situation level S

When an element is extracted, it is assigned a situation level. The situation level is an analogy to the energy level in the quantum physics. It indicates the level of inheritance for the extracted element. If the situation level of an element A is less than the situation level of another element B, the element A is supposed to be in a class closer to the root of inheritance tree than the class that contains the element B. Elements that have the same trigger time are placed at the same situation level.

(2) Multiplicity M

The multiplicity indicates whether different elements have the same identifier or not. If the multiplicity of an identifier is greater than one, it indicates that the identifier stands for more than one element. When the extracted element is an attribute, it has a unique identifier and the multiplicity is one. When the extracted element is a method, the element may share the identifier with other elements. Those elements are placed at the same identifier space but at different situation levels. Figure 2(a) and 2(b) show these images.

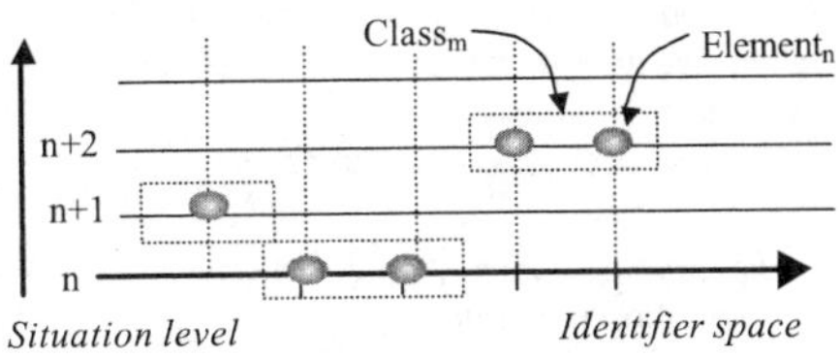

Figure 2(a). Multiplicity for attributes

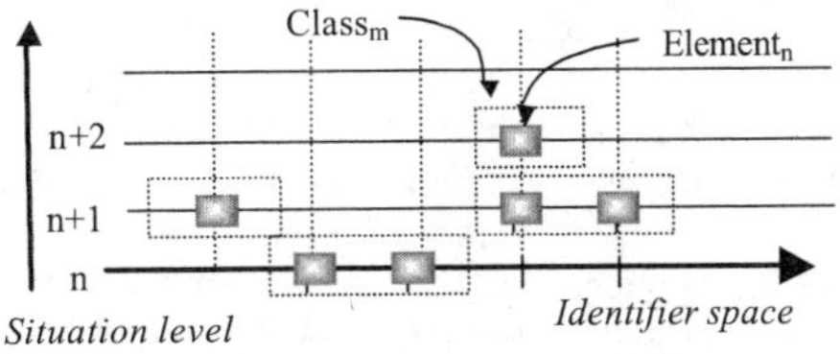

Figure 2(b). Multiplicity for methods

4. APPLICATION TO THE DERIVATION OF DESIGN PATTERNS

Quantizing operations and characteristics of elements are not only effective for extracting attributes and classes but also effective for deriving the design patterns [3]. In this section we demonstrate that the design patterns for typical structures are derivable by using the quartering operations and characteristics of elements. The rationales for this demonstration are as follows:

i) If we can find a correspondence between the sequence of application of the quantizing operations and characteristics of elements and the derivation of design patterns, we may find new design patterns by changing the sequence of the applications.

ii) In the place of the design pattern application, the sequence of application of the quantizing operations and characteristics of elements may determine the class structures. In other words, *a design pattern may be expressed as a sequence of operations to the software field.* Also, introducing meta-rules to reduce the sequence of operations makes it possible to reduce a complex class structure into a simple class structure that preserves the semantics of the class.

We chose the four typical design patterns to illustrate the processes of the design pattern derivations by the applications of the quantizing operations to the software field and the extraction of the characteristics of elements of software.

(1) Adapter: interface to objects

The "adapter" design pattern emerges when we have a class with a stable method, e.g. the Target class in Figure 3(a), and would like to add new features without changing the interface. Figure 3(a) shows that Target class and Adaptee class are combined with Adapter class without changing the original interfaces. We can start to distill this pattern through extracting Request() method of Target class and SpecificRequest() method of Adapter class from the software field, and placing them at the appropriate position on the base level of class Target. Figure 3(b) illustrates this situation.

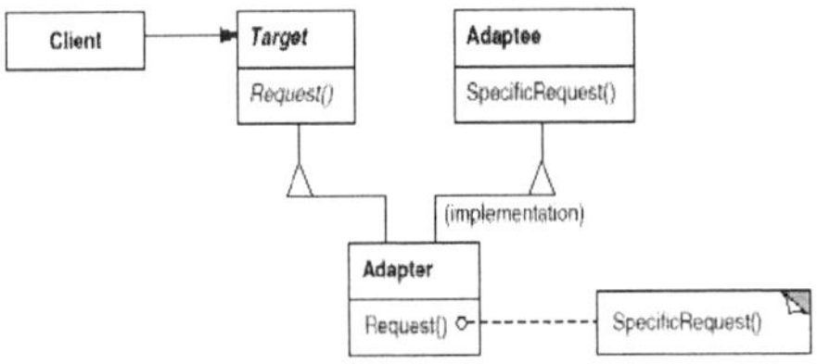

Figure 3(a). Structure of the "adapter" pattern

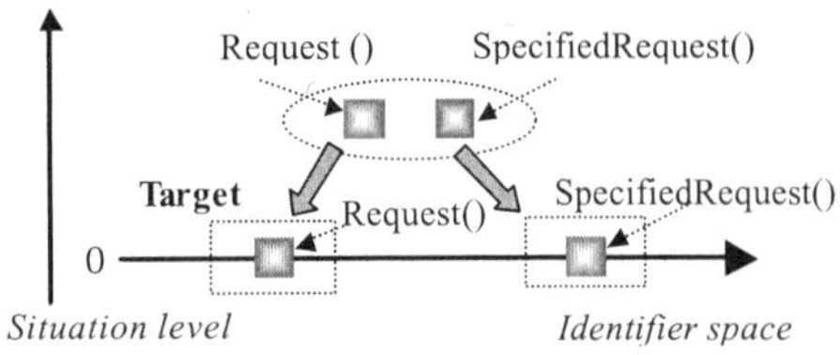

Figure 3(b). Placing elements in the identifier space on the base situation level

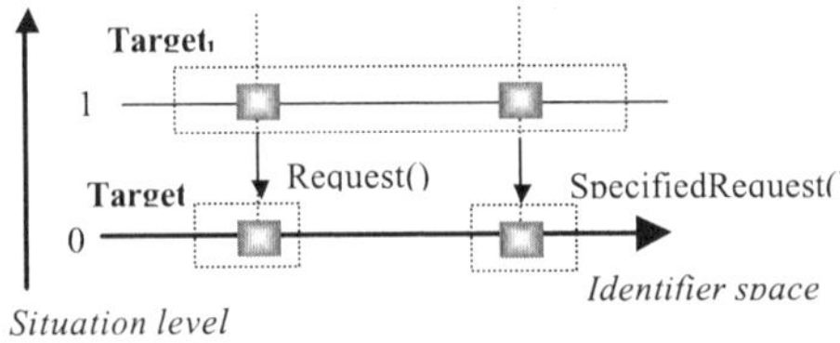

Figure 3(c). Positioning corresponding to the Adapter pattern

Then we need to add a new element (method), Request() with the same trigger time as the existing methods Request() and SpecificRequest() to this software field. Since the identifier is the same, the new method is placed at the same position with the existing method Request(). But it must be set on the different situation level because of the constraint of multiplicity. After doing the same thing with another new method SpecificRequest(), we obtain the final positioning as shown in Figure 3(c). The situation that more than one method with the same identifier placed on the different situation level in the software field indicates there is inheritance relation. Therefore, the positioning shown in Figure 3(c) is corresponding to the class structure shown in Figure 3(a).

(2) Bridge: implementation of objects

The "bridge" design pattern emerges when we try to separate the interface and the implementation of a class and to make it easy to extend as shown in Figure 4(a).

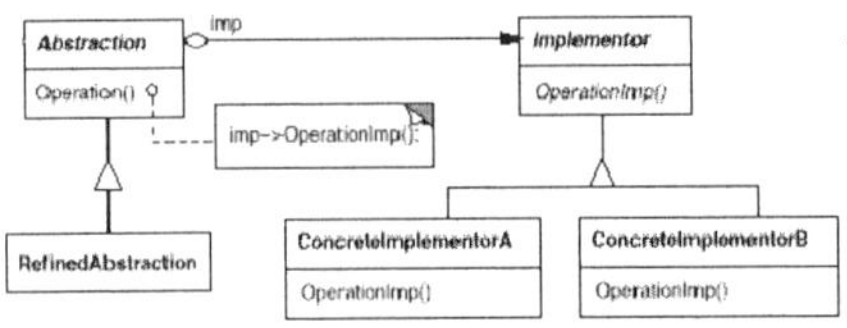

Figure 4(a). Structure of the "bridge" pattern

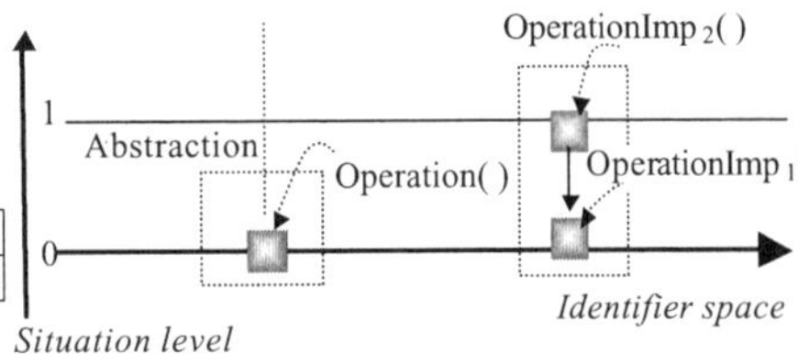

Figure 4(b). Positioning corresponding to the bridge pattern

The characteristic of this pattern is that there are several methods sharing the same name, e.g. the Operation() method in Figure 4(a), and each of them will be implemented at different trigger times. The positioning in the identifier-situation level space would be like shown in Figure 4(b). Unlike Adapter pattern, it is known that there would be several implementations for Operation(), we place its implementations at the different positions. Due to the constraint of multiplicity, we cannot place those implementations on the same situation level. We have to place them on different situation levels shown in Figure 4(b). When we extract several OperationImp$_2$() at the same trigger time, we need to place them at different positions on the same situation level. The positioning shown in Figure 4(b) is corresponding to the class structure shown in Figure 4(a).

(3) Composite: construct of hierarchical objects

The "composite" design pattern emerges when we try to construct hierarchically structured objects with component specific parts and nesting components as shown in Figure 5(a). The characteristic of this pattern is that it is known that several methods sharing the same name are implemented at the same trigger time. The positioning of this case in the software field is shown in Figure 5(b).

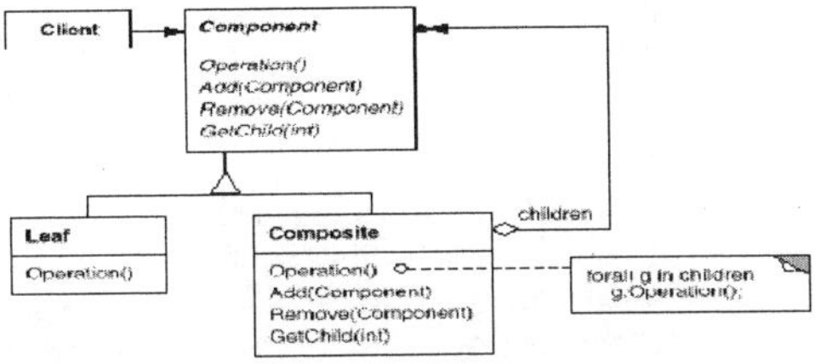

Figure 5(a). Structure of the "composite" pattern

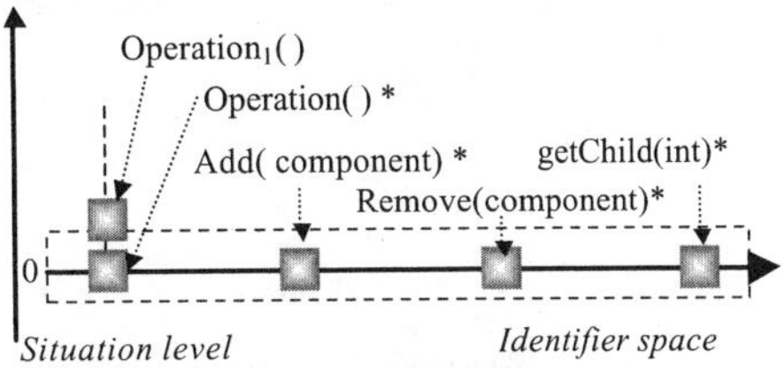

Figure 5(b). Initial positioning corresponding to the Composite pattern

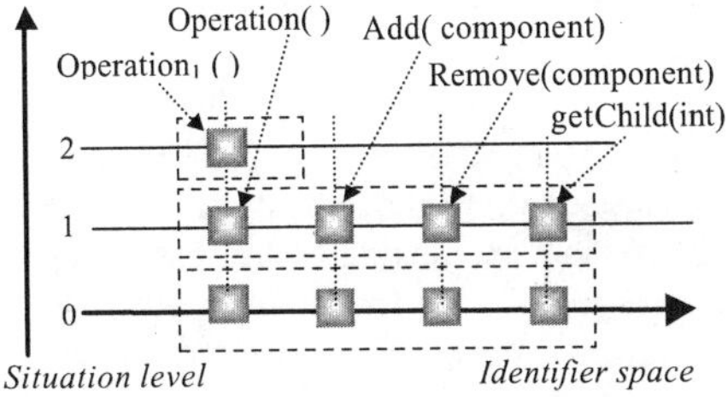

Figure 5(c). Positioning corresponding to the Composite pattern

The methods with asterisk (*) stand for methods that have several implementations. The fact that they have multiple implementations is known at the same trigger time. Since they have the same identifier, they are placed at the same position in identifier space. Due to the constraint of multiplic ity, however, they are placed on the different situation levels.

Methods named Operation() may contains methods extracted at the different trigger time. Even though Operation$_1$() is placed at the same position on the identifier space, it has different trigger time from other methods Operation() and placed on the different situation level. Therefore, the positioning shown in Figure 5(c) is corresponding to the class structure shown in Figure 5(a). The recursive association in Figure 5(a) is determined by whether classes separated at the different situation levels have repetition or not.

5. CONCLUSION

It is demonstrated that the typical design patterns can be derived from the software field by using quantizing operations and characteristics of elements (methods). When such operations are refined, it may be possible to derive optimized class structure by optimizing the adapting order of the operations.

REFERENCES

[1] I. Jacobson, G. Booch, J. Rumbaugh, "The Unifield Software Development Process," Addison Wesley (1999)

[2] Mikio Ohki, Kohei Akiyama, "A Proposal of the Conceptual Modeling Criteria and their Validity Evaluation," IEICE VOL.J84-D-1 No.6 pp.723-735(2001)

[3] Gamma, Helm, Johson & Vissides, "Design Patterns: Elements of Object-Oriented Software," Addison-Wesley (1995)

[4] Chidamber, Kamemer, " A Metrics Suite for Object Oriented Design, "IEEE Trans. SE Vol.20, No.6 pp.476-493 (1994)

[5] Takako Nakatani, Tetuo Tamai, "A Study on Statistic Characteristics of Inheritance Tree Evolution," Proceedings of Object-Oriented Symposium, pp.137-144(1999)

[6] Mikio Ohki, Shoijiro Akiyama, "A Class Structure Evolutional Model and Analysis of its Parameters," IPSJ Vol.2001 No.92 SE-133-3 pp.15-22(2001)

·Knowledge-based Software Engineering
T. Welzer et al. (Eds.)
IOS Press, 2002

A Design of Agent Oriented Search Engine for Web Documents

Hirokazu Aratani, Shigeru Fujita, Kenji Sugawara
Chiba Institute Of Technology, Dpt., of Computer Science,
2-17-1, Tudanuma,Narashino,275-0016,Japan

Abstract. There are much information on the WWW. Each information is written by natural language. The searcher who want to retrieve information from WWW use index page such as yahoo or search engine such as google. The aim of information search is depended on each situation, hence information retrieval as mechanically is not satisfied for the each requirement. In this paper, we described how to retrieve information from web page which is formated as text/html. Our approach is based on agent oriented information component framework.

1 Introduction

As WWW is developed rapidly, information expressed in natural language have been increasing on WWW. To search information from WWW, many search engines, represented by Yahoo, Google, etc, is used generally. These search engines show the ranking caused from simple text correspondent with search keywords or number of links from other site as retrieval result. However, the purpose of information retrieval is various, and it is difficult to meet enough a retrieval request depending on various situation.

So, we have developed new information retrieval system which searches information with different process from usual information retrieval by using autonomous software agent (hereafter, it abbreviates Agent). Our retrieval system corresponds Agent to the text/html, which is target of retrieval, at 1 on 1, and each Agent evaluates its text/html with comparing contents of text/html about whether it includes some information related to search keywords or not. And the evaluation affects retrieval result of our system. In this paper, we describe the design of our agent oriented information retrieval system.

2 The Design of Agent Oriented Information Retrieval

2.1 Changing to Information Component

Assuming that web page, which is target of retrieval, is expressed with suitable HTML format, our system acquires information of links to other site from the web page, and word index of each web page is created by morphological analysis. Our retrieval system uses the link information and word index as information component, and we called these information Primary Source.

The reason why we use a web page as information component is (a) It can't always assume that a series of web pages which compose a certain page are on the single host machine, (b) There is not neccesarily strong correlation between several text/html files which compose

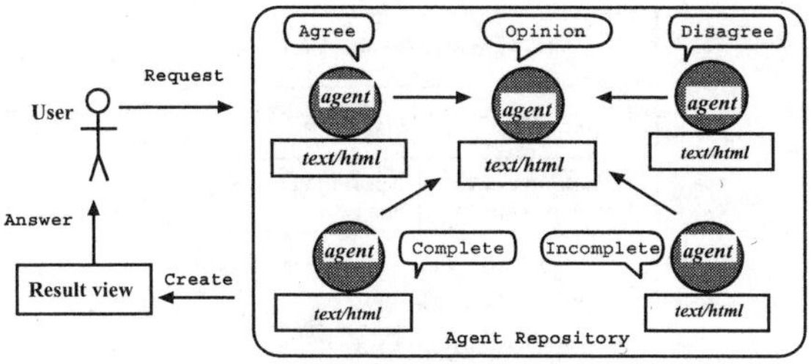

Figure 1: Conceptual Model of Information Component Use System

a web site, (c) It is finally possible that an information is restored by binding information components when information shown to searcher who is requesting information is over the several text/html. We design following 4 functions to the information component.

1. It judges whether a web page has some information relating to search keywords or not.

2. It points to other web page seemed to include some information relating to search keywords.

3. It judges truth to search keywords.

4. It shows support/un-support to the judgment of truth shown by other web page.

With above functions, in group of information components, (a) an information component recommends itself or other information component seemed to be related to search keywords, (b) an information component compensates some words for search keywords, and it judges truth again, (c) an information component shows relation of judgement shown by other information components. With these functions, group of information components recommends web page to searcher.

2.2 *Information Component Use Model*

Our retrieval system changes information included in web page to information component, and uses it as information source. Figure1 shows conceptual model of information component use model.

In figure1, "Agent Repository" is processing environment of the information component. "text/html" is information which is target of processing on this system and an element composing web page. "Agent" is an autonomy object corresponded to text/html. "User" is a worker who searches requesting information. "Keywords" is words inputted by searcher for information retrieval. "Result View" is created by each agent with its cooperative processing, and retrieval result is shown to searcher with it. "Opinion" is expressed when an information component judges its text/html relating directly to search keywords. "Agree","Disagree","Complete" and "Incomplete" are expressed to Opinion, and it shows relation between agents.

Following shows the process order of this system. First, a searcher inputs some words for retrieve. Second, an agent in the repository expresses itself as candidate of retrieval result requested by a user. Third, in addition to expressed agents, agents recommended by other one also express itself. Fourth, all the agents in repository evaluate other agent's express such as

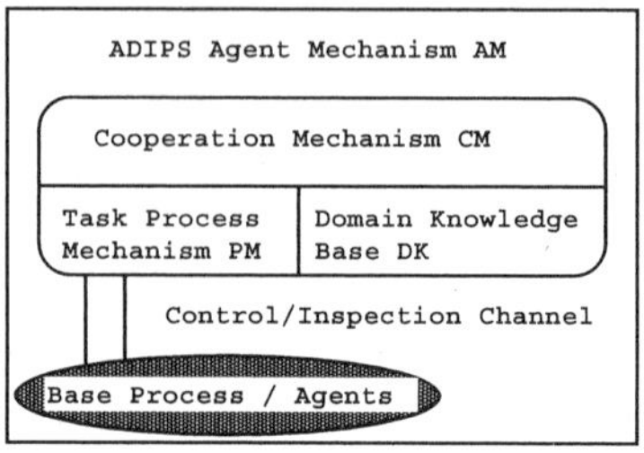

Figure 2: ADIPS agent architecture

agree, disagree, complete and incomplete. Finally, as a result view of retrieval, opinions shown by expressed agent are marged.

Opinion, Agree, Disagree, Complete and Incomplete are expressed by each agent in repository. When an agent is corresponded to text/html, which is information component, relating to search keywords directly, its agent expresses "Opinion". Then, if an agent agrees to the Opinion, its agent expresses "Agree". If an agent disagrees to the Opinion, its agent expresses "Disagree". If an agent can't express "Agree" or "Disagree" clearly, but can support the Opinion, its agent expresses "Complete". If an agent can't express "Agree" or "Disagree" clearly, and can't also express "Complete", its agent expresses "Incomplete". URL of text/html corresponded to agent expressed Opinion are shown to user as a retrieval result. In case there are many Opinions, which Opinion should be shown to user depends on the parameter decided when a result view has been created. Most simple rule of the parameter is in order of Opinions getting more "Agree" and less "Disagree". By changing this rule, our retrieval system can show various result view to searcher.

2.3 Agent Architecture

We use a structure of ADIPS framework we study and develop for the agent for creating infomation conponent from text/html.

The ADPS framework supports to develop Agent-based Distributed Information Processing Systems. The ADIPS framework, has two subsystem: (1) ADIPS workplace which is an operational environment of the agents and (2) ADIPS repository which is a database of class agents. A class agent is instantiated to an instance agent in the ADIPS workplace. These subsystems are implemented as a distributed system on networked workstations.

The agents in the ADIPS workplace make an organization to provide services for the users using the extended contract net protocol provided in the ADIPS framework for agents to cooperate among them. An architecture of the ADIPS agent, shown in Figure2 consists of three parts,i.e.,

$$\text{ADIPSAgent} = \langle \text{CM}, \text{PM}, \text{DK} \rangle.$$

CM is a cooperation mechanism using the cooperation protocol based on the KQML[2] and the extended contract net protocol.

PM is a task process mechanism to deal with the specified tasks, such as video conference services.

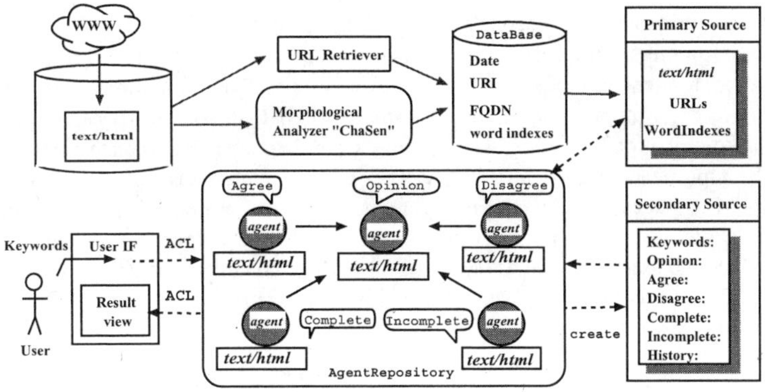

Figure 3: Agent Oriented Information Retrieval

DK is a mechanism to manage domain knowledge of each agent to represent its abilities, knowhow to realize the functions using PM,

CM, and knowhow to adjust the functions according to the situation.

DK consists of a message parser, the message handlers and the agent scripts. The message parser classifies a message from the CM and selects a message handler to deal with the message.

A message handler is a set of procedures to deal with the message based on the knowledge written in the agent scripts provided by the ADIPS framework. The detailed forms of scripts are defined according to each domain of knowledge.

2.4 Process of Agent Oriented Information Retrieval

To get many text/html, which is target of retrieval, from WWW, we use existing search engine because of restriction of our local resources.

Our retrieval system gets information of links to other site from text/html, and creates word index of text/html with morphological analyzer "Chasen". We called this link information and word index Primary Source, and it is used by agent of our retrieval system as information source when agents processes in repository cooperatively.

When a user inputs search keywords to retrieval system, group of agents in repository is inquired with ACL(Agent Communication Language) formed broadcast which means "Do you have information related to search keywords?".

If a text/html has related information to it, agent corresponded to the text/html expresses Opinion, and other agent expresses one of "Agree", "Disagree", "Complete", "Incomplete" to the Opinion. If an agent has expressed "Agree", it means the agent has affirmed word index of agent expressing Opinion. If an agent has expressed "Disagree", it means the agent has denied word index of agent expressing Opinion. If an agent has expressed "Complete", it means the agent has judged word index of agent expressing Opinion to be proper expression, although it can't express "Agree" or "Disagree" clearly. If an agent has expressed "Incomplete", it means the agent has been able to express none of "Agree", "Disagree" or "Complete".

When our retrieval system processes for retrieval, all agents in repository surely select one of the five expressions, and information of these expressions, for example the number of Opinion or the number of Agree to the Opinion, is stored in database as processing log.

We call this processing log Secondary Source. After next time, to getting more "Agree" or "Complete" and less "Disagree" or "Incomplete", Secondary Source is used from agents.

After each agent in repository has expressed one of five expressions, a result view of retrieval must be shown to user. A rule of ranking of URL shown to user can be changed by changing combination of "Agree", "Disagree", "Complete" and "Incomplete". If the rule is set so that the Opinion expressed more "Disagree" or "Incomplete" gets higher score, user will be able to get web pages including negative contents to search keywords. It is most ordinary rule that the Opinion expressed more "Agree" or "Complete" gets higher score, and in this case, user will be able to get web pages including affirmative contents to search keywords.

Figure3 shows conceptual model of our information retrieval.

2.5 Examination of the method of evaluation experiment

The our agent oriented information retrieval can show web pages having various view points, goals and purpose, to user as retrieval result with comparing contents of web pages and evaluating the expressions, "Agree", "Disagree", "Complete" and "Incomplete", with cooperative communication of agents.

For example, web page including some movie's reputation can be considered to be a web page in which its creator's viewpoints or goals are reflected strongly. If such web pages are searched by usual search engines, in case search keywords are affirmative for the movie, web page including affirmative reputation would be retrieved, or in case search keywords are negative for movie, web page including negative reputation would be retrieved.

Hence, it is difficult for searcher to know what reputation is ordinary on WWW. Our retrieval system can be expected that web pages including various reputation for the movie can be retrieved in spite of whether search keywords are affirmative or not for the movie, because our retrieval system can provide various retrieval result by changing the rule of combination of the expressions of agents.

Now, we are considering the evaluation experiment for proving that our retrieval system can get web pages including various movie's reputation as shown in Figure4. The example of expression by agent is shown in Table 1.

3 Conclusion

In this paper, we describe design of agent oriented search engine for web documents which shows to user that raking of number of agree, disagree, complete and incomplete from other agents.

Agent	Expression	Keyword on web page
Agent A	opinion	MovieA, reputation, good
Agent B	Agree	MovieA, good
Agent C	Disagree	MovieA, no good
Agent D	Complete	MovieA, reputation
Agent E	Incomplete	book, watch

Table 1: The example of expression by Agent

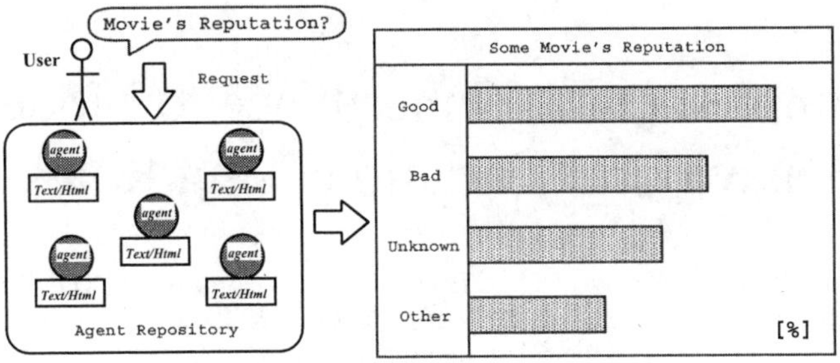

Figure 4: Example of Evaluating Experiment

On our system, these agents corresponding to each web pages from exiting search engine's result. These agents communicate each other to get more agree and complete and less disagree and incomplete, therefore proposed system provides the point view about opinion on the Internet community automatically. This mechanism will support for sercher who does not know about something with out misdirection from ill structured web network.

References

[1] Dieter Fensel, Mark A. Musen **ed.**, "The Semantic Web: A Brain for Humankaind", IEEE Intelligent Systems, March/April, (2001).

[2] T.Finin. J.Weber, G.Wiederhold, M.Genesereth, R.Fritzson, D.McKay, J.McGuire, R.Pelavin, S.Shapiro, and C.Beck. "DRAFT specification of the KQML agent communication language plus example agent policies and architectures," http://www.cs.umbc.edu/kqml/kqmlspec/spec.html, (1993).

[3] L.S. Frank, Singular Perturbations I, North-Holland, Amsterdam (1990).

[4] Kuwabara, K., Ishida, T., and Osato, N.: AgenTalk: Coordination Protocol Description for Multiagent Systems. Proc. First International Conference on Multi-Agent Systems (ICMAS '95) p. 455 (1995)

[5] Fujita, S., Hara,H., Sugawara,K., Kinoshita,T., Shiratori,N., Agent-Based Design Model of Adaptive Distributed Systems, Applied Intellignece 9, 57-70(1998)

[6] "Chasen", `http://chasen.aist-nara.ac.jp/`

Knowledge-based Software Engineering
T. Welzer et al. (Eds.)
IOS Press, 2002

Complementing Inheritance to Model Behavioural Variation using Roles

Dimitrios THEOTOKIS, Anya SOTIROPOULOU, Georgios GYFTODIMOS
University of Athens, Department of Informatics & Telecommunications
Panepistimiopolis, Ilissia, Athens

Abstract. Kind-specific variations are modelled in class-based object-oriented languages using the inheritance relationship. Consequently, inheritance is the mechanism for modelling incrementally "kind-of" variations, and subsequently a vehicle for reuse. Yet, in practice, inheritance is also used for specialisation, sub-typing, inclusion, etc.. As a result, those notions (orthogonal from a conceptual viewpoint) are examined under the same prism, a fact that restricts modelling of behavioural changes in existing object hierarchies. This is the case because inheritance fails to accommodate for an equally fundamental notion to that of objects and their relationships, namely that of roles. Although definitions of the role concept and of the use of roles in modelling object-oriented systems abound in literature, we maintain that only a few acknowledge the intrinsic role of roles in modelling behavioural variations. After presenting the issues related with modelling variations using the inheritance relationship and discussing existing approaches to overcome the limitations that occur, we present a role-based approach and a model to complement inheritance in order to achieve behavioural evolution in a flexible, consistent, and extensible manner. A key feature of the proposed model is the runtime behavioural modification of objects in terms of the addition and removal of roles.

1 Introduction

The need to alter – enhance or modify – the behavioural landscape exposed by objects, is common in object-oriented software [8,9,16]. This is due to the changes that the conceptual model, upon which the software is build, undergoes. Class-based object-oriented languages and methodologies approach behaviour evolution – the addition, modification, and removal of behaviour – by means (a) of inheritance and editive changes on existing class hierarchies, and (b) aggregation/parameterisation plus inheritance [1, 6, 17]. Both techniques, although effective to a certain degree in achieving kind-specific variations, do not provide the expressiveness required to model changes that (a) are not necessarily related with the inheritance relationship, that is they are not kind-specific, such as a person *becomes* a student, rather than a person *is* a student, (b) are effective for a period of time, that is, a person who has become a student, temporarily, becomes an employee over the summer holidays, (c) denote characteristics that do not directly relate with the entity modelled by a class, but are mere extensions to it and thus do not call for specialisation, and (d) are not known during the development phase that is they are unanticipated changes. However, the absence of a notion complementary and orthogonal to that of inheritance enforces the use of the latter, when modelling behavioural changes [4]. This leads to a number of problems, including but not limited to class explosion, common ancestors dilemma, name collisions, homonymous attributes [10]. Such problems are resolved using conditional programming, a technique that hinders reusability and, most importantly, behavioural evolution – since it requires editive changes on existing code. Moreover, the fact that a sub-class's reference(s) to its super-class(ess) is(are) bound at compile-time leaves little room for manoeuvring when attempting to accommodate for behavioural variations, particularly when such variations must be realised during the run-time.

Although a number of alternatives to class-based inheritance have been proposed as a remedy to the problems mentioned above, such as mixin-based inheritance [5] and design patterns [6], none addresses the accommodation of behavioural evolution in an effective way.

Mixins and mixin-methods [13, 14], although they are an enhancement of object-based inheritance with respect to encapsulation, have several problems, which are related to their too narrow design space. The "Object" abstraction is not only responsible for supplying behaviour, but also for defining, structuring and composing it. Specifying the applicable extensions as named attributes of the object introduces problems, which decrease the flexibility of the approach. First, all possible extensions of an object's behaviour have to be definitely specified when the basic functionality of the objects is defined; there is actually no separation between both kinds of behaviours – the variations are part of the default behaviour definition of the object. However, when implementing some base behaviour, it is impossible to predict all possible future desired extensions (variations) of it. Thus, adding some new extension means introducing it somewhere in the existing object hierarchy, resulting in a decrease of flexibility by not being able to uncouple the dependencies enforced by inheritance, especially if the unforeseen extension has to be inserted into an object situated near the top of the hierarchy. Again, due to the overloaded model, a performed extension cannot be cancelled anymore. Consequently the approach does not support temporal variations, which are important for an adaptable behaviour. Additionally, a mechanism for flexible scope control that supports internal encapsulation is missing.

Design patterns are realised in terms of aggregation/parameterisation plus inheritance. Consequently, the static binding of super references and the predetermined type of self references of the aggregates and/or parameters leave little room for behavioural changes, especially unanticipated ones that expose different types.

Both approaches simply elevate the problem in a higher level of abstraction. This is the case because such alternatives rely mainly on the use of inheritance and aggregation/parameterisation for this purpose. The absence of an explicit, well-defined, robust and orthogonal modelling construct, to decouple the concepts of basic and acquired behaviour and, as result, relax the rigidness of the behavioural landscape introduced by the fixation of super references and parameter types respectively during the compilation phase, is evident.

In terms of conceptual modelling the representation of acquirable characteristics is achieved through the notion of roles [2,3,7,12]. Sowa distinguishes between natural types "that relate to the essence of the entities" and role types "that depend on the accidental relationship to some other entity" [11 p. 82]. Consequently, bank *Account* is a natural entity whose objects will always be of type *Account* during their lifetime. A *Shared* account on the other hand is not a natural type, in fact it is a role that an account object may acquire for a period of time in order to expose behavioural characteristics associated with multiple owners, as well as the basic behaviour defined in the *Account* class. Moreover, treating *Shared* as a role implies that there is no loss of identity when the requirement for an account object to have multiple owners no longer holds. The account object remains an *Account*.

The key idea underlying the role concept is a simple and natural one. It is based on the fact that a natural type, in other words a unit that describes basic behavioural characteristics, during its lifetime may be exposed to unanticipated changes which it may acquire or lose without loosing its identity. The latter is the fundamental notion of role-based modelling.

Following this, roles model unanticipated changes in the most effective way since they can be attributed to an entity on demand, exist as a behavioural enhancement of that entity for as long as the context they model is valid. Furthermore, there is no limitation as to how many roles an entity can play simultaneously.

In this paper we present a role model to complement the inheritance relationship so that modelling of behavioural variations can be realised independently of the use of inheritance, thus avoiding the drawbacks introduced by the latter. For this purpose we describe the necessary language constructs, semantics and data structures that will accommodate the dynamic nature of role assignment.

2 Modelling Behavioural Variations

2.1 Modelling Behavioural Variations Using inheritance

Inheritance either single, multiple or mixin-based is used for extending existing definitions (classes). In as such, derived definitions (subclasses) of one or more classes incorporate delta changes of a common ancestors. Through the inheritance relationship a subclass inherits all of its parents characteristics and may extend them, override them, or use them as is. For this purpose, a subclass is statically bound to its super-class, a fact that occurs during the compilation phase. Consequently, derived definitions are interlocked with their corresponding original definitions.

Despite the fact that an object of a given class can be treated as an object of all of the classes' super-classes through polymorphism, binding statically the super reference at compile time and the self reference at instantiation time implies (a) that it becomes impossible to alter the behavioural characteristics of an object, and (b) that the object in question will, during its lifetime, expose the behaviour represented in its classes. Needless to say that if new behavioural requirements occur, these can only be modelled in terms of new sub-classes. It becomes evident that the more new classes are introduced the more complex the behavioural landscape becomes due to the inter-relationships that exist amongst classes and that software maintenance becomes more complicated. This situation leads to the class explosion phenomenon. Consider the running example of Figure 1. Assume that the required behavioural landscape of the banking system is such that the following type of accounts are needed: *Account*, *SharedAccount*, *ATMAccount*, *HistoryAccount*, *SharedATMAccount*, *SharedHistory-Account*, *ATMHistoryAccount*, *SharedATMHistoryAccount*. Figure 2 illustrates the required behavioural landscape using single inheritance, multiple inheritance and mixin-based inheritance.

Figure 1: Behavioural landscape of a banking system: Roles played by an account

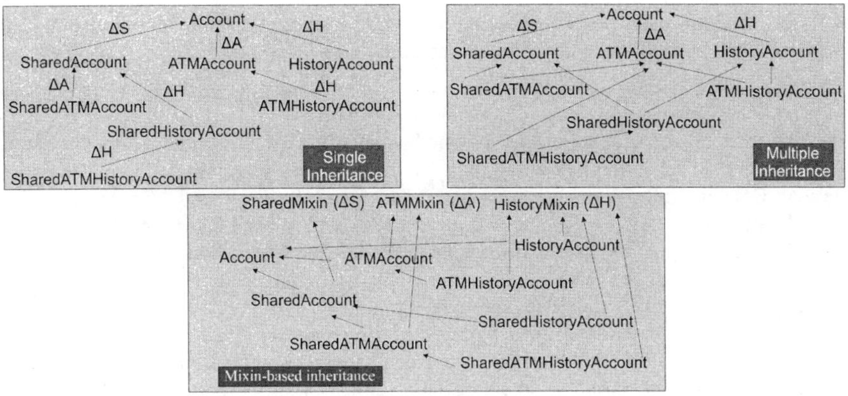

Figure 2: Three approaches to behavioural evolution using inheritance

Although modelling the required behavioural landscape is possible using the three different approaches to inheritance, there are some serious drawbacks associated with each approach.

Consider the single inheritance approach. In order to model the *SharedATMAccount* it is necessary to replicate the behaviour of *ATMAccount* in the sub-class of *ShareAccount*. Similarly, for the *SharedATMHistoryAccount*, the behaviour of *HistoryAccount* needs to be replicated. Replication implies the addition of specific behaviour editively. This complicates reusability since changes to the *ATMAccount* class are not automatically inherited by the *ShareATMAccount* class and the *SharedATMHistoryAccount* class respectively and require editive changes on those two classes in order to reflect the modifications that the *ATMAccount* undertakes. Furthermore, if both the *ATMAccount* and *HistoryAccount* classes define a field or method with the same name but different semantics, for instance the method *debit*, in replicating the code of those two classes it is necessary to cater for the occurring name conflicts using conditional logic, a task that again limits the flexibility of the class with respect to reuse, maintenance, and its behavioural evolution. This is known as the homonymous attributes problem [15].

Multiple inheritance on the other hand, although it resolves the problem of code replication, results in complex and often tangled hierarchies, which are difficult to maintain, extend and reuse. Naming collisions still occurs in this approach as well and are resolved with blocks of conditional programming. Multiple inheritance introduces a number of problems, associated with it, such as homonymous attributes [10] and common ancestors dilemma [15], both of which are resolved again with the use of conditional logic.

Finally, in contrast with single and multiple inheritance, where delta-changes of a given class are directly embedded in its subclasses, in mixin-based inheritance delta-changes remain unbound or free in classes known as mixin-classes. Such classes are first class entities and exist independently of the class they modify. Mixin classes define only behaviour associated with the delta changes of a base class and as such cannot be instantiated. More importantly they are not structurally bound in some specific place in the inheritance hierarchy. As such, they are defined once and can be reused in the definition of classes. Clearly, mixin-based inheritance resolves the problem of the common ancestors dilemma encountered in multiple inheritance, but does not address the problem of homonymous attributes. To compound all of the above, the addition of another variant complicates further the behavioural landscape and makes behavioural evolution and reuse problematic since it requires extensive editive changes, that cause side-effects related to the above mentioned problems.

2.2 Modelling Behavioural Variations Using Design-Patterns

Design patterns [6] were proposed as a remedy to the problems introduced by inheritance aiming primarily in achieving better reusability and secondarily in accommodating behavioural evolution. Behavioural patterns and in particular *State*, *Strategy* and *Visitor* as well as structural patterns, such as *Bridge*, *Decorator* and *Proxy*, have been proposed for this purpose [6]. For instance, the *Visitor* pattern allows one to define a new operation without changing the classes of the elements on which it operates. The *Decorator* pattern allows one to issue additional functionality to a class with sub-classing.

Key to design patterns is the separation of the *variation object* from the *base object*. The variation object is the one that undergoes behavioural modification. In order to loosely couple these objects, the variation object becomes either an attribute of the base object, or is passed as an argument to it. This relationship is thus expressed either through aggregation or parameterisation. This is known as the aggregation/parameterisation plus inheritance technique. Due to this, it becomes evident that the drawbacks of using inheritance are carried into the use of design patterns, particularly with respect to behavioural evolution. Thus, although design patterns provide an excellent vehicle for consistent and well structured design, they contribute little to reuse and even less to behavioural evolution in an environment where behavioural changes occur dynamically [18].

3 The ATOMA Role Model

The ATOMA role model was developed in order to better model cross-cutting behavioural changes related to the evolution of the behavioural landscape, without having to take care for the various drawbacks introduced by inheritance. An implementation of the model exists and is based on the Java programming language. In this section we present the model and focus on the characteristics that make the model suitable and effective in realising modifications of the behavioural landscape of objects in a dynamic, transparent and natural way.

3.1 What is a role

In the context of the ATOMA role model, roles are used for specifying behavioural variations on a basic theme. In other words roles are used to model behavioural variations, even cross-cutting ones, to an object's basic behaviour. In as such, roles may be used to classify objects, but in contrast to class-based classification, role-based classification is multiple and dynamic.

In our approach we assume that a role is an encapsulated entity that specifies both state (properties) and behaviour (methods). Its behavioural landscape is specific and well defined. A role is only an adjustment of some basic behaviour defined either by an object or another role already assigned to an object. We also assume that an object may acquire and relinquish roles dynamically during its lifetime, may play different roles simultaneously, and that it may play the same role several times. Moreover, we advocate that an object looses all of its roles when it is destructed, that instances of the same role may exist concurrently, and that roles may be assigned to both objects and classes. An object role implies that the role in question modifies an object's behavioural landscape, while a class role means that all instances of that class will possess the role in question.

Role assignment can be done either during the instantiation of objects or during their lifetime. The former is realised by providing the role as an argument to the object's constructor. The latter is achieved by means of the *acquire* and *relinquish* methods provided by the implementation of the ATOMA role model.

3.2 *Role types*

Three types of roles are defined in the ATOMA role model, namely *specialisation roles*, *connectivity roles* and *class like roles*.

Specialisation roles: A specialisation role specifies a behavioural variation of an object or another role. At the syntactic level specialisation roles are identified by the expression **alters <when>**. For instance the expression **R alters B when E** where R is a role, B the behavioural landscape of an object or another role and E an event, denotes that role R specifies a behavioural variation on B's behavioural landscape when the event E takes place. According to the running example of Figure 1, role ATM is a specialisation role for account objects.

Table 1: Specialisation roles

Role X { ... } alters B
Role X { ... } alters B when E
Role X { ... } alters B when E = condition
Role X { ... } alters B when condition

Table 2: Connectivity Roles

Role X { ... } combines (Y,X)
Role X { ... } combines (Y, Z) when E
Role X { ... } combines (Y, Z) when E = condition
Role X { ... } combines (Y, Z) when condition

Connectivity Roles: Connectivity roles, as their name implies, connect two behaviour specification modules by specifying the relationships that exist between their methods in order to construct a structure that exposes a higher level of functionality. The syntactic variations of connectivity roles are presented in Table 2.

Class-like roles: Class-like roles resemble classes in that they provide full functionality (they do not refer to any super parameter), but cannot exist on their own. Usually they are the terminal elements of a role hierarchy. For instance, a role describing a cross-cutting aspect of account functionality, say, that of synchronisation and recovery, will be realised as a class-like role. This is because it defines a complete behavioural landscape in the sense that there is no super reference and at the same time the behavioural landscape it exhibits cannot exist independently of other behavioural landscapes.

3.2.1 Conditional role assignment

An optional part of the syntactic definitions of roles in the **when** clause, whose syntax is presented by the following grammar:

WhenClause	::	**when** EventSpecification
EventSpecification	::	WithEventName | withoutEventName
WithEventName	::	EventName ConditionPart
ConditionPart	::	e | '{' ConditionSpecification '}'
WithoutEventName	::	ConditionSpecification[1]
EventName	::	Identifier

The existence of the **when** clause in the definition of a role associates the role with an event name and/or some particular conditions which specify when the behavioural variations that the role realises will be applied. In other words, when the role will become "part" of the behavioural landscape of an object. According to Tables 1 and 2, there are four distinct cases in role specification.

[1] A ConditionSpecification is any Boolean expression.

1. There is no **when** clause in the role's definition. This suggests a default role. Default roles are applied immediately when the object that they modify is instantiated.
2. There exists an event specification associated with the role definition, but no condition. The role will be applied to an object, when the event specified in the role's definition occurs.
3. There exists a condition without an event. In this case the role will be applied to an object iff the condition holds.
4. There exist an event specification and a condition associated with the role definition. For a role to be applied to an object under this scenario the event must take place and the condition must be met.

This categorisation introduces a notion of prioritisation in role assignment. Roles of the fourth category are placed last in the role queue of an object. Similarly roles of the third category are placed before roles of the fourth category in the role queue, and are preceded by roles of the second category. Roles of the first category precede roles of the second category. Roles of the same category are placed in an object's role queue on a first-come-first-served basis.

Consider an object with a method say *doSomething*. Assume that the object's role queue contains four roles, say r_1, r_2, r_3, r_4, of the first, second, third and fourth category, respectively, which all define the *doSomething* method. When a call to the object's *doSomething* method is issued, the evaluation sequence due to role prioritisation will be as follows: Firstly r_4's *doSomething* will be evaluated. Then r_3's *doSomething* method will be executed and so on and so forth. Finally, the definition of the object's *doSomething* method will be considered. Allowing for this prioritisation of the execution sequence of the behavioural landscape provides the means to simulate method overriding and method selection, based on the principle of the most specific super class, without however having to incorporate the respective semantics of inheritance. Most importantly prioritisation introduces a notion absent in class-based object models, that of on demand changing the execution order of related methods. Broadly speaking this could be considered as changing an object's inheritance hierarchy on demand. Following inheritance-based terminology it means that classes can change position in the hierarchy graph on demand, and after an object's instantiation. Thus, making the least-specific class, the most-specific one and vice-versa.

3.3 Modelling Behavioural Evolution with Roles

The internal representation of roles in the ATOMA model is achieved using a complex structure namely an atom, depicted in Figure 3.

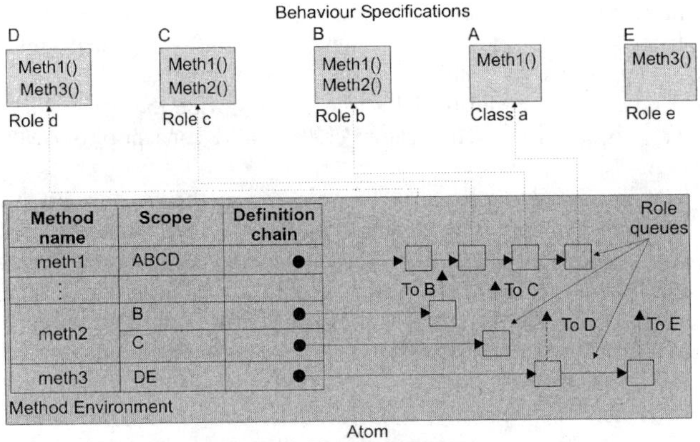

Figure 3: The atom structure

An atom consists of a method environment, a structure that depicts at any given time an object's current behavioural landscape. The method environment is a name space that holds (a) the names of the methods in the object's current behavioural landscape, (b) the scope of these methods, and (c) pointers to the definitions of these methods as these exist in the object itself. When a role is assigned to an object the object's method environment is updated according to the following:

1. If the role defines an new method, that method is added to the method environment, its scope is defined and a pointer is created to reference the method's implementation in the role's class.
2. If the role defines an existing method, in other words if that method overrides an existing one, then the scope and pointer characteristics of that method are updated to reflect the change.

The scope for each method defines the execution sequence to be followed during the evaluation of given method and is guided by the rules governing role prioritisation, as those described in Section 3.2.1.

When a role is removed the object's method environment is updated accordingly. For each object in the system an atom is created upon the object's instantiation. The atom contains the object's method environment and provides the necessary infrastructure for method evaluation and delegation.

4 Roles vs. Inheritance and Design Patterns

In this section we briefly present the advantages the ATOMA role model presents in conjunction to inheritance and design patterns, when viewed from the perspective of behavioural evaluation and reuse.

- Single, multiple and mixin-based inheritance, object migration and polymorphism: Since roles are encapsulated it becomes evident that problems associated with homonymous attributes, common ancestors dilemma, name conflicts, code replication and object migration are elevated thus making code free of conditional logic. The dynamic nature of roles resolves issues related to the static binding. Moreover, roles may be used to accommodate polymorphism.

- Multi-facet inheritance: An object may at a given time have two or more roles of the same type, say a shared account, can have more than one roles of type owner. This feature cannot be expressed in terms of single, multiple or mixin-based inheritance.
- Overriding: Under the proposed model a role may override the behavioural landscape of the object or role is applied to. This feature enhances the concept of overriding as realised by inheritance.
- Sub-typing: By assigning a specialisation role on another role, sub-typing is present without the issues that emerge from the use of inheritance for this purpose.
- Substitutability: Under the ATOMA role model substitutability is not supported. Since it would make little sense to say that a shared account can be used where an account can be used. However, the resulting structure that encapsulates both the account object and the shared object (role) can be treated either as an account, wherever that is applicable, or as shared.
- Context independent applicability: Consider a collection of heterogeneous objects. Furthermore, consider the need to enhance the behavioural landscape of these collection's objects with behaviour that records all operations performed on them, that is a history mechanism. Under the ATOMA role model this is achieved by assigning a History role on each of the collection's objects. By contrast on inheritance-based systems this would imply the addition of a class in the inheritance hierarchy of each object found in the collection.
- Design patterns: Design patterns attempt to overcome the issues introduced by inheritance using aggregation/parameterisation plus inheritance. This implies that design patterns do not resolve the problem associated with static binding and *a priori* known object types.

The dynamic nature of the ATOMA role model resolves these issues in a natural way since roles are not *a priori* parts of an object, nor does an object know the role types it may acquire.

5 Conclusions

Having identified the limitation of inheritance and design patterns in modelling and realizing the evolution of the behavioural landscape of objects, we proposed the ATOMA role model to complement classical object models. Dynamic roles can support conceptual models of many applications and as such can be considered as an alternative to inheritance with respect to reusability and behavioural evolution. The proposed role model incorporates the notions of classical object-oriented models such as encapsulation, overriding, polymorphism, object identity, specialisation in a transparent and orthogonal way. Furthermore, role priorities enhance classical object-oriented models in that they provide the means to evaluate behaviour according to a particular state of an object without needing conditional logic, which is always hard-coded and reduces the flexibility for reuse and behavioural evolution. Role ordering enables further prioritisation of the evaluation of the methods of an objects, hence allowing fine grained control over the object's behavioural landscape. Dynamic role acquisition and loss allow for the runtime modification of an object's behavioural landscape. Needless to say that the proposed role model enhances reusability since no rigid design decisions are embedded in the definition of entities.

Our future work is focused on issues concerning the persistency of objects that are behaviourally enhanced by roles as well as temporal aspects of such persistency. In particular, we aim in incorporating the ATOMA role model in object-oriented database management system with temporal characteristics.

6 References

1 P. America, A behavioural approach to subtyping in object-oriented programming languages, *Philips Research Journal*, 44(2-3):365-383, 1989

2 A. Albano, R. Bergamini, G.Ghelli, R.Orsini, An Object Data Model with Roles, in Proc.of 19th VLDB Conference, pp. 39-51, 1993

3 E. Bertino, G. Guerrini, Objects with Multiple Most Specific Classes, in Proc. of ECOOP 1995 Conference, volume 952 of LNCS, pp. 102-126, Springer-Verlag, 1995.

4 G. Booch, *Object-oriented Analysis and design*, Addison-Wesley, 2nd edition, 1994.

5 G.Bracha, *The Programming language Jigsaw: Mixins, Modularity and Multiple Inheritance*. PhD Thesis, University of Utah, March 1992.

6 E.Gamma, R.Helm, R.Johnson, J.Vlissides, *Design Patterns, Elements of Reusable Object-Oriented Software*, Addison-Wesley, 1994.

7 G.Gottlob, M.Schref, B.Roeck, Extending object-oriented systems and roles *ACM Transactions on Information Systems*, 14(3):286-296, 1996

8 W.Harrison, H.Ossler, Subject-oriented programming (a critique of pure objects). In Proc. of 8th ACM OOPSLA 93, vol. 29, no. 10 of *ACM SIGPLAN Notices*, pp. 411-428, ACM Press, 1993

9 G.Kiczales, J.Lamping, A.Mendhekar, C.Maeda, C.V.Lopes, J.M. Loingtier, J.Irwin, Aspect-oriented programming. In M.Aksit and S.Matsuoka, editors, Procs of the 11th ECCOP 97, vol. 1241 of LNCS, pp. 220-243, Springer-Verlag 1997. Invited talk.

10 J-L Knudsen, Name collisions in multiple classification hierarchies In S.Gjessing and N.Nygaard, editors, Proc. of 2nd ECOOP 88, vol. 322 LNCS, pp. 21-40, Springer-Verlag, 1988

11 F.J.Sowa. *Conceptual Structures: Information Processing in Mind and Machine*. Addison-Wesley, 1984

12 F. Steinman, On the Representation of Roles in Object-Oriented and Conceptual Modelling, *Data and Knowledge Engineering*, 35(1), pp. 83-106, Elsevier 2000.

13 P. Steyaert, W. Codenie, T. D'Hondt, K. De Kondt, G. Lucas and M. Van Limberghen "Nested Mixin-Methods in Agora", in O. Nierstrasz (ed) Procs of the 7th European Conference on Object-Oriented Programming ECOOP 93, LNCS 707, pp. 197-219, Springer-Verlag 1993.

14 P. Steyaert, and W, De Meuter, "A Marriage of Class-Based and Object-Based Inheritance Without Unwanted Children" in W. Olthof (ed.) Procs. Of the 9th European Conference on Object-Oriented Programming ECOOP 95, LNCS 952, pp. 127-145, Springer-Verlag 1995.

15 A.Taivalsaari *Towards a taxonomy of inheritance mechanisms in Object-Oriented Programming*, PhD thesis, Licentiate Thesis, Sept.1991

16 D. Theotokis, *Object-oriented development of Dynamically modifiable Information Systems using Components and Roles*, PhD Thesis, Dept. of Informatics and Telecommunications, Univ. of Athens, Sept. 2001 (in Greek)

17 D. Theotokis, A. Sotiropoulou, G. Gyftodimos and P. Georgiadis. "Are Behavioural Design Patterns Enough for Behavioural Evolution in Object-Oriented Systems?" in Procs 8th Panhellenic Conference in Informatics, 2001, Vol. 1, pp. 90-99.

18 J.Vllissides The trouble with observer. *C++ Report*. September 1996

Knowledge-based Software Engineering
T. Welzer et al. (Eds.)
IOS Press, 2002

Patterns for Enterprise Application Integration

Matjaž B. JURIČ, Ivan ROZMAN, Tatjana WELZER, Marjan HERIČKO, Boštjan BRUMEN, Vili PODGORELEC
University of Maribor, Faculty of Electrical Engineering and Computer Science, Institute of Informatics, Smetanova 17, SI-2000 Maribor, e-mail: matjaz.juric@uni-mb.si, http://lisa.uni-mb.si/~juric/

Abstract. Enterprise application integration (EAI) is the very important for each information system. Due to its heterogeneity, application integration is also a difficult task. This article presents sound solutions for common design and architectural challenges in integration, based on the component approach to integration. The major contribution of the article is the definition of six new integration patterns and the discussion of their applicability for intra-EAI and inter-EAI (or B2B) integration.

1. Introduction

Enterprise application integration (EAI) is becoming the key success factor for information systems [1]. With the growing requirements for information access and e-business, the need for integrated applications is higher than ever. First, it is necessary to allow for application integration within a company, which we call intra-EAI. Second, there are growing needs to ensure inter-EAI or business-to-business (B2B) integration [1].

Concrete integration problems and the corresponding solutions are seldom identical at the first glance. Careful analysis of integration projects, however, shows that integration problems and their solutions can be classified into common categories. Thus, patterns can be used to describe common integration problems and their solutions. Patterns in software engineering are a proven solution to the problems in a given context [2, 3, 4].

In this article we present the results of the analysis and experience with several integration projects. We present common integration solutions and we call them *integration patterns*. Integration patterns, presented in this article, are *design* and *architectural patterns*. They help us to understand the different design solutions and architectures for integration and allow us to choose the best solution for our problem. They allow us to look at the integration problems from a certain abstraction level. Integration patterns, defined in this article, provide a sound solution, for the intra-EAI as well as for the inter-EAI. They are suitable for the component based approach to EAI, as defined in [1]. Integration patterns are platform and programming language independent, and can thus be used on any suitable platform and with any programming language.

The review of the related publications has shown that not much has been done on the definition of the integration patterns. The [5] defines two integration patterns, the Access Integration and the Application Integration. Both are process patterns, therefore not directly comparable with the design and architectural patterns, presented in this article. The author of [6] defines the Data Access Object (DAO) pattern for accessing the data of integrated systems. The DAO pattern has been included in the J2EE Design Patterns catalog, maintained by Sun Microsystems. The DAO pattern forms a basis for integration patterns, presented in this article. The author of [7] defines two process patterns: Scenario Partitioning, and State

Machine Integration. Again, these are process patterns, therefore not directly comparable to patterns in this article. In [8] the author gives a brief description (one paragraph) of some integration design patterns, including Direct Data Mapping pattern, which is comparable to our Data Mapping pattern; Hierarchical Multi-Step Pattern, comparable to our Integration Mediator pattern; Direct Request Pattern, comparable to our Integration Façade pattern; and Peer Service Pattern, comparable to our Integration Mediator pattern. Please notice however, that patterns in article [8] are just briefly described in a few sentences, without a formal description of the pattern design and the other usual elements of a pattern description. In [9] the author presents four B2B patterns. The Direct Application B2B pattern presents how to directly integrate applications between enterprises. The Data Exchange B2B pattern shows XML based architecture for data transfers between enterprises. Closed Process Integration B2B pattern identifies the principal participant responsible for the managing processes. Open Process Integration B2B pattern introduces the notion of shared processes. The latter two are process patterns, therefore not comparable to the patterns in this article. The Direct Application and Data Exchange patterns, on the other hand, focus on point-to-point integration and lack formal definition. They differ considerably from patterns in this article, which are broker and mediator based. Also, patterns presented in this article are general enough to use for inter and intra-EAI.

The overview of the related literature has shown that integration patterns, presented in this article, are original contributions to this field.

In the next sections of this article we will present the following integration patterns: in section 2 we will present the Integration Broker pattern, in section 3 the Integration Wrapper pattern, in section 4 the Integration Mediator pattern, in section 5 the Virtual Component, in section 6 the Data Mapping pattern, and in section 7 the Process Automator pattern. We will describe the patterns using a non-formal pattern representation, as used by several patterns catalogs, including [10, 11]. In section 8 we conclude the paper with final remarks and outline the future work.

2. Integration Broker Pattern

2.1. Context

When integrating applications within a company or between the companies, we are usually required to achieve the integration between several different applications. Connecting each application with each other is not a valuable solution, because it increases the dependencies – complexity. Thus the maintenance becomes very difficult.

2.2. Problem

In point to point integration the application interaction logic is coupled with both integrated applications. This makes both applications highly dependable on each other, which makes their maintenance complicated and time consuming. Small changes to one application could require modifications to all the other connected applications.

In fact, the maintenance of an integrated system will be more time consuming and costly than the maintenance of the applications themselves, which will make the benefits of integration less obvious. Considering that in a typical integration scenario we are faced with many such applications (often more than fifty), the point to point approach becomes unusable, because it leads to an exponential increase in complexity.

2.3. Forces

- Separation of responsibilities for different operations is required between applications, which need to be integrated.
- An application should provide a common integration interface, which solves the complexity and does not require building interoperability interfaces for each integration scenario.
- The integration logic should be separated for easier maintenance.
- The clients should not see the details of integration.
- The clients should not see the internal structure of applications being integrated.
- The communication model should not be limited; rather the best solution should be used for each application.

2.4. Solution

Integration broker describes the architectural approach to integration of many different applications. It overcomes the disadvantages of point to point integration. Integration broker minimizes the dependencies between integrated applications and provides one or more communication mechanisms between applications. The Integration broker is an abstraction for middleware technologies and is realized with a combination of middleware technologies, offered by the J2EE platform. It provides the necessary services, such as transaction, security, naming, lifecycle, scalability, management, rules, routing and brokering, and so on.

Integration Broker will be used by applications, needed to be integrated, to achieve integration on different levels. Applications will access the integration broker transparently through interfaces in programmatic or declarative ways. Programmatic ways means that applications will have to implement code to use the infrastructure services. The declarative ways, on the other hand, enable that we just mark specific applications and declare which services they should use and the infrastructure takes care of the details of invoking a service.

The transparency of the provided services for the applications will also depend on the selected technology. Communication, brokering, and routing services can be, for example, implemented transparently with the use of object request brokers, which mask remote method invocations to such a level that they look like local method invocation to the developers. A message oriented middleware on the other hand will require that the application creates a message and that it parses incoming messages and reacts to them accordingly. Declarative transaction and security services can provide services to applications without adding any code to the application, and so on.

Integration broker opens the path to build the integration layers step by step and reuse the previous results. It is not based on the point to point communication between applications. Thus, it can reduce the n to n multiplicity to n to 1, which reduces the complexity and simplifies the maintenance. The structure is shown in Figure 1.

The Integration broker defines the roles of each application for a certain integration interaction. For each interaction, one or more applications require certain services from a certain application. The applications that require services are called “client applications”. The application that provides the service is called the “server application”. Please note that the client and server roles are defined for a certain interaction only and can change during the execution. Usually all applications will have both roles – they will act as a server application for certain interactions and a client application for the other interactions.

The Integration broker does not only connect the applications, but bases the integration on contracts between the applications. These contracts are usually expressed as interoperability interfaces. The interoperability interfaces define what services the client applications can request from the server applications.

Interoperability interfaces define the relations between applications on which the applications depend. Interfaces define the coupling between integrated applications as long living contracts. They provide a façade through which the client applications access the interoperability services and encapsulate the applications. As long as the interfaces stay unchanged we can replace parts or the whole server application without influencing any client application. Therefore a lot of effort has to be put into the definition of the interoperability interfaces.

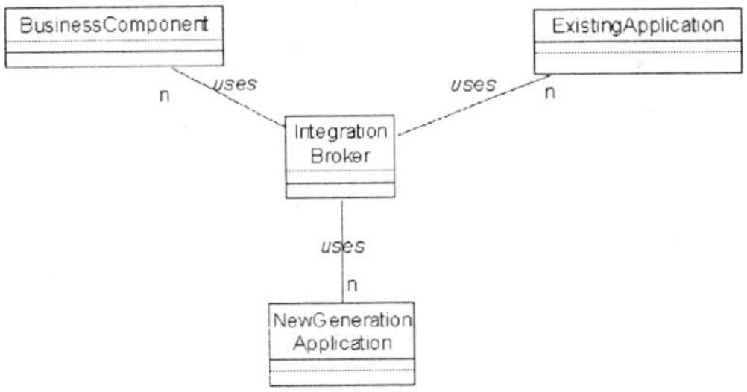

Figure 1: Integration broker pattern

Integration Broker should support one or more of the following communication models:

- Synchronous one to one communication, where the client requires immediate response from the server and waits (blocks) for the response.
- Deferred synchronous one to one communication, where the client asks for a response later or is notified by the server (call back or event).
- Asynchronous one to one communication, where the client does not require an answer from the server, nor does it require for the server to be online by the time of submitting the request.
- Asynchronous one to many communication, where a single client can communicate with more servers. This model is also called "publish and subscribe".

Typical representatives of Integration Broker pattern are common middleware technologies, particularly remote method invocations (object request brokers) and message oriented middleware. Integration Broker pattern is usually implicitly used in integration. This pattern requires one or more middleware products, which implement the functionality. As today a high level of abstraction is achieved, this pattern is not modeled in the design time. However, the architecture has to be aware of this pattern and should adapt the communication requests between the components.

2.5. Consequences

- The number of connections between applications is reduced, which also reduces the level of coupling between the integrated applications
- The dependencies between the applications are defined as contracts in form of interoperability interfaces
- If the interfaces are carefully designed we can replace parts or the whole application without influencing other involved applications
- The location transparency is achieved

- The maintenance effort and costs are therefore reduced to an acceptable level

2.6. Related Patterns

This pattern is related to all other integration patterns, covered in this chapter. It is also related to the GoF Mediator pattern.

3. Integration Wrapper Pattern

3.1. Context

Providing programmatic access to the existing applications is important for reusing the functionality of the existing applications and developing new solutions. The existing applications may not provide APIs, or the provided APIs might not be sufficient.

3.2. Problem

If we want to reuse the functionality of the existing application, we have to access them somehow. The most obvious possibility is to access them through the application programming interfaces (APIs) that existing applications provide. Sometimes, however, existing applications will not provide any APIs to access their functionality, not even the proprietary ones. Or, they will provide only a subset of functionality through the APIs, but we would need to access the other functions as well.

3.3. Forces

- For integrating and reusing the existing applications we need to access them programmatically
- Through the API access we can reuse data and functionality of the existing applications
- Accessing the application through the APIs is better than going into the database directly, because we do not avoid the business logic

3.4. Solution

The Integration Wrapper pattern is about layered approach to adding APIs to existing applications. This means that the services and the functionality of the existing applications are exported to the other applications, thus enabling interoperability and integration. Its motivation lies in the Adapter pattern (GoF), however the goal of Integration Wrapper is to provide reusable interfaces for multiple clients to access the wrapper simultaneously.

Figure 2: Integration Wrapper pattern

To develop the wrappers, we will build a layer around the existing application and add the necessary interfaces. We will call the added application interfaces a wrapper and the modified existing application will be called a "wrapped existing application". The Integration Wrapper has two major objectives. First, it should provide open, reusable interoperability interfaces. Second, it should convert the calls to the reuse the services and functionality of existing application. For the latter the Integration Wrapper can reuse the already provided APIs, or need to add such APIs. The structure of the Integration Wrapper is shown in the Figure 2.

Generally, the wrapper can add APIs in an intrusive or non-intrusive way. There are two possibilities how to add wrappers to the existing applications:

- We can modify the existing applications and provide the missing access
- We can use screen scraping or terminal emulation to access the functionality though the user interfaces.

One criterion that will influence the decision between modifying the existing applications and using screen scrapping or terminal emulation will be the availability of source code and the required tools. We have to make sure that the versions of source code are complete and reflect the current executable code. If we do not have the source code and all the tools and the libraries necessary to build the working executable of the existing application our only choice will be to utilize the user interface wrapping (discussed a little later).

Even if we have the source code and all the required tools, we might choose not to modify the existing applications and rather use screen scraping or terminal emulation. The reasons can be that we do not want to risk introducing bugs into existing application, that we are not familiar with the technology of existing application, and so on.

Even before we select one of these choices, we have to identify the operations through which we will access the existing application functionality. We will figure this out with the analysis of the existing application. We have to analyze the application, and we must focus on what we actually need. The Integration Wrapper pattern is related to the Integration Broker pattern. The structure of the wrapper depends on the type of communication. If we use synchronous communication style, such as remote method invocation, then the infrastructure will force typed communication and will check the operation signatures. When using the asynchronous communication, the wrapper is responsible for decomposing the messages.

3.5. Consequences

- Integration Wrapper enables programmatic communication with existing applications
- It enables reuse of the services and the functionality of the existing applications
- It hides the details of internal structure of the existing applications, their technologies, the programming model, and the communication details
- It reduces the complexity and decouples the clients

3.6. Related Patterns

Integration Broker, Virtual Component, GoF Adapter

4. Integration Mediator Pattern

4.1. Context

When integrating applications, the integration logic often needs to be separated from all the involved applications and also needs to be encapsulated, which minimizes dependencies, increases the reuse, and simplifies the maintenance.

4.2. Problem

In cases when we have the existing applications, which need to be integrated with each other, or where a common functionality is distributed among several applications and/or duplicated in several existing applications, we often need integration logic, which will solve these problems and represent a service or a functionality in a common way to its clients. The clients should not be aware of the complexity, hidden inside the mediator.

4.3. Forces

- The existing applications often need to be integrated among each other
- Certain functionality is often distributed among more than a single existing application
- Certain functionality is often duplicated in more than one existing application
- The interaction between the applications is complex
- The clients should not be aware of this complexity

4.4. Solution

The Integration Mediator acts like a controller for the involved existing applications and provides an interface for the clients. It should be aware of the existing applications and include the interaction logic to fulfill certain higher-level operations which require complex interaction with the existing and/or newly developed applications. The integration logic, contained inside the Integration Mediator can be used for different integration levels, such as data level integration or function and method level integration. The Integration Mediator should not access the existing applications directly. Rather, it should use the integration wrappers. The structure of the Integration Mediator is shown in the Figure 3, and shows the client, integration wrappers, and the mediator.

Generally, there are two forms of the integration mediators: Single step or Stateless; and Multi step or Stateful. Stateless mediators are used for those integration scenarios, where the maintenance of the state during an interaction with the existing applications is not necessary. This means that the way the mediator acts depends only on the response from the existing applications. Examples are routing and brokering, and vocabulary transforming. A typical example of stateless mediator is an XSLT engine.

Stateful Integration Mediator is used when we have to keep track of the previous interactions with applications. The mediator then accumulates the data about the previous interactions and uses this information for further interactions. Stateful Integration Mediators are also those based on events, where they remember events and after all required events have been triggered, they perform a certain action on the activity.

Stateful Integration Mediators require that the state is managed and sometimes even persisted. State persistence might be needed for the interactions with the existing applications, which take a longer time and thus must be able to survive system shutdowns. Such long lasting interactions might be very complex, lasting from a few minutes to hours or even days.

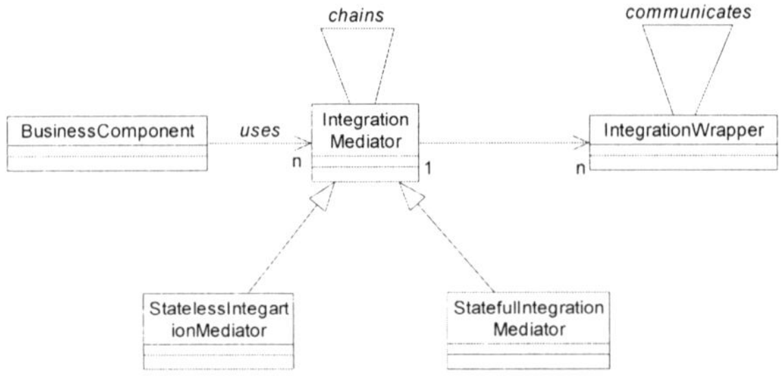

Figure 3: Integration Mediator pattern

4.5. Consequences

- Application dependencies are minimized
- The integration logic is encapsulated and decoupled from the participating existing applications and new clients
- Maintenance is simplified as the integration logic is centralized rather than distributed among existing applications
- Services can be built on top of the functionality, provided by the mediator, thus they do not have to be aware of the complexity of the existing applications

4.6. Related Patterns

Integration Wrapper, Virtual Component, GoF Mediator, GoF Façade.

5. Virtual Component Pattern

5.1. Context

Accessing the services of an integrated information system can vary, particularly if the integration system uses a variety of existing applications, implemented in different technologies. Accessing these services directly would require that the clients possesses the knowledge of the internal structure of the information system. Virtual components provide a common, unified access point to the services, thus acting as a façade to the existing applications.

5.2. Problem

Clients, accessing the integrated information system should not be aware of the complexity of the existing applications and should not access them directly. Integrated information system is also more than just connected existing applications. Integrated information system should provide new services and functionalities. They should be exposed to the clients in a common, uniform way. If clients would access the existing applications directly, they would be too highly coupled with them, making the maintenance and the replacement very difficult.

5.3. Forces

- Existing applications do not provide the high level services and functionalities, required by clients
- Clients should not be aware of the complexity of the information system
- Client should use high level services

5.4. Solution

Virtual Component pattern provides a solution for integrating the existing applications with the clients. The pattern has its motivation in the Façade pattern, however, the Virtual Component pattern is targeted towards the integration and provides reusability and the ability to re-engineer and replace the applications behind the virtual component with the actual, modern implementation. Integrated information system based on the Virtual Component pattern is a system that looks like a newly developed information system where in fact it reuses the functionality of the existing applications.

Virtual components do not differ from the newly developed components from the perspective of the clients. Both provide the functionality through the interfaces. The concept of virtual components will therefore allow us to make existing applications look like new developed components and to mix existing and new applications in all and any possible way.

Virtual Component pattern encapsulates the details that the existing applications contribute to satisfying requests and the methods by which they are satisfied. On one side, the virtual component presents the exiting application through abstract interoperability interfaces. On the other side, the virtual component communicates with the integration wrappers and the integration mediators. This is shown in the Figure 4.

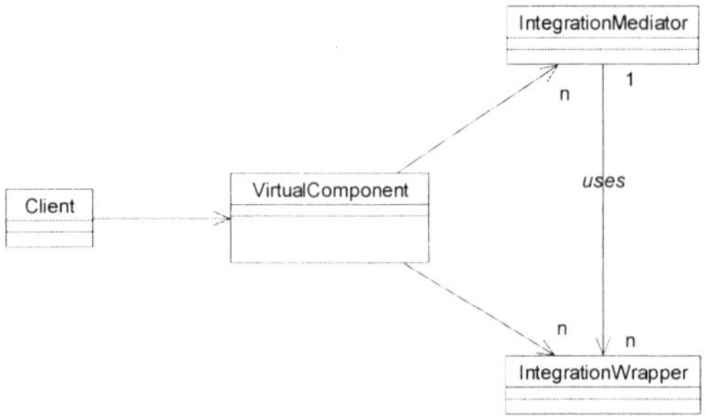

Figure 4: Virtual Component pattern

Virtual component might be for example an order placing component, which provides a simple interface to place an order and internally accesses the existing systems like a payment system, an inventory system etc. Virtual component, together with the abstract interoperability interfaces present an application view that is implementation independent. If we keep the abstract interface constant, the other applications are not aware of any changes that are done on the original application. Thus, there is no need for modifying other applications that depend on the original application when a change is made. In other words, client virtual components are unable to determine how the server virtual components are implemented.

The Integration Broker pattern influences the way in which a virtual component will be actually implemented. In each case the virtual component masks the complexity of the existing applications that implement the high level business functionality in the background.

Virtual components are deployed on the business logic tier. They will be built in several stages during the integration. The different virtual components will expose the interfaces that will offer different abstraction levels to access the functionality. Therefore, we will organize the virtual components into several sub tiers on the business logic tier.

The virtual components on a lower level will take care of the technology adoption, and will be built on data level and application interface level integration. Virtual components on higher levels will transform the high level business request into a series of lower level calls to different low level virtual components for the existing applications. High level virtual components will also do some data conversions and adoptions to finally reach the goal of implementing the functionality through the reuse of existing applications.

We will typically use virtual components for one or a combination of the following functions:

- Virtual components encapsulate functionality of existing applications and present them in the same way, or some rearranged way. Virtual components can, for example, present exactly the same functionality that can be found in the existing application APIs. In this

case they just mask the technology differences and are called lower level virtual components.
- Lower level virtual components implement the code that translates the method invocations into one or more calls to APIs of the existing applications and databases accesses. This code will often have to do parameter transformations, alignment of data types, and other transformations to mask the technology differences between the J2EE technologies and the technologies used by the existing applications. In more simple terms, the lower level virtual components will act as adapters between the new and the existing applications.
- Virtual components can provide a different, higher level interface and thus mask the way existing applications implement their APIs, too. Such virtual components are called higher level virtual components and their interfaces should be defined based on a global design model, which we will discuss later in this paper.
- Virtual components can encapsulate several existing applications and help in maintaining the transaction integrity and the security.
- Virtual components are also useful to encapsulate or abstract persistent data. For this purpose the virtual components can access EIS databases directly or though provided protocols. In this case they will often also implement the validation logic. This is an extra level of security, which might not have been handled by the old application that will keep the database in a consistent state.
- Virtual components can provide a unified access to several EIS databases and can handle different combinations of databases in the background. Alternatively, they can use APIs to access data, if those APIs are provided by the existing applications.
- Virtual components will often be layered, thus higher level virtual components will aggregate the behaviors of lower level virtual components and provide the higher level of abstraction required for multiple levels of abstraction of EIS application functionality.
- Virtual components can also be used to map technical differences. A particularly useful scenario is to adapt synchronous and asynchronous communication models.

5.5. Consequences

- Virtual components provide a unified view on the services and the functionality of integrated information system
- Virtual components abstract the details of the information system, thus providing a sort of façade
- Virtual components provide high level, business process oriented interfaces for interoperability
- They enable easy replacement with newly developed components as long as the interfaces remain unchanged

5.6. Related Patterns

Façade, Integration Wrapper, Integration Mediator, Integration Broker.

6. Data Mapping Pattern

6.1. Context

When integrating the existing applications, the data often needs to be moved from one application to other. Access to the databases of existing applications varies from the type of datastore (relational, object, hierarchical, flat files, and so on.) and the way data is accessed (directly to the database, through application, physical, and so on.).

6.2. Problem

The data mapping logic can become complex, therefore it is preferable if it is encapsulated and decoupled for the existing applications. This way the data mapping logic is less coupled with the existing applications, which improves maintenance.

6.3. Forces

- Data needs to be moved between the existing applications
- Data is stored in different formats in the existing applications
- Accessing the data varies from the type of storage and the access technologies
- The data mapping logic should be separated and should not be complicated with technical details.

6.4. Solution

The Data Mapping pattern is used to encapsulate and abstract the data mapping logic for transferring, replicating and updating data between the related integrated existing applications. This pattern accesses the data store, either directly through DAO, or wrappers.

The Data Mapping pattern comes in two variations: the Direct Data Mapping; and the Multi Step Data Mapping. The Direct Data Mapping pattern handles the mapping, where data needs to be moved from a certain data store to the other, without transformations. The Multi Step Data Mapping also transforms the data. The structure of the pattern is shown in the Figure 5.

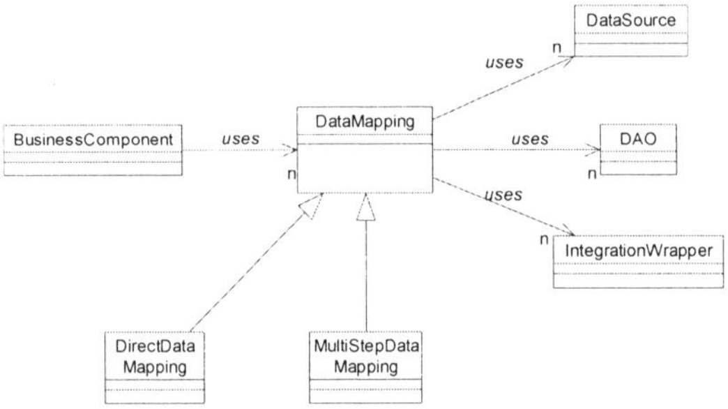

Figure 5: Data Mapping pattern

6.5. Consequences

- The data mapping logic is encapsulated and decoupled from the participating existing applications and their data stores.
- Data dependencies are minimized.
- Maintenance is simplified as the data mapping logic is centralized rather than distributed among the existing applications.
- Business components can use the functionality, provided by the Data Mapping pattern, thus they do not have to be aware of the data complexity of the existing applications.

6.6. Related Patterns

Integration Wrapper, Integration Mediator, Data Access Object.

7. Process Automator Pattern

7.1. Context

System interactions should often be hidden and abstracted by the process controller. The dependencies between the business process controllers and the system logic of the information system should also be minimized.

7.2. Problem

The services of an integrated information system should be exposed to the clients though high level methods, which reflect their business processes. A typical business process method will require an interaction with different virtual components and integration mediators. This interaction should not be delegated to the clients, because this enhances the complexity, increases the maintenance effort, and does not allow us to use declarative transaction management.

7.3. Forces

- Services of the integrated system should be exposed as high-level business process methods
- The business process interaction logic should be abstracted and encapsulated on the middle tier
- Clients should not be responsible for making the necessary operation invocations
- Business process logic should often be performed inside transactions
- The dependencies between process automation control and the information system technology should be minimized

7.4. Solution

Process Automator pattern enables to gather and encapsulate the business process logic and thus enables to minimize the dependencies between the business process automation logic and information technology system logic. All interactions are hidden by the process automator controller. This pattern helps to improve the quality of business processes, reduces the process execution costs and reduces the necessary time. Therefore, this pattern is highly appropriate for defining integration process within and between the companies.

The Process Automator pattern sequences the activities of a business process and delegates steps to the corresponding parts of the information system. It does this using virtual components and integration mediators, through which the automator components access the functionality of the existing applications. The process automator, however, can access the newly developed components as well. The structure is shown in Figure 6.

Common uses for the Process Automator pattern are the definition of the business activities, the timers, and process context informators. It comes in two variations: Closed Process Automator; and Open Process Automator. The difference is exclusively in the semantic understanding of both types of processes. The Closed Process Automator implements a process, which is managed internally and externalizes the key process activities only through the data exchange. The clients are able to monitor the activities within the process, but cannot actively participate in their execution. The Open Process Automator enables sharing of business process between the clients. Such processes are managed by more than one client and are particularly useful for inter EAI, or B2B integration, where a single process is shared by more than one company.

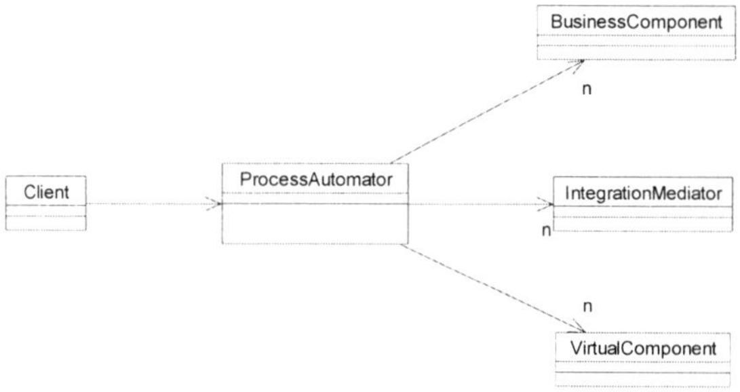

Figure 6: Process Automator pattern

7.5. Consequences

- The architecture allows easy analysis of business processes, their bottlenecks, utilization, downtime, and so on.
- Flexibility is achieved for redefining the business proceses
- The process automator components are aligned with the business managers view, which reduces the semantic gap between IT and management
- With the connection to the virtual components and the integration mediators, a highly flexible integration architecture can be defined

7.6. Related Patterns

Virtual Component, Integration Mediator.

8. Conclusion

The major contribution of this article is the definition of six new integration patterns: Integration Broker pattern, Integration Wrapper pattern, Integration Mediator pattern, Virtual Component pattern, Data Mapping pattern, and Process Automator pattern. These integration patterns are a result of a systematical analysis and identification of common integration problems. They represent sound solutions for these common integration problems and have been verified according to the "rule of three", that is, they have been successfully implemented in several integration projects.

The presented integration patterns are useful for intra-EAI as well as for inter-EAI and B2B integration. We have followed the principle that successful inter-EAI and B2B integration can be built on a well-defined intra-EAI only. Therefore, the integration patterns have to be applied step by step, first to enable the intra-EAI integration. Then we should build B2B interactions on top of an integrated architecture. In this context all the presented patterns are important. However, the process automator pattern is the one that deserves a special consideration. Typically, we will apply this pattern when implementing shared business processes. Our future research will be focused on how to apply these patterns using the most important component based architectures.

References

[1] Matjaz Juric with Ramesh Nagappan, Rick Leander, S. Jeelani Basha, Professional J2EE EAI, Wrox Press Inc; ISBN: 186100544X, December 2001

[2] Alexander Christopher, Sara Ishikawa, Murray Silverstein, A Pattern Language: Towns, Buildings, Construction, Oxford University Press, ISBN: 0195019199, 1979

[3] Richard P. Gabriel, Patterns of Software: Tales from the Software Community, Oxford University Press; ISBN: 0195121236, May 1998

[4] Erich Gamma, Richard Helm, Ralph Johnson, and John Vlissides, Design Patterns: Elements of Reusable Object-Oriented Software, Addison-Wesley Pub Co; ISBN: 0201633612, January 1995

[5] IBM Patterns for e-business, IBM Developer Works, http://www-106.ibm.com/developerworks/patterns/

[6] Torbjörn Dahlén, Integration Tier Patterns for the J2EE Platform, Sun Microsystems, Inc., 2001

[7] Francis Bordeleau, Behavior Integration Patterns – Ph.D. Thesis, Carleton University, School of Computer Science, 2001

[8] Andre Yee, Making EAI Work in the Real World: EAI Patterns, http://eai.ebizq.net/enterprise_integration/yee_3.html

[9] Andre Yee, Order Out of Chaos: Understanding B2B Integration Patterns, http://b2b.ebizq.net/ebiz_integration/yee_1.html

[10] Deepak Alur, John Crupi, Dan Malks, Core J2EE Patterns: Best Practices and Design Strategies, Prentice Hall PTR, ISBN: 0130648841, June 2001

Knowledge-based Software Engineering
T. Welzer et al. (Eds.)
IOS Press, 2002

A Proposal of Class Cohesion Metrics Using Sizes of Cohesive Parts

Hirohisa AMAN[1], Kenji YAMASAKI[1], Hiroyuki YAMADA[1], Matu-Tarow NODA[1]

[1]*Department of Computer Science, Ehime University,*
Bunkyo-cho 3, Matsuyama, Ehime 790–8577, Japan
aman@cs.ehime-u.ac.jp

Abstract. Cohesion is one of traditional and important software attributes. This could be used to assess object-oriented class design. Several metrics have been proposed in order to capture class cohesion in terms of connections among methods within a class. These metrics are based on (1) the number of sets of connected methods, or (2) the density of method connections within the class, but they do not consider sizes of sets of connected methods. In this paper, two new metrics for class cohesion have been proposed, which are focusing on sizes of sets of connected methods, with considering strength of method connection. These proposed metrics are analytically verified using a mathematical framework.

1 Introduction

Cohesion is one of software attributes representing the degree to which the components are functionally connected within a software module[1]-[3]. This notion could be applied to object-oriented software: An object class corresponds to a module, whose attributes and methods correspond to module components. In general, highly cohesive class tends to have high maintainability, reusability and reliability[4], so that class cohesion would be one of criteria used for assessing class design. In order to measure class cohesion, several metrics have been proposed : 'Lack of Cohesion in Methods' (*LCOM*)[5]-[8], 'Tight Class Cohesion (*TCC*)', 'Loose Class Cohesion (*LCC*)'[7], 'Information flow-based Cohesion (*ICH*)'[9]; see [4] for details of them. These metrics are based on (1) the number of sets of connected methods, or (2) the density of method connections within the class, but they do no consider sizes of sets of connected methods. In this paper, two new metrics for class cohesion have been proposed, which are focusing on sizes of sets of connected methods, with considering strength of method connection. The proposed metrics satisfy the mathematical properties of cohesion metrics proposed by Briand and others[10].

2 Models and Metrics

Preliminary to developments of metrics, we present several underlying definitions.

Definition 1 (binary relation on methods).
Given a class. Let M be the set of methods within the class. We define a binary relation $S : M \rightharpoondown M$ as

$$S = \{ (u, v) \in M \times M \mid u \text{ invokes } v \}.$$

Then we define the *reflective transitive closure* $S^* : M \rightharpoondown M$ as

$$S^* = \left\{ (u, v) \in M \times M \;\middle|\; (u = v) \vee \left(\bigvee_{n \geq 1} u \; S^n v \right) \right\}, \tag{1}$$

where $S^n = S^{n-1} \circ S \;\; (n \geq 2)$, and $S^1 = S$. ("$\circ$" indicates the composition of relations[11].) ■

Based on S^*, we represent indirect relationships between method and attribute, as well as direct relationships between them.

Definition 2 (method accesses to attributes).
Given a class. Let M be the set of methods, and A be the set of attributes, within the class. For any $m \in M$, $a \in A$, we define the following predicates *ac*, *wr* and *re* :

$$ac(m, a) \overset{def}{\Longleftrightarrow} m_0 \in M \text{ s.t. } [\, (m \; S^* m_0) \wedge (m_0 \text{ accesses } a) \,], \tag{2}$$

$$wr(m, a) \overset{def}{\Longleftrightarrow} m_0 \in M \text{ s.t. } [\, (m \; S^* m_0) \wedge (m_0 \text{ writes data onto } a) \,], \tag{3}$$

$$re(m, a) \overset{def}{\Longleftrightarrow} m_0 \in M \text{ s.t. } [\, (m \; S^* m_0) \wedge (m_0 \text{ reads data from } a) \,]. \tag{4}$$

■

The predicate *ac* considers not only direct access to attribute but also indirect access to attribute via access-methods. *wr* and *re* are focusing on data-writing and data-reading through attribute access. Using the above three predicates, we introduce two graph models.

Definition 3 (weak-connection graph).
Given a class. Let M be the set of methods, and A be the set of attributes, within the class. We define *weak-connection graph* as an undirected graph $G_w(V, E)$, where $V = M$ and

$$E = \{ \{u, v\} \in M \times M \mid \exists a \in A \text{ s.t. } (\, ac(u, a) \;\wedge\; ac(v, a) \,) \}. \tag{5}$$

■

Definition 4 (strong-connection graph).
Given a class. Let M be the set of methods, and A be the set of attributes, within the class. We define *strong-connection graph* as a directed graph $G_s(V, E)$, where $V = M$ and

$$E = \{ (u, v) \in M \times M \mid \exists a \in A \text{ s.t. } (\, wr(u, a) \;\wedge\; re(v, a) \,) \}. \tag{6}$$

■

When two or more methods access to one attribute, those methods seem to share the attribute. The weak-connection graph represents attribute-sharings.

Furthermore, accesses to attributes include data-readings and data-writings. If a method writes data onto an attribute, and another method reads data from the attribute, then a dependent relationship might be occurred between the methods. Such relationship is emphasized by the strong-connection graph.

```
public class C {
    private int a1, a2;
    public void m1(int x){ a1 = x; }
    public void m2(int y){ a2 = y; }
    public int m3(){ return a1 + a2; }
    public void m4(){ m1(0); }
}
```

Figure 1: An example of class written in Java.

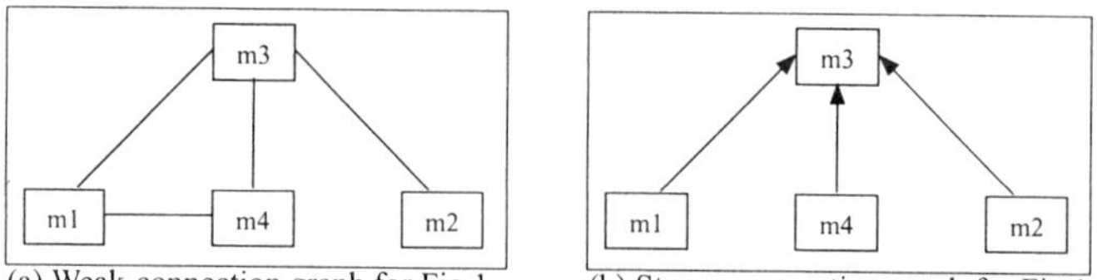

(a) Weak-connection graph for Fig.1 (b) Strong-connection graph for Fig.1

Figure 2: Weak-connection graph and strong-connection graph for the class shown in Fig.1.

For example, consider a class shown in Fig.1. According to Defs.3 and 4, we obtain the weak-connection graph and the strong-connection graph shown in Fig.2 :

ac(m1, a1), ac(m3, a1) and ac(m4, a1) are true, so that the edges {m1,m3}, {m1,m4} and {m3,m4} are shown in Fig.2(a);

'm4 invokes m1', 'm1 writes data onto a1' and 'm3 reads data from a1', so that wr(m1, a1), wr(m4, a1) and re(m3, a1) are true. Thus the edges (m1,m3) and (m4,m3) are shown in Fig.2(b);

etc.

While the strong-connection graph is sensitive to directions of attribute accesses, the weak-connection graph is insensitive to them. In other words, the weak-connection graph seems to be optimistic about method connections, but the strong-connection graph looks pessimistic about them.

Using the weak-connection graph and the strong-connection graph, we propose two metrics for class cohesion.

Definition 5 (Optimistic Class Cohesion (OCC)).

Given a class C. Let M be the set of methods, and A be the set of attributes, within C. Consider the weak-connection graph $G_w(V, E)$, where $V = M$ and E is in Eq.(5). Let $n = |M|$.

For each method $m_i \in M (i = 1, \ldots, n)$, let $R_w(m_i)$ be the set of methods which are reachable by m_i on $G_w(V, E)$:

$$R_w(m_i) = \{\ m_j \in M \mid \exists m_{k_1}, \ldots, m_{k_p} \in M \ \text{s.t.}\ \{m_{k_s}, m_{k_{s+1}}\} \in E \ (s = 1, \ldots, p-1),\ m_i = m_{k_1},\ m_j = m_{k_p},\ i \neq j\ \}. \tag{7}$$

We define *Optimistic Class Cohesion* (*OCC*) for class C as

$$OCC(C) = \begin{cases} \max\limits_{i=1,\ldots,n} \left[\dfrac{|R_w(m_i)|}{n-1} \right], & (n > 1), \\ 0, & (n = 1). \end{cases} \tag{8}$$

■

$|R_w(m_i)|/(n-1)$ denotes the percentage of methods to be reachable by m_i on the weak-connection graph ('-1' means excepting itself). *OCC* is the maximum value of them. That is, *OCC* quantifies the maximum extent of attribute-sharings among methods within the class. For example, in the case of Fig.2,

$$R_w(\mathrm{m1}) = \{\mathrm{m2}, \mathrm{m3}, \mathrm{m4}\}, \quad R_w(\mathrm{m2}) = \{\mathrm{m1}, \mathrm{m3}, \mathrm{m4}\},$$
$$R_w(\mathrm{m3}) = \{\mathrm{m1}, \mathrm{m2}, \mathrm{m4}\}, \quad R_w(\mathrm{m4}) = \{\mathrm{m1}, \mathrm{m2}, \mathrm{m3}\}.$$

Thus $|R_w(\mathrm{m1})| = \cdots = |R_w(\mathrm{m4})| = 3$. We can calculate as $OCC = \max[3/(4-1)] = 1.0$.

Definition 6 (Pessimistic Class Cohesion (PCC)).

Given a class C. Let M be the set of methods, and A be the set of attributes, within C. Consider the strong-connection graph $G_s(V, E)$, where $V = M$ and E is in Eq.(6). Let $n = |M|$.

For each method $m_i \in M (i = 1, \ldots, n)$, let $R_s(m_i)$ be the set of methods which are reachable by m_i on $G_s(V, E)$:

$$R_s(m_i) = \{\, m_j \in M \mid \exists m_{k_1}, \ldots, m_{k_p} \in M \text{ s.t. } (m_{k_s}, m_{k_{s+1}}) \in E \ (s = 1, \ldots, p-1), \ m_i = m_{k_1}, \ m_j = m_{k_p}, \ i \neq j \,\}. \tag{9}$$

We define *Pessimistic Class Cohesion* (*PCC*) for class C as

$$PCC(C) = \begin{cases} \max\limits_{i=1,\ldots,n} \left[\dfrac{|R_s(m_i)|}{n-1} \right], & (n > 1), \\ 0, & (n = 1). \end{cases} \tag{10}$$

■

$|R_s(m_i)|/(n-1)$ denotes the percentage of methods to be reachable by m_i on the strong-connection graph. *PCC* is the maximum value of them. That is, *PCC* quantifies the maximum extent of dependent relationships among methods within the class. This would be the maximum size of highly cohesive part of the class. For example, in the case of Fig.2,

$$R_s(\mathrm{m1}) = \{\mathrm{m3}\}, \quad R_s(\mathrm{m2}) = \{\mathrm{m3}\}, \quad R_s(\mathrm{m3}) = \{\}, \quad R_s(\mathrm{m4}) = \{\mathrm{m3}\}.$$

Thus $|R_s(\mathrm{m1})| = |R_s(\mathrm{m2})| = |R_s(\mathrm{m4})| = 1$ and $|R_s(\mathrm{m3})| = 0$. We can calculate as $PCC = \max[1/(4-1), 0/(4-1)] = 1/3$.

3 Analytical Evaluation of Metrics

Briand, Morasca and Basili have proposed a mathematical framework (BMB framework) including properties to be satisfied by several types of software metrics[10]. The supported types of metrics are 'size', 'length', 'complexity', 'coupling' and 'cohesion'. Note that BMB framework provide necessary conditions of software metrics, because the framework does not include the all properties to be satisfied by those metrics.

In BMB framework, a software is represented by a graph model in which vertexes are corresponding to software components, and edges are corresponding to coupling relationships between the components. BMB framework have suggested the following four properties to be satisfied by cohesion metrics. For the sake of convenience, we will write the cohesion of class C as $\mu(C)$.

Property 1 : $\forall C \ \mu(C) \in [0, max]$, where max is a positive constant number.

Property 2 : Let $G(V, E)$ be the graph model of a class C. Then $E = \phi \implies \mu(C) = 0$.
Property 3 : Consider two classes C and C' whose models are $G(V, E)$ and $G(V, E')$, respectively. Then $E \subseteq E' \implies \mu(C) \leq \mu(C')$.
Property 4 : Consider two classes C_1 and C_2 whose models are $G_1(V_1, E_1)$ and $G_2(V_2, E_2)$, respectively. Let C_{12} be a class whose model is $G_{12}(V_1 \cup V_2, E_{12})$, where $E_1 \cup E_2 \subseteq E_{12}$, i.e., C_{12} is composed of C_1 and C_2. Then $(E_1 \cup E_2 = E_{12}) \wedge (E_1 \cap E_2 = \phi) \implies \max[\ \mu(C_1),\ \mu(C_2)\ ] \geq \mu(C_{12})$.

3.1 OCC

OCC satisfies the above four properties. We now show the proof for the property 4 only, for the lack of space; the proofs for the remaining properties could be derived from the definitions of *OCC* and R_w easily.

Proof for Property 4 :

Let C_1 has n_1 methods m_i^1 $(i = 1, \ldots, n_1)$, C_2 has n_2 methods m_i^2 $(i = 1, \ldots, n_2)$, and C_{12} has n_{12} methods m_i^{12} $(i = 1, \ldots, n_{12})$, respectively. Let $R_w^1(m_i^1)$ be the set of reachable methods by m_i^1 on $G_1(V_1, E_1)$, $R_w^2(m_i^2)$ be the set of reachable methods by m_i^2 on $G_2(V_2, E_2)$, and $R_w^{12}(m_i^{12})$ be the set of reachable methods by m_i^{12} on $G_{12}(V_1 \cup V_2, E_{12})$, respectively.

(i) Case $n_1 = n_2 = 1$: From the definition and property 2, $OCC(C_1) = OCC(C_2) = OCC(C_{12}) = 0$. Thus, $\max[OCC(C_1), OCC(C_2)] = OCC(C_{12})$.

(ii) Case $n_1 > 1$ or $n_2 > 1$: This case may be $n_1 + n_2 \geq n_{12}$. Let $n_1 + n_2 - n_{12} = p\ (\geq 0)$. We will describe $m^1_{n_1-p+k} = m_k^2$ $(k = 1, \ldots, p)$, without loss of generality. In constructing C_{12} from C_1 and C_2, we add no edge to their weak-connection graphs. Thus

$$R_w^{12}(m_i^{12}) = \begin{cases} R_w^1(m_i^1), & (i = 1, \ldots, n_1 - p), \\ R_w^1(m_i^1) = R_w^2(m^2_{i-n_1+p}), & (i = n_1 - p + 1, \ldots, n_1), \\ R_w^2(m^2_{i-n_1+p}), & (i = n_1 + 1, \ldots, n_{12}). \end{cases}$$

Since $n_1, n_2 \leq n_{12}$,

$$\frac{|R_w^{12}(m_i^{12})|}{n_{12} - 1} \leq \frac{|R_w^1(m_i^1)|}{n_1 - 1}, \quad (i = 1, \ldots, n_1), \quad \text{and}$$
$$\frac{|R_w^{12}(m_i^{12})|}{n_{12} - 1} \leq \frac{|R_w^2(m_j^2)|}{n_2 - 1}, \quad (i = n_1 - p + 1, \ldots, n_{12};\ j = i - n_1 + p).$$

Thereby we get

$$\max_{i=1,\ldots,n_1} \left[\frac{|R_w^{12}(m_i^{12})|}{n_{12} - 1} \right] \leq \max_{i=1,\ldots,n_1} \left[\frac{|R_w^1(m_i^1)|}{n_1 - 1} \right] = OCC(C_1), \quad \text{and}$$
$$\max_{i=n_1-p+1,\ldots,n_{12}} \left[\frac{|R_w^{12}(m_i^{12})|}{n_{12} - 1} \right] \leq \max_{\substack{i=n_1-p+1,\ldots,n_{12} \\ (j=1,\ldots,n_2)}} \left[\frac{|R_w^2(m_j^2)|}{n_2 - 1} \right] = OCC(C_2).$$

From these,

$$\begin{aligned} OCC(C_{12}) &= \max_{i=1,\ldots,n_{12}} \left[\frac{|R_w^{12}(m_i^{12})|}{n_{12} - 1} \right] \\ &= \max \left\{ \max_{i=1,\ldots,n_1} \left[\frac{|R_w^{12}(m_i^{12})|}{n_{12} - 1} \right], \max_{i=n_1-p+1,\ldots,n_{12}} \left[\frac{|R_w^{12}(m_i^{12})|}{n_{12} - 1} \right] \right\} \\ &\leq \max \{\ OCC(C_1),\ OCC(C_2)\ \}, \end{aligned}$$

for all classes such that $E_1 \cup E_2 = E_{12}$ and $E_1 \cap E_2 = \phi$. ∎

3.2 PCC

In the above proof, replace '*OCC*' with '*PCC*', 'R_w' with 'R_s', and, 'weak-connection graph' with 'strong-connection graph', respectively. Then we can get the proof for *PCC*.

4 Conclusions and Future Works

We have proposed two metrics for class cohesion, *OCC* (*Optimistic Class Cohesion*) and *PCC* (*Pessimistic Class Cohesion*). If two or more methods access to one attribute directly or indirectly, those methods seem to share the attribute. Such sharing is a kind of connections among methods. *OCC* quantifies the maximum extent of such connections within a class. This would be the maximum size of cohesive part of the class.

When methods access to attributes, those accesses include data-readings and data-writings. By focusing on such differences in accesses, we can consider dependent relationships among methods, which would be strong connections among methods. *PCC* quantifies the maximum extent of such dependent relationships within a class. This would be the maximum size of highly cohesive part of the class.

According to BMB framework, we have showed that *OCC* and *PCC* satisfy necessary conditions of cohesion metrics.

The future works include the followings : (1) to study relationships among *OCC*, *PCC* and existing metrics using many experimental data; (2) to discuss the usefulness of BMB framework in the software engineering discipline.

References

[1] G.J. Myers, Software Reliability-Principles and Practices, John Wiley & Sons, Inc. (1976).

[2] M. Page-Jones, The Practical Guide to Structured Systems, 2nd ed., Yourdon Press (1988).

[3] E. Yourdon and L. Constantine, Structured Design, Englewood Cliffs, Prentice Hall (1979).

[4] L.C. Briand, J.W. Daly and J. Wüst, A Unified Framework for Cohesion Measurement in Object-Oriented Systems, Empirical Software Eng. : An Int'l J. **3**(1) (1998) 65–117.

[5] S.R. Chidamber and C.F. Kemerer, A metrics suite for object-oriented design, IEEE Trans. on Software Eng. **20**(6) (1994) 476–493.

[6] M. Hitz and B. Montazeri, Chidamber and Kemerer's metrics suite : a measurement theory perspective, IEEE Trans. on Software Eng. **22**(4) (1996) 267–271.

[7] J.M. Bieman and B.-K. Kang, Cohesion and reuse in an object-oriented system, Proc. ACM Symp. Software Reusability (1995) 259–262.

[8] B. Henderson-Sellers, Software Metrics, Prentice Hall (1996).

[9] Y.-S. Lee, B.-S. Liang, S.-F. Wu and F.-J. Wang, Measuring the coupling and cohesion of an object oriented program based on information flow, Proc. International Conference on Software Quality (1995).

[10] L.C. Briand, S. Morasca and V.R. Basili, Property-based software engineering measurement, IEEE Trans. on Software Eng. **22**(1) (1996) 68–86.

[11] D.F. Stanat and D.F. McAllister, Discrete mathematics in Computer Science, Prentice-Hall (1977).

[12] H. Aman, H. Yamada and M.T. Noda, A Proposal of Class Cohesion Metrics focusing on Sizes of Cohesive Parts, Technical Report of IEICE **KBSE2001–19** (2001).

Knowledge-based Software Engineering
T. Welzer et al. (Eds.)
IOS Press, 2002

Construction of a Fuzzy Grammar from a Set of Sentences

Vladislav KUBÍČEK, Jaroslav ZENDULKA
BUT FIT, Božetěchova 2, 612 66 Brno, Czech Republic

Abstract. A non-terminal fuzzy regular grammar is introduced and a method for its construction from a given set of sentences presented in this paper. The grammar is used to describe the relations between the occurrences of symbols in a set of sentences. It can be used to describe a set of sentences (for example a set of images with discovered elementary shapes) and such a description can be employed to retrieve similar sentences (for example images) or to analyze sentences (for example text). The fuzzy value in the grammar indicates the probability of using a given production generating a symbol and is given by the probability of the occurrence of the symbol in the set of sentences. The method of grammar construction was verified by an experimental system. Some results of experiments are presented in the paper too.

1 Introduction

The description of images is the key problem of content-based image retrieval and image processing in general. The abilities of comparing images depend on the method of their description. The problem has two possible solutions. We can use either a human-made description or an automatically created vector of features derived from an image to be described. Each of these approaches has some disadvantages.

The human-made description is based on the semantics of the image, but its subjectivity makes it less usable for content-based retrieval. Furthermore, it is impossible to prepare such a description for large image databases. The feature vector is usually based on visual features that can be easily derived from images and so the description reflects neither semantics nor syntax of images.

The grammar systems are good for a syntax description. Even if there some types of grammars have been developed for the image description, they are not often used. The reason is simple: it is difficult to detect a grammar for a set of images. We can construct a grammar and then use it to generate sentences of the corresponding language, but the opposite task - to detect a grammar from sentences of a language, is not easy. That is why there are many examples of using a grammar to produce decorations or recurrent pattern [1, 2]. The use of a grammar to describe images is not so common. We know only two examples. The first one concerns a work in which a few paintings by Picasso were described by means of a grammar. The second one is a proposal of a method to recognize a written text represented as an image, which is based on a fuzzy grammar [3].

The use of grammars constructed from a set of sentences is more general. They can be used not only for image description, also for text correction and in other application domains. But the grammar is usually constructed manually [1, 4, 5].

There are some works trying to use image syntax [6, 7]. Our approach is different. We propose a system detecting and describing the syntax by the grammar system, which is automatically constructed. The works of Miroslav Novotný [8] are dedicated to the grammar construction. He constructs the infinite grammar from sentences and then performs its reduction. We try to generate a minimal grammar directly from the sentences using knowledge about the sentences. There is one important simplification in our approach compared with the classical use of grammars. We consider only occurrences of symbols in sentences, not their order.

In our work, we use the term *symbol* (or a terminal symbol) for a fragment of information that represents a syntactical unit and the term *sentence* for a sequence of symbols. Symbols in a text could be words and symbols in an image description could be some image features, for example shapes. Section 2 introduces a non-terminal fuzzy regular grammar, which is used in our method. The description of the method is presented in Section 3. Section 4 describes an experimental system that was implemented for experiments. Some results of the experiments are summarized in Section 5.

2 Non-terminal fuzzy regular grammar

To describe the occurrence, we consider neither the order of symbols in a sentence (also spatial relations in the case of images) nor their multiplicity. It is only the presence of the symbol in a sentence what is important for grammar construction and for generating descriptions from the grammar.

We can use a *regular grammar* $G=(N, T, P, S)$ to express the occurrence of symbols for any set of sentences, because the occurrence depends only on a presence of other symbols, not on its context where N, T, P, S are respectively the non-terminal alphabet, the terminal alphabet, the set of production rules, and the starting symbol.

Although the regular grammar can describe a language represented by a given set of sentences, it does not express the probability of sentence occurrences in the set, which can be useful in some applications. Therefore, we introduce fuzzy values that are given by the probability to the grammar. We call the grammar *non-terminal fuzzy regular grammar*. It is similar to a fuzzy grammar presented in [3] where the fuzzy value f is the probability of using a given production to generate a sentence, i.e. $f = PS/NS$ where PS is the number of sentences for generation of which the production was used and NS is the number of all sentences. In our non-terminal fuzzy grammar, the fuzzy value expresses the probability of using a given production.

Formally, the *non-terminal fuzzy regular grammar* is a five-tuple $FG=(N, T, P, S, f)$ where N, T, P, S are respectively the non-terminal alphabet, the terminal alphabet, the set of production rules, the starting symbol, and $f=\{f_i|i=1, 2, ..., n\}$ is a set of fuzzy values for the productions in P. The number of fuzzy values n is equal to the number of productions. The value f_i is the probability of using the i-th production.

The only form of the productions is $<a>\rightarrow b<b>$ where $<a>$, $<b>\in N$ and $b\in T$. We use a notation, in which a non-terminal of a regular grammar produced by a given production is denoted as a derived terminal symbol in angle brackets, except the starting non-terminal S.

The sum of fuzzy values of productions with the same left side is in the closed interval [0,1]. If the sum is less than 1, then there is a probability that no production will be used. In this case, the non-terminal will be replaced by an empty symbol. In other words, it is a probability of the production $<a>\rightarrow\varepsilon$, where $<a>$ is a non-terminal with the sum less than 1 and ε denotes an empty symbol.

The non-terminal fuzzy regular grammar is a fuzzy variant of the regular grammar, except the absence of the productions of the form $<a>\rightarrow b$ where $<a>\in N$ and $b\in T$, which

Table 1: The dependence table a) sentences of an example and conditional probabilities of the symbol occurrences, b) the dependence table.

a)

	p(b | c) = ½
a	p(c | b) = ½
abc	p(a | b,c) = ½
bc	p(b | a,c) = ½
	p(c | a,b) = ½

b)

A\B	a	b	c	a,b	a,c	b,c
a	x	0	0	x	x	½
b	0	x	½	x	½	x
c	0	½	x	½	x	x

are replaced by using fuzzy values. Furthermore, the fuzzy value enables to control the probability of a sentence derivation.

Because we use the grammar only to describe the occurrence of symbols in a sentence, each symbol can occur in a sentence at most once, and therefore there are no cyclic productions. That is the reason why we will use the term *set of symbols* for a set of symbols presented in a sentence or its fraction.

3 The method of grammar construction

To construct the grammar describing the occurrence of symbols, we need to know dependencies between the occurrences. The existence of the dependency is sufficient to construct a classic regular grammar; the rate of the dependency is necessary for a fuzzy grammar.

Our method of grammar construction is based on a *conditional probability* of symbol occurrences in a sentence $c = p(a_1|a_2..a_m) = p(a_1..a_m)/p(a_2..a_m)$, used to express the relationships between the symbols. A simple example of sentences and conditional probabilities of their occurrences can be found in Table 1a. It is a probability, that a sentence containing symbols $a_2..a_m$, contain also a symbol a_1, It can be seen as a dependency of the symbol a_1 on a set of symbols $a_2..a_m$.

The detection of dependencies (conditional probabilities) is the first step of grammar construction. An approach similar to the Apriori method [9,10] used for mining association rules can be applied, except there is no threshold for the conditional probability.

The method of occurrence dependencies is presented in [11] and will not be described here. Table 1 also shows organization of dependencies in so called *dependency table*. The *dependency* of a symbol a_i on a set of symbols $b_j = a_2..a_m$ we mark as $c_{i,j} = p(a_i \mid b_j)$. The set of all symbols $a_i, a_2..a_m$ will be called a *dependency set*.

The sets of symbols are grouped to levels according to their cardinality. In our example in Table 1b, there are two levels.

The second step is the grammar construction itself. For each dependency $c_{i,j} > 0$, productions generating a sentence with symbols a_i and b_j must be created. If we created productions directly from the sentences, the grammar would have too many productions. To minimize the number of productions created during construction, it is important to process sets of symbols in an appropriate order. We use levels mentioned above for this ordering. The ordering within a level is by the value of so called summary dependency $p\text{-}sum(a_1..a_m) = \prod_{i=1..m} p(a_i)$.

The processing order of symbols in a set to be processed is also important because it also influences the number of created productions. The symbols with high occurrences in the processed sets of symbols should be preferred, because it increases the probability of its reuse for generation other sentences.

The following algorithm can generate the grammar:
Input: The dependency.
Output: The non-terminal fuzzy regular grammar.

1) Summarize dependencies of each symbol a_i on all set of symbols b_j, $sum_i=\Sigma c_{i,j}$. For all $sum_i<1$ insert a production $S \rightarrow a_i\langle a_i\rangle$. Insert a_i to T, $\langle a_i\rangle$ to N, and $1-sum_i$ to f as a fuzzy value of the production.
2) For all levels of sets of symbols do
   2.1) While there is some unprocessed dependency relation on the level do
   2.1.1. Find the unprocessed dependency set set_{big} with the biggest summary dependency *p-sum* (set_{big}) on this level.
   2.1.2. Find the best existing non-terminal *N-best*, generating a part of the set_{big}. *N-best* = $\langle a_1a_2..a_n\rangle$ for $S \Rightarrow a_1\langle a_1\rangle \Rightarrow a_1a_2\langle a_1a_2\rangle \Rightarrow \ldots \Rightarrow a_1a_2..a_n\langle a_1a_2..a_n\rangle$ where $\{a_1,a_2,..,a_n\}\subset set_{big}$ with maximal $p\text{-}sum(a_1a_2..a_n)$ for suitable $\{a_1,a_2,..,a_n\}$.
   2.1.3. Increase the fuzzy value of all productions used to generate the *N-best* non-terminal, by the probability $c_{i,j}$. These are the productions $S \rightarrow a_1\langle a_1\rangle$, $\langle a_1\rangle \rightarrow a_2\langle a_1a_2\rangle$, ..., $a_{n-1} \rightarrow a_n\langle a_1a_2..a_n\rangle$ if $\langle a_1a_2..a_n\rangle$ is *N-best*.
   2.1.4. Create productions and corresponding terminals, non-terminals, and fuzzy values necessary to generate remaining symbols in set_{big}. These are the symbols from set_{big} that are not generated before *N-best*, i.e. $set_{big} - \{a_1,a_2,..,a_n\}$. Process the symbols in the order of the number of their occurrences in sets of symbols from the biggest to the smallest.
   2.1.5. Mark all dependency relations between symbols from set_{big} as processed.

In step 1, the algorithm creates productions necessary to generate all sentences containing one symbol because the dependency is a relation between at least two symbols. These dependencies are processed in step 2 where the levels are processed one by one.

The step 2.1.1 ensures the best order of processing on the level. The step 2.1.2 finds the existing productions, which can be used to processing symbols of the set of symbols. We use a notation indicating the symbols that are generated before the non-terminal is generated. The steps 2.1.3 and 2.1.4 modify fuzzy values of reused productions and create new productions. The step 2.1.5 restricts dependency sets necessary to process in next iterations.

4 Experimental system

An experimental system has been implemented. Its objective is to verify a functionality of the method. The identity of a source set of sentences (we will call them as *source sentences*) from which the grammar was generated and the languages generated by the grammar (we will call them as *generated sentences*) was checked. In addition, the number of generated productions was evaluated. The optimality of the computations was not the objective of the experimental system.

The system implements the algorithm described in Section 3 with a small difference. We do not compute probabilities, but only numbers of occurrences, similarly to the Apriori algorithm [9], which accelerates the algorithm.

The experimental system consists of four main parts: the generator of the source sentences, the dependency table constructor, grammar constructor, and the identity checker.

The source sentences are generated randomly. The generator uses the number of the sentences, their maximal length, and the number of symbols used in the sentences as parameters. The symbols can appear multiply in a generated sentence.

Figure 1: The average number of sentences necessary to generate the set of source sentences.

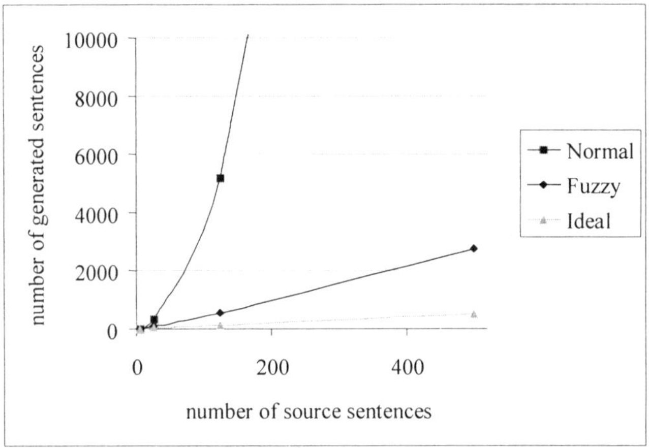

The sentences are pre-processed before the dependency table is constructed. The multiple symbols are substituted by only one symbol and the sentences are sorted according to their length. The dependency table construction was implemented according to [11].

The grammar constructor implements the algorithm from Section 3. We have tested creation of both the classic regular grammar and the non-terminal fuzzy regular grammar. The same constructor was used for both grammars. The only difference was in including fuzzy values in the case of the non-terminal fuzzy regular grammar.

Having constructed the grammars, it was used to generate sentences. The generated sentences were generated by random application of the productions than can be applied. For fuzzy grammar, the fuzzy values were used as a rate of the selection. Finally, the generated sentences were compared with source ones on presence and completeness.

5 Experimental results

The first test verified the functionality of the method. The test was executed for different lengths of sentences (5, 10, 15, 20), different maximal number of used items (5, 10, 15, 20), and different number of sentences (5, 25, 125, 500). The sentences were generated by the grammar until all source sentences are generated.

Figure 1 compares the average number of sentences necessary to generate all source sentences by the regular grammar and the non-terminal fuzzy grammar. The average values were computed from the test results for different lengths of sentences and number of symbols. The ideal value marks the same number of the generated sentences as the source sentences. The higher number of the generated sentences results from the fact that some sentences can be generated several times. The result shows the advantage of the fuzzy grammar where the fuzzy values can be employed to control the generating process.

The test confirmed that the grammars generate the language identical with the source one.

The second experiment shows the dependencies of the number of productions on number of symbols, sentences, and on the length of sentences. Figures 2 and 3 present the average number of generated productions of the non-terminal fuzzy regular grammar. Figure 2 corresponds to source sentences with 20 different symbols.

Figure 2: The number of productions for sentences with maximal 20 different symbols.

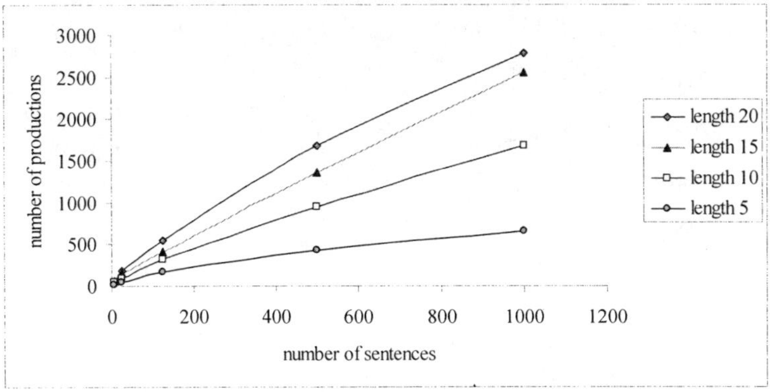

The dependency of the number of productions on the length of sentences is linear because the number of productions that must be applied is linearly dependent on the length of the sentence. With the increasing number of the sentences, the number of productions approaches a limit given by all possible combinations of symbols in a maximal sentence. This is shown very well in Figure 3 for sentences of the maximal length 5. The source sentences of maximum 10 different symbols were used in the experiment the results of which are in Figure 3. Compared Figure 2 and Figure 3, we can see that the number of the productions grows greatly with number of the symbols.

The last experiment evaluated the time complexity of the method. We used the same parameters of the source sentences as in the previous experiment. The results for 20 different symbols are shown in Figure 4 and for 10 different symbols in Figure 5.

As we have mentioned before the experimental system is not optimised. Experiments were done on a Pentium Celeron 660MHz computer with 64 MB RAM.

The number of symbol combinations mainly influences the time complexity because all combinations have to be processed. The number of the combinations is given by the length of sentences and by the number of different symbols.

Figure 3: The number of productions for sentences with maximal 10 different symbols.

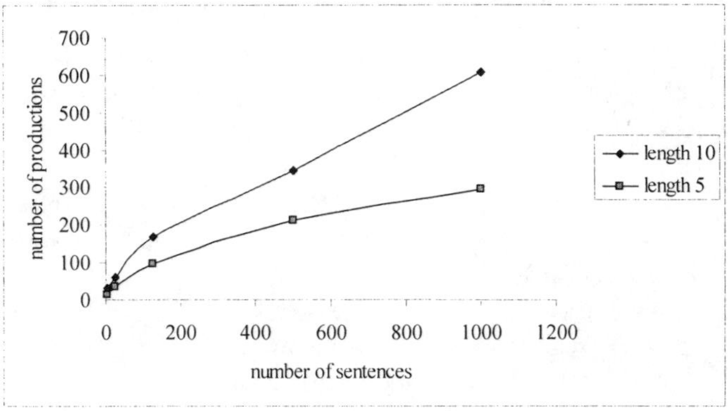

Figure 4: The method time complexity for sentences with maximal 20 different symbols.

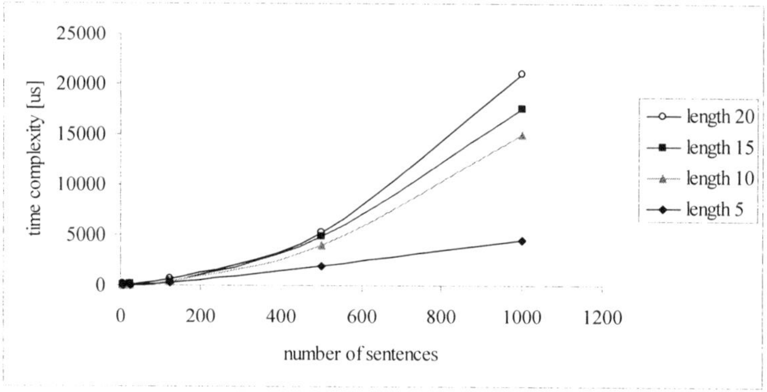

6 Conclusions

The method of grammar construction can be useful in some fields of the information technology for syntax description. Our method is based on a conditional probability and the resultant grammar describes the relations of symbol occurrences in sentences. We have introduced a non-terminal fuzzy regular grammar for this purpose. It can be considered as a variant of a fuzzy grammar. The functionality of the method was verified by means of an experimental system.

In future we would like to study the method properties in more details, optimise the method by developing a more effective algorithm and its implementation, and to apply the method in the field of image retrieval.

This work has been supported by the Grant of FRVS MSMT, FR1794/2002/G1 2002 "Knowledge discovery for similarity search in multimedia databases " and by the long-term grant project of Ministry of Education No. MSMT 262200012 "Research of information and control systems".

Figure 5: The method time complexity for sentences with maximal 10 different symbols.

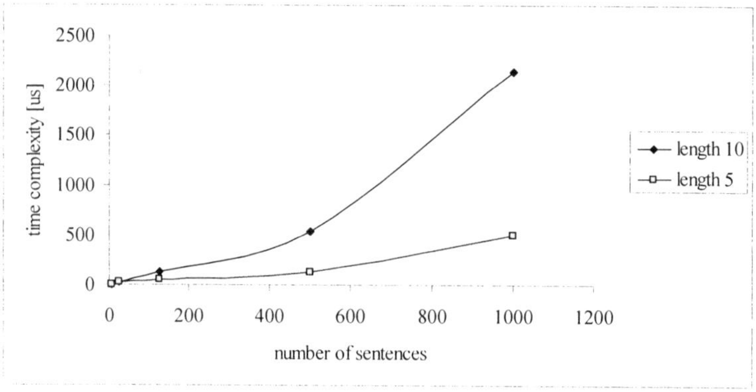

References

1. Michal Klodner: *Informatické struktury vizuální komunikace*, thesis UIVT FE VUT Brno 1999, p. 85.
2. A. Habel, H. J. Kreowski, S. Taubenberger: *Collages and patterns generated by hyperedge replacement*, Languages of Design 1, Elsevier Science, ISSN 0927-3034, 1993, p. 125-145.
3. G. F. DePalma, S. S. Yau: *Fractionally fuzzy grammars with application to pattern recognition*. In: Fuzzy sets and their applications to cognitive and decision processes, Academic Press, ISBN 0-12-775260-9, New York 1975, p. 329-351.
4. G. Bouma: *Extracting Dependency Frames from Existing Lexical Resources*, In: Proceeding of the NAACL Workshop on WordNet and Other Lexical Resources: Applications, Extensions and Customizations, Somerset, NJ, 2001.
5. Y.Ishihara, A.Ohsaki, H.Seki and T.Kasami: *Assignment of Data Types to Words in a Natural Language Specification*, IEICE Transactions on Information and Systems E79-D, 6, 820-828 (1996-06).
6. M D Alder, G Lim, C J S deSilva: *The Syntax of Images*, Technical Report TR95-01, Centre for Intelligent Information Processing Systems, The University of Western Australia, http://ciips.ee.uwa.edu.au/Papers/Technical_Reports/1995/01/Index.html, January 1995.
7. C. A. Goble, C. Haul, S. Bechhofer: *Describing and Classifying Multimedia using the Description Logic GRAIL*, In: Proceedings of the SPIE 96 Conference Storage and Retrieval for Image and Video Databases IV SPIE Vol 2670, San Jose, California, USA, 1-2 February 1996.
8. M. Novotný: *Reduction of Pregrammars*, Fundamenta Informaticae. ISSN 0169-2968, 1998, vol. 1998, no. 33, s. 295-306.
9. J. Han, M. Kamber: *Data Mining: Concepts and Techniques*, Morgan Kaufmann Publishers, ISBN 1-55860-489-8, San Francisco 2000, p. 550.
10. M. J. Zaki, *Parallel and Distributed Association Mining: A Survey*, In: IEEE Concurrency, special issue on Parallel Mechanisms for Data Mining, Vol. 7, No. 4, December 1999, p. 14-25.
11. V. Kubíček: *A Construction of a Grammar*, In: Proceedings of ISM 2002, 8 p. (accepted for)

Knowledge-based Software Engineering
T. Welzer et al. (Eds.)
IOS Press, 2002

Algebraic Theory of Production Systems*

Stefanuk, V.L.
Institute for Information Transmission Problems, Russian Academy of Sciences, Bolshoy Karetny per. 19, 101447 Moscow, Russia
Zhozhikashvili , A.V.

Abstract. The paper presents a novel approach to the production system description. The approach is called algebraic one as it is based on the mathematical category theory. The definition of theory of category productions (tc-productions) proposed in the paper is the result of generalization of various types of productions found in the literature. It is as strict as the definition in original production theory by Post, yet it is essentially more general as it covers a number of production systems found in Artificial Intelligence and elsewhere.
The algebraic production language was developed with the purpose to keep the language only general enough to cover the most typical production systems. In fact it is shown that proposed formal constructions naturally stem from a restricted set of requirements concerning such systems.
Being independent from knowledge content and data formats used in production systems the definition is rigorous enough to be used in formal studies.
Mathematically the definition of productions is as perfect as the formal definitions of rules acting upon character strings typical for mathematical logic. It allows to built a strong theoretical base for the study of various problems including generation of new rules and reuse of knowledge or knowledge-based systems.

1 INTRODUCTION

Production or rule knowledge bases are widely used in Artificial Intelligence systems. The term "production" was born in mathematical logic. By the production E. Post [1]

---

* This research was partially supported by grant from the program "Mathematical modeling, Intellectual computer systems and non-linear mechanical systems control" of Russian Academy of Sciences, project # 2.24, and by grant from Russian Fund for Basic Research, project #02-01-00955.

understood a rule for conversion of symbol strings. Similar rules were introduced by A. Markov [2] in his definition of a normal algorithm. Later the productions were found in computer linguistics. N. Chomsky [3] used them in his theory of formal grammars. We will refer to the productions used in the mentioned above studies as the classical ones.

Afterwards the production systems were widely spread over the area of Artificial Intelligence. In this area the productions were understood in a general way as rules having certain conditions of applicability and producing some actions when the conditions were fulfilled. There were published studies devoted to the production systems in this general understanding of the term [4,5,6].

However, in the process of transition to such a general understanding of productions the mathematical rigorousness, inherent for original studies of production systems, has been lost. In mathematical logic productions were defined in a formal language. It allowed to give mathematical formulations for the problems related to the systems of production. Meanwhile in the works on production systems in the area of AI similar questions were raised only with the reference to the production system as a whole. Yet without a strict definition of the single productions meaning, the authors of such works are doomed to restrict themselves with the general considerations only. In the best case they can base their studies on considerations of how productions act, unable to speak on how the productions are to be designed to produce such actions.

Let us give some examples. In the mentioned above study on the formal grammars N. Chomsky proposed a classification of such grammar based on the type of the productions admitted by a grammar. The grammars were distributed over four levels, beginning with most powerful grammar, grammar without restrictions, and ending with the most weak grammar, the regular one. Without a formal theory for the production systems in a generalized understanding, one can not expect to obtain such a classification. Meanwhile such a classification would be a serious new step in the theoretical studies devoted to the generalized production systems usually met in AI, or, more generally, to the intelligent knowledge-based systems.

Another problem which may be formulated and solved for classical production systems is the problem of what operations may be performed with the productions of a given type. The formal grammar classification was developed in this direction. Thus, it was shown that the production system implementing the unrestricted grammar is equivalent to Turing machine, while a production system defining a regular grammar is equivalent to a finite automaton. Such results would be very important for generalized production systems. For instance, in rule-based expert systems some attachment procedures are used rather intensively, which are fired after a corresponding rule is being applied. It is important to find out, which of these procedures perform actions, achievable with help of original productions, i.e. the attached procedures are introduced only for the sake of effectiveness, and which of them perform something that was not possible without the attached procedures.

Many studies related to the generalized production systems seems to be incomplete because it is impossible to reformulate involved notions in terms of a production structure. Let us consider, for example, the commutative property of production systems. The commutativeness means that the result of application of two productions does not depend on the order of their application [6]. The systems using such productions are generally less complicated. Only the performance may be influenced by the choice of the order of application, not the final result. For classical productions, which use character strings, it is possible to formulate a number of formal assumptions sufficient for the production system to have the commutative property. It is impossible to carry these assumptions over the productions in a generalized sense, as there are no strict definitions for the production. The production composition is another example. For classical productions it is possible to formulate the conditions on a pair of productions, which guarantee that after successful application of the first production the second one also will be applicable, and to show how to construct a single production which will be equivalent to the sequential application of productions constituting the pair. Such a result may not be directly extended to generally understood productions.

Let us point to one more direction of study which would be impossible without having a formal theory of production systems. We have in mind the systems that are able to modify their production knowledge bases during the performance. There may be various reasons for such medication such as performance rate, the reduction of the knowledge base size, and etc. Besides that, the learning systems may form new productions. Let us give a simple example. Let some production system contains the productions $ABC \to BAC$, $CAB \to CBA$, $ABCD \to BACD$, $CABD \to CBAD$. These productions suppose the hypothesis that the neighboring symbols A and B always may be interchanged with each other. It means that all these productions may be replaced with the following single production: $AB \to BA$. It is clear that this may be an erroneous hypothesis. Nevertheless generation of such a hypothesis constitutes an important step in learning. Such hypotheses may be accepted or rejected depending on whether they lead to correct or erroneous conclusions. For classical productions it is easy to formulate an algorithm which allows from productions $ABC \to BAC$ and $ABD \to BAD$ to built the production $AB \to BA$. For the more widely understood productions such an algorithm may be described only superficially due to the lack of any strict language for description of such productions.

2 PROBLEM FORMULATION

The paper presents a novel approach to the production system description. The approach is called algebraic one as it is based on the mathematical category theory. The definition of theory of category productions (tc-productions) proposed in the paper is the result of generalization of various types of productions found in the literature. It is as strict as the definition in original production theory by Post or Markov, yet it is essentially more general as it covers a number of production systems found in Artificial Intelligence and Computer Science.

Below are typical examples of production systems, which may be described with the use of the language proposed in this paper:

1. The rules of string transformation like those used in the normal algorithm of Markov. Moreover, within the frames of the algebraic approach some more complex transformation rules may be implemented. For example, the rule $XaY \to YaX$ meaning that if a string contains the character "a", then the preceding substring and the substring which follows the character "a", may be interchanged.

2. The rules of transformation of algebraic expressions, say the rule $X(Y+Z) \to XY + XZ$ meaning an implementation of the distributive identity.

3. The rules implementing a standard logic inference, for example the rule $\forall_x P(X) \quad Q(X)$ allows to infer $Q(c)$ from the clause $P(c)$. More complex construction related to a predicate language may also be expressed in the language described in the paper, for example, the unification operation which is used in theorem proving by the resolution method.

4. The rules of additions and removals described by N. Nilsson and used in the system STRIPS [7].

5. The rules used in the works on natural language understanding such works by Bobrow [8].

6. Many types of rules used in Expert Systems.

Careful analysis of artificial intelligence systems leads to the conclusion that the use of our algebraic approach to production systems may be extended to the systems with the knowledge base consisting from a large number of arbitrary components, which are not tightly connected to each other. Such a component reacts to a certain condition. If the current situation satisfies the condition the component is activated to transform the situation. This process repeats itself until a requested result is obtained (or a decision is made that the result is not attainable). Not only the production systems are arranged in this way where the components are productions with associated conditions of applicability and algorithms of application. The same arrangement is found for the system using some other technologies, say, blackboard architecture, demon-based architecture, and etc. It means that an effective formal technique intended for productions, may be used also to study of systems of another type.

Yet, in our approach we tried to find a formal language which is not too general than it is necessary for the most typical production systems. In fact it is shown that proposed formalism naturally stems from a restricted set of requirements concerning such systems.

3 ALGEBRAIC APPROACH TO THE DESCRIPTION OF PRODUCTIONS

Let us start the exposition of the essence of our algebraic approach.

3.1 Situations and patterns

A typical classical production looks like $s \to t$, where s and t are some strings of symbols. The left side of the production describes to where the production may be applied. The right side describes what is obtained after its application. In our approach we also will consider a production as something consisting from two parts, referred to as the left and the right side of the production, however the left side now describes the situation in which the production may be applied, the right one describing the situation, which will be created after its application.

Some complication consists in the fact that classical productions do not contain a description of the whole situation to which the production is applicable. Thus, the production $s \to t$ says that the string to which the production is applicable, must contain the part s. There is no other information in this production concerning what else the string may contain. As a result of application of this production the part under consideration, s, should be replaced with the substring t. A direct generalization of this circumstance requires that only certain fragment of the situation, not the situation as whole is shown in the left part of the production, providing that the right part contains the thing that should replace this fragment. Though in case of strings the operation of substitution of one string instead of another brings no problems, in a more general case it is not that simple to replace one fragment with another. It is not permitted, for example, to offer the following production acting on graphs "If a graph contains subgraph G it should be replaced with the subgraph H", as it is not clear at all how the subgraph H should be inserted into the graph which is left from the original graph after the removal of G from it. Note, that one of the approaches to the extension of formal grammars onto graphs resulted in the proposal of an algebraic graph grammars [9,10] based on the category theory, the approach reminding the one used in present paper.

Thus, we start from the point that the left side of the production must describe the situation, in which it is applicable, however some contextual fragments of the situation may be omitted. In the same time the description should explicitly demonstrate the kind of relationship among the parts of the situation which are still present and those, which were omitted. For this reason the above mentioned production $s \to t$ we prefer to write as $XsY \to XtY$. The symbols X and Y do not denote some concrete substrings. They represents the variables that may be substituted with some arbitrary substrings. The expression XsY explicitly shows the interrelation among the present in the classical production string s and omitted strings X and Y. In this way we are able to show in the production how to arrange the substring t, which substitutes s, with the rest parts of the string.

The description of the situation, containing the information on its certain fragments and on the connections of the fragments with the rest of the situation, we will refer to as the situational pattern (template), or simply the *pattern*. The difference between the pattern and the description of concrete situation lies in the following: the pattern contains information about some fragments, it shows the way these fragments are connected with the rest of the pattern, yet the fragments themselves are not written down. To accommodate the latter there are some slots which may accept various data. When the missing data are entered, the pattern transforms to the description of the concrete situation. These process of reduction the pattern to a concrete situation by way of adding to it some missing data is referred to as a *concretization* of the pattern. The data added to the pattern are called *concretizaters* of the pattern. In general, each pattern may admit various concretizers. In result the pattern may be transformed into different situations. It means that a certain *set of concretizers* is associated with each pattern.

The following question is frequently raised. Is it possible to concretize the pattern in a way that in the result of the concretization one would obtain a given situation? The operation allowing to answer the question is called the *matching* of situation with the pattern. The purpose of the operation is to show if among the set of concretizers of the given pattern there exists such a concretizer, which after its use may lead to the given situation. If the answer is positive one, the situation is said to match the pattern, and normally the found concretizer bears certain information on the specific features of the given situation which makes it different from other situations matching the same pattern.

As it was emphasized before, the pattern does not bear information on the content of the concretizer, though it points how the concretizer should be inserted, how its elements should be combined with other components of the pattern. Let S be a set of all possible situations, and let X be the set of the concretizers for a given pattern. The pattern must show how some concretizer converts it into a situation, i.e. to give a certain mapping $\varphi: X \to S$. This consideration is crucial for our further formal constructions. It possible to consider the mapping $\varphi: X \to S$ as a formal definition of the pattern, provided that the situation $s \in S$ is considered to match the patter if there exists a concretizer $x \in X$ such that $\varphi(x) = s$.

3.2 Theory of category language

In simple cases it is possible to consider only one set of situation S and restrict the consideration with patterns of the form $\varphi: X \to S$, where various sets may play the role of the set of concretizers X, φ being various mappings. In more complicated cases it is necessary to take into consideration several different sets of situations. In particular the set of concretizers of one pattern may be viewed as the set of situations for another pattern. Let us consider one important case, when it is required.

A pattern (template) may be used to identify certain class of related situations: the class will include those situations which match a given pattern. If it becomes necessary to distinguish within the class some narrow subclass, it may be achieved with the help of some other pattern. The material for matching with this new pattern will be the result of match of the situation with the first pattern, i.e. the concretizer obtained in the process of matching. This means that if the mapping $\varphi: X \to S$ plays the role of the first pattern, then as the second, narrowing, pattern one should take a mapping $\psi: Y \to X$, in which the role of the set of situations is played by the set of concretizers of the first pattern. In order to define whether some situation $s \in S$ is the member of the class defined with pattern $\psi: Y \to X$, one first need to learn if the situation s is a member of the class defined with the pattern $\varphi: X \to S$, i.e. to find such $x \in X$ that $\varphi(x) = s$. Then one has to look for a concretizer $y \in Y$ (provided that such a concretizer does exist), such that $\psi(y) = x$. It is obvious that above procedure is the same as to match the situation s against the pattern $\psi\varphi: Y \to S$, which naturally to be referred to as the *composition* of the patterns $\psi: Y \to X$ and $\varphi: X \to S$. Other examples of the use of the set of concretizers of one pattern as the set of situations for another one, are the operations of composition and generalization of productions which we will be discuss in what follows.

The above discussion leads us to the following construction. In order to built a system of patterns it is necessary to show which sets may play the role of a set of situations or a set of concretizers (as we saw above it is reasonable to combine these two kinds of sets as the set of concretizers of one pattern may play the role of a set of situations for some other pattern), and to show also what mappings may be used in the patterns. We will require that the class of all such mappings should be closed with respect to the operation of composition. To finish our theory all the identical mapping are to be included in this class of mappings.

Now we see that in order to define a system of patterns one has to define a concrete category, i.e. a subcategory of category of sets and mappings. Any two objects X and Y of the category and a corresponding morphism $\varphi: X \to Y$ of this category defines a pattern. The set Y will be referred to as the set of situation for this pattern. The set X will be referred to as the set of its concretizers. A situation $y \in Y$ is considered matching the pattern, if for some $x \in X$ one has $y = \varphi(x)$.

3.3 TC-productions

Now it is possible to give a definition of a production. Let a subcategory of category of sets is given. The production from the set S to the set T is the diagram $S \leftarrow X \rightarrow T$, where X is an object of the category, $\varphi : X \rightarrow S$ and $\psi : X \rightarrow T$ being its corresponding morphisms. Such a productions will be referred to as a tc-productions. Thus, the tc-production is a pair of patterns with a common set of concretizers, these patterns being referred to as the left and right part of the production. A tc-production is considered to be applicable to the situation $s \in S$ if it matches the pattern $\varphi : X \rightarrow S$, i.e. if $s = \varphi(x)$ for some $x \in X$. The result of application of the production is the situation $t \in T$ defined with the formula $t = \psi(x)$. Thus, to obtain the result one has to concretize the right side of the production in the same way as the left side was concretized under a successful match with the original situation.

It is more frequently occurs that the result of the action of a tc-production will be a situation belonging to the same set as the original situation. This special case follows from the general definition by assuming additionally that $S = T$. Under this condition the production system may perform in an ordinary way: some next production may be applied to the result of the first production and so on. Note that the concretizer x is not uniquely defined, in general, from the condition $s = \varphi(x)$, hence the application of the tc-production is not a unique operation.

The formulated definitions are as faultless from mathematical point of view as the typical definitions in mathematical logic of productions intended to work with strings of symbols. Our definitions open a possibility to study from a formal mathematical perspective those problems which were mentioned at the start of the present paper. Thus, the classification of production systems may be based on the classification of categories which describe the situations, patterns, and operations of matching and concretization associated with the production system under consideration. The categories may be classified, in turn, on the base of constructions which are used in the given category, or whether the direct products do exist in this category, or the sums, or the cores, and etc.

As an example of the use of the technique of tc-productions we will show how certain notions may be implemented in this language associated with production systems of common type. We mentioned above that for the productions in a wide sense of the word it is possible to define the notion of composition by describing how the composition acts, yet it is not possible to show how the composition may be built from the original data. For comparison we will show that it can be done for the case of tc-productions. Let $S \leftarrow X \rightarrow T$ and $T \leftarrow Y \rightarrow R$ be two productions. Let us construct the pullback

$$\begin{array}{ccc} T & \leftarrow & Y \\ \uparrow & & \uparrow \mu \\ X & \leftarrow & Z \\ & \nu & \end{array}$$

Now the production $S \leftarrow Z \rightarrow R$ may be considered as the composition of productions $S \leftarrow X \rightarrow T$ and $T \leftarrow Y \rightarrow R$.

Here is another example. How to formulate the conditions on the arrangement of productions that are sufficient ones for the productions to be commutative? We will rely on the following considerations. Let us imagine that the two productions act on different parts of the situation. In this case their actions are independent. The application of one of the productions does not touch the area which the other production is working upon. In result of the sequential application of these productions two fragments of the situation are changed independently, and besides the order of these changes is inessential.

Without our mathematical formalism we should restrict themselves with these wordy description of above. Yet, in the language of tc-productions a precise formulation may be given. Let $S \leftarrow X \rightarrow S$ and $S \leftarrow Y \rightarrow S$ be two productions. Let us imagine that we found the object Z and morphisms $\lambda_1, \lambda_2 : Z \rightarrow X$, , $\mu_1, \mu_2 : Z \rightarrow Y$, such that the diagram

$$\begin{array}{ccc} S & \xleftarrow{\psi_j} & Y \\ \varphi_i \uparrow & & \uparrow \mu_i \\ X & \xleftarrow[\lambda_j]{} & Z \end{array}$$

is a pullback for $i = 1,2$, $j = 1,2$ (it is the way to write down that the productions acts on different fragments of the situation). Then the productions are commutative.

Let us give a rigorous proof for this assertion. Let first production transformed the situation s into the situation t, let the second production transformed the situation t into the situation w . In accordance with above given definitions it means that for some $x \in X$ the formulae $\varphi_1(x) = s$, $\varphi_2(x) = t$, $\psi_1(y) = t$, $\psi_2(y) = w$ are valid.

Due to the second and the third equations we conclude that an element $z \in Z$ may be found for which $\lambda_1(z) = x$, $\mu_2(z) = y$. Then the relation $s = \varphi_1(x) = \varphi_1(\lambda_1(z)) = \psi_1(\mu_1(z))$ is true. It means that the second production is applicable to the situation s and will transform it into the situation $\psi_2(\mu_1(z)) = \varphi_1(\lambda_2(z))$. To this situation the first production may be applied in its turn, that transforms it into the situation $\varphi_2(\lambda_2(z)) = \psi_2(\mu_2(z)) = \psi_2(y) = w$. We see that the application of the second production first and then the first production similarly transforms the situation s into the situation w, i.e. the productions do commute. This condition is not necessary, it is only a sufficient one. Moreover, it may be formulated for categories in which the pullbacks exist, otherwise the condition will be more complex. Similar approach is used in [11].

4 CONCLUSION

In conclusion we will list again the possible directions where the use of the proposed algebraic approach may be useful both for theoretical studies and for applications.

This approach may be used for some classification of production systems on the base of categories associated with the systems. In the frames of algebraic approach a correct answer may be obtained as what procedures may be implemented with the production systems and which can not be reduced to the productions of a given type in principle. The algebraic approach may be used to design and study of algorithms of production inference. Such algorithms may be studied with rigorous mathematical methods, and in the same time the area of their application may be wide enough. In the language of tc-productions the algorithms of automatic formation and transformation of production systems may be described. Finally, the language of tc-productions may be used in computer tools for the design of production systems. A significant part of the work within these tools will be done in a universal style, independently from the concrete data, while the data will only define which category should be chosen for the most correct presentation of such data.

REFERENCES

[1] Post, E., Formal reduction of the general combinatorial problem, *American J. Math.*, **65**, 197-268 (1943).

[2] Markov, A. , 1954, *A theory of Algorithms*. National Academy of Sciences, USSR

[3] Chomsky N. ,1963, *Formal properties of grammars*, Handbook of Mathematical Psychology, vol. II Ed. Luce R., Bush R., Galanter E., NewYork.

[4] Newell, A., and Simon, H.A., 1972, Human Problem Solving, Englewood Cliffs, NJ: Prentice-Hall.

[5] Waterman, D.A. and Hayes-Roth, F. (eds.), *Pattern-directed Inference Systems*, Academic Press, New York, 1978.

[6] Nilsson, N.J., *Principles of Artificial Intelligence*, Tioga Pub. Co., Palo Alto, CA, 1980, and Springer-Verlag, Berlin, 1982.

[7] Fikes, R.E., Hart, P.E. and Nulsson, N.J., Learning and executing generalized robot plans, *Artificial Intelligence* **3,** 251-288, (1972).

[8] Bobrow D.G., *Natural Language Input for a Computer Problem-Solving System*, Semantic Information Processing, edited by M.Minsky, the M.I.T Press, Cambridge, Massachusetts, 1968.

[9] Ehrig H., Introduction to the Algebraic Theory of Graph Grammars, *Lecture Notes in Computer Science*, **73**, 1-69, (1978).

[10] Michael J. Healy, Category Theory Applied to Neural Modeling and Graphical Representations. *Paper NN0648 in IJCNN at Como, Italy (revised version).*

[11] A.Zhozhikashvili, V.Stefanuk., Theory of Category Patterns for AI problems. *Proceedings of RAN: Theory and Control Systems*, **5**, 5-16, (1999).

Knowledge Management for Business Processes

Knowledge-based Software Engineering
T. Welzer et al. (Eds.)
IOS Press, 2002

Early Experience of a Dynamic Application Downloading Platform for Multi-Application Smart Cards

Eikazu NIWANO† Masayuki HATANAKA†
Junko HASHIMOTO† Shuichiro YAMAMOTO††
†*NTT Information Sharing Platform Laboratories,*
3-9-11, Midori-cho Musashino-shi, Tokyo 180-8585 Japan
††*NTT Data, 1-21-2, Shinkawa Chuo-ku, Tokyo 104-0033 Japan*

Abstract. The demand for multi-application smart card platform has been increasing in various business sectors recently. When it comes to the actual implementation of the platform, however, network-based dynamic downloading in a CI (Card Issuer)- SP (Service Provider) separated environment has not made much progress. This paper proposes our multi-application smart card platform that uses licensing and policy management technologies to enable CI and SP to reflect their own business policy flexibly via network. It also describes a prototype implementation, and early evaluation from the point of business sector as well as the application download performance. With these evaluations, we will show the proposed technology is applicable to various business domains and it can be of practical use.

1. Introduction

In the 25 years since smart cards were first proposed, they have become steadily more widespread. Domestic card market in Japan rose to 26.5 million cards (including 8 million IC telephone cards) in 1999 and 44.7 million cards (including 11 million IC cards) in 2000. Sales are expected to double to 86.2 million (including 15 million IC telephone cards) in 2001. Card demand worldwide is expected to increase from 1.4 billion cards in 1999 and 1.8 billion in 2000 to 3 billion in 2003.

A feature of smart cards is their use for personal authentication and carrying secure information. This puts smart cards in high demand as a key device for providing secure services in our network society.

To make it easy to adapt cards to different types of services, a mechanism (information sharing platform for smart cards) is required that allows the network and cards to work together smoothly. This enables secure card issue, operation, and application download after the cards are issued. Although progress is being made on this concept, we do not yet have a smart card platform that supports application download after the card has been issued in a practical manner.

In this paper, we present the cost-sharing smart card model that provide dynamic application download on a smart card. Next section describes the existing smart card platforms. Then Section 3 explains the cost-sharing smart card model and Section 4 gives a prototype implementation issues. Section 5 discusses experiences and effectiveness of the proposals and performance considerations. Section 6 describes the related researches. Finally, Section 7 summarizes and presents future work.

2. Smart Card Platform

For worldwide standardization, MasterCard-driven MULTOS[1]and Visa-driven VOP (Visa Open Platform)[2]are the two major international standardization organizations. GP (Global Platform)[3] or the extended version of VisaCard's VOP is also being discussed in the international organizations for standardization.

2.1 VOP/GP (VISA Open Platform/Global Platform)

VOP (VISA Open Platform) is a platform that VisaCard camp designed for the operation management of JavaCard-based multi-application smart cards. To promote the widespread use of the multi-application smart cards across business fields, GP is working on the standardization of infrastructures for card issuance and maintenance, application maintenance, terminals, and AP download after card issuance (post-issuance loading). Visa International has transferred a license of the VOP specifications to GP so that GP can maintain the specifications and use them for the development and promotion of the cards. GP is promoting standardization of online AP download and token-based operation right management, but it does not take card memory domain management into consideration. There are no practical GP applications yet.

2.2 MULTOS/MAOSCO Platform

MULTOS is a platform that Mondex/MasterCard camps designed for the operation management of multi-application smart cards. This CI-driven card management architecture places a Registration and Certification Center (RC) at the top of the hierarchy that authenticates cards and card applications and CI starts AP downloading after being delegated from an AP service provider (SP). MULTOS defines operation rules for card issuance management but not for online AP download yet. With regard to card memory domain management, MULTOS defines the whole domain space management and it does not define the details about memory management for each AP. MULTOS adopts token-based operation right management for its standard. This platform, however, takes no considerations about authenticating SP. The reason is that MAOSCO Ltd. basically controls all the card management in accordance with the company policy.

3. Cost-sharing Smart Card Model

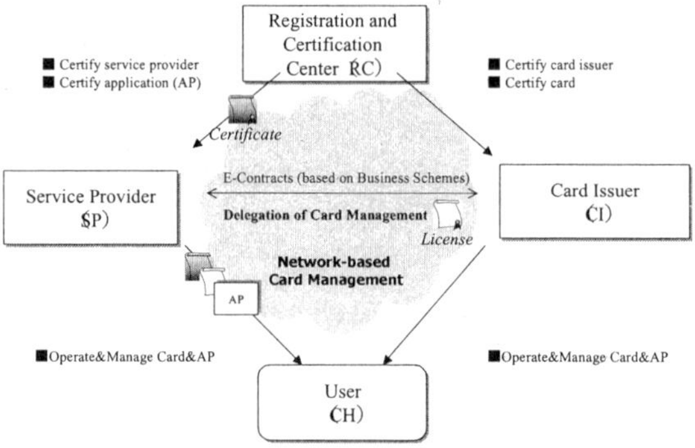

Figure 1. Entity model

The common smart card platform needs to allow various services, such as public, billing, and transportation services, to coexist on the same smart card. It is necessary to separate SPs and card issuer (CI) to put multiple services together on the same card. The free memory domain of the smart card can be rented to the third-party SP. We call this concept as cost-sharing smart card model. It has the RC to ensure smart CIs and SPs. As CIs and SPs are independently defined, card holder (CH) can use best suitable applications of SPs by selecting candidate services allowed by the CI. The business relationship among players of the cost-sharing model is as follows. CIs make the card memory rental contract with service providers to load their applications. Thus, CI can collect fees for card management and operation cost from SPs and also CHs.

As Figure 1 shows, the cost-sharing smart card model includes CI, SP, RC, and CH. CI issues smart cards and provides rental spaces on smart cards for SPs. SPs provide smart card applications for CHs. RC established to register CI, Card, SP and applications. CHs use smart card applications provided by SPs. CHs should download applications securely onto the smart cards before using them. SPs should have delegated rights to use memory spaces of smart cards from CI. CI and SPs are certificated each other by RC.

4. Prototyping

4.1 Functions

As shown in Figure 2, 6 functions are supported to SP operator menu. They are Card Issuer Management, Card Holder Management, Application Management, Policy Management, Billing Management and Audit Trail Management. The card issuer management is used to record CIs who provide rental card spaces. The card holder management is used CHs who uses APs provided by the SP. The application management is used to manage downloadable applications. The billing management is provided to see billing information at time of downloading. The audit trail management is provided to keep logs of transactions. The Policy Management menu is provided to change operation policy such as card operation.The same kinds of menus are provided to CI and CH.

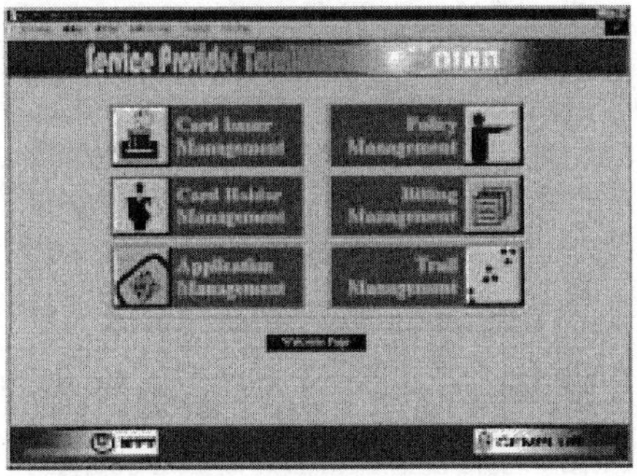

Figure 2. Operator menu of service providers

4.2 High Performance Java Card

By extending JavaVM reference[4], we have developed "Sapphire" [5] JavaVM that runs on an ELWISE card that was also developed by NTT as the world's first smart card having 1MB of nonvolatile flash memory.

The JavaCards now available in the market have the upper limit of 32Kbyte memory capacity and downloadable applications are limited in number even though the Cards are called multi-application smart cards. When we want to implement Card Manager that provides a wide range of functions such as multi-application management or AP online download, the cards requires 20Kbyte memory space at least. If we download the Card Manager onto the currently available JavaCards, the number of APs and the size of the Applications become small. Therefore we need to have a smart card having larger memory space like Sapphire. The Sapphire is designed to resolve these issues, providing a large 1Mbyte of flash memory capacity implemented on an ELWISE card.

The ELWISE is a contact-type multi-purpose smart card. Equipped with special circuitry capable of handling multiple encryption schemes and a large nonvolatile memory (more than ten times the size of conventional card memories), the card can be used for a wide range of services such as electronic payments, multimedia data communications, and medical applications. The card allows a number of conventional single-purpose card applications to be integrated into a single ELWISE card.

4.3 System Configuration

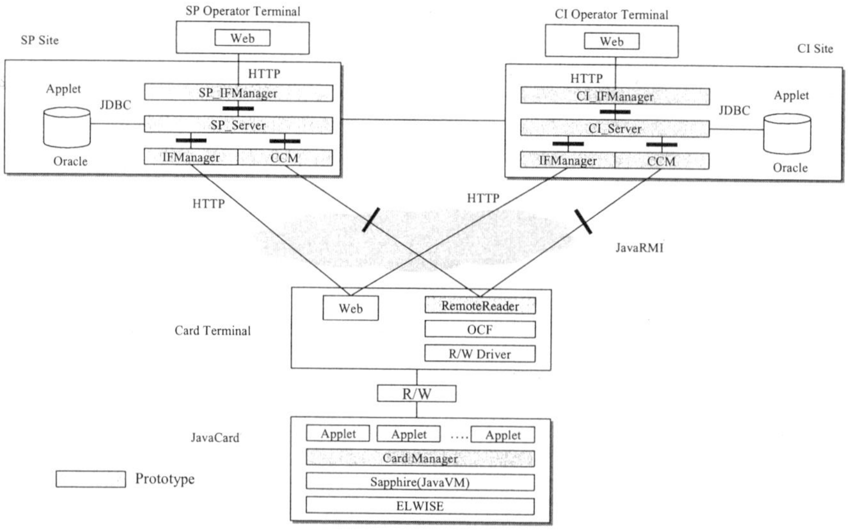

Figure 3. System configuration

The prototype system consists of smart cards, terminals and servers as shown in Figure 3.

The card manager, CM, is developed on JavaCard VM. The remote reader, RR, is developed on terminal. CI server and SP server communicate smart cards via the remote reader.

The CM was implemented on the smart cards to communicate with the servers for card management. The functions include CM status management, AP management including download function, policy management, security management, transaction management, PIN management, and shared information (profile) management.

The RR is installed on the terminal. RR sends and receives APDU messages between the servers and Open Card Framework (OCF) on smart cards. OCF is a standard set of Java packages and classes independent of smart card OSs and terminals.

The RC server issues a certificate electronically to an AP provided by SP. In this prototype, we issued it offline.

The CI and SP servers are developed using layered architecture.

The IFmanager and card communication manager (CCM) provide the interface between user terminal and server. The CCM refers to card profile information to identify types of JavaCards being used, and controls communications depending on the card type.

The SP processes license requests while CI issues licenses. For the AP download license, SP sends the download request to CI whenever SP needs it. In respect to renting a card space (tenant management), we created the space for applications required at time of download.

The CI and SP servers manage cards and applications. The CI and SP IF Server provide the interface between operator and server.

HTTP is used for Web terminal interface including CH, SP and CI. JavaRMI is used for the communications between the CI and SP servers and between the servers and terminals. JDBC is used for database communications.

4.4 Example of download sequence

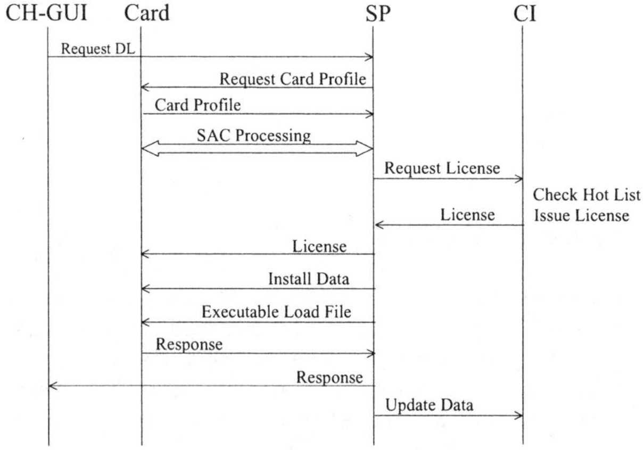

Figure 4. Application download sequence

Figure 4 shows an example of the download sequence. First, CH sends a download request to SP, then SP server and CM start using an asymmetric cryptography (RSA) to authenticate the CH. After the authentication, the session key is generated to be used for all the encryption process within the same session. This security transaction processing is called as SAC.

Next, SP requests CI to delegate a license on the AP download for the CH, CI sends it to the SP. At this point the AP download license is issued. In the course of this process, CI checks hot list and confirms that the CH is valid. SP and AP are checked by the licenses issued by RC.

Now, SP starts downloading the card application onto a smart card with the download license and RC-issued application registration certificate.

By confirming the validity of the download license, CM starts downloading the AP. The on-card transaction management copes with network failure and ensures secure download.

In case of all the download process finishes successfully, CM sends success response to SP. Then SP response it to the CH via terminal, and update billing data by using a billing management function to pay CI for the rents of CI card memory domain as a download fee.

4.5 Operation Management

SPs and CIs can remotely manage their applications and information on smart cards independently. CIs also can lock a smart card when it is lost or unauthorized access comes in. These kinds of erroneous smart cards are managed by a hot list. By using policy operation rules, it can be changed dynamically after a smart card issuance. Examples of policy rules are as follows.

Ex1) If valid(SP_Id) then issue_license(SP_Id).

Ex2) If invalid(Card_Id, Hot_list) then refuse(Card_Id).

This kind of policy rules are simple but useful tool to describe card management operations.

CI manages all the information of issued smart cards and CHs. It also manages downloadable applications and the relationship between smart cards and applications.

Secure transaction between CHs and SPs are necessary to provide. No unauthorized access, tampering and data leakage are allowed. It is necessary to get back to a normal operation when communications and any other types of errors occur.

5. Early experiences

In this chapter, we will report on the opinion evaluations of the proposed technology.

5.1 Responses in the demonstrations

We have received excellent responses in the demonstrations as the first prototype achieved secure online AP download in a CI-SP separated environment. For example, NTT and Gemplus jointly participated[6] in "Cartes2000", the world's largest smart card exhibition held in Paris from October 24th through 26th 2000, where we received an excellent response. "Le Monde", a French newspaper wrote an article about our prototype system entitled "our dream of making the smart card our next generation computer" in their November 6th issue[7]. In the article, Mr. Michel Alberganti commented, "Our long awaited dream may not come true tomorrow, but it is just around the corner that the piles of plastic cards and coins stuffed into our wallets will be totally replaced by ONE smart card".

The respondents also shared the same view that the market for multi-application will be 2 to 4 years ahead of us. This shows the progressiveness of our proposal.

With regard to multi-application, most of the respondents said it difficult to coexist with public and private smart card APs. For example, medical APs may be difficult to coexist with public transportation families. Although we must pay attention to such skeptical opinions on general-purpose multi-application smart cards, such opinions also depend on situation. For example, Japanese government plans to deliver national identification smart card and provide its memory domain to private sector applications. In this case, it is highly expected secure AP download and management functions.

5.2 Accepted as the Japanese multi-application smart card standard

NICSS (the Next generation Ic Card System group) [8] is working on the standardization mainly for public sectors in Japan. In case of administrative smart cards, it is important to reduce production cost by mass production with common smart card platform. Therefore, NICSS standardized the first draft specification including the cost-sharing model in April 2001 based on our proposal. The model is called as the NICSS framework. This shows the usefulness of our technologies.

The Ministry of Economy, Trade and Industry (METI) of Japan started "The IT-City research project" based on the NICSS framework from January 2002[9]. By re-designing the prototype and integrating the function of outsourcing memory domain management, we have developed the product version [10][11]. And it has already been applied to the 14 cities all over Japan.

5.3 Applicability

As mentioned above, IT-City project of Japanese government accepted the cost sharing model based on our proposal. This shows the applicability of the proposal to the administrative sector as well as private sectors, because smart card applications of IT-Cities include private sectors such as service points and digital money.

5.4 Flexibility

As the market analysis results revealed that the needs vary among business sectors. Therefore, it is necessary to extend and customize basic functions with policy rules. The high evaluation of the cost sharing and policy control indicates the possibilities of establishing a new card business by realizing flexible communications between CI and SP using policy control mechanism. The proposed policy rules can be used to manage licenses and execute transactions on licenses. By maintaining these licensing and policy management via network, the rules of access and execution control required for card operation can be changed dynamically. This mechanism allows CI and SP to independently establish their policy and licensing operations so that their smart card business scheme becomes feasible.

5.5 Performance improvement

To put this technology into practical use, improving the performance is an issue. In the prototype system we implemented on card CM and security functions by using Java code. It is necessary to translate these codes into native codes to improve performance. Actually speaking in the commercial version of system we implemented them in native code.

6. Related technologies

6.1 Multi AP smart card platform

Although MULTOS adopts a very strict framework based on the Registration and Authentication Center as the core to authenticate every entity, it only starts discussing the online AP download.

VOP and NICSS, on the other hand, are recommending architecture that allows CI to delegate authority to SPs for AP download. There are, however, some issues to solve. VOP only provides static authority delegation. NICSS only standardize cost-sharing reference models.

We have developed the policy and licensing technologies to enhance VOP/NICSS platform technology and provided a mechanism of dynamic operation right control among various entities

6.2 Card management system

The Card Management System (CMS) and Application Management System (AMS) are

now having important roles to control evolving APs on huge number of smart cards.
Many internet based smart card researches has been proposed. They treated smart cards as a server. Guthery et al. [12] proposed the way to treat Java card as a mobile Web server. Rees et al. [13] proposed a WebCard can be seen as an internet node.
Vandewalle et al. proposed JC-RMI to give the remote object invocation interface for applets on a smart card. The GemXpresso RAD tool[14] generates a Java Card proxy from the card applet interface, and the proxy communicates with the card applet with APDUs. Thus the client AP can use the proxy as the card applet.

Rohs et al. [15] proposed the JiniCard provides smartcard middleware to retrieve smart card services over the internet. When a JiniCard is plugged somewhere, the JiniCard explore determines the capabilities of the card, then Jini registers the card and provides lookup services through Java interfaces. As its services are automatically registered, the JiniCard become available over the network thanks to Jini services.

Lorphelin [17] proposed the smartX framework to download new smart card APs on various terminals. The smartX engine is installed on the target terminals. The smartX applications are described in SML(Smart Markup Language). For example, SML provides <Apdu> tag to describe APDU command. SmartX terminal applications are developed by two blocks: the AP process and the AP protocol. The AP protocol is described in the SML dictionary and is card-specific. The AP process encapsulates the AP logic and compiled into Java applet. As the card-specific block is downloaded if necessary, this can be minimize the AP downloading time.

Chan et al. [18] proposed the Java Card Web Servlet (JCWS) to provide a seamless access interface between a Web browser and a JavaCard. The JavaCard is viewed as a repository of Web-enabled object, HTML pages, data objects, and JavaCard Applets.

Urien et al. [19] proposed an internet smart card, @Card, works as an internet node including a web server and a trusted proxy. @Card has been implemented in a JavaCard and runs internet client and server AP. They also developed SmartTP looks like a TCP and connects smart agents located in both smart cards and terminals.

Bergner et al.[20] proposed a mechanism for connecting small devices to CORBA services. The architecture consists of smart card event broker on a smart card and a smartcard proxy in a terminal. The smart card proxy includes a proxy event broker and applet proxies. The smart card event broker and the proxy event broker communicates each other.

Urien[21] have realized an experimental XML script parser on smart cards. The XML script parser is invoked from an embedded web server. It can have access to all embedded resource4s and manage connections to remote servers.

Donsez et al. [22] proposed a JMS-SOAP based platform to connect multi-AP smart cards, and both to discover smart card services and requests for services. JMS is a Java based specification of Message Oriented Middleware (MOM). A SOAP proxy provides the facilities that allow distributed clients to discover and use the services on a smart card.

These approaches differ from ours in that they provide the middleware connecting applications in the distributed environment and smart cards. It is also possible to combine these approach and ours. For example, our CM can be extended to have these distributed facilities.

7. Conclusion

In this paper, we have proposed a smart card information platform and analyzed the effectiveness based on the prototype system.

Through field trials, we will continue to discuss and evaluate the applications to the administrative sector, and establish a framework of offering the applications to a wide rage of business fields like medical, e-commerce and communications. We will push forward with network-based application download onto various types of mobile gears like cards and mobile phones (SIM) from low-end to high end. We would also like to promote the activities to make this platform technology as an international standardization.

Some issues relating to the multi-application smart card technology remain to be tackled. Future technology development will allow us to keep multiple applications in one card, but this also means that the more information one card can hold, the more complicated things become when we come to submit the various paperwork required to have the card re-issued if the card is lost, stolen or damaged. To cope with this situation, we must either keep multiple smart cards with the same authorities and information, or we must have a one-stop platform service agent on the server that can re-issue applications and restore the applications to their previous status prior to losing the card. We expect smart cards will be able to communicate with various other types of device such as mobile phones, IC card public pay phones, cars, ATMs, television sets, and game machines. We also require platform technology that can connect between these devices flexibly if we are to fully utilize the possibilities of these backyard information systems. Various kinds of platform and OS products have been developed for smart cards, and we believe the technology for connecting different smart card platforms will be developed and standardized further.

Acknowledgements

First we would like to thank co-researcher Hideki AKASHIKA who worked for NTT Information Sharing Platform Laboratories. We also would like to thank Mr. Shoichi SENDA and Mr. Shohei TAKEUCHI who are senior research engineers in NTT Information Sharing Platform Laboratories for their helpful discussions. We also wish to thank Mr. Seiichi IDO, Executive Director of NTT Information Sharing Laboratory Group.

References

[1] MULTOS, http://www.multos.com
[2] OP(VOP), http://www.visa.com/nt/suppliers/open/main.html
[3] Global Platform, http://www.globalplatform.org
[4] JavaCard, http://www.javasoft.com/products/javacard/index.html
[5] Suzuki, K., Hirata, S. and Yamamoto, S., Sapphire-A JavaCard VM for 1-MB Flash Memory Smart Card, NTT REVIEW, vol.14, No.1, pp.20-22, 2002.
[6] NTT&Gemplus Collaborative project report, http://www.ntt.co.jp/news/news99/9910/991013.html
[7] Our Dream of Making the Smart Card into a Genuine Computer, French newspaper Le Monde, 2000.11.6
[8] NICSS, http://www.nicss.gr.jp/main.htm
[9] IT-City Project, http://www.itcity.jp/
[10] Toji, R.; Wada, Y.; Hirata, S.; Suzuki, K., A network-based platform for multi-application smart cards, Proceedings. Fifth IEEE International Enterprise Distributed Object Computing Conference, 2001., 2001, pp. 34 -45.
[11] NICE, http://www.nice.ntt.de/
[12] Guthery, S., Kehr, R., Posegga, J., How to turn GSM SIM into a Web Server, In Dommingo-Ferrer, J., Chan, D., Watson, A. Eds., 4th IFIP TC8/WG8.8 Working Conference on Smart Card Research and Applications, 2000, pp.209-222.
[13] Rees, J., Honneyman, P., Webcard: a Java Card Web Server, In Dommingo-Ferrer, J., Chan, D., Watson, A. Eds., 4th IFIP TC8/WG8.8 Working Conference on Smart Card Research and Applications, 2000, pp.209-222.
[14] Vandewalle, J. and Vetillard, E., Developing Smart Card-Based Applications Using Java Card,
[15] Rohs, M., Vogt, H., and Kehr, R., Platic goes Internet: Issues in Smartcard Middleware, JavaCard Workshop, 2000, Cannes.

[16] Kehr, R., Rohs, M., and Vogt, H., Mobile Code as an Enabling Technology for Service oriented Smartcard Middleware. In proc. Of the 2nd International Symposium on Distributed Objects and Applications, pp.119-130, 2000.
[17] Lorphelin, X., Internet and smart Card Application Deployment, http://www.smartx.com
[18] Chan, A., Cao, J., Chan, H, and Young, G., A Web-enabled framework for smart card application in health services, CACM, Sept., 2001, Vol.44, No.9, pp.77-82.
[19] Urien, P., Saleh, H., and Trizraoui, A., Internet Card, a smart card for internet, http://proms2000.kt.agh.edu.pl, Protocols for Mutimedia Systems, 2000.
[20] Bergner, K., Rausch, A., Sihling, M., and Vilsmeier, C., CORBA and the Java Card - Connecting Small Devices to a Standard Event Service,
[21] Urien, P., Programming Internet Smartcard with XML Scripts, in Attali, I., and Jensen, T. Eds.: E-smart 2001, LNCS 2140, pp.228-241, 2001.
[22] Donsez, D., Jean, S., Lecomte, S., and Thomas, O., Turning Multi-applications Smart Cards Services Available from Anywhere at Anytime: A SOAP/MOM Approach in the Context of Java Cards, in Attali, I., and Jensen, T. Eds.: E-smart 2001, LNCS 2140, pp.83-94, 2001.

Knowledge-based Software Engineering
T. Welzer et al. (Eds.)
IOS Press, 2002

Building Business Application Development Environment With Multi-Grain-Size Repository

Koichi TERAI, Masahiko SAWAI, Naoki SUGIURA, Noriaki IZUMI and Takahira YAMAGUCHI
{terai, sawai, sugiura, izumi, yamaguti}@ks.cs.inf.shizuoka.ac.jp
Dept. Computer Science, Shizuoka University
3-5-1, Johoku, Hamamatu, Shizuoka, 432-8011 Japan

Abstract. In order to build the Web-based application as a shopping site on the Web, various ideas from the different viewpoints are required, such as enterprise modeling, workflow modeling, software development, and so on. From the above standpoint, this paper proposes an integrated environment to support the whole development process of analysis, design and implementation of business application. In order to reuse know-hows of various ideas in the business application development, we devise the multi-layered repository, which consists of coarse-, middle-, and fine-grain-size repositories that correspond to the enterprise models, workflow models, and software models, respectively. We also provide a methodology that rebuilds heterogeneous information resources required for the business applications development into a multi-grain-size repository based on ontologies. The contents of the repositories are modeled by the is-a, has-a, and E-R relations, and described by the XML language. We have implemented JAVA-based prototype environment with the tools dealing with the multi-layered repository and confirmed that it supports us in various phases of business application development including business model manifestation, detailed business model definition and an implementation of business software applications.

1 Introduction

Due to the recent trend of e-business, e-commerce site is broadly expanded, and it has become more difficult to make a success in a web-business than ever before. Because of the reason, it is becoming much more important how rapidly web-shop can be constructed from business idea to deploy the idea into the marketplace. The deployment of a business idea means decision making on the strategy of company, designing workflow, and developing business application. In order to implement the business idea as shopping site, various know-hows should be involved and stored as accessible repository, which is described in formal way to support the development of application and the reflection of the change of idea and strategy. Because the contents of the repository include various sorts of information, these different contents are required to be interoperated.

In this paper, we construct special repositories for Web-shop development and an environment for managing the repositories. The repositories consist of coarse-, middle-, and fine-grain-size repository that corresponds to enterprise modeling, workflow modeling, and software development, for each (shown as Figure 1). For the interoperation of the repositories, we describe each repository's contents by XML according to the unified model of is-a, has-a, and general relations. We have implemented a prototype

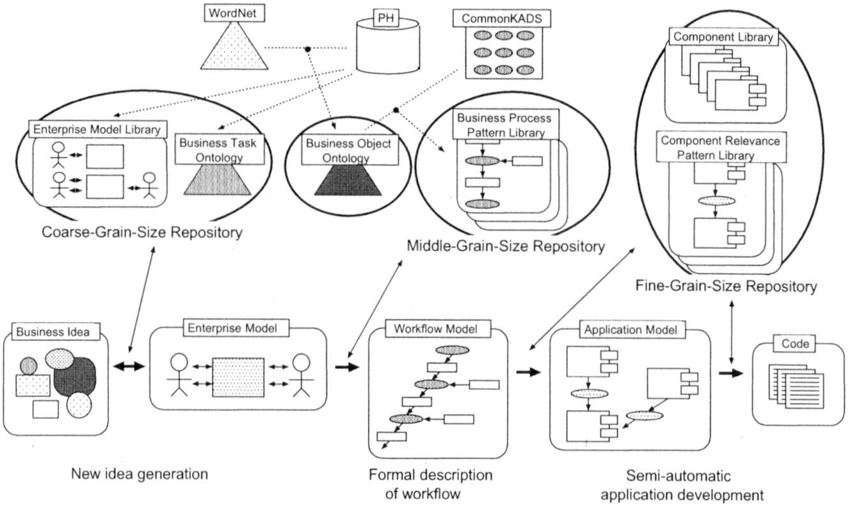

Figure 1: Overview of our environment

environment by using Java language. The environment can generate program codes from business idea, and is able to extend to existing web-shop according to the new idea so that the change is reflected on web-shop application. By applying the environment to case studies, we've confirmed a change of a business logic can be reflected on the structure of Web-shop application.

2 Design of Multi-Grain-Size Repository

Proposed environment is based on multi-grain-size repository, which consists of coarse-, middle-, and fine-grain-size repository. In this section, we show the design of the repositories of the different grain-size.

2.1 Design of Coarse-Grain-Size Repository

2.1.1 Enterprise Model Library

A new business idea is not emerged as a detailed model like workflow models but as abstract concepts such as enterprise models, best practices and so on. In order to reuse enterprise model for the development of business applications, we construct enterprise model library by analyzing case studies of enterprise models that are provided in the *e*-business Process Handbook of MIT[5].

The Process Handbook's case studies of enterprise model contain has-a relations among business tasks that make up each business of the enterprise model. The case studies are described as English text. For example, famous online bookstore Amazon.com has the task structure that top level tasks are made up with "Buy", "Sell", "Manage", and these business tasks have followed-level tasks such as "Receive", "Attract audience to web site", "Manage resources by type of resource", and so on.

We exploit actors (such as customer, supplier, and so on) appearing in case study enterprise model and interactions among those actors. Five classes (Distributor, Creator, Broker, Extractor, Service Provider) are categorized according to the type of the interaction among actors (show Figure 2).

2.1.2 Business Task Ontology

It is difficult for a machine process to use the *e*-business Process Handbook as it is because of its semantic ambiguous with informal concepts such as "what", "how", and so on. Due to this semantic problem that formal definitions like "is-a" or "has-a" relationship are not given, we rebuild *e*-Process Handbook based on the business object ontology and formalize into the business task ontology, which contains formal inheritance structure of task properties.

A task that frequently appears in case studies is regarded as a generic task and is placed as an upper concept of is-a relation's hierarchy. Constructed business task ontology is shown in Figure3. In this ontology approximately 500 tasks are defined.

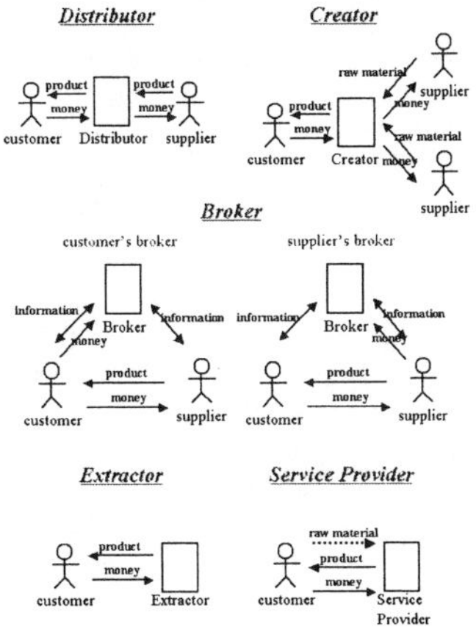

Figure 2: Interaction Types

2.1.3 Business Object Ontology

Terminologies in defining a business are not always identical. In order to reuse common concepts of business definitions, we construct business object ontology to formalize the taxonomy and to specify the relation between business objects.

We employ the WordNet[2] as a general ontology that contains over 17,000 concepts, in order to reuse of general concepts in the construction the business object ontology. Main objects of the business object ontology are extracted from *e*-business Process Handbook because it has large amount of business processes.

First, we exploit terminologies from case studies, and then with respect to the degree of frequency and the abstraction in the terminology obtained from the case studies, we identify the structure of business objects based on WordNet. Figure 4 shows constructed business object ontology.

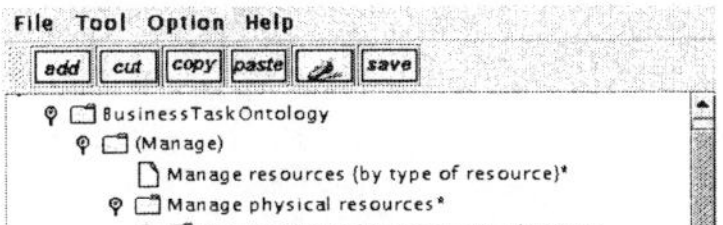

Figure 3: Business Task Ontology

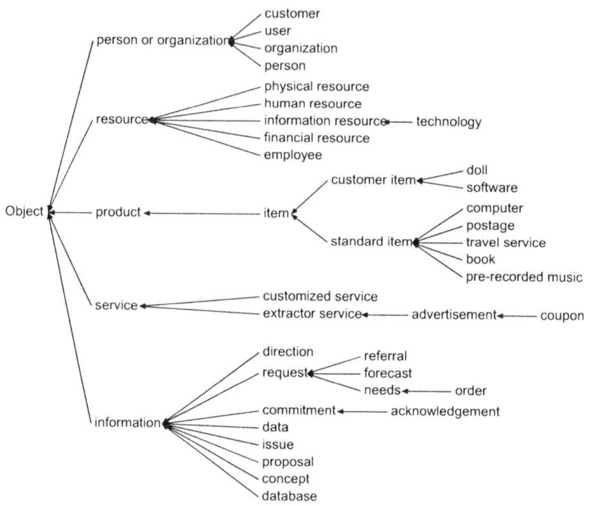

Figure 4: Business Object Ontology

2.2 Design of Middle-Grain-Size Repository

To deploy the enterprise model obtained from the coarse-grain-size repository, we transfer the enterprise model into the workflow model by extending additional information of working process. In order to support the transformation, we devise the middle-grain-size repository as a library of business objects and business process methods.

The middle-grain-size repository is obtained by the following way. First, in order to define the business objects and the business process methods as the primitives of workflow models, concepts on the business object ontology are employed as the business objects. The business process methods are obtained as 16 methods from CommonKADS[1, 4] inference primitives. Second, in order to bridge the levels of coarse-grain-size and middle-grain-size, a business process pattern is provided, which is a semantic unit of workflow model(show Figure 5). We assume business process pattern for each task is provided by business domain specialist. By analyzing business tasks on the coarse-grain-size, the frequent patterns are given, which are named business process patterns. Finally, by mapping information between two levels and merging business process patterns according to the tasks on the coarse-grain-size, we obtain the workflow model of the enterprise model.

2.3 Design of Fine-Grain-Size Repository

To obtain the executable application of Web-store from the model of the middle-grain-size repository, we provide a repository of software library as a fine-grain-size repository. In order to help us to write a program code of a system, a fine-grain-size repository contains business components, relevance information of components, and information of their use.

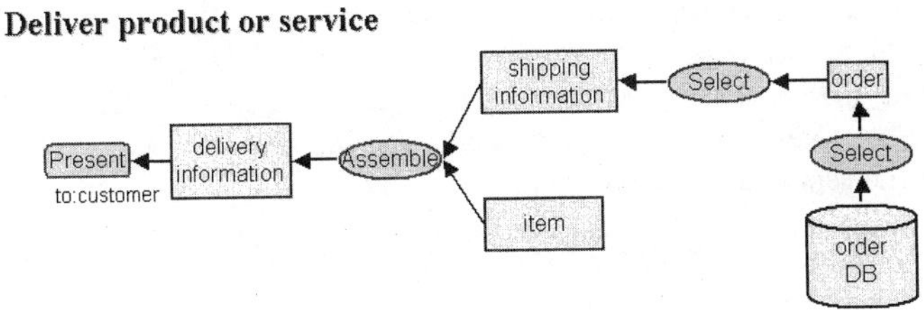

Figure 5: Example of Business Process Pattern

A business component is a software package, which is used in various business applications[3]. There is an issue in what granularity and sort the business component should be implemented. From a standpoint of a target application of Web-store management, we have defied seven business components by analyzing commercial business component package: Order, Shopping Cart, Inventory, Customer, Delivery, Catalog, and Payment. Each business component has API information described with XML.

Business components collaborate in specific situation, for example, when the customer order, the shipping information and billing information are passed from Customer component to Order component.

We have exploited these components collaboration from existing e-commerce sites and web-shop development packages and made library as relevance patterns of components. To generate e-business application code from workflow model, we exploit component relevance patterns from workflow model, merge the patterns by considering common object among patterns, and finally generate code by referencing meta data contained in the pattern.

There are several types of participants in developing Web application such as an application architect, page designers, and Java programmers. Our environment not supports page design now but generate simple input field (HTML). Application architecture is fixed by underlying web application framework (Struts of The Jakarta Project in this case study), but it is can be changed by implementing adaptation code for each framework. Java code is generated from component relevance pattern.

3 Implementation of Prototype Environment

3.1 Design of Tool

Proposed environment supports business application development through enterprise modeling, workflow modeling, and business application development. Each model dealt with by each modeling step is basically composed of objects and relations. The object corresponds to such as actor, business object, inference primitive, component, and so on. The relations are defined based on the objects defined. Because these models can be shown graphically (show Figure 6) as the related objects, we are able to implement our environment as GUI application in order to deal with models easily. In the application, we can edit the model by intuitive way such as clicking, dragging, and so on.

We describe the repository's data with XML so that we can deal with those data with DOM or SAX and can easily add new information by introducing new name tag without changing existing tool. Additionally the use of XML makes the repositories interoperatable.

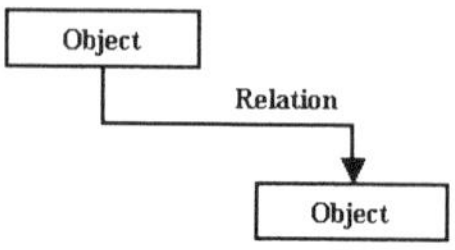

Figure 6: Model Primitive

3.2 Detailed Implementation of Environment

Implemented environment consists of three tools: enterprise model editor, business process editor, and component relevance pattern editor that support enterprise modeling, workflow modeling, and business application development respectively. Each editor is shown Figure 7, Figure 8, and Figure 9.

At first, we select existing enterprise models that contain the feature of new e-business idea. In Figure 7, existing enterprise model is listed in the left frame of window. Then, we merge business task hierarchies contained in each selected enterprise model. We can manage business tasks of two models and remove some business task from them. Finally we define merged business tasks as a new enterprise model and name it. This enterprise model is passed to the business process editor.

After obtaining the enterprise model, we transfer the enterprise model into a workflow model by using the business process editor. When we select a business task, candidates of the business process pattern are obtained. By selecting one of those business process patterns, the model of the business process pattern is given. When we finish extracting all business process patterns, we merge obtained patterns by considering common business object among patterns. Not only we merge common business objects, but also, we can unify objects by referring the business object ontology.

Finally, when we complete merging patterns, we obtain the workflow model. This workflow model is given to the component relevance pattern editor.

As specified e-business idea as a workflow model, we write a system code of it. The component relevance pattern editor supports us to make codes. The workflow model and business process primitives contained in the workflow model are shown in the editor window. For each business process primitive, it is specified in the list whether component relevance pattern can be exploited from it or not. When we complete selecting all the patterns from the candidate patterns, finish exploiting, these patterns are joined by merging common objects among patters. If there is no common object, new patterns are introduced from component relevance pattern library. Finally we name it and register it as a new pattern. Selecting one pattern from the list of patterns, we obtain the code of the pattern at the lower right of the window.

The whole process above enables us to prototype and to manage Web-stores according to business idea. We have applied case studies, and the result of the application confirms us that we are able to manage the various information corresponding to the three repositories.

4 Discussions

We confirmed that this support environment help us to develop business application. Now we have several future works to develop business application more efficiently and effectively.

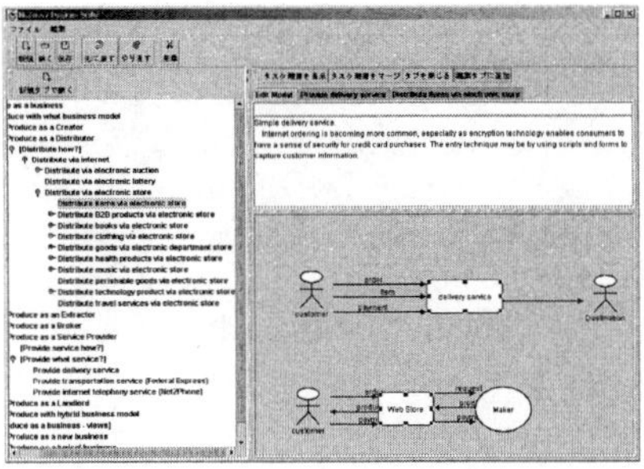

Figure 7: Enterprise Model Editor

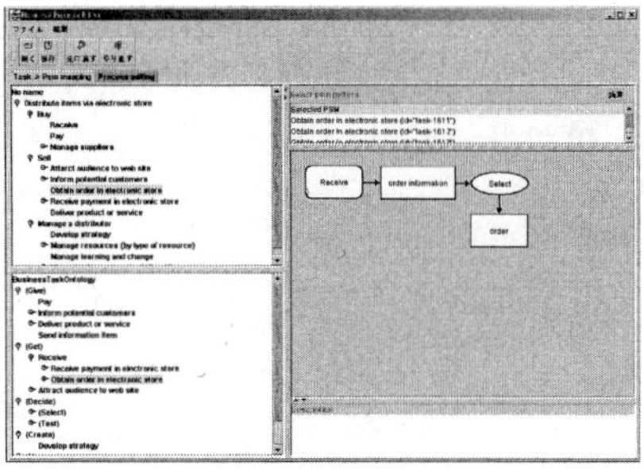

Figure 8: Business Process Editor

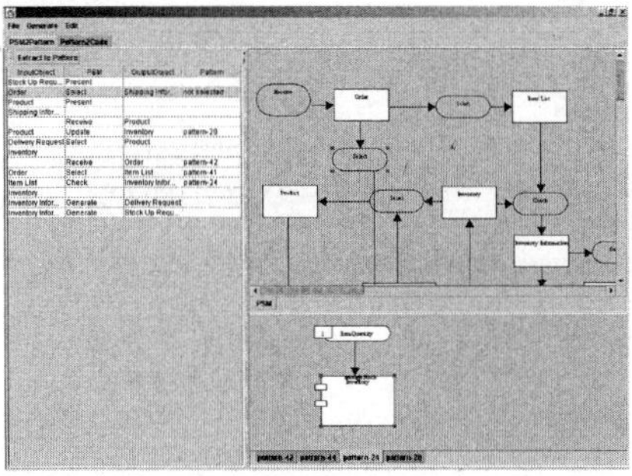

Figure 9: Component Relevance Pattern Editor

Our workflow model is composed of the CommonKADS's inference primitive and business object contained in the business object ontology. With the inference primitive and the business object, we can define a workflow model of several granularities. The inconsistency of the granularity makes it difficult to develop business application from workflow model automatically.

In this study, at the development process from the workflow model to business application, we mainly focused on implementing business logic. We assume that actual development of business application should be considered on 3 separated layers: presentation, business logic, and data management, because each layer should be managed independently.

Our environment is now under extended construction according to these requirements.

5 Conclusion

In order to succeed shopping site on the Web in recent broad expansion of e-commerce site, it is important to deploy the new idea into the marketplace quickly as is in the form of a business application. We proposed the integrated support environment for business application development based on Multi-Grain-Size Repository to support development of business applications from models. The Multi-Grain-Size Repository consists of coarse-, middle-, and fine-grain-size repository, and support enterprise modeling, workflow modeling, and application development respectively. These repositories are constructed based on existing repositories such as *e*-business Process Handbook, Word-

Net, and CommonKADS.

We have implemented a prototype environment with Java language as GUI application. In order to interoperate the models among three levels of the repository, contents of the repository are based on the common semantics written by XML. Our environment consists of enterprise model editor, business process editor, and component relevance pattern editor. Each editor deals with each aspect of business application development and manages repositories. By coding repository contents with XML, each editor exchanges the input information or output product seamlessly each other.

References

[1] Breuker, J., and W. Van de Velde. COMMONKADS LIBRARY FOR EXPERTISE MODELING. IOS Press, and Ohmsha.
[2] Fellbaum, C. ed. WordNet. The MIT Press, 1998.
see also URL: http://www.cogsci.princeton.edu/~wn/
[3] Herzum, Peter, and Oliver Sims. Business Component Factory. John Wiley & Sons, 1999.
[4] Schreiber, Guus, et al. KNOWLEDGE ENGINEERING AND MANAGEMENT. The MIT Press, 1999.
[5] The MIT Process Handbook Project: http://ccs.mit.edu/ph

Knowledge-based Software Engineering
T. Welzer et al. (Eds.)
IOS Press, 2002

A Discussion on Aggregation Constraint for Business Process Modeling in an Example of Building Construction

Seiya AMAN[3], Toshifumi KAI[5], Masaaki HASHIMOTO[1], Yoshiaki TEGOSHI[2], Toyohiko HIROTA[4], Keiichi KATAMINE[1]
e-mail: hasimoto@ai.kyutech.ac.jp
[1] *Kyushu Institute of Technology, 680-4 Kawazu, Iizuka, 820-8502 Japan*
[2] *Hiroshima Institute of Technology, 2-1-1 Miake, Saeki-ku, Hiroshima, 731-5143 Japan*
[3] *Fujitsu FIP Corporation, Time 24 Bldg., 2-45 Aomi, Koto-ku, Tokyo, 135-8686 Japan*
[4] *Kyushu Sangyo University, Fukuoka, 813-8503 Japan*
[5] *Matsushita Electric Works, Ltd, 1048 Kadoma, Kadoma-shi, Osaka, 571-8686 Japan*

Abstract. With the goal of developing a usable technique for sophisticated business process modeling, we discuss here an aggregation constraint of processes in an example of building construction. We first analyzed actual building construction, and made an object model of resources, products and processes in the building construction. Then, we formalized the aggregation constraints on the object model. The aggregation constraints are classified into the indispensable and additional constraints. By applying the indispensable aggregation constraints, we have developed a prototype system which automatically generates a construction schedule from the design documents. The system also evaluated the generated schedule with the additional aggregation constraints. Then, the schedule was revised by hand. We discuss here the aggregation constraints from various viewpoints. In the future, we plan to develop an aggregation constraint concerning construction cost, a sophisticated algorithm for solving some of the aggregation constraints and a constraint for determining aggregation hierarchy.

1 Introduction

In order to improve the reliability and productivity of sophisticated software such as business process scheduling and management, it is very important to know exactly what is required of the software. For this reason, the technique of business process analysis and modeling has been undergoing improvement.

The contemporary versatile user requirements for products and services have been increasingly requiring the diversified and proper-scale production instead of the mass production. A production batch must be precisely scheduled for efficient diversified and proper-scale production. The batch can be determined by means of *aggregation* of products and processes. Aggregation is one of the main techniques of business process analysis and modeling, so aggregation technique should be studied.

In the field of building construction, the buildings themselves are different from each other. That is, building construction is one of the best examples of the diversified and proper-scale production [1]. Therefore, we have been studying the aggregation technique in the example of building construction.

We found that building construction schedules are made based on the design documents of the building [2]. All parts of the building are described in the documents. An example of *a primitive process* in construction would be the process for constructing a part in a specific work, such as assembling iron reinforcing bars [3]. On the other hand, construction management uses *a full-day process* in scheduling. Workers arrive at a construction site in the morning and work there the full

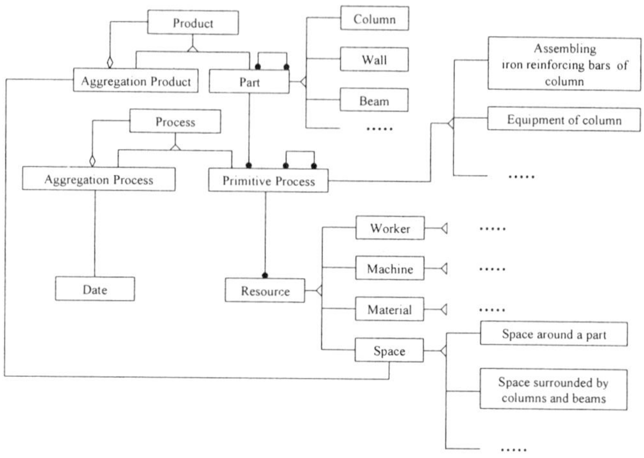

Fig. 1 Object diagram of building construction.

day, leaving in the evening [4, 5]. In this example, the relationship between the primitive and full-day processes must be studied in order to schedule the construction process from design documents. We first analyzed the construction process using the documents of actual building construction and by interviewing construction managers. Then, we formalized the relationship between the primitive and full-day processes as *an aggregation constraint* on the processes.

Here we discuss the aggregation constraint. In this paper, Section 2 outlines a domain model of building construction, Section 3 describes the constraint conditions of process aggregation in the model, Section 4 illustrates a computer-assisted prototype system supporting building construction scheduling by applying the aggregation constraint and Section 5 discusses the aggregation constraint.

2 Domain Model of Building Construction

As a result of the analysis of the actual domain of building construction, we determined that there are three important concepts in the domain: *products, processes* and *resources.* Products are parts that are components of buildings such as columns and beams. Processes are the work to build products such as assembling iron reinforcing bars and covering with concrete. Resources are workers, machines, materials and work-spaces. A resource is usually occupied when a process is carried out. The relationship among them is specified using the object diagram in Fig.1. The execution sequence among the processes is determined by the following factors:

(1) Execution dependency constraint between parts

A part is supported by other parts in a building. Therefore, all parts have a relationship to other

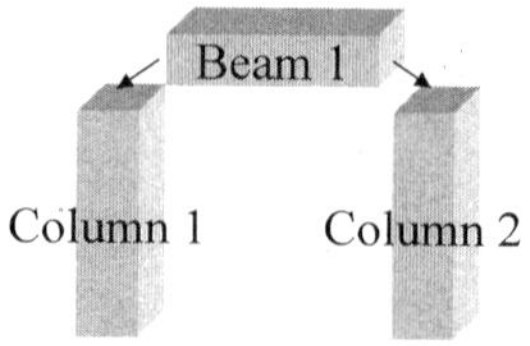

Fig. 2 Existence dependency constraint between parts.

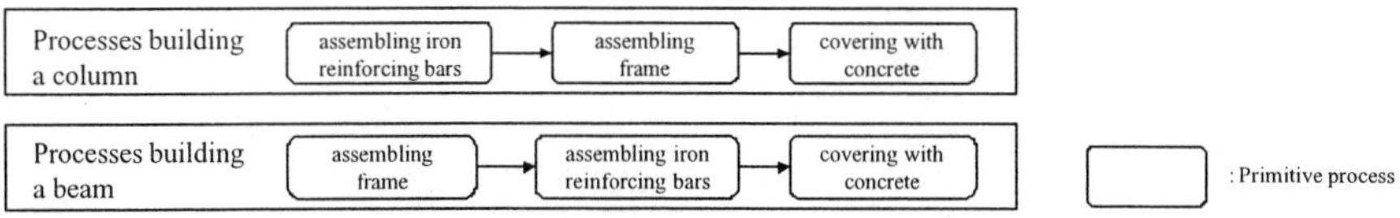

Fig. 3 Primitive processes example of an execution sequence.

parts. We call this condition the existence dependency constraint. When a part is built, its supporting parts must be finished. An example is shown in Fig.2. When a beam 'Beam1' is built, its supporting columns 'Column1' and 'Column2' must be finished. The arrows in the figure express the existence dependency constraint.

(2) Primitive processes and the execution sequence

A primitive process is defined as a process for constructing a part in a specific work such as assembling iron reinforcing bars. The execution sequence of primitive processes is decided for each kind of part. For example, the execution sequence of the primitive processes that build a column is shown in the upper part of Fig. 3. Assembling iron reinforcing bars is the first process. The second is assembling a frame. Covering with concrete is last. However, in the case of a beam, the first process is assembling the frame, and the second is assembling the iron reinforcing bars, as shown in the lower part of the figure.

(3) Occupancy condition of resource

Each primitive process occupies resources. If the resources are occupied by other processes, the primitive process is postponed until the resources are released. Figure 4 shows the model of resource occupancy.

(4) Standard work amount of human-power

The data of the standard work amount performed per unit of human-power is specified by the construction industry sector. The data are used for estimating the cost price and term of the construction.

(5) Exceptional matter

If a problem due to the weather or transportation happens, it is necessary to postpone practicing the process and increase the number of workers.

(6) Aggregated process

An aggregated process is a full-day process of construction which is manageable for a general contractor. This is a full-day process because workers arrive at a construction site in the morning and work there the full day, leaving in the evening. The aggregated process is created by applying a constraint condition of aggregation to the primitive processes, as shown in Fig.5. The aggregation

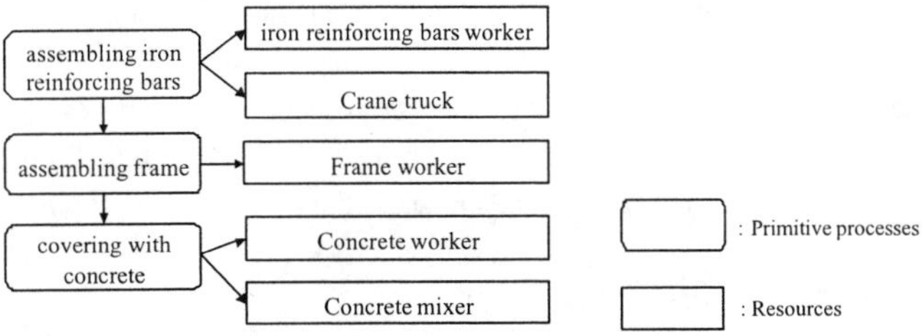

Fig. 4 Model of resource occupancy.

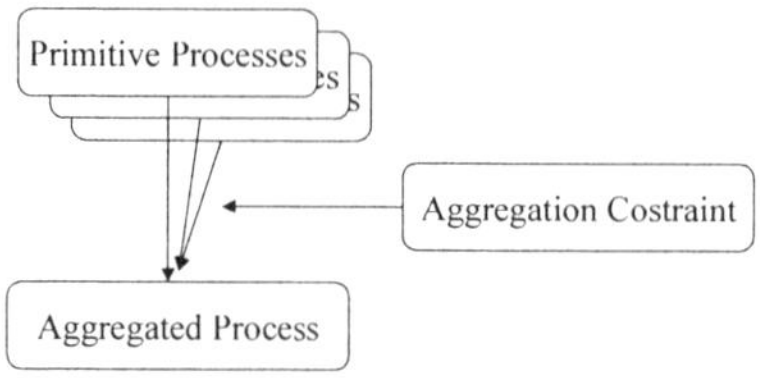

Fig. 5 Aggregation of primitive processes.

constraint is described in the next section.

3 Constraint Condition of Process Aggregation

This section classifies the aggregation constraint conditions and formalizes them.

3.1 Classification of constraint conditions

The constraint conditions of process aggregation are complicated. Therefore, we classified them into two groups: indispensable and additional conditions. The indispensable conditions must be always applied, while the additional conditions have an arbitrary priority of application. The priority is changed according to construction conditions by the experience and knowledge of construction experts.

(1) Indispensable constraint condition

(a) Work party

A work party repeats the same kind of process for many parts. Therefore, the primitive processes that the same work party practices are aggregated.

(b) Full-day process

The process aggregated with the same work party is divided into day by day. The work time of a day can be changed, since overtime work is allowed.

(2) Additional constraint condition

(a) Selection of a part to be constructed next

A work party constructs some parts continuously in a day. The parts that will be near each other in the building are selected for work efficiency.

(b) Managerial limitation of number of workers

A construction manager cannot manage an unlimited number of workers. Therefore, the number of workers in a construction site is limited. This limitation influences the term of construction.

(c) Competition for space

From the viewpoint of work efficiency, more than two work parties usually never go into the same space at the same time. The space, for example, can be defined as one surrounded by four columns. When the term of construction is required to be shortened, the size of space occupied by a work party can be changed.

(d) Competition for resources

The workers and large machines may be busy at other construction sites, and the days on which these resources are available may be limited. The processes that use these resources must be carried out during the available days.

(e) Continuous work of the same party

It is efficient to have the same party work on continuous days at the same construction site.

3.2 Formalization of constraint conditions

We formalized the constraint conditions in order to process them with computers. We have made the functions of the constraint conditions that are difficult to formulate. We are still studying the formalization of the last two constraint conditions in the previous subsection.

(1) Work party

P1.RESOURCE == P2.RESOURCE == P3.RESOURCE == ---.

'Pn (n = 1, 2, 3, - - -)' specifies a primitive process. 'RESOURCE' specifies a work party. Then, P1, P2, P3, - - - belong to the same aggregated process.

(2) Full-day process

P1.WORK_TIME + P2. WORK_TIME +
P3. WORK_TIME + --- ? WORK_TIME_OF_A_DAY .

'WORK_TIME' means work time of each primitive process. Then, P1, P2, P3, - - - belong to the same aggregated process within time 'WORK_TIME_OF_A_DAY'.

(3) Selection of a part to be constructed next

Some patterns for selecting the next part to be constructed are determined by the program functions. The parts have position data with the coordinate form. 'PATTERN 1' selects the next part in a straight line distance. 'PATTERN 2' chooses the next part in a certain division.

(4) Managerial limitation of number of workers

AP1. WORKER_NUMBER + AP2. WORKER_NUMBER +
AP3. WORKER_NUMBER --- ? WORKER_NUMBER_OF_A_DAY .

'APn (n = 1, 2, 3, - - -)' specifies an aggregation process. 'WORKER_NUMBER' means worker number of each aggregation process. Then, AP1, AP2, AP3, - - - are decided within the number 'WORKER_NUMBER_OF_A_DAY'.

(5) Competition for space

P1.SPACE != P2.SPACE != P3.SPACE != ---.

'SPACE' specifies a space occupied by each primitive process. Then, P1, P2, P3, - - - occupy different spaces.

4 A prototype System of Computer-Assisted Scheduling

We have developed a computer-assisted scheduling system that applies our domain model of building construction[6]. The system provides a draft of a schedule automatically from the building design data and construction specifications that determine the sequence of primitive processes. The draft of a schedule can be revised manually. The system adds the revision points as new constraint

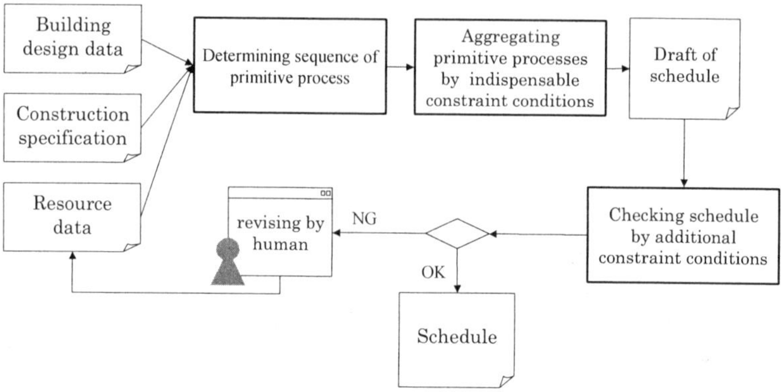

Fig. 6 Flow of scheduling in the system.

conditions and produces a revised schedule.

The system aggregates primitive processes by using the indispensable constraint conditions. The system also checks the schedule by using the additional constraint conditions. Figure 6 shows the flow of scheduling in the system.

We have developed an editor that shows the construction schedule. The editor displays a bar chart that is used in actual building construction. An example of such a bar chart is shown in Fig. 7. In the bar chart, the horizontal axis shows time, and the vertical axis shows process. A bar shows an aggregation process. Figure 8 shows an example of checking the schedule.

5 Discussion

This section discusses the constraint conditions of process aggregation which are described in this paper.

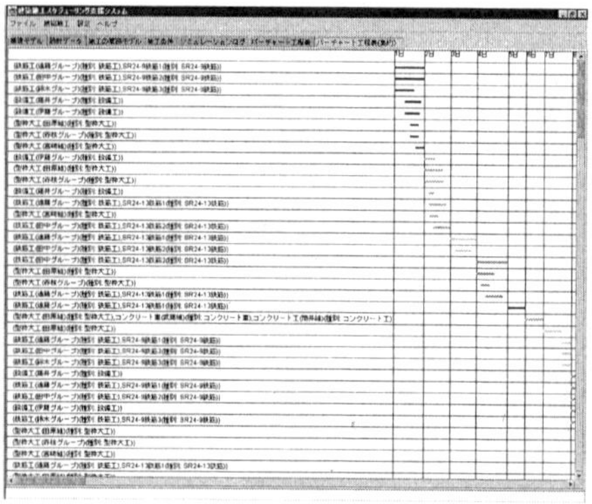

Fig. 7 Sample bar chart.

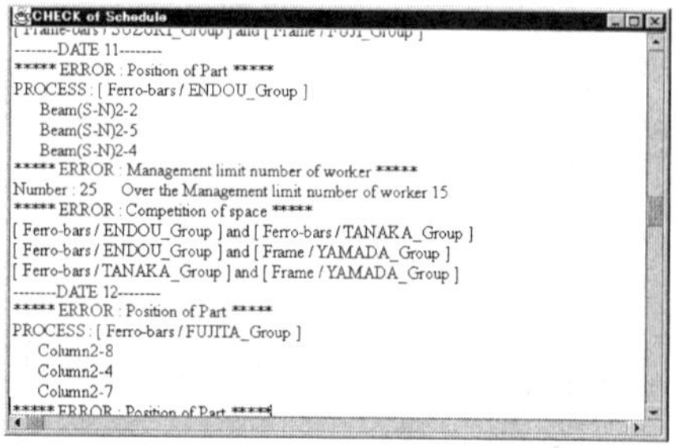

Fig. 8 Example of checking the schedule.

(1) Formality of aggregation constraint

We studied the constraint conditions of process aggregation and formalized them. Then, we developed a prototype system of construction scheduling by applying the formalized constraint conditions. The system has correctly processed them. Thus, the constraint conditions possess the formality.

Of course, there are complicated constraint conditions, such as the selection of the part to be constructed next, which are difficult to formalize using simple arithmetic expressions. Such conditions are specified as pre-defined functional patterns, the details of which are implemented using the programming language in our prototype system. A sufficient set of such patterns should be studied.

(2) Checking and revising the schedule

In our prototype system, several alternative schedules are made on the basis of the indispensable constraint conditions by assigning a resource to processes randomly when the resource competes. Then, the schedule with the shortest term is automatically chosen. The schedule is checked with regard to the additional constraint conditions. If some problems are found in the check, the schedule is revised by humans. Therefore, the various constraint conditions having high priority can be satisfied on the schedule. The method checking and revising schedule has been introduced in our research since automatic generation of schedule satisfying all the constraint conditions is impractical.

(3) Aggregation constraint by resources

Almost of the aggregation constraint conditions that we have studied originate in resources. The reason is that processes are aggregated from the viewpoint of efficient use of resources. The efficient use of resources is one of the main concerns of construction management which schedules the full-day aggregated processes.

(4) Aggregated process and product

We have discussed the aggregation of processes. On the other hand, the concept of aggregated products is also useful for specifying a range to be constructed in a day. However, the aggregated products cannot be defined by themselves. They are defined by using the aggregated processes. Therefore, we have been studying the aggregation of processes.

(5) Related works

Aggregation was introduced as an abstraction which was important in conceptualizing the real world [7, 8]. At present, aggregation abstraction is one of the main concepts in the object-oriented analysis and modeling [9, 10]. The problem of solving the consistency of aggregation constraints was shown to be NP-hard [11, 12]. Production planning in an industry was discussed on the base of aggregation of products [13].

(6) Future work

We have not yet made a constraint condition concerning construction cost. The cost is one of the main concerns of scheduling. Therefore, the constraint condition concerning cost should be studied. Automatic generation of schedule satisfying all the constraint conditions is impractical as mentioned above. However, it would be valuable for our study that some of the additional constraint conditions are taken into account of the automatic generation. The constraint condition 'Continuous work of the same party' specifies a set of full-day aggregated processes. It means that the set is an aggregation of the aggregated processes. Therefore, hierarchical aggregation should be studied.

6 Conclusion

We have discussed process aggregation by analyzing the actual examples of building construction. The details of aggregation originate in the need for an efficient use of resources. The reason is that the efficient use of resources is one of the main concerns of construction management. The aggregation has been formalized as constraint conditions on the object model of resources, products and processes in the construction domain. The constraint conditions have been classified into the indispensable and additional constraints.

Using the prototype system applying the formalization, we were able to produce a schedule automatically using the indispensable constraint conditions. Moreover, the system can check the schedule using the additional constraint conditions. If some problems are found in the check, the schedule is revised by humans.

In the future, we plan to develop an aggregation constraint concerning construction cost, an algorithm for solving some of the additional constraints, and a constraint for determining aggregation hierarchy.

References

[1] K. Miyata, M. Kudou and S. Funatsu, The Management of Building Construction Schedule (in Japanese), Kashima Publishing, Tokyo, 1991.

[2] Y. Shinyashiki, M. Hashimoto, T. Hirota, K. Katamine, Y. Tegoshi, A Case Study on Architectural Construction Process Modeling - Process Aggregation and Constrains -. Proceedings of the Third Joint Conference on Knowledge-Based Software Engineering, IOS Press, pp. 299-302, 1998.

[3] Business Process Society of Building Construction, Business Process Primer of Building Construction (in Japanese), Syoukoku Company, Tokyo, 1994.

[4] T. Sayou. The Management of Building Construction (in Japanese), Kashima Publishing, Tokyo, 1992.

[5] S. Uchida. The Building Construction (in Japanese), Ichigaya Publishing, Tokyo, 1992.

[6] T. Miura, M. Hashimoto, Y. Tegoshi, T. Hirota and K. Katamine. A Product-Centric Process Modeling of Building Construction (in Japanese), Report of Information Processing Society of Japan, Vol. 2000, No. 45, pp.43-48, 2000.

[7] J.M. Smith and D.C.P. Smith, Database Abstractions: Aggregation, Communications of the ACM, Vol. 20, No. 6, pp. 405-413, 1977.

[8] J.M. Smith and D.C.P. Smith, Database Abstractions: Aggregation and Generalization, ACM Transactions on Database Systems, Vol. 2, No. 2, pp. 105-133, 1977.

[9] J. Rumbaugh, M. Blaha, W. Premerlani, F. Eddy and W. Lorensen, Object-Oriented Modeling and Design, Prentice-Hall, p. 500, 1991.

[10] Object Management Group, Inc., OMG Unified Modeling Language Specification, Version 1.4, 2001.

[11] C.L. Pape, Constraint Propagation for Ordering, Abstraction and Aggregation, Journal of Experimental & Theoretical Artificial Intelligence, Vol. 10, No. 1, pp. 63-76, 1998.

[12] K.A. Ross, D. Srivastava, P.J. Stuckey and S. Sudarshan, Foundations of aggregation constraints, Theoretical Computer Science, Vol. 193, No. 1-2, pp. 149-179, 1998.

[13] P. Richard and C. Proust, Maximizing benefits in short-term planning in bottle-glass industry, International Journal of Production Economics, Vol. 64, No. 1-3, pp. 11-19, 2000.

Knowledge-based Software Engineering
T. Welzer et al. (Eds.)
IOS Press, 2002

Using Mobile Devices for Personalized Information

Kimmo Salmenjoki, Riku Jäntti
Department of Computer Science
University of Vaasa
Box 700
65100 Vaasa
Finland

Abstract. The introduction and extensive usage of Internet and Intranet in information systems have left the restriction of excessive information intact so far. XML is often seen as a closely related technique to HTML due to its tagging system. How ever, all major software vendors are appreciating XML as a new way of seeing and sharing information sources.
First we will give a comprehensive overview of the techniques available for the mobile and PDA devices. Secondly we address the advantages and disadvantages of personalization, which has become the main solution for the information overflow in the web environment. In this scope we will see how information systems and their construction are affected due to the requirements of the new mobile networks and end devices. We include some examples how existing web pages can include the usage of mobile extensions. We will also see some future prospects of small devices both in the educational and business environments.

1. Introduction

In this paper, the use of personal mobile devices, especially mobile phones and personal digital assistant (PDA) devices, for personalized knowledge management applications is investigated. By personalized information, we refer to information and knowledge management services that can be adapted according to user's preferences and the capabilities of his terminal. Applications that are based on these adaptive systems are called context-aware applications in [5]. Similar discussion to ours, but focusing on personalized multimedia services can be found in [7].

There exist powerful and commonly used software platforms for web applications such as Java and XML that could be used as a basis of personalized information services. However, not all mobile terminals support these environments and even if they do, they might have some devices dependent restrictions on them. Since the goal is to have transparent adaptive services, there should be some protocol for service capability negotiations between the server and the mobile device. Furthermore, the access methods of the different terminals vary: a mobile device could access the network via wireless local area network (WLAN) or via mobile phone network such as GSM/GPRS or UMTS or even access it through a phone line modem or fixed local area network.

This paper is organized as follows: In section 2, the most important existing and upcoming platforms for personalized mobile services are reviewed. Section 3 discusses the role of personification in web based services. In section 4, possible data integration architectures are discussed. In section 5 we focus on combining the previous data integration patterns with mobile services. Finally, section 6 concludes the paper with overall solutions for system integration and interoperability.

2. Mobile Application Platforms

The emerging third generation (3G) mobile networks will provide tools for handling terminals with variety of access methods with different operational capabilities while providing service personalization. The 3G core network is designed to handle variety of radio access networks (RANs) such as GSM/GPRS RAN, UTRAN, BRAN, and even WLAN (see e.g. [9]). It provides also gateways to many fixed networks, the most important of which are the public switched telephony networks (PSTNs) and the Internet. The mobile execution environment (MExE), see [1, 2, 3, 4, 11], specifies standard classmarks that define what kind of platforms are supported by the mobile device. The MExE server provides standard means of negotiating the mobile terminal's and network's supported capabilities. It also provides tools for personalization of information in terms of information representation. Unfortunately, MExE is operator dependent. That is, it only works in the operators own network. This problem will eventually be solved with the virtual home environment (VHE) concept [13], which allows transparent access to services even when the mobile is roaming in a foreign network.

The MExE server provides means of capability and content negotiations between terminals and the mobile network. The negotiation may take place at service initiation or on a dynamic basis. It could, for instance, be triggered by the change in mobile equipments capabilities (e.g. external monitor and keyboard is connected to it). Capability negotiations include choice of execution environment based on both the service providers and mobile terminals capabilities. For instance, certain service could be accessed either using WAP or Java applets. Content negotiation is used in order to obtain the best representation of the information including conversions from standard protocols to their equivalent wireless derivatives. Content negotiation can also be used for the personalization of the information. Services are provided by applications executing in the client or server or both. It is notable that MExE allows services, in which two mobile terminals directly interact with each other without the use of operator's or third party's MExE servers. In addition, MExE implements security functions that allows authentication the source and content of services to be downloaded. It allows the user to control what services to download and which functions the services can perform in his terminal.

Mobile terminals are divided into classmarks based on the supported execution environments. Current specification defines three classmarks; new will be added based on needs and technological progress:

- **Classmark 1: WAP Enviroment**
  This classmark is indented for mobile phone type of devices with very limited screens and numerical keypads. The supported execution environment is wireless application protocol WAP. WAP is converted to/from HTTP v1.1 in the WAP gateway.
- **Classmark 2: PersonalJava Environment**
  This classmark specifies communicator type of phones and multimedia phones with possible colour screens and sophisticated input devices, such as touchpad, voice control etc. The PersonalJava application environment is the standard Java environment optimised for consumer electronics devices designed to support WWW content including Java applets. The personal Java API is a feature subset of Java 2 Platform Standard Edition (J2SE) with some optional Java packages and API

modifications necessary for the needs of small portable devices. Classmark 2 also supports JavaPhone API, which is a vertical extension to the PersonalJava platform that defines APIs for telephony control, messaging (SMS, UDP datagrams and WAP datagrams), address book, and calendar information, etc. In addition to JavaPhone API, classmark 2 has MExE API that specifies support for networking protocols not directly supported by PersonalJava or JavaPhone APIs including HTTP v1.1, HTTPS and mailto, and optionally Gopher, FTP, and file protocols.

- **Classmark 3: J2ME CLDC Environment**
  This classmark is indented for resource-constrained devices (low processor speed, small memory space etc.). It utilizes Java 2 Platform Micro Edition (J2ME) with Connection Limited Device Configuration (CLDC) and Mobile Information Device Profile (MIDP).

So from above we see that Java technologies provide a unified platform for application development both in fixed and mobile network environments. In what follows we will consider how the application and data will relate to these networks.

3. Web Based Applications with Personification and Mobility

In this chapter we will see how the role of user and user needs have changed due to the technology changes mentioned above. Web as a platform is open-ended web browser window to any information sources. Both information providers and user recognized that this results in a chaos of information, where neither the owner or the user of these information sources are satisfied. Web developers have started to work on this dilemma by building web sites for registered users, where the user is identified and hence becomes like a traditional IT application user. The role of registration is twofold: to get information about the (possible) customer and to provide a unified user experience with adapted content (and additional advertisements). In operating system level windows environment the trend has been to give the user his information on the desktop, independently weather that information is located on the local PC or in the outside network environment. Also the network is accessed hierarchically, switching between Internet and PC or between Internet versus Intranet environments. Internet gateways and proxies to PC and finally mobile and WLAN technologies have made the network more ubiquitous.

In the end devices, mobile phones have always been personalized, as they have mostly been used for personal communication. Originally PC computers stand for personalized computers, both from the OS and application point of view, but are only now starting to live up to their original name. The newest major possibilities here are that these networks and various end devices will become tools for information so that one can fluently work on different devices, networks and applications, as it best fits one's preferences (a unified user experience). Examples of this kind of IT usage are Geographic Information System (GIS), location and user preference applications (like unified messaging or usage of Resource Description Framework (RDF) for improved personalization). To enable this information synchronization, network roaming and information organization are the critical factors. A working example of this kind is the usage of calendar and email applications on PDA devices like IPAQ. In the following figure we describe the present organization of the IT systems with both their traditional and mobile components:

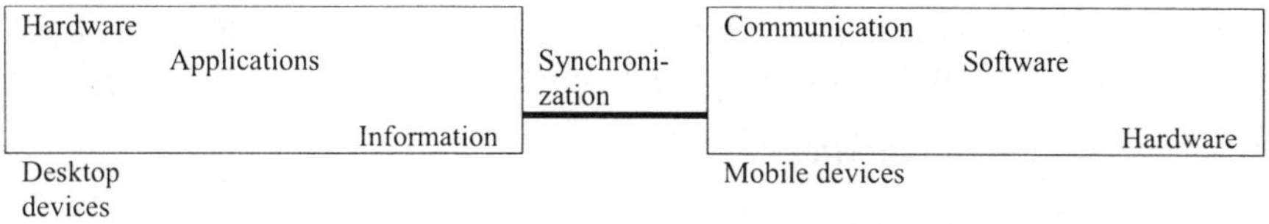

Figure 1. Mobile usage with respect to traditional IT applications

Here the various parts in the picture represent different levels and possible configurations of personification, where in mobile devices hardware is more central that in the information centric desktop environment. In traditional applications, information is mostly file (and directory) centric and in mobile applications the information is mostly managed from within the applications totally in a user centric manner. In mobile devices there is less room for changing the applications, but all customisation is done through the user preferences. One necessary component for unified user experience is synchronization, which is also being standardized in the SyncML initiative, see [15].

4. Data Integration and Networked Applications

With the above development the focus of IT is changing from databases and application integration to enhanced user presence with user preferences, ubiquitous networking and knowledge integration. Here various XML based technologies are working examples of this kind of development. Technically this approach is using open XML, SOAP and UDDI technologies with various ontologies (like EDI/XML or Biztalk.org) to share information between organizations (and companies). For further details on XML technologies see [17] for example.

The possibilities for tighter integration are fourfold: platform centric, network centric, device centric or information centric. Here the end devices are continuously developing, but figure 1 above gave basically the two opposite approaches presently existing. The convergence or networks and devices goes towards more ad hoc type usage of networking in a unified manner from the user's point of view. The amazing thing is that mobile and PDA devices can compensate for their restricted physical abilities through applications and tighter integration as presented.

We describe each possible information organization and new data integration trends in figures 2 to 5 with some present descriptive examples:

Platform centric data integration

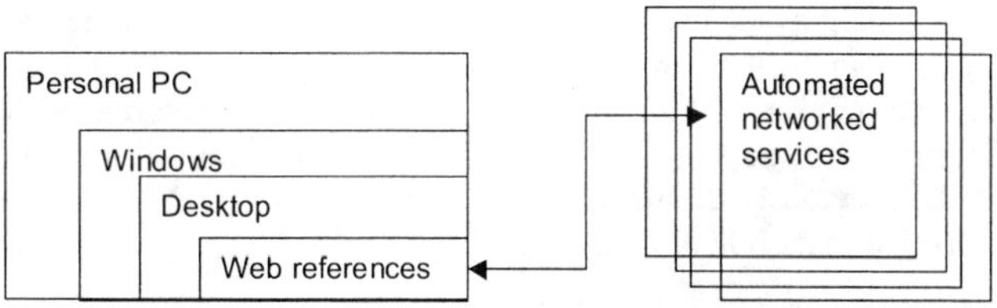

Figure 2. Platform centric web services (like Microsoft .Net or Java web services, [12])

This service concept is a driving force for web based application development in the near future. This has the advantage of providing coherent information with parameterized service queries or proxy type adaptation for the user. The main problem with this approach is the ownership of the customer information and customer access.

Network centric data integration

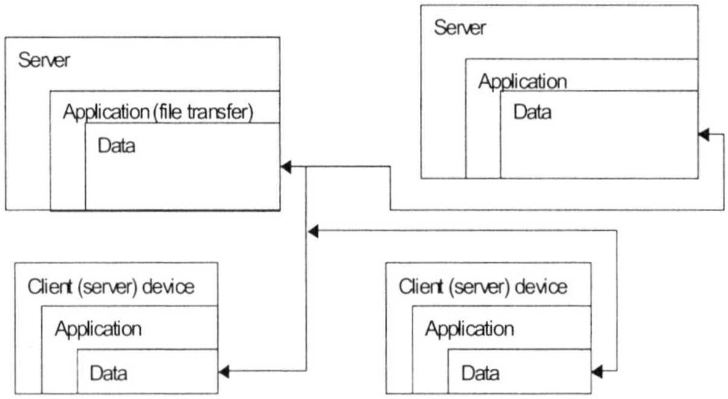

Figure 3. Network centric peer to peer computing (like Napster application or Sun's JXTA)

In this approach the roles of the traditional server and client parts are relaxed: each device is a node in the network acting both as a server and client. Here the main problem is the illegal usage of data. Music and movie industry have faced serious threats due to this type of copying of multimedia information on the networks. There are also cases where people have used MP3 players to copy application software from computers to portable devices.

Device centric data integration

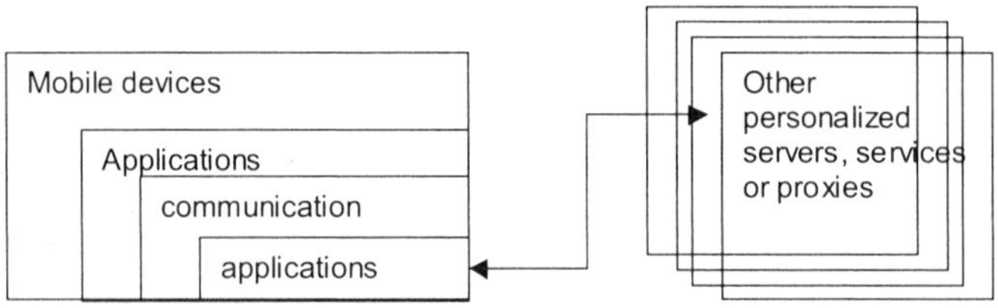

Figure 4. Device centric (present mobile and PDA usage with WAP and XHTML)

In this approach the tendency is to develop applications integrated to the end devices, and use networked and web technologies to adapt the content as necessary. The main interest in this approach has been around application architectures and adapting content to various end devices, for more details see [6]. Here XHTML, RDF and SyncML are the related XML technologies that will improve the integration especially in mobile environments. With the near future inclusion of the previously discussed Java technologies like J2ME and MExE new applications can be loaded to mobile devices, too.

Information centric data integration

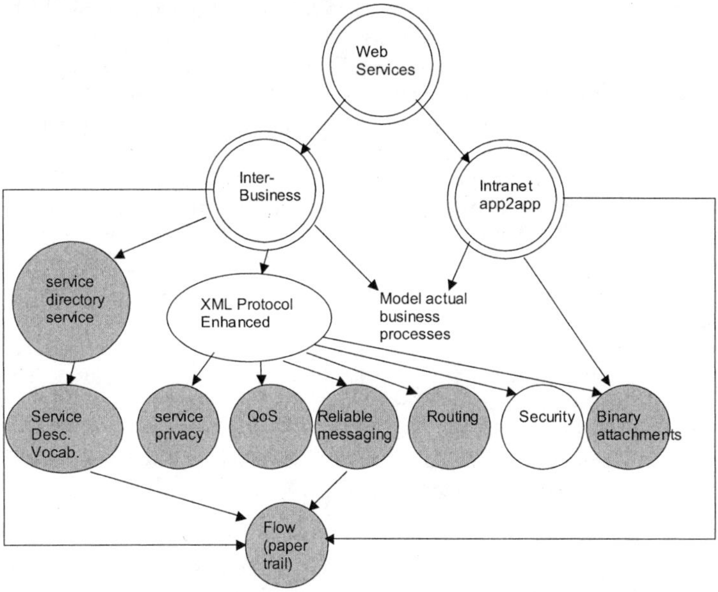

Figure 5. Information centric (XML Protocol enhanced web services), original source http://www.w3.org/2001/04/roadmap/ws.svg

In this approach one is looking for combining the previously discussed networking and XML technologies using common dictionaries and shared ontologies, which enable a tighter exchange of strictly defined data sources. The connection between services and VHE is that the service can use authentication, routing etc functions provided by the network through the common framework interface of OSA. One problem here presently is a scattering of the XML technologies, especially in the Schema section, and vendor and user commitment to these standards (instead of inventing new ones like Microsoft's C# or Nokia's Mobile Internet Technical Architecture MITA efforts). Gradually, when the applications will contain in-build XML usage, a tighter integration of various networked information sources will be enabled. In Figure 5 above web services will finally enable the change from traditional paper trail into electrical transactions. The critical components to require from the network systems are service privacy, QoS, reliable messaging, routing, security and binary attachments.

5. Service portability and openness – the Virtual Home Environment and Open System Architecture

Personalization of services requires that the service provider keeps track of user profiles. In a personalized setting the user must be able to define certain look and feel and functional properties for his mobile terminal. Some of this personification information can be stored locally in terminal and hence be available regardless of the access network. There are, however, several drawbacks with this concept. User could have several terminals in his disposal, the memory of the terminal could be very limited for storing such information, and a lot of bandwidth would be wasted by transmitting this information from mobile to the service provider.

In the virtual home environment concept (VHE), the user has the same personalized individual interface and service mix available in his mobile terminal regardless of which network he is currently using. In that case, the network has to take care of transmitting user profiles, charging information, service information, etc. from the user's home network, i.e. the network storing this information and in charge of charging the user, to the access network he currently is using. Although this concept sounds simple, the involved signalling tasks from the network side are demanding.

In a 3G network, Customized Applications for Mobile Enhanced Logic (CAMEL, [13]) service capability is extension of the Intelligent Network (IN) concept utilized e.g. in GSM and PSTN systems. While IN is network specific and does not carry information from network to network, CAMEL is designed to handle also mobility and roaming between networks. With networks that implement both CAMEL and MExE it is possible to achieve truly ubiquitous personalized mobile services.

VHE is currently under standardization [14]. It promotes the view that 3G service architecture called Open System Architecture (OSA) should be a layered architecture, with standardized interfaces between the layers. The OSA APIs are implemented over a distributed processing environment, making the actual runtime location of services insignificant. These properties of OSA enable the network operators to be less dependent on particular vendor's products, but more importantly third party service providers to access the network resources in a standardized manner making them less dependent on single carrier provider's network.

VHE/OSA is joint effort of the Third Generation Partnership Project (3GPP), International Telecommunication Union (ITU), and Universal Telecommunication Systems Forum. That is, it is driven by the telecommunications industry and teleoperators. Another stakeholder in the service development process is the Parlay Group [11], which has been formed to support creation of communications applications by specifying and promoting open APIs that intimately link IT applications with the capabilities of the communications world. The convergence trend between telecommunications world and the rest of the IT world can be seen in the co-operation between VHE/OSA development group and the Parlay group.

The VHE/OSA model is shown in figure 6. Applications access the service capabilities through a common framework interface. The key component of both OSA and Parlay is the framework server and its API. These allow the applications to discover the available network functionalities. The service capability servers such as MExE provide functionalities to construct services. These functionalities are grouped into logically coherent interface classes called Service Capability Features (SCFs). The SCFs offer a generalized view of the network functionality to third party application developers via standardized interfaces.

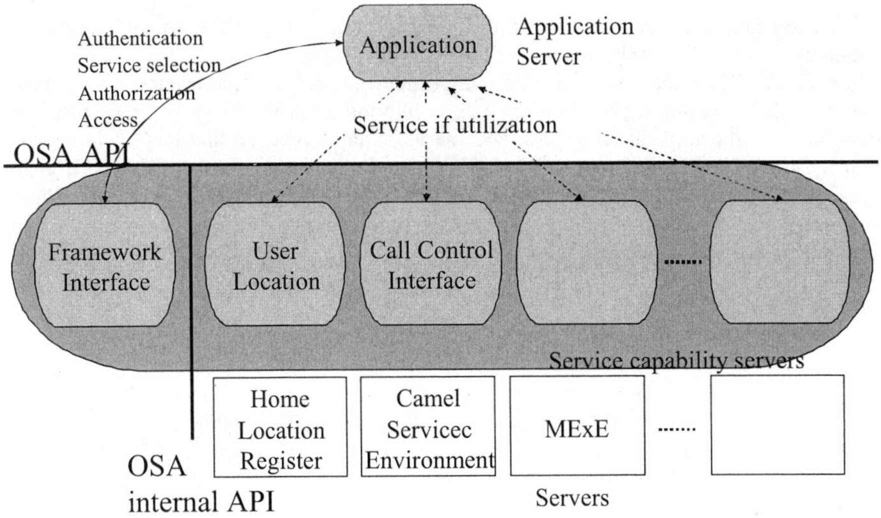

Figure 6. VHE OSA model

In figure 6 we note that the critical network properties, like service privacy and QoS, of Figure 5 can be obtained via the OSA API interface.

6. Concluding remarks- user centric services

In the previous chapter we saw the trends in present web based application and service development with upcoming standards for mobile platforms. When the services will include more automated features utilizing the user settings and preferences using the previously discussed XML technologies like RDF, we will see fully integrated personalized services, where the user is embedded in a network of transparent devices discreetly serving his needs and interrupting his other activities as little as possible. The critical factors in this development are the UI issues, application and data integration and user preferences and acceptance. Figure 7 gives an idea of a transparent user view, which can dependent also on time and user location. Also the activation of the application can be provided by the online web services components.

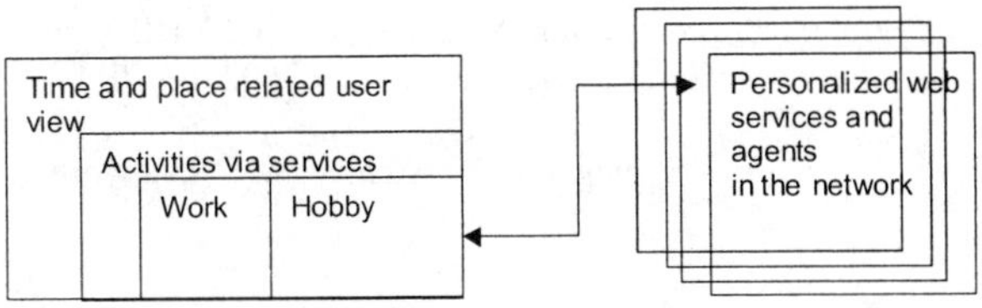

Figure 7. User centric or fully personalized services (like unified messaging applications, GIS based applications or RDF based calendar and communication applications)

With more personalized devices and integrated applications users can start to use ubiquitous computing and various existing networks in the vicinity of the user according to his preferences, timing and personal activities. Pervasive computing will become ubiquitous so that computers are a natural extension of our everyday life.

Finally IT is moving from information management into knowledge management and "knowledge based applications" in efforts like the Semantic Web by W3C, see [16]. Some parts of the application have to become more agent type, so that they communicate with the user and his preferences when necessary, but are also able to help the user by working independently of the user using only his preferences and networked information sources (possibly communicating with user's other agent and other networked agent applications and web based services).

7. References

[1.] 3GPP TS 22.057 V4.0.0 (2000-10) 3rd Generation Partnership Project Technical Specification Group Terminals Mobile Execution Environment (MExE) Service Description, Stage 1 (Release 4), 2000.

[2.] 3GPP TS 22.057 V4.0.0 (2000-10) 3rd Generation Partnership Project Technical Specification Group Terminals Mobile Execution Environment (MExE) Service Description, Stage 2 (Release 4), 2000

[3.] 3GPP TS 22.121 v4.0.0 "Virtual Home Environment" (Release 2), 2000

[4.] 3GPP TS 22.12 v4.0.0 "Virtual Home Environment/Open Service Architecture", 2000

[5.] P. J. Brown, J.D. Bovey, and X. Chen, "Context-aware applications; From the laboratory to the marketplace," IEEE Personal Communications, October 1997, pp. 58 - 63.

[6.] J. Burkhardt, H. Henn, S. Hepper, K. Rintdorff, T. Schäck, "Pervasive computing," Addison-Wesley, 2002.

[7.] Y.-F. Chen, H. Huang, R. Jana, S. John, S. Jora, A. Reibman, and B. Wei, "Personalized Multimedia Services Using A Mobile Service Platforme," In Proc. IEEE Wireless Communications and Networking Conference WCNC 2002, Vol 2., Mar 2002, pp. 918-925.

[8.] F. Daoud and S. Mohan, "Strategies for Provisioning and Operating VHE Services in Multi-Access Networks," IEEE Communications Magazine, January 2002, pp. 78-88

[9.] H. Kaaranen, A. Ahtiainen, L. Laitinen, S. Naghian, V. Niemi: UMTS Networks, John Wiley, 2001

[10.] Parlay http://www.parlay.org/

[11.] G. Stone, "MExE Mobile Execution Environment White Paper," MExE Forum, December 2000, (http://www.mexeforum.org/MExEWhitePaperLrg.pdf)

[12.] Sun Inc: Java web services website, (http://java.sun.com/webservices/), 2002

[13.] TSG SA WG1 Specifications, (http://www.3gpp.org/TB/SA/SA1/specs.htm), 2002

[14.] VHE: Virtual Home Environment organization, 2002

[15.] W3C: XML standard, (http://www.w3c.org/XML/), 2002

[16.] W3C: Semantic Web effort, (http://www.w3.org/2001/sw/), 2002

[17.] WDVL (Web Developers Virtual Library): XML section, (http://wdvl.internet.com/Authoring/Languages/XML/), 2002

Program Understanding, Reuse, Knowledge Discovery

Knowledge-based Software Engineering
T. Welzer et al. (Eds.)
IOS Press, 2002

An Automatic Method for Refactoring Java Programs

Seiya YAMAZAKI
Graduate School of Science and Technology, Keio University
3-14-1 Hiyoshi, Kouhoku-ku, Yokohama 223-8522, Japan

Morio NAGATA
Dept. of Administration Engineering, Faculty of Science and Technology
Keio University
3-14-1 Hiyoshi, Kouhoku-ku, Yokohama 223-8522, Japan

Topic: Program understanding, programming knowledge, learning of programming, modeling programs and programmers.

Abstract. In order to increase productivity of the software development, it is desired to write understandable and reusable programs. Thus, a refactoring method, which transforms programs into understandable ones, has been an attracted research issue. Existing refactoring tools only replace a specified part of the program with another text by the programmer. However, it is difficult to find the part of the program to be replaced. Thus, we think that the tool should refactor programs automatically. Moreover, it should tell the programmers the refactoring strategy to be applied. This paper proposes a tool refactoring Java programs automatically. Our tool provides the following two common facilities for refactoring small parts of given programs. The first one is to hide methods of a class. For example, if a public method is used only within own class, the method is replaced with the private one. The other facility is to reduce the scope of a variable. For example, a variable is used only within "for", "while", or "if" statement in a method, the variable is declared where the statement is needed. Our tool has succeeded in refactoring many Java programs automatically.

1. Introduction

Software products have become too large to be understood and modified by programmers. Refactoring [1] is one of the ways that transform programs into understandable and modifiable ones without changing those behaviours. In refactoring, the first step is to understand a current structure of the program. The second step is to improve the structure. The third one is to rewrite the source by hand. The final step is to execute and test the rewritten source program. In the future, it is easier for the same programmer or the other programmers to understand the refactored programs than original programs.

Though refactoring is so attractive to the programmers, it has not been used yet. When the programmers would like to apply refactoring to their programs, there are four difficulties; in specifying the part of the program to be replaced; in specifying the method of refactoring to be carried out; in understanding the processes of refactoring; and in carrying out refactoring. In most cases of applying refactoring, programmers have to improve programs by hand. Therefore, it often causes much trouble.

There exist several tools for supporting refactoring, for example "Xrefactor"[2], "jFactor"[3], and "jBuilder 6 Enterprise"[4]. These tools only substitute a part of the program into another text. Thus, these tools cannot resolve above issues.

2. An Outline of Our Automatic Method for Refactoring

We propose an automatic method for supporting programmers to refactor their Java programs. Methods of refactoring to be applied usually depend on a certain situation. If there exist several possibilities of refactoring, the tool cannot always determine a particular method automatically. The following two methods can be always applied to improve programs without depending on the situation.

- To hide methods of a class
- To reduce scopes of variables

It is assumed that any Java program is transformed into an XML form by Javaml [5] before applying our method.

3. To Hide Methods of a Class

We can hide some methods of a class by reducing their scopes. After our proposed tool confirms that a method is not used in the other classes, it transforms the method into a localized one. For example, if a public method is used only in own class, the method is transformed into the private one. If a public method is used within its subclasses, it is transformed into a protected one. If a protected method is used only within own class, it will be transformed into a private one.

3.1 Example

```
class ClassA{
      public method(){
      }
}
class ClassB extends ClassA{
      ClassA instance = new ClassA();
      private foo(){
         instance.method
      }
}
class ClassC{
      private foo(){
      }
}
class ClassD{
      private foo(){
      }
}
```

→

```
class ClassA{
      protected method(){
      }
}
class ClassB extends ClassA{
      ClassA instance = new ClassA();
      private foo(){
         instance.method
      }
}
class ClassC{
      private foo(){
      }
}
class ClassD{
      private foo(){
      }
}
```

If our tool transforms above program, the following processes are executed. The first process is to detect "method()" in the ClassA, and "foo()" in the ClassB. The second process is to find that "method()" is used in the ClassB.

The third process is to understand that ClassB's parent class is ClassA. The final process is to transform the "public method" into protected one because the public method in the ClassA is used only within its subclasses.

3.2 Steps of hiding methods of a class

- [Step1] Get all names of methods and classes.
- [Step2] Inspect where the method is used.
- [Step3] Get an instance of the method.
- [Step4] Get a name of the class appeared on the instance.
- [Step5] Examine a parent-child relationship between the original class and the referred class.
- [Step6] Modify the method to be localized if the method is not used in another class.
- [Step7] Transform the Javaml format into the Java program.

In step3, we search the following pattern to get an instance of the method.

instance.method

In step4, we search the following pattern to get the name of a class.

ClassA instance = new ClassA();

3.3 Exceptional cases

Above method almost succeeds in refactoring programs. However, there are some exceptional cases.

3.3.1 the same constructor

At first, in case that there are the same constructor in a class. For example, if

ClassA instance = new ClassA(); ***ClassB instance = new ClassB();***

are in the same class, the tool might get a different class name.

3.3.2 Factory method

Next, suppose that the program produces an instance by using a factory method, for example,

```
class FMFactory1 extends FMFactory{
  public FMFactory1(String s){
    super(s);
  }
  public FMBase getInstance(){
    return new FM1(msg);
  }
}
```

Above program does not include ***ClassA instance = new ClassA ();*** , therefore the tool cannot find out this pattern.

4. To Reduce Scopes of Variables

In case that a variable is used only within "for", "while", and "if" statements in a method, the variable is declared where the statement is used.

4.1 Example

```
void foo(){                          void foo(){
    int i = 0;
    if(someCondition){      ──►          if(someCondition){
        i = 1;                               int i = 1;
    }                                    }
}                                    }
```

If our tool transforms above program, the following processes are executed. The first process is to detect "int i = 0;" The second process is to search for "i" from behind the variable in the method description except the conditional branch. In case of that there are no other "i", the tool declares "int" in front of "i = 1" in the conditional branches.

4.2 Steps of Reducing Scopes of Variables

- [Step1] Search ***int variable = number;***
- [Step2] If the variable is used only in the conditional expressions, then the declaration "int" is moved into the conditional expressions.
- [Step3] Transform the Javaml format into the Java program.

4.3 Exceptional cases

In some cases, our method fails to transform the programs into correct ones.

4.3.1 long, double and float

The tool does not support long, double, and float constructors.

4.3.2 incorrect transformation

```
void foo(){                          void foo(){
    int i = 0;
    if(someCondition){      ──►          if(someCondition){
        j= i;                                j= int i;
    }                                    }
}                                    }
```

Above transformation shows a wrong case. This kind of a program is transformed by our method. However, there are no initialization of "i" in the transformed program. Thus, the program cannot be compiled.

4.4 Improved Reducing Scopes of Variables

```
void foo(){
    int i = 0;
    if(someCondition){
        j= i;
    }
}
```

→

```
void foo(){

    if(someCondition){
        int i = 0;
        j= i;
    }
}
```

To eliminate ***4.3.2 incorrect transformation***, we changed the way of reducing scopes of variables. The first process is to detect "int i = 0;" The second process is to search for "i" from behind the variable in the method description except the conditional branch. In case of that there are no other "i", the tool declares "int i = 0;" in front of "i" in the conditional branches.

4.4.1 Steps of Improved Reducing Scopes of Variables

- [Step1] Search ***int variable = number;***
- [Step2] If the variable is used only in the conditional expressions, then the declaration "int i = 0;" is moved into the conditional expressions.
- [Step3] Transform the Javaml format into the Java program.

There is no change in steps of hiding methods of a class. The change is in the way of "the declaration is moved into the conditional expressions." Not only "int" is moved into the conditional expressions, but also "int i = 0;" is moved as it were. Though this method has to move more text than former way of reducing scopes of variables, it can be always applicable. We adopt this improved one.

5. Concluding Remarks

Our tool successfully modified many Java programs in above situations. We set two criteria of automatic transformations. The first one is that a programmer decides the execution of refactoring. The second one is that a transformation is carried out when the programmer understand the difference between the original program and the transformed program. After the transformation, programs will be converted to be understandable, reusable, and modifiable ones for programmers by applying refactoring. In other words, refactoring is a method for programmers. Therefore, our tool always notices to programmers when refactoring is applied. Moreover, the notification will be useful information when the programmer writes the same kind of the program in the future.

We would like to explain our tool's advantage in terms of maintenance of programs. Both proposed ideas are concerned with *scope*. Our tool can reduce scopes of methods or variables. When a programmer maintains programs, which have the reduced scopes, he/she can watch them without paying attention to the vanished scopes.

```
class ClassA{
    public method(){
    }
}
class ClassB extends ClassA{
    ClassA instance = new ClassA();
    private foo(){
      instance.method
    }
}
class ClassC{
    private foo(){
    }
}
class ClassD{
    private foo(){
    }
}
```

→

```
class ClassA{
    protected method(){
    }
}
class ClassB extends ClassA{
    ClassA instance = new ClassA();
    private foo(){
      instance.method
    }
}
class ClassC{
    private foo(){
    }
}
class ClassD{
    private foo(){
    }
}
```

Reducing scopes of methods (Scope of "method()")

If a programmer who does not use our tool, he/she must watch the program with paying attention to scope of "method()" as left side of above figure. If a programmer who uses our tool, he/she watches only the reduced scope of "method()" as right side of above figure.

```
void foo(){
    int i = 0;
    if(someCondition){
        i= 1;
    }
}
```

→

```
void foo(){

    if(someCondition){
        int i=1;
    }
}
```

Reducing scopes of variables (Scope of "i")

If a programmer who does not use our tool, he/she must watch the program with paying attention to scope of "i" as left side of above figure. If a programmer who uses our tool, he/she watches only the reduced scope of "i" as right side of above figure.

Our tool can reduce valid scopes of methods or variables, which should be checked, for programmers to understand their programs easily.

References

[1] Martin Fowler, Refactoring: Improving the design of existing code, Addison Wesley Longman, 1999
Refactoring Home Page http://www.refactoring.com/
[2] Xrefactory: A Refactoring Browser for Emacs http://xref-tech.com/speller/
[3] jFactor: Refactoring tools to professional Java IDE http://www.instantiations.com/jfactor/
[4] jBuilder 6 Enterprise: The leading Java TM development solution http://www.borland.com/jbuilder/
[5] Javaml: An XML-based Source Code Representation for Java Programs
http://www.cs.washington.edu/homes/gjb/JavaML/

Knowledge-based Software Engineering
T. Welzer et al. (Eds.)
IOS Press, 2002

A Concept-Oriented Approach to Support Software Maintenance and Reuse Activities

Dirk Deridder
Programming Technology Lab
Vrije Universiteit Brussel, Brussels, Belgium
Dirk.Deridder@vub.ac.be - http://prog.vub.ac.be/

Abstract. A major activity in software development is to obtain knowledge and insights about the application domain. Even though this is supported by a wide range of tools and techniques, a lot of knowledge remains implicit in the resulting artefacts (e.g. class diagrams). Examples of such implicit knowledge are amongst others the links between the different artefacts, the knowledge that is lost as a result of iterative refinements, and the knowledge that is regarded common sense by the involved parties. Most of this knowledge resides in the heads of the stakeholder, the domain experts, and the developers. As it is likely that they can no longer remember it or that they are no longer available when software reuse and maintenance activities are initiated, this poses a problem. In this paper we present ongoing research in which we focus on our use of an ontology as a medium to tackle this problem. Making the different kinds of knowledge explicit will be accomplished by representing them as concepts in the ontology. Subsequently we will link these concepts to the artefacts created during analysis, design and implementation. This enables a bi-directional navigation between the concepts and the artefacts which consequently will serve as a vehicle to start reuse and maintenance activities.

1 Introduction

During the software development life-cycle the system to be built is conceived through and documented by different kinds of artefacts. Besides modelling the final solution, these artefacts (such as class diagrams) reflect our knowledge about the application domain to a considerable extent. Unfortunately a lot of this knowledge remains implicit and most often resides in the heads of the different people concerned. The most important of this implicit knowledge are amongst others the links between the different artefacts, the knowledge that is lost as a result of iterative artefact refinements, and the knowledge that is regarded as common sense by the involved parties. This includes the link between the conceptual artefacts and their concrete realizations in the implementation.

Especially in the context of software maintenance and reuse activities it is imperative to have access to the afore-mentioned knowledge elements. This is not surprising, for these activities require a major effort in understanding the existing system. For achieving this understanding, it is helpful if you can rely on the people who were involved with the development of the original system. In practice however it is likely that they are no longer available or, if they are available, that they no longer have the specific knowledge you seek. As a result you will spend a major part of your time trying to figure out which concepts are represented by which parts of the code, and vice versa.

On top of this it is likely that the artefacts are not always internally consistent as well as externally consistent. Both types of consistency refer to the correct and consistent usage of terminology and concepts. For internal consistency this usage is confined to one artefact. In the case of external consistency it boils down to the consistent and correct usage between different artefacts. Most of the time these inconsistencies are a direct result of the implicitness of knowledge such as the links between the artefacts. Let's say that a person wants to consider a certain artefact for reuse, both violations of consistency will be quite confusing and will seriously hamper performing this task.

To overcome these problems we propose the use of an ontology as a store for this knowledge and as a driving medium to support the persons who are charged with executing reuse and maintenance activities. For this purpose the different concepts, that are represented in the artefacts, will be defined and stored in the ontology. To obtain an initial set of concepts we will complement the already existing application engineering cycle with a domain engineering cycle. This combination is quite similar to the *dual life-cycle* as presented by Reifer in [6]. Subsequently these concepts will be "glued" to the different (elements of) artefacts through extensional and intensional concept definitions. This will enable a bi-directional navigation between the concepts represented in the conceptual artefacts (e.g. `Car Fleet Management`) and their concrete realizations in the code (e.g. a group of classes).

This research was partially performed in the context of the SoFa project ("Component Development in a SOftware FActory : Organization, Process and Tools"). During this project we delimited our scope of investigation to *Business Support Systems*. Such systems are characterized by the fact that they support knowledge intensive, enterprise critical processes that are cooperatively performed by groups of knowledgeable business workers. In what follows we will assume that the applications of which we speak comply to this characterization.

In this paper we will mainly focus on the concept-part of the approach we envision. Since this depends heavily upon the use of an ontology we will provide a detailed description in Section 2. In it we will briefly discuss our motivation for selecting ontologies as a medium for our approach. Next we will elaborate on our view on ontologies where we will present a notion of concept networks and concept roles. To conclude the section we will present the SoFaCB (SoFa ConceptBrowser) ontology tool. In Section 3 we will sketch how we put this ontology tool into effect to support reuse and maintenance activities. In this section we will present intensional and extensional concept definitions as a way to couple concepts to artefacts/code. To end the section we will propose task ontologies as a way to overcome the gap between broad concepts and their narrow concrete realizations.

2 An Ontology in a Concept-oriented Approach

In computer science there are many different interpretations of what an ontology is or should be. Most of the time this interpretation is depending heavily upon the application in which the ontology is used. We prefer to use the popular but rather abstract definition of Gruber [4], being that an ontology is an explicit specification of a conceptualization. If we instantiate this definition for our work we get that an ontology represents a certain view on an application domain, in which we define the concepts that live in this domain in an unambiguous and explicit way. An important aspect of an ontology, which we believe is not covered by the definition of Gruber, is the referential role that this explicit specification (the concepts) plays. This means that it is used as a work of reference and that there exists a strict commitment from the users towards the meaning of these concepts i.e. an *ontological commitment* is enforced. To avoid confusion we would like to stress that it is not our goal to create rigorous formal ontologies for the application domains under consideration. Instead we prefer a lightweight approach where it is desirable but not necessary to end up with a set of concepts that is usable as a standard for a larger community.

In the following subsection we will motivate the choice of an ontology as a medium for our approach. Next we will zoom in on our view on an ontology in terms of a concept network and the way the concepts in such a network can play different roles depending on the application context. We will conclude this section with a brief discussion of our lightweight ontology tool SoFaCB.

2.1 Ontology as a Medium : Motivation

If we keep our definition in mind and we retake the issues of implicit knowledge and internal/external consistency, it should become clear why we chose an ontology as a medium for our approach.

First of all, since an ontology is supposed to be an *explicit* specification of a conceptualization, it is natural to use it to capture and store this knowledge. That way we obtain a means to share this knowledge, which would otherwise remain inside the heads of the people who built the original system. Secondly, since an ontology is intended to define the kinds of things that exist in a domain, it provides a number of standard concepts to capture and organize these things. Examples of such concepts are identity, essence, and the subsumption relationship. Thirdly, since the knowledge is now made available in an explicit form it becomes possible to refer to it from within the different artefacts. This will greatly reduce the above-mentioned consistency problems which is mainly a result of the enforced ontological commitment from the artefact-creators towards the used terminology and concepts. Moreover this explicit specification will also prove beneficial for the comprehensiveness of the artefacts they produce. This could be attributed to the fact that a novice to the software system will have a cross-referenced dictionary-alike documentation of the artefacts to his or her disposal.

2.2 Concept Networks and Concept Roles

In Figure 1 we show an example of a partial concept network which we will use throughout this text. To enhance readability we will refer to these concepts by their preferred-label instead of their unique concept numbers. The `Toy Example` domain contains three concepts (clouds): `Car Fleet Management`, `Car`, and `Company Car`. In the `core` domain we have only shown two principal concepts: `Concept`, and `Domain`. All of these concepts are defined by their surrounding definitions. These definitions are connected to the concepts by relations (arrows). For instance for the `Car` concept, the definition slots used are: `has-preferred-label`, `has-definition`, and `has-image`. To introduce a new concept it suffices to "instantiate" the concept `Concept` and fill in the corresponding definition slots. Doing so you obtain a network structure that is very similar to conceptual graphs [8].

In a concept network we adhere the view that every element in it is a concept. This means that the relations we use are also represented by concepts. Thus the system is said to be self-contained. To group a set of related concepts we have introduced a `Domain` concept. The

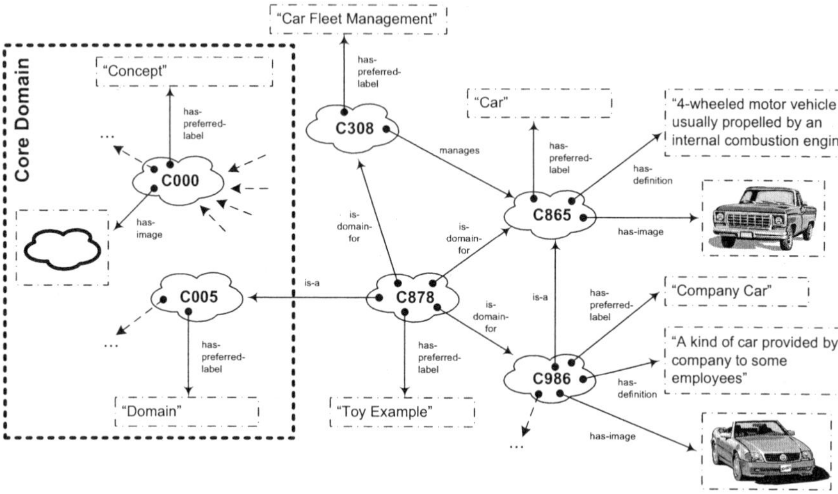

Figure 1: An example of a partial concept network

semantics of this is that concepts can belong to many domains. As shown in the example, the `Domain` concept belongs to the `core` domain. This domain can be seen as an ontology for the concepts in the right part of the figure since these are described in terms of it.

If we generalize this observation we get three 'concept roles' in an ontology : a core role, a domain structural role, and an application role. These roles correspond to *virtual layers* in the ontology, where the concepts in the (bottom) application layer are described in terms of the concepts in the (middle) domain structural layer which are finally described in terms of the concepts in the (top) core layer. In our example you find concepts such as the `Manages` relationship in a domain structural role. The core role is taken up by concepts such as `Concept`, `is-a`, ..., enabling us to create the `Company Car` concept for instance. Finally we have concepts with an application role such as `Car`, and `Car Fleet Management`. Note that concepts can shift their roles according to the context in which they are used. For example if we describe the concepts for a specific car fleet management application, then the `Car` and `Company Car` concepts will be used in a domain structural role.

2.3 *The SoFaCB Ontology Tool*

Many excellent tools for building and managing ontologies are already available [1, 2]. Since we pursued a lightweight approach and since we wanted to gain experience in the do's and don'ts in this field, we nevertheless decided to create our own lightweight tool from scratch. In this light we found the report [3] from the creators of Protégé very useful. This report presents the evolution of their work and several issues regarding ontology tool building.

In Figure 2 we present a snapshot of the SoFaCB tool in which we visualize the concept `car` from the example in Figure 1. The value types for concept definitions that are currently allowed are limited to text, images, and concepts. Note that what is shown in the right pane of the browser is the on-the-fly HTML-translation of the underlying concept network for the

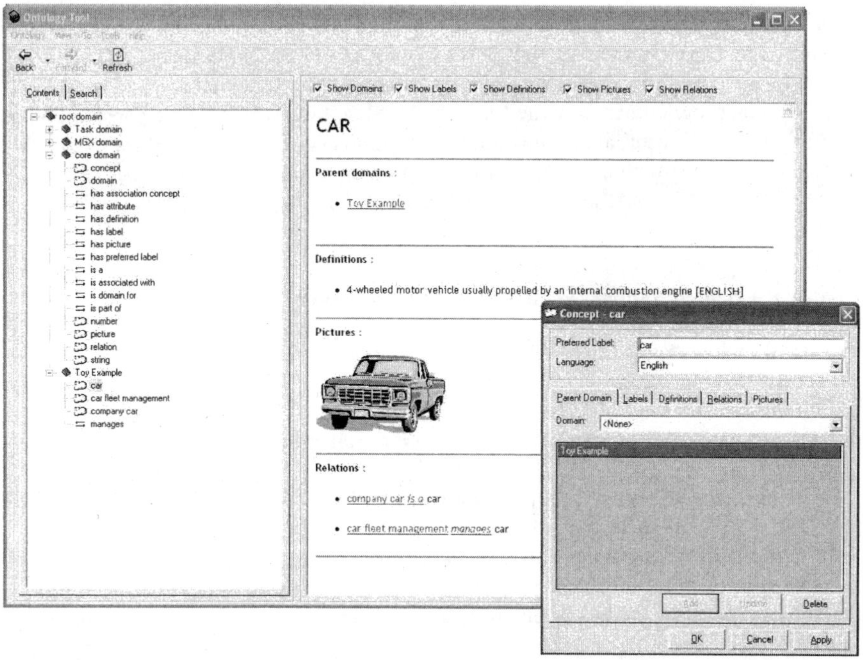

Figure 2: A snapshot of the SoFaCB tool. The left pane of the browser shows the available concepts, and the right pane shows the details of the selected concept. The smaller window on the foreground is used to enter values for the definition slots of a new concept.

selected concept.

Since a lot of domain models are represented as UML diagrams (class diagrams and activity diagrams) we have included a Rational Rose importer that translates these models into a concept network representation.

Besides being lightweight, our prototype tool was also intended to be as generic as possible. With this we mean that the number of hard-coded concepts had to be limited (or ultimately non-existent). This objective becomes difficult to obtain when confronted with the higher level concepts. Examples of such (core) concepts are `concept`, `association`, `is-a`, ... By keeping these concepts soft-coded it becomes possible to adapt the tool from within itself. This is in part facilitated by our data model, which we kept as simple and as generic as possible, and the fact that the tool directly uses certain concept definitions to provide its functionality. A very simple example of the latter is the "fluffy cloud" image attached to the concept `concept`, which is used by the tool as an icon in the tree-view. More advanced uses of this reflective behavior would be to change the template for the definition slots (and corresponding user interface) for creating a new concept.

As a result of a number of non-functional requirements in the project that supported this research, we were not able to carry this genericity to its limit. For instance, in the current version it is not possible to alter some of the definitions of the core concepts because many of them are hard-wired into the tool. Presently we have started work on a new version of the tool in Smalltalk in which we will eliminate this issue. In it we will also include intensional and extensional concept definition types in SOUL (Smalltalk Open Unification Language) [9]. SOUL is an interpreter for Prolog that runs on top of a Smalltalk implementation. Besides allowing Prolog programmers to write 'ordinary' Prolog, SOUL enables the construction of Prolog programs to reason about Smalltalk code. Amongst others this enables declarative reasoning about the structure of object-oriented programs and declarative code generation. The use of these intensional and extensional concept definition types will be explained in section 3.

3 Concept-oriented Support for Reuse and Maintenance

As we stated in the introduction, we will complement the application engineering cycle with a domain engineering cycle. Central to both cycles will be the ontology, which is used as the point of reference for the concepts. Initially the domain engineering cycle will provide the core set of concepts and relations that are used in the artefacts constructed in the application engineering cycle.

Whenever a reuse activity is initiated we will use the ontology to locate the asset to be reused. This is done by identifying the concepts needed to accomplish the reuse action, and by using the attached extensional and intensional concept definitions to locate the artefacts that 'implement' them. A similar approach is followed to support maintenance activities. In the following subsection we will briefly introduce the idea of both concept definition types.

3.1 Linking Concepts to Artefacts

Intensional and extensional concept definition types were based on the idea of software views as described in Mens *et al.* [5] and will make it possible to connect the concepts in the ontology to actual Smalltalk entities. An extensional definition will summarize all the entities to which we want to link a certain concept. Conversely an intensional definition will be represented by a SOUL-'formula' which makes it possible to calculate the corresponding Smalltalk entities. The former definition type is easy to formulate (just enumerate the entities), but is rather static and of limited use in highly evolving implementations. The latter can sometimes be very difficult to formulate (a logic rule must be formulated that describes the Smalltalk entities you want) but provides a highly dynamic and very powerful mechanism for code reasoning/querying purposes.

Even now that we have identified a mechanism that allows us to connect concepts to artefacts/code, one main question remains unanswered : How do you link very broad concepts (such as `Car Fleet Management`) to scattered code entities (such as a group of classes)? The answer to this question lies in the use of task ontologies which we will describe in the next subsection.

3.2 Describing High-level Concepts with Task Ontologies

We have based our idea of task ontologies on task models as described by Schreiber *et al.* in the *CommonKADS* methodology [7]. Task models allow us to abstract and to position the different tasks within a business process. A task is a subpart of a business process that represents a goal-oriented activity. Popularly stated, a task model provides a decomposition of high level tasks into subtasks together with their inputs/outputs and I/O flow that connects them. The actual implementation of a task is described by one or more task methods. It is the decomposition of the high-level tasks into subtasks that we use to decompose broad (task-oriented) concepts into narrower concepts. This makes it possible to bridge the gap between broad concepts and Smalltalk entities.

To validate the idea of task ontologies we have set up an experiment in which we used the prototype tool to create a simple ontology which enabled us to express *task ontologies*. Consequently we used these concepts in the task ontology to describe the task models of a certain domain. Within this research project we have successfully used SoFaCB to describe a set of task models in the broadcasting domain. In this case you find concepts such as `Task`, `Input`, `Task Method`, ... in a domain structural role. The core role is taken up by concepts such as `Concept`, `is-a`, ..., enabling us to create the `Task` concept for instance. Within the broadcasting domain we have concepts with an application role such as `Transmission Schedule Management` (as a `Task`), `Pre-transmission Schedule` (as `Input`), `Transmission Schedule Deviations` (as `Input`), and `Post-transmission Schedule` (as `Output`). Remember that concepts can shift their roles according to the context in which they are used. For example if we describe a task method (a concrete implementation of a task), then the `Transmission Schedule Management` concept will be used in a domain structural role. To bridge the gap between the broad `Transmission Management` concept and the code, we will decompose it into subtasks such as `Verify Schedule`, `Generate Schedule Difference`, ...

Providing a business analyst with a task model makes it possible to direct him/her to ask a client questions about the needed task method with respect to the abstract task model. When basic components are created that correspond to the general tasks in the task model, it consequently becomes possible to propose a solution within the boundaries of the existing technological infrastructure. With respect to reuse these task models can thus be used to guide business analysts in performing a business analysis in which the task models are instantiated and adapted to satisfy specific customer needs.

4 Conclusion

In this paper we have presented an ontology as a medium for a concept-oriented approach to support software maintenance and reuse activities. This approach uses the ontology to capture (implicit) knowledge in software development artefacts as concepts. In this explicit form it becomes possible to share these concepts that would otherwise remain hidden with the people originally involved in the development of the system. Moreover it becomes possible to use the ontology as a point of reference which will improve the consistency of the software artefacts produced. As a means to link concepts to artefacts/code we propose the use of intensional and extensional concept definition types in SOUL. These will serve as a vehicle that enables a bi-directional navigation between both sides. To overcome the ‘conceptual gap’ between broad concepts and fine-grained (scattered) implementation artefacts we have presented task ontologies. Even though the research we presented here is still in its infancy we were already able to successfully validate some of these ideas in the IWT research project SoFa. During this project we successfully used our SoFaCB ontology tool to represent a task ontology within the broadcasting domain with which we supported business analysts in advocating reuse.

Acknowledgements

This work has been supported in part by the SoFa project ("Component Development and Product Assembly in a Software Factory : Organization, Process and Tools"). This project was subsidized by the Institute for the Promotion of Innovation by Science and Technology in Flanders (IWT) and took place in cooperation with MediaGeniX and EDS Belgium.

References

[1] O. Corcho, M. Fernández-López, and A. Gómez Pérez. IST project IST-2000-29243 : OntoWeb - Ontology-based information exchange for knowledge management and electronic commerce : D1.1. technical roadmap v1.0. http://babage.dia.fi.upm.es/ontoweb/wp1/OntoRoadMap/index.html, 2001.

[2] A.J. Duineveld, R. Stoter, M.R. Weiden, B. Kenepa, and V.R. Benjamins. Wondertools? A comparative study of ontological engineering tools. In *Proceedings of the 12 th International Workshop on Knowledge Acquisition, Modeling and Mangement (KAW'99)*, Banff, Canada, 1999. Kluwer Academic Publishers.

[3] W. Grosso, H. Eriksson, R. Fergerson, J. Gennari, S. Tu, and M. Musen. Knowledge modeling at the millennium – the design and evolution of protégé-2000. In *Proceedings of the 12 th International Workshop on Knowledge Acquisition, Modeling and Mangement (KAW'99)*, Banff, Canada, 1999.

[4] T.R. Gruber. Towards principles for the design of ontologies used for knowledge sharing. In N. Guarino and R. Poli, editors, *Formal Ontology in Conceptual Analysis and Knowledge Representation*, Deventer, The Netherlands, 1993. Kluwer Academic Publishers.

[5] K. Mens, T. Mens, and M. Wermelinger. Maintaining software through intentional source-code views. Software Engineering and Knowledge Engineering (SEKE2002), Ischia, Italy, 2002.

[6] D. J. Reifer. *Practical Software Reuse.* Wiley Computer Publishing, 1997.

[7] G. Schreiber. *Knowledge Engineering and Management - The CommonKADS Methodology - A software engineering approach for knowledge intensive systems.* MIT Press, 2000.

[8] J.F. Sowa. *Conceptual Structures - Information Processing in Mind and Machine.* The Systems Programming Series, Addison-Wesley, 1984.

[9] R. Wuyts. *A Logic Meta-Programming Approach to Support the Co-evolution of Object-Oriented Design and Implementation.* PhD thesis, Vrije Universiteit Brussel, Programming Technology Lab, Brussels, Belgium, 2001.

Knowledge-based Software Engineering
T. Welzer et al. (Eds.)
IOS Press, 2002

Meta-data and ER Model Automatic Generation from Unstructured Information Resources

Javier Gramajo, David Riaño
Department of Computer Engineering and Mathematics
Universitat Rovira i Virgili, Tarragona, Spain
{jgramajo, drianyo}@etse.urv.es

Abstract

The huge amount of data in the Internet requires sophisticated tools to retrieve information. Here we introduce GINY, a framework that allows us to retrieve and reuse the information that is available in the Internet, GINY generates a data structure which is based in an ER model or generates a resource description framework RDF.

1 Introduction

The amount of data in the Internet has grown rapidly since its conception in 1969. With the introduction of search engines we can access the Web and use the information retrieved.

The best search engines claim that they can deal with the whole Web. That is to say, they can continue indexing the entire Web as it grows.

The Web is a distributed, dynamic, and rapidly growing information resource, which presents difficulties to traditional, information retrieval systems. Those systems were designed for different environments and have typically been used for indexing a static collection of directly accessible documents. The nature of the Web brings up important questions as whether the centralized architecture of the search engines can deal with the expanding number of documents? and if they can regularly update their databases to detect modified, deleted, and relocated information?

The answers to these questions impact both on the best search methodology to use when searching the Web and also on the future of the Web search technology. Any serious search system has to define three aspects which are, the information that is been looked for, the description of the search that it is been made, and the data structure that is been used to store the information retrieved. So, a search engine can be interested in either the data that is on the Web or the links to the source pages (metadata), and also in organizing the search criteria and the returned information as a list of terms, as a database or as an ontology.

For example, the system Jasper [1] is based on the search and organization of web page links according to the interest of a set of users which is expressed as a dynamic list of keywords that the system searches in the web pages. On the contrary, TSIMMIS [2] is concerned with the integration of data that comes form heterogeneous sources in an Object Exchange Model (OEM) that can be locally accessed. Recent works as On2broker [3] show the increasing need of using ontologies to represent the search condition and the data retrieved, as well.

In this paper we introduce a new methodology that allows us to transform a retrieved data set from an Internet search in a conceptual Entity-Relationship Data Model (ER), that can be translated into a Relational Database or into a RDF Knowledge-base format that is used to store the web retrieved data.

Section 2 describes the GINY's framework [4] where that methodology has been implemented. Section 3 describes the process used to obtain the conceptual ER Data Model and the DDL and RDF database and knowledge-base generators. Finally, section 4 contains some tests and results of the process, and section 5 some conclusions and future work.

2 Description of the GINY's Framework

GINY is a framework that allows us to get a content structure automatically. We selected an unsupervised Clustering [5] process to find the structure that should store the information about a domain that is represented as a keyword (*domain name*) and a set of properties (*domain description*).

As figure 1 shows, GINY is organized as a front-end where users make queries and obtain answers on a centralized database. Simultaneously, users can define search domains that are managed by the Search Definition Ontology Module. The back-end takes a search domain and uses a search engine to retrieve web information about the selected domain ontology. This information is used by the Data Structure Extractor to obtain a conceptual ER model to store the retrieved data. This model can produce both a DDL script that defines a relational database or a RDF description of a knowledge-base that are able to store the retrieved information.

To understand the functioning of these components a route through the model is displayed in figure 1. Whenever a user wants to make a query he has to define an ontology that describes the domain of interest, the query is sent to the search engine that looks for web pages that contain information that is related to the search ontology. These pages are analyzed by the Natural Language Analyzer that represents the answer as a data table. Finally, that table is given to the Data Structure Extractor Module that generates the data and knowledge structures and fills them with the web information that the user can access with SQL queries.

This work is about the description of some Artificial Intelligence techniques applied by the Data Structure Extractor in order to automatically obtain a conceptual data model that is transformed into DDL or RDF files. The rest of the GINY components are described in [4].

3 The Description of the Data Structure Extraction Process

GINY's main contribution is to transform a data matrix with interesting information into a conceptual data model that is implemented as a relational database or a resource description knowledge-base. During this process, an unsupervised clustering algorithm is used.

3.1 The Input Data Matrix

The data obtained from the Internet is organized in a data matrix where each column represents a feature of the data and the rows contain the values associated to that features. This is interpreted as an extension of the intension that the search ontologies in section 2 describe. From the database perspective it is possible to view the matrix as an entity where the rows are the registers and the columns the attributes of the entity in a Entity-Relationship model

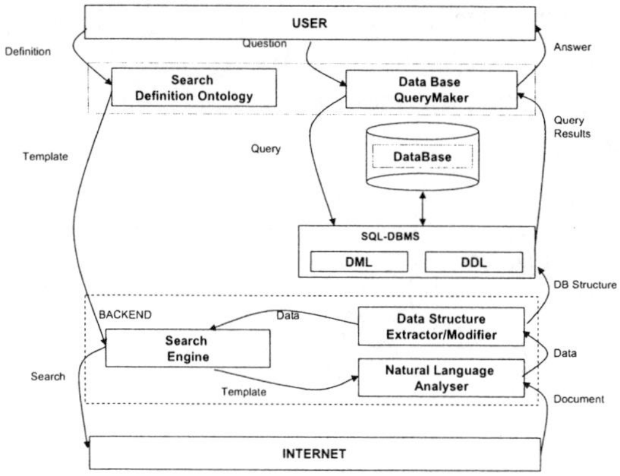

Figure 1: GINY's Framework Model.

(ER). The extraction of the data structure is a procedure in which the initial matrix is used to construct an ER model.

3.2 The ER Conceptual Model Generation

Figure 2 describes the process of transforming a single entity structure (data matrix) into a ER model. This process starts with the *entity discovery* procedure. This procedure uses the Pearson's correlation function to compute a distance matrix that shows the degree of correlation between the features in the data matrix. The matrix values are taken in their absolute value because we are interested in the degree of the relation between the features (magnitude) and not in the character of the relation (sign).

Once the distance matrix is obtained we apply the Johnson's algorithm [5] to determine the clusters. Each cluster contains a highly correlated subset of features that are not very correlated to the features in other clusters. This drives the process toward the construction of optimal groups of features that GINY interprets as the entities of the final ER model. In the Johnson's algorithm clusters are determined from a changing pivot value that relates the two most correlated features. This can be made using two strategies: *Single-Link* and *Complete-Link*. The difference between them depends on the selection criterion that takes features with the less minimum correlation or with the less maximum correlation, respectively.

The number of clusters representing the model entities is determined by an input parameter called *ClustersNumber*, which can vary between one and the maximum number of columns of the data matrix.

Now, the *relationship discovery* process starts (see figure 3). GINY uses the minimal-square function to reduce similar data within the same entity. The parameter *ValueThreshold* defines the concept of similarity in a range between 0% and 100%. If the value of the minimal-square function is smaller than the parameter, one of the two compared rows is removed. This process is applied to each cluster obtaining a percentage of reduction *LevelReduction*.

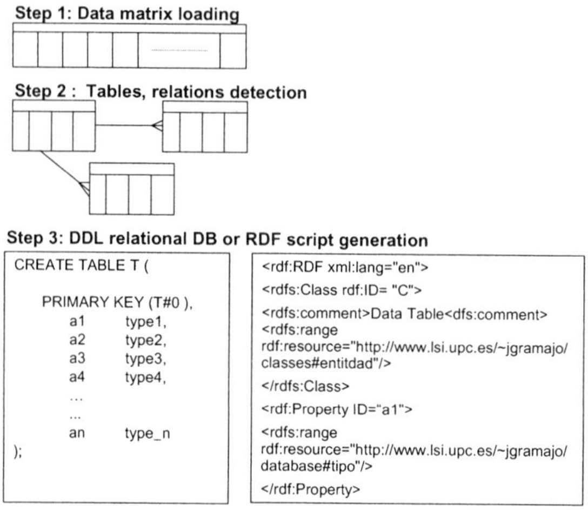

Figure 2: Steps to get conceptual data model.

Any two reduced entities define an M:N relationship, if only one of the entities is reduced the relationship is 1:N, and if none of them is reduced the relationship is 1:1.

3.3 Script Generation

As figure 2 shows, once the ER model is obtained, two kinds of scripts can be generated: a DDL database description and an RDF knowledge-base description.

The DDL (Database Definition Language) script is made of a sequence of SQL [6] commands that construct a relational database that implements the ER model. See figure 4.

The RDF (Resource Description Framework) script contains a meta-data representation schema [7] that represents a knowledge-base that defines the ER model as an ontology. See

```
for i =1..ClustersNumber - 1 {
    Table creation with cluster[i] attributes;
    if (table_level_reduction[i] >  0%)
    then {
        for j = i+1 .. ClustersNumber {
        if (Abs(distances[i,j]) >= Abs (MinValue))
           and (table_level_reduction[j] == 0%)
        then
            Add a reference from cluster[j]
            as a foreign key in table[i];
        }
      }
    }
```

Figure 3: Relations detection algorithm.

```
CREATE TABLE NAME_0
(
    PRIMARY KEY ( NameKey#0 ),
    height     real,
    pblack     real,
    pand       real,
    blackand   real,
    wbtrans    real
);

CREATE TABLE NAME_1
(
    PRIMARY KEY ( NameKey#1 ),
    lenght     real,
    eccen      real,
    blackpix   real
);

CREATE TABLE NAME_2
(
    PRIMARY KEY ( NameKey#2 ),
    area       real,
    meantr     real
);

CREATE TABLE NAME_0_2
(
    PRIMARY KEY ( NameKey#0_2 ),
    FOREIGN KEY ( NameKey#0)
        REFERENCES NAME_0
        ON DELETE CASCADE
        ON UPDATE CASCADE,

    FOREIGN KEY ( NameKey#2)
        REFERENCES NAME_2
        ON DELETE CASCADE
        ON UPDATE CASCADE
);

CREATE TABLE NAME_1_2
(
    PRIMARY KEY ( NameKey#1_2 ),
    FOREIGN KEY ( NameKey#1)
        REFERENCES NAME_1
        ON DELETE CASCADE
        ON UPDATE CASCADE,

    FOREIGN KEY ( NameKey#2)
        REFERENCES NAME_2
        ON DELETE CASCADE
        ON UPDATE CASCADE
);
```

Figure 4: DDL Script from the entity-relation Model ER.

an example in figure 5.

Scripts comes from the ER model where entities are transformed into tables or classes, attributes are transformed into columns or properties, and relationships are transformed into foreign keys or descriptions.

4 Tests and Results

The automatic extraction of the data structure has been tested with two domains from the University of Irvine (UCI) repository: *Bupa* that has 7 attributes and 345 elements and *Page-segments* that has 18 attributes and 210 elements.

Bupa is about blood tests on liver disorders that might arise from excessive alcohol consumption. Each data in the bupa data file represents a single male person. *Page-segments* is about the analysis of text and graphs in documents. The problem consists in classifying all the blocks of the page layout of a document that has been detected by a segmentation process.

All the attributes are numerical and they do not contain missing values. These restrictions eliminate some problems that are not important at this moment.

GINY has set to obtain three clusters (*ClusterNumber* = *3*), the threshold value to 2% (*ThresholdValue* = *0,02*), and the clustering strategy to Complete-Link.

Figures 4 and 5 shows the final scripts. The tables and the classes obtained do not attend to any semantic coherence between columns and properties, but to a storage optimization.

5 Conclusions

Non-structured information in the Internet makes tools as GINY necessary to obtain an structure to contain the information retrieved from distributed data sources.

The inference of a conceptual data model has been solved with a learning algorithm, which allows the generation of two alternative data and knowledge structures. The process

```
<rdf:RDF xml:lang="en"> <rdfs:Class rdf:ID= " name_0">
<rdfs:comment>Data Table<dfs:comment> <rdfs:range
rdf:resource="http://www.lsi.upc.es/jgramajo/classes#Entity"/>
</rdf:Class>

<rdf:Property ID="nameKey_0">  <rdfs:range
rdf:resource="http://www.lsi.upc.es/jgramajo/database#Integer"/>
</rdf:Property>

<rdf:Property ID="mcv"> <rdfs:comment>mcv</rdfs:comment>
<rdfs:range
rdf:resource="http://www.lsi.upc.es/jgramajo/database#real"/>
</rdfs:domain rdf:resource="#name_0"/> </rdf:Property>

<rdf:Property ID="alkphos"> <rdfs:comment>alkphos</rdfs:comment>
<rdfs:range
rdf:resource="http://www.lsi.upc.es/jgramajo/database#real"/>
</rdfs:domain rdf:resource="#name_0"/>
...
```

Figure 5: Script generado Descripción de Contenidos, RDF.

starts with an entity discovery stage, that is followed by a relationship discovery stage, and finishes with the script generation.

Up to now, non-semantic conceptual models for numerical data can be inferred. In the next future GINY can be extended to generate semantic models based on numeric and alphanumeric data by the use of conceptual clustering techniques.

Acknowledgements

This work has been partially supported by h-TechSight under grant number IST-2001-33174 by The European Commission.

References

[1] J. Davies, R. Weeks, and M. Revett. Jasper: Communicating information agents for the www,. In *Web Conf. (Boston MA, Dec.1995), World Wide Web Journal Vol. 1, 1,*, pages 473–482, O'Reilly, Sebastopol CA, 1995.

[2] Sudarshan Chawathe, Hector Garcia-Molina, Joachim Hammer, Kelly Ireland, Yannis Papakonstantinou, Jeffrey D. Ullman, and Jennifer Widom. The TSIMMIS project: Integration of heterogeneous information sources. In *16th Meeting of the Information Processing Society of Japan*, pages 7–18, Tokyo, Japan, 1994.

[3] Dieter Fensel, Jrgen Angele, Stefan Decker, Michael Erdmann, Hans-Peter Schnurr, Rudi Studer, and Andreas Witt. On2broker: Lessons learned from applying ai to the web.

[4] David Riaño and Javier Gramajo. Automatic extraction of data structure. Technical report, Universitat Rovira i Virgili, October 2000.

[5] Anil k. Jain and Richard C. Dubes. *Algorithms for Clustering Data.* Prentice-Hall Inc., 1988.

[6] Judith S. Bowman, Sandra L. Emerson, and Marcy Darnovsky. *The practical SQL Handbook. Using Strcutured Query Language.* Addison Wesley, 3 edition, 1998.

[7] *RDF, Resource Description Framework.* http://www.w3.org/TR/rdfs-schema.

Knowledge-based Software Engineering
T. Welzer et al. (Eds.)
IOS Press, 2002

On Efficiency of Dataset Filtering Implementations in Constraint-Based Discovery of Frequent Itemsets

Marek WOJCIECHOWSKI, Maciej ZAKRZEWICZ
Poznan University of Technology, Institute of Computing Science,
ul. Piotrowo 3a, 60-965 Poznan, Poland
{marek,mzakrz}@cs.put.poznan.pl

Abstract. Discovery of frequent itemsets is one of the fundamental data mining problems. Typically, the goal is to discover all the itemsets whose support in the source dataset exceeds a user-specified threshold. However, very often users want to restrict the set of frequent itemsets to be discovered by adding extra constraints on size and contents of the itemsets. Many constraint-based frequent itemset discovery techniques have been proposed recently. One of the techniques, called dataset filtering, is based on the observation that for some classes of constraints, itemsets satisfying them can only be supported by transactions that satisfy the same constraints. Conceptually, dataset filtering transforms a given data mining task into an equivalent one operating on a smaller dataset. In this paper we discuss possible implementations of dataset filtering, evaluating their strengths and weaknesses.

1. Introduction

Discovery of frequent itemsets is one of the fundamental data mining problems. Informally, frequent itemsets are subsets frequently occurring in a collection of sets of items. Discovery of frequent itemsets is a key step in association rule mining [1] but the itemsets themselves also provide useful information on the correlations between items in the database. Typically, the goal is to discover all the itemsets whose support in the source dataset exceeds a user-specified threshold.

The most popular algorithm performing the above task is Apriori introduced in [3]. Apriori reduces the search space by exploiting the following property: an itemset cannot be frequent if any of its subsets is not frequent. The algorithm iteratively generates candidate itemsets from previously found smaller frequent itemsets, and then verifies them in the database. Apriori can be regarded as a classic algorithm that served as a basis for many Apriori-like algorithms offering various performance improvements in frequent itemset mining or adapted to discovery of other types of frequent patterns. Recently, a new family of pattern discovery algorithms, called pattern-growth methods [5], has been developed for discovery of frequent itemsets and other patterns. The methods project databases based on the currently discovered frequent patterns and grow such patterns to longer ones in corresponding projected databases. Pattern-growth methods are supposed to perform better than Apriori-like algorithms in case of low minimum support thresholds. Nevertheless, practical studies [10] show that for real datasets Apriori (or its variants) might still be a better solution.

It has been observed that very often users want to restrict the set of frequent itemsets to be discovered by adding extra constraints on size and contents of the itemsets. It is obvious that additional constraints for itemsets can be verified in a post-processing step, after all itemsets exceeding a given minimum support threshold have been discovered. Nevertheless, such a solution cannot be considered satisfactory since users providing advanced selection criteria may expect that the data mining system will exploit them in the mining process to improve performance. In other words, the system should concentrate on itemsets that are interesting from the user's point of view, rather than waste time on discovering itemsets the user has not asked for [4].

Many constraint-based frequent itemset discovery techniques have been proposed recently for various constraint models. One of the techniques, called dataset filtering [9], is based on the observation that for some classes of constraints, itemsets satisfying them can only be supported by transactions that satisfy the same constraints. The method is distinct from other constraint-based discovery techniques which modify the candidate generation procedure of Apriori [6][8]. Dataset filtering can be applied to two simple but useful in practice types of constraints: the minimum required size of an itemset and the presence of a given subset of items in the itemset.

Conceptually, dataset filtering transforms a given data mining task into an equivalent one operating on a smaller dataset. Thus, it can be integrated with other constraint-based pattern discovery techniques within any pattern discovery algorithm. In this paper we focus on the integration of dataset filtering techniques with the classic Apriori algorithm for the discovery of frequent itemsets. We discuss possible implementations of dataset filtering within Apriori, evaluating their strengths and weaknesses.

1.1 Related Work

Item constraints in frequent itemset (and association rule) mining were first discussed in [8]. Constraints considered there had a form of a Boolean expression in the disjunctive normal form built from elementary predicates requiring that a certain item is or is not present. The algorithms presented were Apriori variants using sophisticated candidate generation techniques.

In [6], two interesting classes of itemset constraints were introduced: anti-monotonicity and succinctness, and methods of handling constraints belonging to these classes within the Apriori framework were presented. The methods for succinct constraints again consisted in modifying the candidate generation procedure. For anti-monotone constraints it was observed that in fact almost no changes to Apriori are required to handle them. A constraint is anti-monotone if the fact that an itemset satisfies it, implies that all of its subsets have to satisfy the constraint too. The minimum support threshold is an example of an anti-monotone constraint, and any extra constraints of that class can be used together with it in candidate pruning.

In [7], constraint-based discovery of frequent itemsets was analyzed in the context of pattern-growth methodology. In the paper, further classes of constraints were introduced, some of which could not be incorporated into the Apriori framework.

1.2 Organization of the Paper

In section 2 we provide basic definitions concerning discovery of frequent itemsets and review of the classic Apriori algorithm. Section 3 presents possible implementations of dataset filtering techniques within Apriori. Section 4 presents and discusses the results of the experiments that we conducted to evaluate and compare the performance gains offerred by particular implementations of dataset filtering. We conlude with a summary of achieved results in section 5.

2. Background

2.1 Basic Definitions

Let $L=\{l_1, l_2, ..., l_m\}$ be a set of literals, called items. An *itemset* X is a non-empty set of items ($X\subseteq L$). The *size* of an itemset X (denoted as $|X|$) is the number of items in X. Let D be a set of variable size itemsets, where each itemset T in D has a unique identifier and is called a *transaction*. We say that a transaction T *supports* an item $x\in L$ if x is in T. We say that a transaction T *supports* an itemset $X\subseteq L$ if T supports every item in the set X. The *support* of the itemset X is the percentage of transactions in D that support X. The problem of mining frequent itemsets in D consists in discovering all itemsets whose support is above a user-defined support threshold.

Given two itemsets X and Y such that $Y\subseteq X$, $X' = X \setminus Y$ (the set difference of X and Y) is called a *projection* of X with respect to the subset Y. Given a database D and an itemset Y, a *Y-projected database* can be constructed from D by removing transactions that do not support Y, and then replacing the remaining transactions by their projections with respect to Y.

2.2 Review of the Apriori Algorithm

Apriori relies on the property that an itemset can only be frequent if all of its subsets are frequent. It leads to a level-wise procedure. First, all possible 1-itemsets (itemsets containing 1 item) are counted in the database to determine frequent 1-itemsets. Then, frequent 1-itemsets are combined to form potentially frequent 2-itemsets, called candidate 2-itemsets. Candidate 2-itemsets are counted in the database to determine frequent 2-itemsets. The procedure is continued by combining the frequent 2-itemsets to form candidate 3-itemsets and so forth. The algorithm stops when in a certain iteration none of the candidates turns out to be frequent or the set of generated candidates is empty.

3. Dataset Filtering Within the Apriori Framework

In our simple constraint model we assume that a user specifies two extra constraints together with the minimum support threshold: the required subset S and the minimum size threshold s. Thus, the problem consists in discovering all frequent itemsets including S and having size greater than s. We assume that a user may specify both extra constraints or only one of them. If the latter is the case, $S = \varnothing$ or $s = 0$, depending on which constraint has been omitted. The constraints we consider are simple examples of item and size constraints. However, it should be noted that these constraints are more difficult to handle within the Apriori framework than their negations: the requirement that a certain set is not included in an itemset and the maximum allowed size of an itemset. The latter two constraints are anti-monotone and therefore can be handled by Apriori in the same way the minimum support constraint is used.

On the other hand, the constraints we consider can be handled by dataset filtering techniques. It is obvious that itemsets including the set S can be supported only by transactions also supporting S, and itemsets whose size exceeds s can be supported only by transactions of size greater than s. Therefore, according to the idea of dataset filtering, the actual frequent itemset discovery can be performed on the subset on the source dataset consisting from all the transactions supporting S, and having size greater than s. It should be noted that frequent itemsets discovered in the filtered dataset may also include those not supporting the item or size constraints (the post-processing itemset filtering phase is still required).

The correctness of application of dataset filtering for our constraint model comes from the fact that the number of transactions supporting itemsets satisfying the constraints will be the same in the original and filtered datasets. It should be noted that the support of itemsets not satisfying user-specified constraints, counted in the filtered dataset, can be smaller than their actual support in the original dataset, but it is not a problem since these itemsets will not be returned to the user. Moreover, this is in fact a positive feature as it can reduce the number of generated candidates not leading to itemsets of user's interest. Since we assume that a user specifies the minimum support threshold as a percentage of the total number of transactions in the source dataset, in all implementations of Apriori with dataset filtering, during the first iteration the required number of supporting transactions is derived from the support threshold provided by a user and the total number of transactions found in the dataset.

Regarding integration of dataset filtering with the Apriori algorithm, there are two general implementation strategies. The filtered dataset can either be physically materialized on disk during the first iteration or filtering can be performed on-line in each iteration. We also observe that if the required subset is not empty, the idea of projection with respect to the required subset can by applied to reduce the size of the filtered dataset (meaningful if the filtered dataset is to be materialized) and the number of iterations. In such a case, frequent itemsets are being discovered in the projected dataset and then are extended with the required subset with respect to which the projection has been performed. If apart from the required subset constraint, the minimum size threshold is also present, projection has to be coupled with filtering according to the size constraint. Thus, we have four possible implementations of dataset filtering within the Apriori framework, leading to the following four Apriori variants (all the algorithms presented below take a collection D of transactions, the minimum support threshold, the required subset S, and the minimum size threshold s as input, and return all frequent itemsets in D satisfying all the provided constraints).

Algorithm 1 (Apriori on materialized filtered dataset)

```
begin
  scan D in order to:
    1) evaluate minimum number of supporting
       transactions for an itemset to be called frequent (mincount)
    2) find L1 (set of 1-itemsets supported by at
       least mincount transactions supporting S and having size > s);
    3) materialize the collection D' of transactions from D
       supporting S and having size > s;
  for (k = 2; Lk-1 ≠ ∅; k++) do
  begin
    /* generate new candidates using a standard Apriori procedure */
    Ck = apriori_gen(Lk-1);
    if Ck = ∅ then break;
    forall transactions d ∈ D' do
      forall candidates c ∈ Ck do
        if d supports c then
          c.count ++;
        end if;
```

```
    Lk  = { c ∈ Ck | c.count ≥ mincount};
  end;
  output itemsets from ∪k Lk having S as subset and size > s;
end.
```

Algorithm 2 (Apriori with on-line dataset filtering)

```
begin
  scan D in order to:
    1) evaluate minimum number of supporting
       transactions for an itemset to be called frequent (mincount)
    2) find L1 (set of 1-itemsets supported by at
       least mincount transactions supporting S and having size > s);
  for (k = 2; Lk-1 ≠ ∅; k++) do
  begin
    /* generate new candidates using a standard Apriori procedure */
    Ck = apriori_gen(Lk-1);
    if Ck = ∅ then break;
    forall transactions d ∈ D do
      if d supports S and |d|>s then
        forall candidates c ∈ Ck do
          if d supports c then
            c.count ++;
          end if;
      end if;
    Lk  = { c ∈ Ck | c.count ≥ mincount};
  end;
  output itemsets from ∪k Lk having S as subset and size > s;
end.
```

Algorithm 3 (Apriori on materialized projected dataset)

```
begin
  scan D in order to:
    1) evaluate minimum number of supporting
       transactions for an itemset to be called frequent (mincount)
    2) find L1 (set of 1-itemsets supported by at
       least mincount transactions from S-projected dataset D' of
       transactions from D supporting S and having size > s);
    3) materialize the S-projected dataset D' of transactions from D
       supporting S and having size > s;
  for (k = 2; Lk-1 ≠ ∅; k++) do
  begin
    /* generate new candidates using a standard Apriori procedure */
    Ck = apriori_gen(Lk-1);
    if Ck = ∅ then break;
    forall transactions d ∈ D' do
      forall candidates c ∈ Ck do
        if d supports c then
          c.count ++;
        end if;
    Lk  = { c ∈ Ck | c.count ≥ mincount};
  end;
  forall itemsets X ∈ ∪k Lk do
    if |X∪S| > s then output X∪S;
    end if;
  end;
end.
```

Algorithm 4 (Apriori with on-line dataset projection)

```
begin
  scan D in order to:
    1) evaluate minimum number of supporting
       transactions for an itemset to be called frequent (mincount)
    2) find L1 (set of 1-itemsets supported by at
       least mincount transactions from S-projected dataset D' of
       transactions from D supporting S and having size > s);
  for (k = 2; Lk-1 ≠ ∅; k++) do
  begin
    /* generate new candidates using a standard Apriori procedure */
    Ck = apriori_gen(Lk-1);
    if Ck = ∅ then break;
    forall transactions d ∈ D do
      if d supports S and |d|>s then
        forall candidates c ∈ Ck do
          if d supports c then
            c.count ++;
          end if;
      end if;
    Lk = { c ∈ Ck | c.count ≥ mincount};
  end;
  forall itemsets X ∈ ∪k Lk do
    if |X∪S| > s then output X∪S;
    end if;
  end;
end.
```

4. Experimental Results

In order to compare performance gains offered by various implementations of dataset filtering, we performed several experiments on a PC with the *Intel Celeron* 266MHz processor and 96 MB of main memory. The experiments were conducted on a synthetic dataset generated by means of the *GEN* generator from the *Quest* project [2], using different item and size constraints, and different values of the minimum support threshold. In each experiment, we compared execution times of applicable implementations of Apriori with dataset filtering and the original Apriori algorithm extended with the post-processing itemset filtering phase.

The source dataset was generated using the following values of *GEN* parameters: total number of transactions = 10000, the number of different items = 1000, the average number of items in a transaction = 8, number of patterns = 500, average pattern length = 3. The generated dataset was stored in a flat file on disk.

We started the experiments with varying item and size constraints for the fixed minimum support threshold of 1.5%. Apart from measuring the total execution times of all applicable Apriori implementations, we also registered the selectivity of dataset filtering constraints (expressed as the percentage of transactions in the database satisfying dataset filtering constraints). Figures 1 and 2 present execution times of various implementations of extended Apriori for size and item constraints of different selectivity (PP – original Apriori with a post-processing filtering phase, OL – on-line dataset filtering, MA – dataset filtering with materialization of the filtered dataset, POL – on-line dataset projection, PMA - projection with materialization of the projected dataset).

As we expected, the experiments showed that the lower the selectivity of dataset filtering constraints, the better the performance gains due to dataset filtering or projection are likely to be as compared to the original Apriori. It is obvious that the selectivity of a particular dataset filtering constraint depends on the actual contents of the database. In general, we observed that item constraints led to much better results (reducing the processing time 2 to 8 times depending on constraint selectivity and filtering implementation method) than constraints referring only to itemset size (typically reducing the processing time by less than 10%). This is due to the fact that frequent itemsets to be discovered are usually smaller than transactions forming the source dataset, and therefore even restrictive size constraints on frequent itemsets result in weak constraints on transactions.

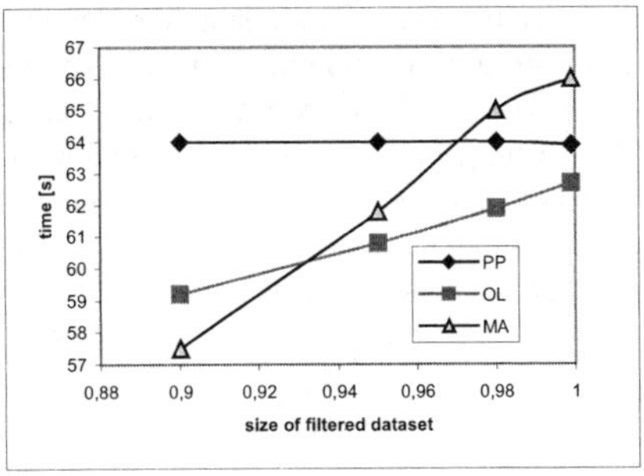

Fig. 1. Execution times for different values of selectivity of size constraints

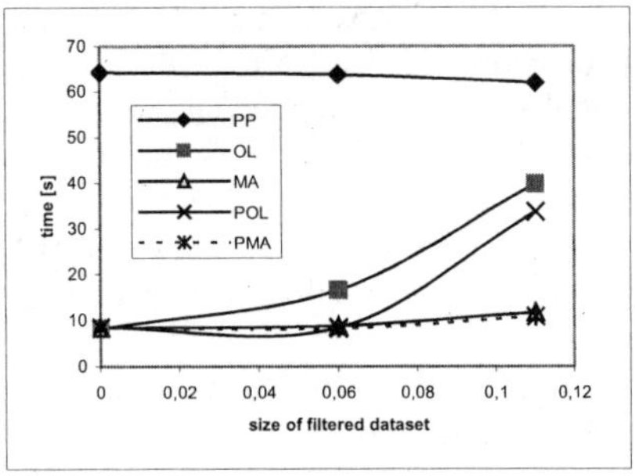

Fig. 2. Execution times for different values of selectivity of item constraints

In case of item constraints, all the implementations of dataset filtering and projection were always more efficient than the original Apriori with a post-processing constraint verifying step. Projection led to better results than filtering, which can be explained by the fact that projection leads to the smaller number of Apriori iterations (and slightly reduces the size of transactions in the dataset). Implementations involving materialization of the filtered/projected dataset were more efficient than their on-line counterparts (the filtered/projected dataset was relatively small and the materialization cost was dominated by gains due to the smaller costs of dataset scans in candidate verification phases). However, in case of size constraints rejecting a very small number of transactions, materialization of the filtered dataset sometimes lead to longer execution times than in case of the original Apriori. The on-line dataset filtering implementation was in general more efficient than the original Apriori even for size constraints (except for a situation, unlikely in practice, when the size constraint did not reject any transactions).

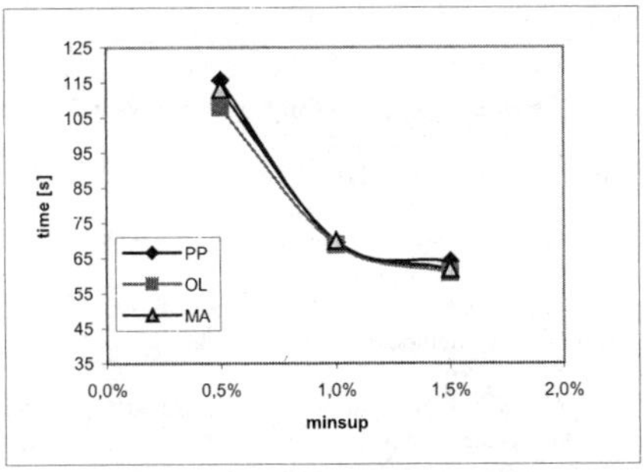

Fig. 3. Execution times for different values of minimum support in presence of size constraints

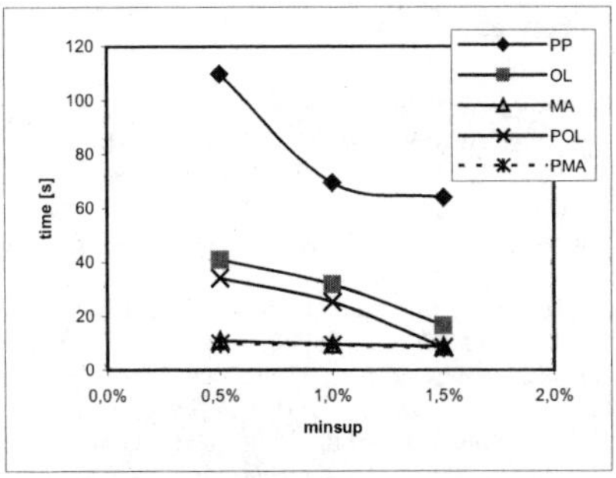

Fig. 4. Execution times for different values of minimum support in presence of item constraints

In another series of experiments, we observed the influence of varying the minimum support threshold on performance gains offered by dataset filtering and projection. Figure 3 presents the execution times for a size constraint of selectivity 95%. Execution times for an item constraint of selectivity 6% are presented in Figure 4. In both cases the minimum support threshold varied from 0.5% to 1.5%. Apriori encounters problems when the minimum support threshold is low because of the huge number of candidates to be verified. In our experiments, decreasing the minimum support threshold worked in favor of dataset filtering techniques, especially in case of item constraints leading to a small filtered dataset. This behavior can be explained by the fact that since dataset filtering reduces the cost of candidate verification phase, the more this phase contributes to the overall processing time, the more significant relative performance gains are going to be (the lower the support threshold the more candidates to verify, while the cost of disk access remains the same). Decreasing the minimum support threshold also led to slight performance improvement of implementations involving materialization of the filtered/projected dataset in comparison to their on-line counterparts. As the support threshold decreases, the maximal length of a frequent itemsets (and the number of iterations required by the algorithms) increases. Materialization is performed in the first iteration and reduces the cost of the second and subsequent iterations. Thus, the more iterations are required, the better the cost of materialization is compensated.

5. Conclusions

In this paper we addressed the issue of frequent itemset discovery with item and size constraints. One possible method of handling such constraints is application of dataset filtering techniques which are based on the observation that for certain types of constraints, some of the transactions in the database can be excluded from the discovery process since they cannot support the itemsets of interest.

We discussed several possible implementations of dataset filtering within the classic Apriori algorithm. Experiments show that dataset filtering can be used to improve performance of the discovery process but the actual gains depend on the type of the constraint and the implementation method. Item constraints typically lead to much more impressive performance gains than size constraints since they result in a smaller size of the filtered dataset. The best implementation strategy for handling item constraints is materialization of the database projected with respect to the required subset, whereas for size constraints the best results should be achieved by on-line filtering of the database with no materialization.

References

[1] R. Agrawal, T. Imielinski, A. Swami, Mining Association Rules Between Sets of Items in Large Databases. Proc. of the 1993 ACM SIGMOD Conference on Management of Data, 1993.

[2] R. Agrawal, M. Mehta, J. Shafer, R. Srikant, A. Arning, T. Bollinger, The Quest Data Mining System. Proc. of the 2nd KDD Conference, 1996.

[3] R. Agrawal and R. Srikant, Fast Algorithms for Mining Association Rules. Proc. of the 20th Int'l Conf. Very Large Data Bases, 1994

[4] J. Han, L. Lakshmanan, R. Ng, Constraint-Based Multidimensional Data Mining. *IEEE Computer* **32** (1999)

[5] J. Han and J. Pei, Mining Frequent Patterns by Pattern-Growth: Methodology and Implications. *SIGKDD Explorations*, December 2000 (2000)

[6] R. Ng, L. Lakshmanan, J. Han, A. Pang, Exploratory Mining and Pruning Optimizations of Constrained Association Rules. Proceedings of the 1998 ACM SIGMOD Conference on Management of Data, 1998.

[7] J. Pei, J. Han, L. Lakshmanan, Mining Frequent Itemsets with Convertible Constraints. Proceedings of the 17th ICDE Conference, 2001.

[8] R. Srikant, Q. Vu, R. Agrawal, Mining Association Rules with Item Constraints. Proceedings of the 3rd International Conference on Knowledge Discovery and Data Mining, 1997.

[9] M. Zakrzewicz, Data Mining within DBMS Functionality. Proceedings of the 4th IEEE International Baltic Workshop on Databases & Information Systems, 2000.

[10] Z. Zheng, R. Kohavi, L. Mason, Real World Performance of Association Rule Algorithms. Proc. of the 7th KDD Conference, 2001.

Knowledge-based Software Engineering
T. Welzer et al. (Eds.)
IOS Press, 2002

Exploiting Informal Communities in Information Retrieval

Christo DICHEV
Department of Computer Science, Winston-Salem State University
Winston-Salem, N.C. 27110, USA
dichevc@wssu.edu

Abstract. Widespread access to the Internet has led to the formation of scientific communities collaborating through the network. Most retrieval systems are geared towards Boolean queries or hierarchical classification based on keyword descriptors. Information retrieval problem is too big to be solved with a single model or with a single tool. In this paper we present a framework for information retrieval exploiting topic lattice generated from a collection of documents where documents are characterized by a group of users with overlapping interests. The topic lattice captures the authors' intention as it reveals the implicit structure of a document collection following the structure of groups of individuals expressing interests in the documents. It suggests navigation methods that may be an interesting alternative to the traditional search styles exploiting keyword descriptors.

I keep six honest serving men
They taught me all I knew:
Their names are What and Why and When
And How and Where and Who.

[Rudyard Kipling, *Just So Stories,* 1902]

1. Introduction

The problem of finding relevant information in a large repository such as Web in a reasonable amount of time becomes increasingly difficult. The findings from traditional IR research, may not always be applicable to large repositories. Document collections, massive in size and diverse in content, context, format, purpose and quality, challenge the validity of previous research findings in IR based on relatively small and homogeneous test collections. A derived challenge is how to support users in order to facilitate their navigation when searching for information in large repository. Browsing and searching are the two main paradigms for finding information. Both paradigms have their limitations. Queries often return search results that meet the search criteria but are of no interest to the user. This problem stems from the extremely poor user model represented by keywords. Two users may have different needs and still use the same keyword query. Nonetheless search engines rank results according to their similarity to the query and thus try to infer the user needs from the lexical representation. Another disadvantage of keyword queries is the inability to exploit other possible variations of search that are available and potentially useful but are outside of keyword match. Next disadvantage is that search is sometimes hard for users who do not know how to form a search query. Frequently, people intuitively know what they are searching but are unable to describe the document through a list of keywords.

Recently, keyword searches have been supplemented with a drill-down categorization hierarchy, that allows users to navigate through a repository of documents by groups and dynamically to modify parts of their search. These hierarchies, however, are often manually generated and can be misleading as a particular document might fall under more than one category. An obvious disadvantage of categorization is that the user must adopt the taxonomy used by those who did the categorization in order to effectively search the repository.

Most of the documents available on the Web are intended for a particular community of users. Typically, each document addresses some area of interest and thus a community centered on that area. Therefore the relevance of the document depends on the match between the intention of the author and the user's current interest. Keyword matching alone is not capable to capture this intention [11]. A great deal of scientific literature available on the Web is intended for example to scholars. For computer science scholars in particular, research papers are often made available on the sites of various institutions. Such examples indicate that scientific communication is increasingly taking place on the Web [10]. However for scientists, finding the information they want on the Web is still a hit-and-miss affair. These trends suggest that decentralizing the search process is a more scalable approach since the search may be driven by a context including topics, queries and communities of users. The question is *what type of topic related information is practical, how to infer that information* and *how to use it* for improving search results.

Web users typically search for diverse information. Some searches are sporadic and irregular while other searches might be related to their interests and have more or less regular nature. An important question is then how to filter out these sporadic, irregular searches and how to combine regular searches into groups identifying topics of interest by observing user's searching behavior. Our approach to topic identification is based on observations of the searching behavior of large groups of users. The assumption is that a topic of interest can be determined by identifying a collection of documents that is of common interest to a sufficiently large group of users.

In this paper we present a framework for identifying and utilizing ad hoc categories in information retrieval. The framework suggests a method of grouping documents into meaningful clusters, mapping existing topics of interest shared by certain users and a method of interacting with resulting repository. The proposed grouping of documents reflects the presence of groups of users that share common interests. Grouping is done automatically and results in an organizational structure that supports searching for documents matching user's conceptual process. Accordingly, users are able to search for similar or new documents and dynamically modify their search criteria. The framework suggests a technique for ranking members of a group based on a similarity of interests with respect to a given user.

2. Topic as Interesting Documents Shared by a Community of Users

Keyword queries cannot naturally locate resources relevant to a specific topic. An alternative approach is to deduce the category of the user queries. Situations where a search is limited within a group of documents collectively selected by a user and his peers as 'appropriate' illustrate a *category* that is relevant to the user's information needs. The major questions are: *what type of category related information is valuable and practical at the same time, how to infer that category information, and how to use it for improving the search results*?

Our method for topic/category identification is based on observations of the searching behavior of large groups of users. The basic intuition is that a topic of interest can be determined by identifying a collection of documents (articles) that is of common interest to a sufficiently large group of users. The assumption is that if a sufficient number of users $u_1, u_2, \dots, u_m$ driven by their interest are searching independently for a collection of documents $a_1, a_2, \dots, a_m$, then this is an evidence that there is a topic of interest shared by all users $u_1, u_2, \dots, u_m$. The collection of documents $a_1, a_2, \dots, a_m$ characterizes the topic of interest associated with that group of users. While the observation on a single user who demonstrates interest in objects $a_1, a_2, \dots, a_m$ is not an entirely reliable judgment, the identification of a group of users along with a collection of documents satisfying the relation $interested\_in(u_i, a_j)$ is a more reliable and accurate indicator of an existing topic of interest.

Additional topical descriptors of scientific literature are the place of publication (the place of presentation). These descriptors when available can support both queries of the type "find similar" and search for new documents. For example, it is likely that researchers working in machine learning will be interested in papers presented in the recent Machine Learning conferences. Yet the papers of ICML 2002 might be new for some of the AI researches. Thus for scientists the term "similar" might have several specific still traceable dimensions:

- Two papers are similar if both were presented at the same conference (in the same session);
- Two papers are similar if both were published in the same journal (in the same section);
- Two papers are similar if both steam from the same project;

That type of similarity suggests a browsing interaction – where user is able to scan ad hoc topics for similar or new materials. Assume that each collection of papers identified by the relation *interested_in*(u_i, a_j) is grouped further following its publication (presentation) attributes. Assume next that user u_i is able to retrieve the collection of documents $a_1, a_2, ..., a_m$ and then browse the journals and conferences of interests. The place and time of publications allow a collection $a_1, a_2, ..., a_m$ to be arranged by place and year of publication. In addition journal and conference names provide lexical material for generating a meaningful name of the collection. They suggest also useful links for search for *similar* or *new* documents.

The Web's transformation of scientific communication has only begun, but already much of its promise is within reach. The amount of scientific information and the number of electronic libraries on the Internet continues to increase [10]. New electronic collections appear daily designed with the needs of the researcher in mind and dedicated to serving the needs of the scientific community by advancing the reach and accessibility of scientific literature. In a practical perspective the proposed approach for identifying a topic of interest is particularly appropriate for *specialized* search engines and electronic libraries. First, specialized search engines (electronic libraries) are used for retrieving information within specified fields. For example, "*NEC ResearchIndex*" (http://citeseer.nj.nec.com/cs) is a powerful search engine for computer science research papers. As a result, the number of users of specialized search engines is considerably smaller compared to the number of users of general-purpose search engines. Second, specialized search engines use some advanced strategies to retrieve documents. Hence the result list provides typically a good indication of the document content. Therefore, when a user clicks on one of the documents the chances to get relevant information are generally high.

The question is: *how to gather realistic document usability information over some portion of the Web (or database)?* One of the most popular ways to get Web usability data is to examine the logs that are saved on servers. A server generates an entry in the log file each time it receives a request from a client. The kinds of data that it logs are: the IP address of the requester; the date and time of the request; the name of the file being requested; and the result of the request. Thus by using log files it is possible to capture rich information on visiting activities, such as who the visitors are and what they are specifically interested in and use it for user-oriented clustering in information retrieval.

The following assumptions provide a ground for the proposed framework. We assume that all users are reliably identifiable across multiple visits to a site. We assume further that if a user (saves/selects) a document it is likely that the document is relevant to the query or to the user's current information needs. Another assumption is that all relevant data of user logs are available and that from the large set of user logs we can extract a set of relations of the type: *(user_id, selected_document)*. The next step is to derive from the extracted set of relations meaningful collections of documents based on overlapping user interests, that is, to cluster the extracted data set into groups of users with matching groups of documents. The last assumption is that within each group documents can be organized (sorted) according to the place and time of publication/presentation.

3. Topic-Community Lattice

Classification of documents in a collection is based on relevant attributes characterizing documents. In most information retrieval applications, the documents serve as formal objects and the descriptors such as keywords serve as attributes. Instead of using the occurrence of keywords as attributes, we use the set of users U expressing interest in a document as a characterization of that document. This enables us to explicate not evident relationship between collection of document and groups of users. In contrast to keywords this type of characterization of documents exploits implicit properties of documents. We will denote the documents in a collection with the letter A. Individual members of this collection are denoted by a_1, a_2 etc., while subsets are written as A_1, A_2. We will denote the group of users searching the collection with the letter U. Individual users are denoted by u_1, u_2 etc., while subsets are written as U_1, U_2.

Given a set of users U, a set of documents A and a binary relation uFa (user u is interested in article a) we generate a classification of documents such that each class can be seen as (ad hoc) topic in terms of groups of users $U_1 \in Pow(U)$ interested in documents $A_1 \in Pow(A)$. Documents share a group of users and users share a collection of documents based on the users interest

$$A_1 = \{a \in A \mid (\forall u \in U_1)\ uFa\}$$

$$U_1 = \{u \in U \mid (\forall a \in A_1)\ uFa\},$$

Within the theory of *Formal Concept Analysis* [12] the relation between objects and attributes is called *context (U,A,F)*. Using the context we generate a classification of documents such that each class can be seen as a topic (category) in terms of the shared users interest in the documents.

Definition. *Let $C = (U,A,F)$ be a context. $c = (U_1,A_1)$ is called a concept of C if $\alpha(A_1)=\{u \in U \mid (\forall a \in A_1)\ uFa\} = U_1$ and $\omega(U_1) = \{a \in A \mid (\forall u \in U_1)\ uFa\} = A_1$. $\pi_A(c) = A_1$ and $\pi_U(c)=U_1$ are called c's extent and intent, respectively. The set of all concepts of C is denoted by B(C).*

	a_1	a_2	a_3	a_4	a_5	a_6	a_7	a_8	.
u_1	1	1	1	1	1	1	1	1	.
u_2	1	1	1	1	1	0	1	0	.
u_3	1	0	0	0	0	1	0	1	.
u_4	0	1	0	0	1	0	1	0	.
u_5	0	0	1	1	0	0	1	0	.
u_6	1	0	1	1	0	0	1	0	.
u_7	0	0	0	0	1	0	1	0	.
u_8	0	0	0	0	0	1	0	1	.
.	.	.	.	.	.	.	.	.	.

Table 1: A partial representation of the relation u_i *is interested in* a_j

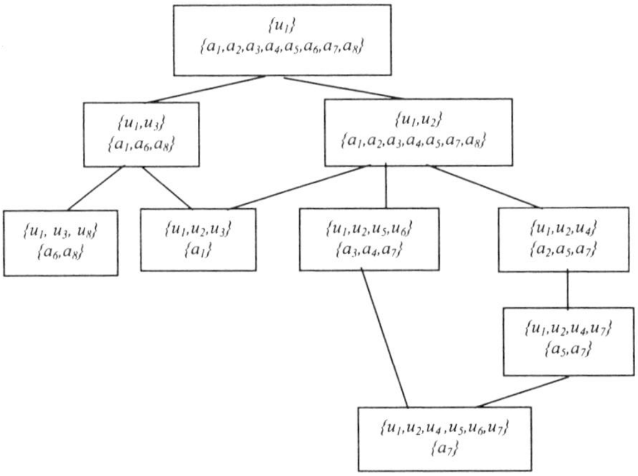

Figure 1: A topic lattice generated from the relation represented in Table 1.

We may think of the set of articles A_u associated with a given user $u \in U$ as represented by a bit vector. Each bit i corresponds to a possible article $a_i \in A$ and is on or off depending on whether the user u is interested in article a_i. We can characterize the relation between the set of users and the set of articles in terms of *topic lattice*. An ordering relation is defined on this set of topics by

$$(U_1, A_1) \leq (U_2, A_2) \leftrightarrow U_1 \subseteq U_2 \text{ or } (U_1, A_1) \leq (U_2, A_2) \leftrightarrow A_1 \supseteq A_2.$$

As a consequence, a topic uniquely relates a set of documents with a set of attributes (users): for a topic the set of documents implies the corresponding set of attributes and vice versa. Therefore a topic may be presented by its document set or attribute set only. This relationship holds in general for conceptual hierarchies: more general concepts have fewer defining attributes in their intension but more objects in their extension and vice versa. The set $C=(U,A,F)$ along with the "≤ " relation form a partially ordered set that can be characterized by a *concept lattice* (referred here as *topic lattice*). Each node of the topic lattice is a pair composed of a subset of articles and a subset of corresponding users. In each pair the subset of users contains just the users sharing interest to the subset of articles and similarly the subset of articles contains just the articles sharing overlapping interest from the matching subset of users. The set of pairs is ordered by the standard "set inclusion" relation applied to the set of articles and to the set of users that describe each pair. The partially ordered set can be represented by a Hasse diagram, in which an edge connects two nodes if and only if they are comparable and there is no other node - intermediate topic in the lattice, i.e. each topic is linked to its maximally specific more general topics and to its maximally general more specific topics. The ascending paths represent the subclass/superclass relation. The topic lattice shows the commonalities between topics and generalization/specialization between them. The bottom topic is defined by the set of all users; the top topic is defined by all articles and the group of users (possibly none) sharing interest in them. A simple example of users and their interest to documents is presented in Table 1. The corresponding lattice is presented in Figure 1.

4. Scientific Communication and Scientific Documents

Widespread access to the Internet has led to the formation of geographically dispersed scientific communities collaborating through the network. Academics are able to communicate and share research with great ease across institutions, countries, and even disciplines. In some cases an individual research has more to do with a dozen colleagues around the world than ones own department. Identification of scientific communities is important from the viewpoint of information retrieval because:

- They are focused on a shared information base that suggest decentralization of the search;
- They are where the semantics resides - communities have shared concepts and terminology;
- They enable community profile creation and thus can support "active information" paradigm versus "active users";
- They can support more natural, not institutionalized directory formation;
- They enable scientific institutions and to more effectively target key audience.

Recently there has been indication of interest in identifying scientific communities [9]. The NEC researchers [7] define a Web community as a collection of Web pages that have more links within the community than outside of the community. These communities are self-organized in that the entire Web graph determines membership. Our notion of communities especially from the viewpoint of their identification differs from NEC definition and is based on shared interests or goals of their members. Rather than attempting to extract communities in our approach we attempt to gain understanding of the shared topic of interest that connects community members. Community identification based on the shared topic of interest enables search tools and individuals to locate specific information by focusing on the items relating community members.

For example, an individual wishing to study the latest scientific findings on data mining research would be able to locate relevant papers, literature, and new developments without wading through the pages of irrelevant material that a normal Web search on the subject might produce. This is possible because this approach assumes local search to generate its results.

Different categories of users are driven by different motivations when searching for documents. Scholars typically search for new or inspiring scientific literature. In such cases keywords cannot always guide the search. In addition the term *new* depends on who is the individual and how current is she with the available literature. Novices or inexperienced researchers may also face some problems trying to get to a good starting point. Typical questions for newcomers in the field are:

- *Which are the most significant works in the field?*
- *Which are the newest yet interesting papers in the field.*
- *Which are the topics in proximity to a given topic?*
- *Which are the most active researchers in the field?*

In effect general purpose search engines do not provide support for such type of questions.

In fact there are three basic reasons for searching and using the scientific literature. Each requires a slightly different process and the use of a slightly different set of information tools.

- Current awareness: keeping current and informed about new literature and current progress in a specific area of interest. This is done in a number of ways, both informally in communications with colleagues and more formally through sources such as those listed in some sites.
- Everyday needs: specific pieces of information needed for experimental work or to gain a better understanding of that work. It may be collaborating data, a method or technique, an explanation for an observed phenomenon, or other similar needs
- Exhaustive research: need to identify "all" relevant information on a specific project. This typically occurs when a researcher begins work on a new investigation or in preparation for a formal publication.

Two information retrieval methods are widely used: Boolean querying and *hierarchical classification*. In the second method, searches are done by navigating in a classification structure that is typically built and maintained manually. Even from scientific perspective the information retrieval problem is too big to be solved with a single model or with a single tool.

5. Support for Topical Navigation

A hierarchical topical structure as the one described in the previous section presents some features that support browsing retrieval task: topics are indexed through their descriptors (users) and are linked based on general/specific relation. User can jump from one topic to another in the lattice; the transition to other topics is driven by the Hasse diagram. Each node in the lattice can be seen as query formed by specifying a group of users, with the retrieved documents defining the result. The lattice supports navigation from more specific to general or general to specific queries. Another characteristic is that the lattice allows gradual enlargement or refinement of a query. Following edges departing downward (upward) from a query produces refinements (enlargements) of the query with respect to a particular collection of documents.

Consider a context $C = (U,A,F)$. Each attribute $u \in U$ and object $a \in A$ has a uniquely determined defining topic. The defining topic can directly be calculated from the attribute u or article a and need not to be searched in the lattice based on the following property.

Definition. *Let $C=(U,A,F)$ be a concept lattice. The defining topic of an attribute $u \in U$ (object $a \in A$) is the greatest (smallest) topic c such that $u \in \pi_U(c)$ ($a \in \pi_A(c)$) holds.*

This suggests the following strategy for navigation. A user $u \in U$ starts her search from the greatest topic c_1 such that $u \in \pi_U(c_1)$, i.e. from the greatest collection of articles interesting to u.

User navigates from topic to topic in the lattice, each topic representing the current query. Gradual refinement of the query may be accomplished by successfully choosing child topics and gradual enlargement by choosing parent topics. This enables the user to control the amount of output obtained from a query. A gradual shift of the topic may be accomplished by choosing sibling topics. Thus a user u searches documents walking through the "topical" hierarchy guided by the relevance of the topics with respect to her current interest. If she wants to see the concepts that are similar to her group then she can browse neighboring topics c_i such that they maximize certain similarity measure with the topic c_1. A simple solution is to measure similarity based on the number of overlapping users in $c_1 = (U_1, A_1)$ and $c_i = (U_i, C_i)$. Thus the browsing behavior can be guided by the magnitude $t = |U_1 \cap U_i|$ for selecting sibling topics. Another indicator of similarity is the place of publication/presentation. Articles at each node are arranged according to their *place* and *time* of publication when available. The names of the dominating journals or conferences are used as lexical source for generating a name of the corresponding topic. The defining concept property suggests also an alternative navigation strategy *guided by articles.* Assume that browsing through the topic lattice user u finds article a interesting to her and wants to see some articles similar to a, that is, articles sharing user's interest with a. Then exploiting the *defining concept property* the user u can jump to the smallest topic such that $a \in \pi_A(c)$, that is to the minimal collection containing a and resume the search from this point by exploring the neighboring topics.

Our supporting conjecture for such type of navigation is that a new document a topically close to documents A_m that are interesting to a user u is also interesting with high probability. More precisely, if a user u is interested in documents A_m, then a document a interesting to her peers U_n ($a \in A_n$, such that $A_n \supseteq A_m$ ($U_n \subseteq U_m$), and $a \notin A_m$) is also relevant. Thus articles $a \in A_n$ that are new to the user u and relevant by our conjecture should be ranked higher with respect to the user u. Therefore in terms of the concept lattice the search domain relevant to the user $u \in U_m$ includes a subset of articles to which other members (i.e., U_k) of the group U_m have demonstrated interest. These are collections of articles A_k of the topic (U_k, A_k), such that $u \notin U_k \subseteq U_n \neq \emptyset$. This strategy supports a topical exploration exploiting the topical structure in the collection of documents. It also touches upon a challenging problem related to efficient recourse exploration: *how to maintain collections of articles that are representative of the topic and may be used as a starting points for exploration.*

Navigation implies notions of place, being in a place and going to another place. A notion of neighborhood helps specifying the other place, relative to the place one is currently in. Assume that a user u is in topic c_1, such that $c_p = (U_p, A_p)$ is a parent topic and $c_2 = (U_2, A_2), \ldots, c_k = (U_k, A_k)$ are the sibling topics, i.e. $U_i \supseteq U_p$, $i = 1,2,..,k$. To support user orientation while browsing a topic lattice we provide the following similarity measurement information. Each edge/link (c_p, c_i) from the parent topic c_p to c_i is associated with two weights W_i and w_i *absolute* and *relative* weight respectively computed according to the following formulae $W_i = |U_i|$ and $w_i = |U_i \cap U_1| / |U_1 + U_2 + .. + U_k|$, $i = 1,2,..,k$. In addition to these quantitative measures each node is associated with a name derived from the place of publication. These names serve as qualitative qualifiers of a topic relative to the other topic names.

The following is a summary of the navigation strategy derived from the above considerations. The decision for the next browsing steps are based on the articles in the current topic and on the weights (W_i/w_i) associated with the sibling nodes. User $u \in U$ starts from the greatest topic c_1 identified by her defining group $U_1 = \pi_U(c_1)$. Arriving at node (U_k, A_k) user u can either refine, enlarge the search or select a new topic in the proximity of the current topic. These decisions correspond to choosing a *descendant, a parent* or a *sibling* topic from the available list; any descendant topic refines the query and shrinks gradually the result to a non empty set of selected documents. The user refines the query by choosing a sequence of one or more links and thus the number of selected documents and remaining links decreases. Correspondingly, the user enlarges the query by choosing a sequence of parent topics (links). In contrast, selecting a sibling topic will result in browsing a collection of articles not seen by that user but rated as interesting by some of her peers. These three types of navigations are guided by the relations between user groups such as set inclusion and set intersection as well as by topic names similarity. The next type of navigation is controlled by selected article. Navigation guided by selected article exploits the defining topic property of an object. By selecting an article a from topic $c_i = (U_i, A_i)$, user is enable to navigate to the minimal collection containing the article a, that is to jump to the smallest topic c such that $A_k = \pi_A(c)$, $A_k \subseteq A_i$. In general traversing the hierarchy in search of documents supported by topic lattice can be viewed as sequence of browsing steps through the topics, reflecting a sequence of applications of the four navigation strategies. Once topic is selected then user can search the papers browsing the corresponding regions associated with place and time of publication. This approach allows users to jump into a hierarchy at a meaningful starting point and quickly navigate to the most useful information. It also allows users to easily find and peruse related concepts, which is especially helpful if users are not sure what they want.

6. Document Relevancy and Topical Hierarchy

In the previous section we described how to identify topics of interest so that users belonging to an ad hoc community of interest can navigate through the articles interesting to some members of the community. However we can reverse the situation and try to predict which members u_i of a given community have indeed similar interest to an user u_1. For those users u_i it might be worth establishing direct communication with u_1 (for example visiting the home page of u_1). Thus we are trying to derive some information side effects. From the available information where user u_1 demonstrates interests to the same objects as u_2 we want to evaluate the likelihood that user u_1 has indeed interests similar to the interests of user u_2 - $similar(u_1, u_2)$. In other words we want to evaluate how similar are their interests? In the suggested predicting method, items that are unique to user u_1 and user u_2 are weighted more than commonly occurring items. The weighing scheme we use (modification of [1]) is the inverse log frequency of their occurrence.

$$similar(u_1, u_2) = \sum_{shared(a)} \frac{1}{\log(freq(shared(a))}$$

In contrast to conceptual clustering [2] where the descriptors are static, in the suggested approach the users who play a role of descriptors are *dynamic*: in general, a user's interest can not be specified completely and her topical interests change over time. Hence, the lattice describing the topical structure is dynamic too. This induces some results based on the following assumptions. A collection of articles A_1 from an existing topic (U_1, A_1) can only be expanded. This is implied by the conjecture that documents, qualified as interesting by user u do not change their status. Therefore, an expansion of the collection of articles with respect to a topic (U_1, A_1) will not impose any change of existing links. Indeed, an expansion of A_1 to A'_1 results in an expansion of all parent (descendent) collections A_m, A_n, such that $A_1 \subseteq A_m \subseteq A_n$, i.e. from $A_1 \subseteq A'_1 \rightarrow A'_m \subseteq A'_n$ and therefore $(U_n, A_n) \leq (U_m, A_m) \rightarrow (U'_n, A'_n) \leq (U'_m, A'_m)$. Analogous relations hold with ancestor nodes. That is, an expansion of an existing collection of articles preserves the structure of the lattice.

Lattices are superior to tree hierarchies which can be embedded into lattices, because they have the property that for every set of elements there exists a unique lowest upper bound (join) and a unique greatest lower bound (meet). In lattice structure there are many paths to a particular topic. This facilitates recovery from bad decision made while traversing the hierarchy in search of documents. Lattice structure provides ability to deal with non-disjoint concepts.

One of the main factors in a page ranking strategy involves the location and frequency of keywords in a Web page. Another factor is link popularity - the total number of sites that link to a given page. However, present page rank algorithms typically do not take into account the current user and specifically her interests. Assume that we have partitioned users into groups associated with their topics of interest (as collections of documents). A modified ranking algorithm can be obtained by extending the present strategy with an additional factor involving the number of links to and from a topic associated with a given user. In this case the page ranking strategy takes into consideration user's interest encoded in the number and the levels of links to a topic associated with a given user. Thus, for a user $u \in U_1$, where (U_1,A_1) is a topic, the page rank of an article a depends on the linkage structure to the articles $a_i \in A_1$ representing the topic of interest of user u. We can interpret a link from article a_i to article a as a vote of article a_i for article a. Thus votes cast by article that are from the users topic weigh more heavily and help to make other pages 'more-important'. This strategy makes page-ranking *user oriented.* Such a strategy promotes pages related to users' topics of interest. From an "active users" perspective this approach enables us to recognize a community of users for which a given article is most likely to be interesting.

An integration of navigation with search based on keyword descriptors will provide an opportunity for different modes of interaction that may be integrated on combined retrieval space. The topic lattice suggests also a partially ordering relation $(\prec)$ for ranking articles returned in response to a keyword request from a user u, assuming that c_0 is the greatest topic such tat $u \in U_0 = \pi_U(c_0)$. Then $a_1 \prec a_2$ if there exist topics $c_1=(U_1, A_1)$ and $c_2=(U_2, A_2)$, $a_1 \in A_1$, $a_2 \in A_2$, such that $| U_1 \cap U_0 | < | U_2 \cap U_0 |$, i.e. the more members of the group U_0 have expressed an interest in a given article the better. This ordering is based on the number of users that has expressed interest in a document. That implies that all articles of the lattice that originate from the same topic are lumped into one rank.

An important characteristic of the lattice classification is that it does not require explicit representation of the objects (documents), due to the fact that it exploits only set inclusion relations. Any set of objects A_1 is identified based on the relation to a group U_1, rather than on specific syntactic properties of their representations. Therefore it can cover objects behind the conventional search forms, such as pdf, images, music files, and compressed archives.

7. Related Works and Conclusion

The quest for relevant information has given rise to two major directions of attack: information retrieval and information filtering. Most retrieval systems are geared towards Boolean queries or hierarchical classification but it has long been recognized in the context of information retrieval that most searches are a combination of direct and browsing retrieval and as a such, a system should provide both possibilities in an integrated and coherent interface [8]. The most challenging test of the information retrieval methods is their application to the Web. The focus of the current efforts of the Web research community is mainly on optimizing the search, assuming active users vs. passive information.

Recently there has been much interest in supporting users through collecting Web pages related to a particular topic [3, 4, 11]. These approaches typically exploit connectivity for topic identification but not for community identification. Community identification does not play any significant role in these methods and therefore user search experience within a community is ignored. Recent work [9] has attempted to find communities by performing analysis of their graph structure. Given a starting point, this method extracts clusters of users in the same "community". Researchers at NEC have developed a new method to enable the identification of communities across the Web [7]. Again, the approach employed for community identification is based on analysis of the Web graph structure and is not explicitly related to resource discovery. A Web community according to this method is a collection of Web pages in which each member page has more hyperlinks within the community than outside it. Rather than attempting to extract communities in our approach we attempt to gain understanding of the topic of interest that connects community members. In collaborative filtering systems [2] items are recommended on the basis of user similarity rather than object similarity. Each target user is associated with a set of nearest neighbor users (by comparing their profiles) who act as 'recommendation partners'. In contrast, in our approach users' similarity is used to build a topical hierarchy supporting search driven by matching topics of interests. A derived benefit of such an approach is that it discloses some implicit relations in documents (such as author's intention) that can guide a search for matching topics of interest. Lattices are appealing as a means of representing conceptual

hierarchies used in information retrieval systems because of some formal lattice properties. Applied to information retrieval they represent inverse relationship between document sets and query terms. Unlike traditional systems that use simple keyword matching, [10] is able to track and recommend topically relevant papers even when keyword based query fails. This is made possible through the use of a profile to represent user interests. Our framework is close in spirit to the application of Galois' concept lattices [4] where each document is described by exactly those terms that are attached to nodes that are above the document node. However in our approach the grouping of documents into classes is based on dynamic descriptors associated with users conducting search on a regular basis.
Web directories represent only one possible classification, which though widely useful can never be suitable to all applications. In our approach *category identification* is part of *community formation* and is based on automatic identification of communities with clustered topical interests.

In this paper we have presented a framework for information retrieval exploiting topic lattice generated from a collection of documents where users expressing interest in particular documents play a role of descriptors. The topic lattice captures the authors' intention as it reveals the implicit structure of a document collection following the structure of informal groups of individuals expressing interests in the documents. Due to its dual nature, the lattice allows two complimentary navigations styles which are based either on attributes or on objects. Topic lattice based on users' interest suggests navigation methods that may be an interesting alternative to the conventional search and navigation styles exploiting keyword descriptors. In addition an integration of these approaches will provide an opportunity for different modes of interaction that may be integrated on combined retrieval space within a coherent system.

References

[1] Adamic L. A and Adar E. Friends and Neighbors on the Web. ***http://www.hpl.hp.com/shl/papers/web10/frequency.html***

[2] Balabanovich, M., and Shoham Y. 1997. Content-based Collaborative Recommendation. *Communications of the ACM* 40(3): 66-72.

[3] Brin, S., and Page, L. 1998. The Anatomy of a Large-scale Hypertextual Web Search Engine. In Proceedings of the 7th *International WWW Conf.*, Vol. 7.

[4] Carpineto, C., and Romano, G. 1996. A Lattice Conceptual Clustering System and Its Application to Browsing Retrieval. *Machine Learning* 24: 95-122.

[5] Chakrabarti, S., van den Berg, M., and Dom, B. 1999. Focused Crawling: a New Approach to Topic-specific Web Resource Discovery. In *Proceedings of the Eight International World Wide Web Conference*, Toronto, Canada, 545-562.

[6] Dichev Ch, Dicheva D., Deriving Context Specific Information on the Web, *Proc. of The WebNet 2001*, Orlando, pp. 296-301.

[7] Flake G.W., Lawrence S., Giles C. L. Efficient Identification of Web Communities In the *Proceedings of the Sixth International Conference on Knowledge Discovery and Data Mining* (ACM SIGKDD-2000), Boston, MA, 2000.

[8] Godin R., Missaoui R., April A. Experimental Comparison of Navigation in a Galois Lattice with Conventional Information Retrieval Methods. *Int. Journal of Man-Machine Studies 38(5):747-767* (1993)

[9] Kumar, R., Raghavan, P., Rajagopalan, S., and Tomkins, A. 1999. Trawling the Web for Emerging Cyber-communities. In *Proc. of the Eight Int. World Wide Web Conference*, Toronto, 403-415.

[10] Lawrence S., Giles C. L. Searching the Web: general and scientific information access IEEE Communications, 37(1):116-122, 1999.

[11] Menczer F., R. Belew: Adaptive Retrieval Agents: Internalizing Local Context and Scaling up to the Web. Machine Learning Journal 39 (2/3): 203-242, 2000.

[12] Wille, R. 1982. Restructuring Lattice Theory: An Approach Based on Hierarchies of Concepts. In: I. Rival (ed.): *Ordered Sets*. Reidel, Dordrecht-Boston, 445-470.

Knowledge-based Software Engineering
T. Welzer et al. (Eds.)
IOS Press, 2002

Searching for Software Reliability with Text Mining

Vili PODGORELEC, Peter KOKOL, Ivan ROZMAN
University of Maribor, FERI
Smetanova 17, 2000 Maribor, Slovenia

Abstract. In the paper we present the combination of data mining techniques, classifying and complexity analysis in the software reliability research. We show that a new text complexity metrics, called α metric as an attribute together with other software complexity measures can be successfully used to induce decision trees for predicting dangerous modules (modules having a lot of undetected faults). Redesigning such modules or devoting more testing or maintenance effort to them can largely enhance the reliability, making the software much more safe to use. In addition our research shows that text mining can be a very useful technique not only for improving software quality and reliability but also a useful paradigm for searching for fundamental software development laws.

1. Introduction

Software evolution and design is a complicated process. Not so long ago, it has been regarded as an art and is still not fully recognised as an engineering discipline. In addition, the size and complexity of software systems is growing dramatically during the last decades. Large systems consisting of many millions lines of code and many modules are not a rarity any more. As the requirements for, and dependencies on, computers become more demanding thus increasing complexity, the possibility of crises from failure increases.

The impact of these failures range from simple inconvenience to major economic damages to loss of lives - therefore it is clear that the 'system' role of software, its quality and resulting design is becoming a major concern not only for system or software engineers and computer scientists, but for all members of society. Thus achieving a maximal level of software quality consistently and economically is crucial. Unfortunately, conventional methods for measuring and controlling quality are not yet successful enough so a more unconventional approach seems to be necessary.

As with systems in management science and economics, software development (the development includes the whole software system life-cycle: from the idea/statement of need to its use and maintenance) has similar system attributes, i.e. as a complex, dynamic, non-linear and adaptive system. Consequently, the aim of our project is to gain a fundamental understanding of software process and software product. The proposed approach uses the science of complexity, various system theories and intelligent system techniques like data mining, text mining and intelligent classifiers.

While reliability is one of the most important aspects of software systems of any kind (embedded systems, information systems, intelligent systems, etc.) the use of text mining and classifying in software reliability research will be presented in the present paper.

2. Software metrics and reliability

During the software development or maintenance, faults are inserted into the code. It has been shown that the pattern of the faults insertion phenomena is related to measurable attributes of the software. For example, a large software system consists of thousands of modules and each of these modules can be characterised in terms of hundreds attribute measures. It would be quite useful to find some laws distinguishing dangerous (modules with potentially many faults) and non-dangerous modules (modules with potentially many faults). But due to the size of the problem it is almost impossible for a human to review all the modules and find such laws – so we decided to use data and text mining and intelligent classifying, employing decision trees, software complexity metrics and long range correlations.

2.1. Software metrics and reliability

The majority of experts in the computing field agree that complexity is one of the most relevant characteristics of computer software. For example Brooks states that computer software is the most complex entity among human made artifacts [15]. There are three possible, not completely distinct, viewpoints about software complexity:

- the classical computational complexity [17, 18],
- traditional software metrics, and
- recent "science of complexity" [16, 2, 7, 9].

Recently two attempts have been made to use the science of complexity in the measurement area. In her keynote speech at FESMA conference 1998 Kitchenham [1] argued that software measurement or estimates and predictions or assumptions based on them are infeasible. This is because software development, like in management science and economics, is a complex, non-linear adaptive system and inaccuracy of predictions is inherently emergent in such systems. As a consequence it is important to understand uncertainty and risk associated with that. Kokol et al [5-10] in their papers represent the similar view but their conclusion is that one not only has to understand the principles and findings of science of complexity but also can use them to assess and measure the software more successfully, for example with the employment of so called α metric. This metric is based on the measurement of information content and entropy and it is known that the entropy is related to reliability – and thereafter α metric is a very viable candidate for software reliability assessment and software fault prediction.

3. Physical background

Many different quantities [3] have been proposed as measures of complexity to capture all our intuitive ideas about what is meant by complexity. Some of the quantities are computational complexity, information content, algorithmic information content, the length of a concise description of a set of the entity's regularities, logical depth, etc., (in contemplating various phenomena we frequently have to distinguish between effective complexity and logical depth – for example some very complex behaviour patterns can be generated from very simple formula like Mandelbrot's fractal set, energy levels of atomic nuclei, the unified quantum theory, etc.- that means that they have little effective complexity and great logical depth). Li [13] relates the complexity with difficulty concerning the system in question, for example the difficulty of constructing a system, difficulty of describing the system, etc. It is also well known that complexity is related to entropy. Several authors speculate that the relation is one to one (i.e. algorithmic complexity is equivalent to entropy as a measure of randomness) [12] but [13] shows that the relation is one to many or many to one depending on the definition of the complexity and the choice of the system being studied.

Using the assumption that meaning and information content in text is founded on the correlation between language symbols one of the meaningful measures of complexity of human writings is entropy as established by Shannon [11]. Yet, when a text is very long it is almost impossible to calculate the Shannon information entropy so Grassberger [12] proposed an approximate method to estimate entropy. But entropy does not reveal directly the correlation properties of texts so another more general measure is needed. One possibility is to use Fourier power spectrum, however a method yielding much more quality scaling data was introduced recently. This method, called long-range correlation [4] is based on the generalisation of entropy and is very appropriate for measuring complexity of human writings.

4. Long-range correlations

Various quantities for the calculation of long range correlation in linear symbolic sequences were introduced in the literature and are discussed by Ebeling [14]. The most popular methods are dynamic entropy, scaling exponent $1/f^{\delta}$, higher order cumulates, mutual information, correlation functions, mean square deviations, and mapping of the sequence into random walk. It is agreed by many authors [4, 14] that the mapping into random walk is the most effective and successful approach in the analysis of human writings.

Long-range power law correlation (LRC) has been discovered in a wide variety of systems. As a consequence the LRC is very important for understanding the system's behaviour, since we can quantify it with a critical exponent. Quantification of this kind of scaling behaviour for apparently unrelated systems allows us to recognise similarities between different systems, leading to underlying unification. For example LRC has been identified in DNA sequences and natural language texts [4, 14] - the consequence is that DNA and human writings can be analysed using very similar techniques.

4.1. Calculation of the long-range power law correlation

In order to analyse the long-range correlation of a string of symbols the best way is to first map the string into a Brownian walk model [4]. Namely, the Brownian walk model is well researched and publicised and the derived theories and methodologies are widely agreed and in addition easy to implement with the use of computer. There are various possibilities to implement the above mapping [6]. In this paper we will use the so-called CHAR method described by Schenkel [4] and Kokol [6]. A character is taken to be the basic symbol of a human writing. Each character is then transformed into a six bit long binary representation according to a fixed code table. It has been shown by Schenkel that the selection of the code table does not influence the results as long as all possible codes (i.e. we have 64 different codes for the six bit representation – in our case we assigned 56 codes for the letters and the remaining codes for special symbols like period, comma, mathematical operators, etc) are used. The obtained binary string is then transformed into a two dimensional Brownian walk model (Brownian walk in the text which follows) using each bit as a one move - the 0 as a step down and the 1 as a step up.

An important statistical quantity characterising any walk is the root of mean square fluctuation F about the average of the displacement. In a two-dimensional Brownian walk model the F is defined as:

$$F^2(l) \equiv \overline{[\Delta y(l,l_0)]^2} - \left[\overline{\Delta y(l,l_0)}\right]^2$$

$$\Delta y(l,l_0) \equiv y(l_0 + l) - y(l_0)$$

where

- l is the distance between two points of the walk on the X axis,
- l_0 is the initial position (beginning point) on the X axis where the calculation of $F(l)$ for one pass starts,
- y is the position of the walk – the distance between the initial position and the current position on Y axis, and

the bars indicate the average over all positions l_0.

The $F(l)$ can distinguish two possible types of behaviour:

- if the string sequence is uncorrelated (normal random walk) or there are local correlations extending up to a characteristic range i.e Markov chains or symbolic sequences generated by regular grammars [13], then

  $$F(l) \approx l^{0.5}$$

- if there is no characteristic length and the correlations are "infinite" then the scaling property of $F(l)$ is described by a power law

  $$F(l) \approx l^{\alpha} \text{and } \alpha \neq 0.5.$$

The power law is most easily recognised if we plot $F(l)$ and l on a double logarithmic scale (Figure 3). If a power law describes the scaling property then the resulting curve is linear and the slope of the curve represents α. In the case that there are long range correlation in the strings analysed, α should not be equal to 0.5.

The main difference between random sequences and human writings is purpose. Namely, the writing or programming is done consciously and with purpose that is not the case with random processes, thereafter we anticipate that α should differ from 0.5. The difference in α between different writings can be attributed to various factors like personal preferences, used standards, language, type of the text or the problem being solved, type of the organisation in which the writer (or programmer) works, different syntactic, semantic, pragmatic rules etc.

5. Evolutionary decision trees

Inductive inference is the process of moving from concrete examples to general models, where the goal is to learn how to classify objects by analysing a set of instances (already solved cases) whose classes are known. Instances are typically represented as attribute-value vectors. Learning input consists of a set of such vectors, each belonging to a known class, and the output consists of a mapping from attribute values to classes. This mapping should accurately classify both the given instances and other unseen instances.

A decision tree [21] is a formalism for expressing such mappings and consists of tests or attribute nodes linked to two or more sub-trees and leafs or decision nodes labelled with a class which means the decision (figure 1). A test node computes some outcome based on the attribute values of an instance, where each possible outcome is associated with one of the sub-trees. An instance is classified by starting at the root node of the tree. If this node is a test, the outcome for the instance is determined and the process continues using the appropriate sub-tree. When a leaf is eventually encountered, its label gives the predicted class of the instance.

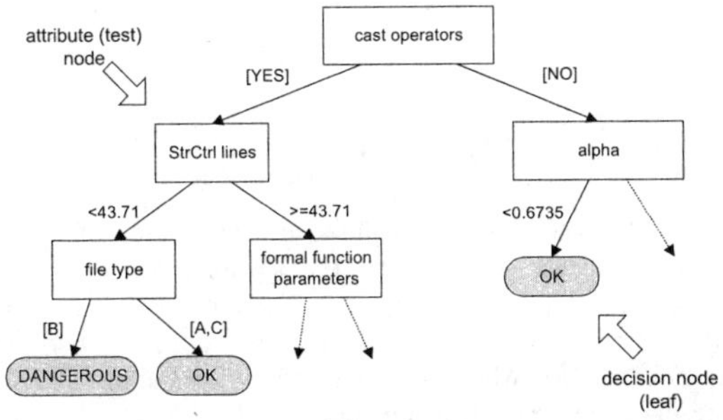

Figure 1. An example of a decision tree.

Evolutionary algorithms are adaptive heuristic search methods which may be used to solve all kinds of complex search and optimisation problems. They are based on the evolutionary ideas of natural selection and genetic processes of biological organisms. As the natural populations evolve according to the principles of natural selection and "survival of the fittest", first laid down by Charles Darwin, so by simulating this process, evolutionary algorithms are able to evolve solutions to real-world problems, if they have been suitably encoded. They are often capable of finding optimal solutions even in the most complex of search spaces or at least they offer significant benefits over other search and optimisation techniques.

As the traditional decision trees' induction methods contain several disadvantages we decided to use the power of evolutionary algorithms to induct the decision trees. In this manner we developed the evolutionary decision support model that evolves decision trees in a multi-population genetic algorithm [20]. Many experiments have shown the advantages of such approach over the traditional heuristic approach for building decision trees, which include better generalisation, higher accuracy, possibility of more than one solution, efficient approach to missing and noisy data, etc.

5.1. The evolutionary decision tree induction algorithm

When defining the internal representation of individuals within the population, together with the appropriate genetic operators that will work upon the population, it is important to assure the feasibility of all solutions during the whole evolution process. Therefore we decided to present individuals directly as decision trees. This approach has some important features: all intermediate solutions are feasible, no information is lost because of conversion between internal representation and the decision tree, the fitness function can be straightforward, etc. The problem with direct coding of solution may bring some problems in defining of genetic operators. As decision trees may be seen as a kind of simple computer programs (with attribute nodes being conditional clauses and decision nodes being assignments) we decided to define genetic operators similar to those used in genetic programming where individuals are computer program trees.

Selection and the fitness function

For the selection purposes a slightly modified linear ranking selection was used. The ranking of an individual decision tree within a population is based on the local fitness function:

$$LFF = \sum_{i=1}^{K} w_i \cdot (1 - acc_i) + \sum_{i=1}^{N} c_i \cdot attr(t_i) + w_u \cdot nu$$

where K is the number of decision classes, N in the number of attribute nodes in a tree, acc_i is the accuracy of classification of objects of a specific decision class d_i, w_i is the importance weight for classifying the objects of a decision class d_i, $attr(t_i)$ is the attribute used for a test in a node t_i, c_i is the cost of using the attribute of $attr(t_i)$, nu is number of unused decision (leaf) nodes, i.e. where no object from the training set fall into, and w_u is the weight of the presence of unused decision nodes in a tree.

According to this local fitness function the best trees (the most fit ones) have the lowest function values – the aim of the evolutionary process is to minimise the value of LFF for the best tree. A near optimal decision tree would classified all training objects with accuracy in accordance with importance weights w_i (some decision classes may be more important than the others), would have very little unused decision nodes (there is no evaluation possible for this kind of decision nodes regarding the training set) and would consist of low-cost attribute nodes (in this manner the desirable/undesirable attributes can be prioritised).

Crossover and mutation

Crossover works on two selected individuals as an exchange of two randomly selected sub-trees. In this manner a randomly selected training object is used to determine paths (by finding a decision through the tree) in both selected trees. Then an attribute node is randomly selected on a path in the first tree and an attribute is randomly selected on a path in the second tree. Finally, the sub-tree from a selected attribute node in the first tree is replaced with the sub-tree from a selected attribute node in the second tree and in this manner an offspring is created which is put into a new population.

Mutation consists of several parts: 1) one randomly selected attribute node is replaced with an attribute, randomly chosen from the set of all attributes; 2) a test in a randomly selected attribute node is changed, i.e. the split constant is mutated; 3) a randomly selected decision (leaf) node is replaced by an attribute node; 4) a randomly selected attribute node is replaced by a decision node.

With the combination of presented crossover, which works as a constructive operator towards local optimums, and mutation, which works as a destructive operator in order to keep the needed genetic diversity, the searching for the solution tends to be directed toward the global optimal solution, which is the most appropriate decision tree regarding our specific needs (expressed in the form of LFF). As the evolution repeats, more qualitative solutions are obtained regarding the chosen fitness function. The evolution stops when an optimal or at least an acceptable solution is found or if the fitness score of the best individual does not change for a predefined number of generations.

6. Fault prediction using decision trees and α metrics

To test the usability of decision trees and fractal metrics α in predicting potentially dangerous modules and in this manner designing reliable software we performed a study in a real world environments. In the example shown bellow we tested a medical software system consisting of 217 modules representing more than 200000 lines of code. For these modules the fault history has been collected over 7 years. The modules have been identified either as OK or DANGEROUS simply by dividing the modules into two classes – bellow and above some fault threshold value (5 faults in our case) [19].

A set of 168 attributes, containing various software complexity measures, have been determined for each software module and the α coefficient has been calculated for each software module using a text processing software developed at our institutions. From all 217 modules 167 have been randomly selected for the learning set, and the remaining 50 modules has been selected for the testing set. Several decision trees have been induced for predicting dangerous modules. In the figure 2 an induced decision tree is presented as an example. The results of classification using induced decision tree is presented in tables 1-3 .

Table 1. Classification results on learning set (number of software modules).

	Classified as OK	Classified as DANGEROUS
OK	108	11
DANGEROUS	4	44

Table 2. Classification results on testing set (number of software modules).

	Classified as OK	Classified as DANGEROUS
OK	30	6
DANGEROUS	4	10

Table 3. Accuracy, sensitivity and specificity of induced decision tree for predicting dangerous software modules (in percents).

	learning set	testing set
accuracy	91.02	80.00
sensitivity	91.67	71.43
specificity	90.76	83.33

Table 4. Accuracy, sensitivity, and specificity on testing set using alternative methods.

	α metric only	**C5/See5**
accuracy	70.0	77.6
sensitivity	66.7	53.1
specificity	72.7	85.6

```
alpha
  |--[<0.63233] OK
  |--[>=0.63233] significance_of_comments
      |--[<1480.04000] StrCtrl_lines
      |   |--[<44.55000] OK
      |   |--[>=44.55000] DANGEROUS
      |--[>=1480.04000] selection_istructions
          |--[<3.79900] DANGEROUS
          |--[>=3.79900] formal_function_parameters
              |--[<19.16200] DANGEROUS
              |--[>=19.16200] significance_of_comments
                  |--[<3026.50800] OK
                  |--[>=3026.50800] DANGEROUS
```

Figure 2. Evolutionary induced decision tree for predicting potentially dangerous software modules.

Above facts showed the usability of decision trees together with various software complexity measures and α metric in software fault prediction. The Table IV shows that the accuracy, when only α metric is used, is about 70% - that means that 70% of modules are correctly classified. When α value is used together with other complexity measures to build the decision tree, the accuracy is increased to 80%, which represents a big improvement, especially regarding the fact that both the sensitivity and the specificity increase. The results, obtained with our method, are also better than those, obtained with C5/See5, especially regarding the balance between sensitivity and specificity.

One of the most interesting characteristic of the induced decision tree (figure 2) is that alpha has been chosen as the most important attribute (root node). This fact shows that α metric is actually useful in predicting dangerous software modules. The combination of α metric with some other software complexity measures as the attributes for decision trees proved to be very successful.

Another important fact is the size of the induced decision tree. As it is very small, regarding the number of possible attributes, it can be concluded that the induced decision tree is highly generalised and is not biased to over-fitting.

Indeed, the decision tree generated presents knowledge which can be transformed into some software design laws, for example

"Modules with low information content (α metric lower than 0.632) are more reliable."

Or a more general law like

"Information content is a good reliability predictor."

These laws or the original decision tree can be used for dangerous module predictions when developing new software systems. We just have to analyse newly developed modules by the attributes (metrics) contained in the decision tree to get a accurate prediction about the reliability of an individual module. Using our approach on various projects, we can possibly generate more laws like above and generalise them to enable more successful software design.

7. Conclusion

In the paper we present the combination of data mining techniques, classifying and complexity analysis in the software reliability research. We show that a new text complexity metrics, called α metric as an attribute together with other software complexity measures can be successfully used to induce decision trees for predicting dangerous modules (modules having a lot of undetected faults). Redesigning such modules or devoting more testing or maintenance effort to them can largely enhance the reliability, making the software much more safe to use. In addition our research shows that text mining can be a very useful technique not only for improving software quality and reliability but also a useful paradigm for searching for fundamental software development laws.

References

[1] Kitchenham, B., "The certainty of uncertainty", Proceedings of FESMA (Eds: Combes H et al), Technologish Institut, 1998, pp. 17-25.
[2] Morowitz, H., "The Emergence of Complexity", Complexity 1(1), 1995, pp. 4.
[3] Gell-Mann, M., "What is complexity", Complexity 1(1), 1995, pp. 16-19.
[4] Schenkel, A., Zhang, J., Zhang, Y., "Long range correlations in human writings", Fractals 1(1), 1993, pp. 47-55.
[5] Kokol, P., Kokol, T., "Linguistic laws and computer programs", Journal of the American Society for Information Science 47(10), 1996, pp. 781-785.
[6] Kokol, P., Brest, J., Žumer, V., "Long-range correlations in computer programs", Cybernetics and systems 28(1), 1997, pp. 43-57.
[7] Kokol, P., Podgorelec, V., Brest, J., "A wishful complexity metric", Proceedings of FESMA (Eds: Combes H et al), Technologish Institut, 1998, pp. 235 - 246.
[8] Kokol, P., "Analysing formal specification with alpha metrics", ACM Software Engineering Notes, 24(1), 1999a, pp. 80-81.
[9] Kokol, P., Podgorelec, V., Zorman, M., Pighin, M., "Alpha - a generic software complexity metric", Project control for software quality : proceedings of ESCOM-SCOPE 99, Shaker Publishing BV, 1999b, pp. 397-405.
[10] Kokol, P., Podgorelec, V., Zorman, M., "Universality - a need for a new software metric", International workshop on software measurement, 1999c, pp. 51-54.
[11] Shannon, C.E., "Prediction and entropy of printed English", Bell System Technical Journal, 1951, pp 30, 50.
[12] Grassberger, P., "Estimating the information content of symbol sequences and efficient codes", IEEE Transactions on Information Technology, 1989, pp. 35, 669.
[13] Li, W., "On the Relationship Between Complexity and Entropy for Markov Chains and Regular Languages", Complex Systems 5(4), 1991, pp. 381 – 399.
[14] Ebeling, W., Neiman A., Poschel T., "Dynamic Entropies, Long-Range Correlations and Fluctations in Complex Linear Structures", Proceedings of Coherent Approach to Fluctations, World Scientific, 1995.
[15] Brooks, P.F., "No silver bullet: essence and accidents of software engineering", *IEEE Computer* 1987, 20(4)10-19, 1987.
[16] Pines, D. (Ed.), "Emerging syntheses in science", Addison Wesley, 1988.
[17] Cohen, B., Harwood, W.T., Jackson, M.I. "The specification of complex systems", Addison Wesley, 1986.

[18] Wegner, P., Israel, M. (Eds.), "Symposium on Computational Complexity and the Nature of Computer Science", Computing Surveys 27(1)5 - 62, 1995.
[19] Pighin, M., Kokol, P., "RPSM: A risk-predictive structural experimental metric", Proceedings of FESMA'99, Technologish Institut, 1999, pp. 459–464.
[20] Podgorelec, V., Kokol, P., "Self-adapting evolutionary decision support model", Proceedings of the 1999 IEEE International Symposium on Industrial Electronics ISIE'99, Bled, Slovenia, IEEE Press, 1999, pp. 1484-1489.
[21] Quinlan, J.R., "C4.5: Programs for Machine Learning", Morgan Kaufmann, 1993.

Software Architecture, Applied Knowledge Engineering

Knowledge-based Software Engineering
T. Welzer et al. (Eds.)
IOS Press, 2002

Symbiotic Information Systems - Towards a Human-Friendly Information System

Haruki Ueno
National Institute of Informatics
2-1-2 Hitotsubashi, Minato-ku, Tokyo
Japan
Tel: +81-3-4212-2516   E-mail: ueno@nii.ac.jp

Abstract Symbiosis is a situation of a system in which every element has its own autonomy and constitute a collaborative community. This type of a community is called a symbiotic community. A Symbiotic Information System (SIS) is an information system which includes human beings as elements and is designed based on the concept of symbiosis. In order to realize an information-based society in the 21st century, every citizen must be allowed to use advanced information systems without any specific training. To realize this situation the information systems must be trained instead of training human beings. This paper discusses the concept of SIS, its background and motivations, study items, goals, case studies, and the way of research, in terms of newly started COE project at NII.

1. Introduction

Nowadays information technology (IT) shows a dramatic progress and obviously, it has been reforming the system of the society largely. It was pointed out for a long time that digitalization of information-based would bring a fusion in the field between communication and broadcast. As a fact, it was more than expected. The globalization of information system carried by the prevalence of Internet promotes every fusion of social informational activities - publication, news, production, distribution, administration, education, daily life, welfare etc. Present communication system with copper wire still has a high usefulness. However, Internet will gain more utility - at least it is certain that information infrastructure as a hardware system will become highly information-oriented, when ultrahigh-speed optical fiber communications network and advanced wireless communications are realized.

In highly information-oriented society, our purpose is to create "anyone, anytime, anywhere" type of information environment - high-tech IT spread over general household, and people receive various kind of service while at home. However, the history shows evidently that advance of software (in a wide sense) is behind the rapid progress of hardware. On looking back at the development of technology, we can see its three phases: First, the technology is available for demonstration and only the researchers can operate it. Then, the trained come to handle it. And at mature phase, everyone come to use it without conscious. Telephone and camera are good examples of matured technology. IT, represented by computer and Internet, has not yet reached the third stage. The fact that the government is working on IT-education or IT-course is nothing but the proof of immaturity of technology. We actually come to be familiar with IT, however it is far from the ideal goal. "Development of trained-computer/information system" way of thinking, instead of training human being, is required. In other words "intelligent information system", more to say, the research and development of "intelligent information infrastructure" is essential. Furthermore, it must be available at reasonable price.

Symbiotic Information System (SIS) ultimately aims at such environment as information system or information infrastructure is indispensable and everyone enjoys the benefit of. The objective of SIS and AI has a lot in common on the point of producing an intelligent computer. Actually, SIS has been studied at various fields. For example, human-friendly machine system, easy-to use computer, various intelligent HI, natural language dialogue, intelligent IR system, constitute the study. However, the research is not enough. It is far from attracting many computerphobe. To solve the problem of "digital divide" will be an extremely significant issue. While the study of IT is in the important position to come up to the needs of society, the study of SIS is especially required to make much of its roll in the society. IT researchers in Japan tend to recognize themes of study in fashion rather than above-mentioned ones. The clues that can be taken from a paper or discussion at the study community are limited. We should start to search a relationship to the society for the goal or theme of study.

In this paper, we would like to examine the study of SIS. The main purpose is not to solve the problem but to pose a problem and give further questions about the study of SIS.

2. What Is SIS?

By Symbiotic Information System, we mean the situation of a system in which human being and information system coexist in a natural way. Although SIS has biologically conceptual relationship to 'symbiosis', it is not used to intend its biological meaning. For reference,

Webster: Biol. the intimate living together of two kinds of organisms, esp. where such association is of mutual advantage: see PARASTISM.

Koujien: the situation in which two kinds of organisms living together and is of benefit to them: ex. Hermit crab and sea anemone, and

Parasitism: the situation in which two kinds of organisms living together and one exploits the other: ex. Vermin

Recently this word is used in a wide sense still more. For example (except our usage): "International Workshop on Biorobotics: Human-Robot Symbiosis, May 1995, Tsukuba" (This book is published by Elsevior as "Robotics and Autonomous Systems 18"[1]. This workshop was held to discuss goal of study in service robot. Its main theme was to discuss human-robot symbiosis.). "James Flanagan, Knowledge Creation- The Symbiotic partnership of University, Government and Industry, Proceedings of Information Environment and International Cooperation for the 21st Century, 2000."([2] the report of plan to promote industry-university cooperative research about IT and case of CAIP Project at Rutgers University. It was a lecture about knowledge-creation based on a case of industry-university cooperative research about Intellectual interface. It was mainly aimed to suggest proper administration for collaborative research as symbiosis between university and company.) Although these examples of usage differ from the original meaning, its nuance remains. The former aims to create a living space in which human beings and robots coexist naturally, while the latter aims for a structure in which university and company coexist to gain a profit at the field of fundamental study of IT by making the best of both domains. The former has close meaning to its original, when we regard robot as quasi being form. The latter intends to represent coexistence of corporations; it is more persuasive than to say "university-enterprise collaboration", for example. (By the way, in Japan recently the word "symbiosis" has often appeared on the newspaper, for examples such as "symbiosis of human and nature". In relation to the matter, there are differences in interpretation between Westerner and Japanese; in western countries, it seems common to regard nature as an object to protect rather than to coexist. This difference may derive from the idea that constitutes each society - monotheism and polytheism. The difference must play an important part on constituting a concept of IT research based on our own idea.)

By symbiosis, we mean: "a situation of a system in which every element has its own autonomy and constitutes a collaborative community". This type of community can be called a symbiotic community. "Symbiotic Information System (SIS) is an information system that includes human beings as elements and designed based on the concept of symbiosis." SIS is mainly constructed by human beings (users) and information system. The information system consists of human interface, operating system, application software, information network, database management system, and contents etc. Each unit can be modeled to acquire autonomy. Naturally, it is able to divide this unit furthermore, since human interface is made up of some intelligent agents.

The purpose of this paper is not to discuss technological theory in detail, but to study the ideal relationship between human being and information system. However, we do not have any paradigm effective to this subject. Thus, we need to do total research on concept formation, modeling, theory, technology development, and feasibility study.

3. Application of SIS

The 21st century is said to be a highly information-oriented society, nevertheless the paradigm required has not yet clarified. However, at least in such society every social person has "right" to enjoy the benefits of the high-tech information service, and an environment in which human beings, machine system, and information infrastructure coexist naturally is essential. Especially the frame to esteem the tradition, culture, and dignity is essential. In fact the present information system supplies only the trained people with its operation, therefore it causes "digital divide". This situation is due to immaturity of paradigm and technology, thus we need to solve the problem fundamentally.

For instance, the birth of computer and prevalence of Windows changed the image of computer before. Though it may not come up to Gutenberg's typography, we can say word processor was an innovator in literal culture. This revolution also has had influence on other application such as CAD software or E-mail. Moreover, Internet affords us to access every type of information worldwide though at home. Likewise, e-commerce has changed the existing business model. Yet, the number of the people who are supplied with ability to operate information technology is so limited that the government has come to handle this issue. How the social system and information service system may be completed, we cannot realize the living space based on information infrastructure, unless the information system becomes user-friendly.

"Anyone, anywhere, anytime" type of information infrastructure has to be the vital necessity for the 21st century. Therefore, the information system must be free from one's age or sex, education, health. It must be operated without any specific education, and every person is to be supplied with the information service in his/her own require. What is most significant is that the information service essential to everyday life must be offered without any specific training or knowledge. In other words, it means, "to train the computer instead of human being". To make an operation of computer more simply it must be technologically improved-so called intelligent computer, intelligent information system is required. This concept leads to the idea of SIS.

Another important thing is that SIS does not necessarily require the technology of high level. It often works enough with existing technology in some cases, or rather; the technology is not yet realized, because of obscurity of what is requested. " i-mode" is a good example of this. Software as well new products are said that they adopt so simple technologies, that development section is strict about their treatment. On the other hand, there are cases that in spite of its obviousness it is hard to attain the goal technologically. For example, neither a robot vision that can recognize a glass nor an art of speech recognition to individuate the voice at party (so called "cocktail party phenomenon") has not realized yet.

At any case, it is significant to define the theme of study after all. Especially in the field of IT, the most effective and appropriate way for the definition is to observe the daily life attentively with the eyes of scientist. Not only a theory and equipment but also such a way of study as to proceed by the trial and error through feasibility study is effective. With this spiral, we can reach to significant goal, and can develop useful technology. This issue is common to every country in the world and therefore it is necessary to study through international collaboration.

4. SIS Research Topics

The long-term goal of SIS is to accomplish the information system for "anyone, anytime, anywhere". Apart from advanced technology for experts, consider now the technique for supporting the people in general. Hence it is necessary to research symbiosis in the relation of human and information system, computer, and robots. IT is required socially to play important roll as to support the information the weak, including the aged and disabled. We can assume as well symbiotic relations between humans (IT works to promote symbiosis of humans, such as groupware or distance learning), computers, and machines. Furthermore, we can also assume symbiosis of information infrastructure and application, or between applications (agents). On research in SIS the elements of the system are to be modeled as agents (autonomous software organisms). With the accurate conception of SIS symbiotic relation between human and natural/artificial environment will be recognized properly especially under Eastern ideas, i.e., Buddhism.

On going in look-ahead basic research, first, it is important not only to make academic contribution (to write a paper), but also to work on general people to diffuse the concept, as their evaluation is usually more adequate than that of pretentious researchers is. For this reason to put an academic demonstration that is easy to understand, interesting, and practical is effective. Though the development of demonstration system may costs a lot, it is essential to maintain the relationship between basic researches and the society.

Second, thus we need to develop the software, the platform for SIS demonstration system (application system). This development is to be itself an important theme in software engineering, because the platform is a sort of advanced program language, and the information modeling of assumed SIS is necessary to configure it. Therefore, the development of SIS operated by the platform will play an important roll in its configuration, realization, and estimation. Moreover, the improvement through such estimation leads to the possibility of practical, multipurpose platform. (C language will not work in this case: it is not only suited to develop the SIS demonstration system, but also to make a technological infection, or to contribute to the software engineering. This would be the main reason why Japan gets behind in developing general purpose software with new concept or function compared with the West.)

Examples of SIS research topics are as follows:

Research on Software Platform (software environments for SIS research)
- Software platform for developing distributed autonomous system
- Quality-of-Service network infrastructure
- Development and execution environment for distributed autonomous intelligent system
- High-performance large-scale multimedia information management system
- Development and execution environment for Multi-agent system, etc.

Basic research for case study (case study ∩ basic research)
- Human-computer cooperative system
- Autonomous intelligent robot
- Intelligent human/ natural interface
- Virtual reality distance conference system
- Adaptive distance learning system
- Ubiquitous information search assistant system
- Evolution system, etc.

5. SIS Researches on Robotics

Consider now the purpose, topics, viewpoint of the study, and elementary research topics taking one of my research fields, intelligent robot (autonomous robot), for instance. Consider the state that human beings and robots coexist naturally as human-robot symbiosis.

5.1 Examples of topics for case study : intelligent robot

The purpose of this study is to develop the all-in-one system that aims to realize human-like construction, figure, function, intelligence, and mind.

1) Research topics related to intelligent robot (varieties of intelligent robot):
autonomous service robot, welfare robot, collaborative robot, remote manipulator robot, autonomous mobile robot, entertainment robot, pet robot, new generation industrial robot
2) Examples of element research essential for studying intelligent robot
robotic vision, task/motion schedule, intelligent control, world model, human interface, natural verbal communication, platform, dynamic environment adaption, monitoring, meaning

understanding, intention understanding, learning system, evolution system, biological model
3) Purpose, function, feature, of each type robot
•service robot:
robot which assists or acts for human. For example, cleaning robot, carry robot, guide robot, communication robot, etc.
•entertainment robot:
robot which acts as an entertainer. The research topic is to study the way human relieves one's stress and recovers oneself.
•pet robot:
robot which acts as pet. The research topic is to study the feature of pet- show lovely behavior, obedience to the master, or to imitate and greet the master, to get familiar with his habit and to sulk when it is not taken care of.
•welfare robot:
robot aims to serve disabled or aged person. For example care-taking robot, self-support assistant robot, walker robot, assistant robot for practice walking or learning language, etc.

5.2 Research in human-robot interface

The issue of this theme is "Is it possible to introduce a paradigm of man-to-man interface into human-robot interface?", since robot is a model of human beings. What we are concerned here is to solve the conceptual and technological problem regarding. To solve this problem we are to make use of existing technology or develop a new technology, which is convincing rather than novel.

•Types of robotic operation :
action-repeat type (industrial robot), handle/button operated type, program operated type, command operated type. Motion energy amplify type (such as, operating a crane with a finger). Cognitive intelligence amplify type (recognizes a faint light, invisible light, inaudible sound, insensible energy).
•Natural interface(based on human-robot communication):
Natural language-based communication. Communication based on expression, action and view. Understanding of meaning and intention. Learning ability (improvement in motion, communication and function).

5.3 Significance of case study: entertainment robot

Though we are considering the research of SIS as a basic study, it is important for the research to be dealt as a case study, or it will lapse into a self-complacent, casual one. The main purpose of the case study is to develop an academic demonstration. Let us examine the research in entertainment robot for example.

1) Examples of demonstration system
respond to humans, imitate the action, chat with people, guide the people, carry a load, follow the people around, and play with people. Robots fawn on each other, show their feelings, act unexpectedly, and communicate through TV picture
2) Academic elements
Voice communication, natural language understanding, intention understanding, modeling of mind, simulation of feelings, formulation of unexpectedness, modeling of cooperation, platform, knowledge system, flexible control, distributed cooperation system, evolutional system, intelligent agent, agent programming, middleware software, multimedia processing, etc.

What is significant is that the demonstration system enables the people to understand its importance immediately, and in addition, the system is realized by academic elements as a result of research on advanced IT. (When an introduction of a paradigm or concept would be the main purpose, the introduction itself is so important that we need not to consider originality of the character technique. For example, though we have only to develop a faster system to overcome its problem in speed, it is impossible to have a lucking paradigm exist.

Why do only a few researchers in Japan as well in the West recognize the fact.)

6. AI and SIS Researches

In this section, related previous researches on AI are roughly summarized and some discussions are made to provide understanding of the role of AI in SIS.

6.1 Perception and affordance

One of the basic research topics on intelligent man-machine interface is about how human or animal perceives the image of objects and the environment. Although the concept of perception is not new, it is rather difficult to obtain the model of human perception. In the 70s, studies on some fields of Artificial Intelligence such as image processing and character recognition were relying on the paradigm of "Data – Feature – Extraction – Identification". However, it turned out that accuracy was not good enough and still far from the level of human. Fuzzy logic and neural-computing were developed after that and better accuracy was obtained under controlled environments. Since then, the research progressed considerably and found more applications in many fields including robot vision. Vision is an important and challenging component, which became an important research domain for young researchers nowadays. A paradigm of "computation with words" presented by Lotfi A. Zadeh [4] seems to be useful in realizing a word-based human-robot interface as an extension of Fuzzy logic. In this paradigm human's way of computation by means of "words" is proposed, instead of traditional way of "computation with numbers".

Affordance theory is a kind of Cognitive Science theories relating to human consciousness system. It was studied and synthesized by James J. Gibson from the 40s to the 60s [3]. The idea started from the question over how a man perceives an object and its environment. Usually it is believed that perception is based on information processing model in which information from the retina is processed, and the object is identified. However, Gibson suggests the hypothesis that perceptive information is not obtained by reasoning, but is something belonging to the object and environment. The object itself affords the information. In perception, the man just "search" for this information: "To perceive them is to perceive what they afford". This hypothesis has been proven by various cognitive-psychology experiments. This idea has a number of supporters, called Gibsonian. "When you are looking for a chair, the chair of a design can be known at a glance" indicates that the chair is emitting affordance, provided that the design is psychologically given. As a result, if a graphical interface is designed based on this affordance theory, the human interface which requires no particular training should be obtained.

6.2 Researches on AI

It is no question that Artificial Intelligence (AI) bears a very important role in research of SIS. This is because SIS is an intelligence system in a wide sense. During the 70s, AI was progressing quickly. It started from the attempts to answer simple questions about human intelligence, and was followed by research on real practical problems which led to development of various scientific demonstration and experiment systems. Generally, by comparing the features with human, new AI research challenges can always be found.

The usefulness of the knowledge processing models and tools attracted wide attentions, and several attempts were made to deploy the system to industry during the 80s. However, it turned out that a practical system could not be realized easily and progress in AI was frozen again. Researchers then turned back to basic researches on his or her own interest with the hope that they would be useful in the future.

Now, it can be considered the time to return to the real problems once again. But instead of basing on someone's proposals, one should aim the research in solving some simple real problems. For example, although the mechanism of evolution is not yet known well, there is a tendency among AI researchers to pick up a problem out of the box, and try to apply an evolution model on it. Out of that model, a number of basic researches and applications are made. When the research topic on that model is exhausted, someone will look for another problem and come up with another model as research material. This repetitive cycle can mislead to perception that progress in AI is advancing rapidly while, in fact, it is not.

6.3 Researches on intelligence

The main research fields on intelligence can be divided into Artificial Intelligence (AI) and Cognitive Science (CS). Both are focusing on realization of the machine (computer software) which posses human intellectual property, and ability to solve problem by itself. While CS emphasizes on investigation and explanation of human intelligence by the methods of experiments and consideration, AI researches focus on realizing the intelligence by computer software. Therefore, CS is psychology and AI is information science. The applications of AI tend to be on knowledge systems and expert systems. Though AI has been using symbolic processing model to explain and implement the intelligence, there are also fields which deal with intelligence by using numerical calculation model such as a fuzzy system or a neural system. Progress is being made in combining results from symbolic and numerical processing sides to realize the system with better intelligence.

In general, dealing with "The problem of realizing human's intelligent ability on a machine" can be considered the research topics on intelligence. Natural language processing, speech recognition, image processing are examples of important research domain to be continued. These functions are important and they will never be realized as a general-purpose system.

Recently, there are also researches which borrow hints from human or animals. Genetic algorithms, Evolution systems, Soft Computing, are some examples. It can be seen that researchers are now carrying out their research from a number of approaches: psychological approach, numerical model approach, knowledge model approach, logical approach, and network model approach, etc. Moreover, not only the intelligence of an individual but the group intelligence also serves as the research topic.

SIS does not post any limit on the methodology used in the research. SIS main research target asks for the ideal symbiosis model between human and the information system. It is recommended that researchers tackle the subject by various methods. It is our hope that SIS will provide a place for researchers and general users to exchange their ideas.

7. Discussions

This paper described the motivation and outline the concepts of the newly launched 5-year COE project on the symbiotic information system (SIS) at NII. Inspired by the need to bring advanced information system to everybody, the project aims to encourage research activities toward better integration of advanced information system in daily life. As an example, an agent-based model for implementation of robot manipulator sharing over the Internet is proposed. Under the proposed model, intelligent components make it possible to construct the system, which allows sharing of multiple robots to multiple web users concurrently with easy-to-use user interface. The system is also extensible by introducing additional functional agents.

Since the project has started a year ago and SIS is too ambitious for us we could not show a concrete idea about the concepts nor technologies at this moment. The reason why we have chosen the topics of autonomous robots, such as, a humanoid robot and a human-friendly robot, as case studies of the SIS research, is

1) a robotic system consists of a variety of autonomous elements, which must collaborate each other in a realistic environment, and

2) a robot is quite attractive in showing the concepts and technologies to ordinary persons. An experimental system has demonstrated some interesting functions even with rather simple mechanisms.

In the next stage of this COE sub-project we are planning to apply the knowledge-based framework, which was developed in an earlier project on an autonomous intelligent humanoid robot Haris [2, 12], in order to append higher intelligence to our robotic system. The image of the knowledge-based software structure is as shown in Figure 1 and 2. Haris receives a human's request in a natural sentence such as "Put a red cup onto a white plate", then understands the meaning, sets a task goal, i.e., "put" in this example, understands the scene by 3D vision, plans a sequence of tasks to achieve the goal, generates robotic commands, and controls the robotic arm and hand. While, the execution is monitored by the vision-based monitoring system. The World model, i.e., a knowledge base, plays a key role in achieving the autonomy. These modules are working together in a framework of distributed agents in a LAN environment. The World model is working as a blackboard in communicating the modules. This software system is designed not only for the Haris arm but also a variety of human-robotic collaboration systems in the SIS framework.

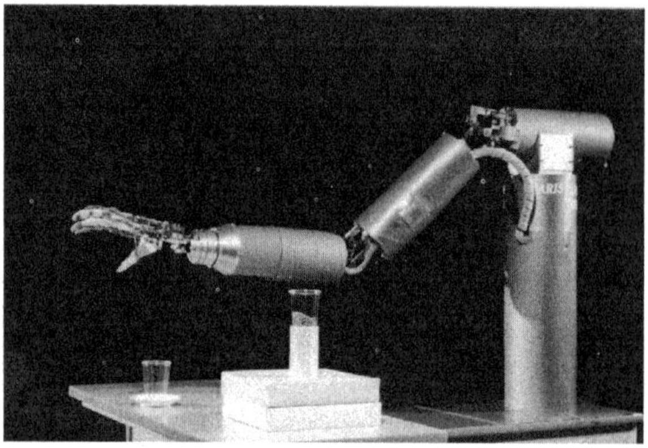

Fig. 1 An overview of the Haris robotic arm.

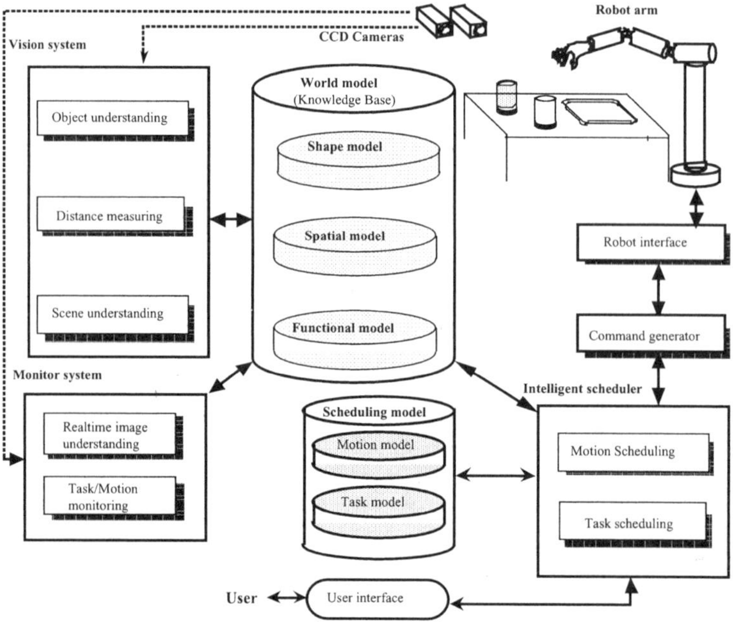

Fig. 2 An overall structure of the knowledge-based system for an intelligent robot in the SIS framework [2, 12].

While, we are developing a human-robot collaboration system including two mobile robots in the framework of SIS, as shown in Figure 2 [11].

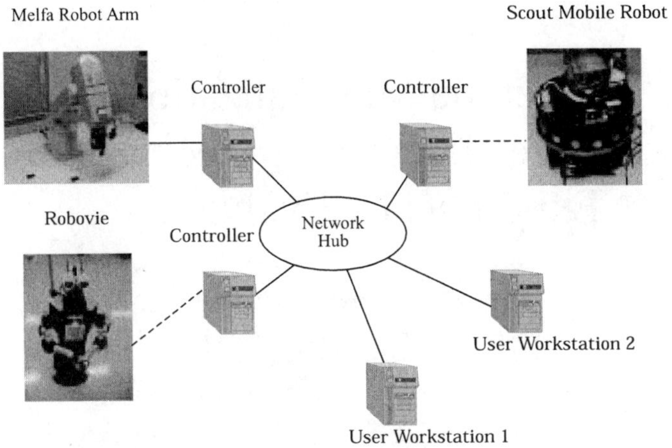

Figure 3. System Diagram of a Svmbiotic Robot Svstem

References

[1] International Workshop on Biorobotics: Human-Robot Symbiosis (Eds. K. Kawamura and T.E. Davis), Robotics and Automation Systems, Vol. 18, Elsevier, 1996.
[2] Haruki Ueno, A Cognitive Science-Based Knowledge Modeling for Autonomous Humanoid Service Robot - Towards a Human-Robot Symbiosis, Proc. 10th European-Japanese Conference on Information Modeling and Knowledge Bases, pp.82-95, 2000.
[3] Masato Sasaki, Affordance: New Theory of Cognition, Iwanamishoten, 1994.
[4] Lofti A. Zadeh, From Computing with Numbers to Computing with Words: From Manipulation of Measurements to Manipulation of Perception, IEEE Trans. Circuits and Systems, Vol.45, No.1, 1999.
[5] Haruki Ueno, Design and Issues of National Institute of Informatics – Discussions on Foundation of IT Basic Research Institute and Its Role, SIG-KBSE99-53, pp.33-40, 2000.
[6] James Flanagan, Knowledge Creation – The Symbiotic partnership of University, Government, and Industry, Proc. Information Environment and International Cooperation for the 21st Century, 2000.
[7] Haruki Ueno, "Encouragement of Research on Symbiotic Informations Systems", COE research proposal.
[8] Masato Sasaki, "Affordance – The New Cognitive Theory", Iwanami Library of Science, 1994.
[9] Ken Taylor and Barney Dalton, "Issues in Internet Telerobotics", Presented at FSR'97 International Conference on Field and Service Robotics at The Australian National University, Canberra, Australia 8-10 December 1997.
[10] Bryan Adams, Cynthia Breazeal, Rodney A. Brooks, Brian Scassellati, "Humanoid Robots: A New Kind of Tool", IEEE Intelligent Systems, July/August 2000, pg. 25-31.
[11] Vuthichai Ampornaramveth, Haruki Ueno, "Concepts of Symbiotic Information System and Its Application to Robotics", Proceedings of the 11th European-Japanese Conference on Information Modelling and Knowledge Bases, pp. 394-407, 2001.
[12] Haruki Ueno, A Knowledge-Based Information Modeling for Autonomous Humanoid Service Robot, IEICE Transactions on Information and Systems, Vol. E85-D, No.4, pp.657-665, 2002

Knowledge-based Software Engineering
T. Welzer et al. (Eds.)
IOS Press, 2002

Method Materialization Using the Hierarchical Technique: Experimental Evaluation

Bartosz BĘBEL, Robert WREMBEL
Poznań University of Technology, Institute of Computing Science
Piotrowo 3A, 60-965 Poznań, Poland
{Bartosz.Bebel, Robert.Wrembel} @cs.put.poznan.pl

Abstract. The application of materialized object–oriented views in an object–relational data warehousing technology is promising. This paper presents a materialization technique of method results in object–oriented views, called *hierarchical materialization*. The hierarchical materialization was implemented and evaluated by a number of experiments concerning methods without input arguments as well as methods with input arguments, for various patterns of method dependencies. The obtained results show that the hierarchical materialization significantly reduces method recomputation time. In this paper we present and analyze the experimental results concerning performance of methods with input arguments.

1. Introduction

New, dynamically growing branches of industry process and store large amounts of data. The information collected in an enterprise is often of different data format and complexity (e.g., relational, object–relational, object–oriented, on-line, Web pages, semi–structured, spreadsheets, flat files) and is stored in information systems that usually have different functionality. As the management of an enterprise requires a comprehensive view of most of its data, one of the important tasks of an information system is to provide an integrated access to all data sources within an enterprise. In practice, data warehousing systems are very often used as a "tool" for data integration. A data warehouse is seen as a set of materialized views. In the process of integrating and warehousing complex data, object–relational data warehouse systems are suitable [3, 4]. In this field, materialized object–oriented views (MOOV) are very promising, however, few approaches have been proposed so far.

We have developed an approach to object–oriented views, called *View Schema Approach* (VSA). In VSA, an *object-oriented view* (OOV) is defined as a *view schema* of an arbitrary complex structure and behavior, composed of view classes. Each *view class* is derived from one or more classes in a database schema. A view class is derived by an OQL-like command defining its structure, behavior, and set of instances [7, 8]. View classes in a view schema are connected by inheritance and aggregation relationships. Several view schemas may be defined in one database and each of them is uniquely identified by its name. Each view schema may be materialized, meaning that all instances of all view classes in a view schema become persistent. Our approach supports also the maintenance of a materialized view schema (cf. [8]).

While materializing an OOV one should consider not only materialization of objects' structure but also objects' methods. The materialization of a method consists in computing the result of the method once, storing it persistently in a database, and then, using the persistent value when the method is invoked, rather than computing it every time the method is invoked. When a method result is made persistent it has to be kept up to date when data used to compute this result change. When method *m* is materialized, it may be reasonable to materialize also the intermediate results of methods called from *m*. We call this technique *hierarchical materialization*. When an object used to materialize the result of method *m* is updated, then *m* has to be recomputed. This recomputation can use unaffected intermediate results that have already been materialized, thus reducing the time spent on recomputation.

There are a few approaches that address method *precomputation*, i.e. materialization, in the context of indexing techniques and query optimization [5, 1, 6] but not in the context of materialized object–oriented views. The work of [5] sets up the analytical framework for estimating costs of caching complex objects. Two data representations are considered, i.e., procedural representation and object identity based representation. In the approach of [1], the results of materialized methods are stored in an index structure based on B–tree, called *method–index*. A method–index on a method *M* stores in its key values the results of the invocation of *M* on the instances of the indexed class. The application of method materialization proposed in [1] is limited to methods that: (1) do not have input arguments, (2) use only atomic type attributes to compute their values, and (3) do not modify values of objects. The concept of [6] proposes data structures supporting materialization of methods and maintenance of materialized results. However, this approach does not take into account the fact that methods depend on each other by calling one method from the other one.

In this paper we briefly present a framework for the hierarchical materialization of method results in object–oriented views (Section 2), discuss its implementation and experimental evaluation (Section 3), and draw conclusions (Section 4).

2. Hierarchical Materialization of Methods

2.1. Overview of Hierarchical Materialization Technique

When *hierarchical materialization* is applied to method m_i, then the result of m_i is stored persistently and additionally, the intermediate results of methods called from m_i are also stored persistently. After the materialization of m_i, the result of the first invocation of method m_i for view object vo_i is stored persistently. Each subsequent invocation of m_i for the same object vo_i uses the already materialized value. When an object vo_i, used to materialize the result of method m_i, is updated or deleted, then m_i has to be recomputed. This recomputation can use unaffected intermediate materialized results, thus reducing the recomputation time overhead.

Methods may have various numbers of input arguments, that can be of various types. Generally, methods that have input arguments are not good candidates for the materialization. However, in our approach, a method with input arguments can be materialized and maintained within acceptable time provided that: (1) the method has few input arguments and (2) each of the arguments has a narrow, discrete domain.

Example 1. Let us consider view classes *V_Computer* – composed of *V_CDDrive*, *V_Disk*, and *V_MainBoard*. *V_MainBoard* in turn is composed of *V_RAM* and *V_CPU*, whose instances are shown in Figure 1. Each view class in this view schema has a method, called *power_cons*, that returns the consumption of electricity power by a computer's component. Power consumed by each instance of *V_Main_Board* is the sum of power consumed by *V_RAM*, *V_CPU*, and *V_MainBoard* itself. Similarly, power consumed by each instance of *V_Computer* is the sum of power consumed by *V_CDDrive*, *V_MainBoard*, and *V_Disk*.

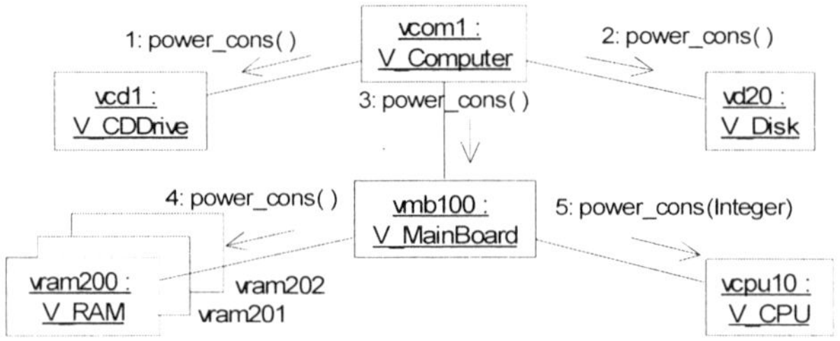

Figure 1. An example of materialized view schema instances

Let us further assume that the instance of *V_Computer*, namely the object identified by $vcom_1$ is composed of objects vcd_1 (the instance of view class *V_CDDrive*), vd_{20} (the instance of view class *V_Disk*), and vmb_{100} (the instance of *V_MainBoard*), which in turn is composed of: $vram_{200}$, $vram_{201}$, $vram_{202}$, and $vcpu_{10}$.

The result of *V_Computer::power_cons* is materialized for the instance of *V_Computer* only when this method is invoked for this instance. Furthermore, all the methods called from *V_Computer::power_cons* are also materialized when they are executed.

Let us assume that the *power_cons* method was invoked for $vcom_1$. In our example, the hierarchical materialization mechanism results in materializing values of the following methods: *V_RAM::power_cons* for objects identified by $vram_{200}$, $vram_{201}$, and $vram_{202}$, *V_CPU::power_cons* for object $vcpu_{10}$, *V_MainBoard::power_cons* for object vmb_{100}, *V_Disk::power_cons* for object vd_{20}, *V_CDDrive::power_cons* for object vcd_1, and finally *V_Computer::power_cons* for object $vcom_1$.

□

2.2. Data Structures

In order to materialize methods in a view class and maintain the materialized results, three additional data structures have been created in an operational data store. These structures, which are described below, are called *View Methods*, *Materialized Method Results Structure*, and *Graph of Method Calls* (cf. [2, 8]).

View Methods (***VM*** for short) makes available the data dictionary information about all methods and their signatures implemented in view classes.

The chain of method dependencies, where one method calls another, is called *Graph of Method Calls* (***GMC*** for short). When materialized method m_j becomes invalid all the materialized methods that use the value of m_j also become invalid. In order to invalidate those methods the content of ***GMC*** is used.

As the same method can be invoked for different instances of a given view class and the same method can be invoked with different values of input arguments, the system has to maintain the mappings between: (1) the materialized value of a method, (2) an object for which it was invoked, and (3) values of input arguments. The mappings are represented in the structure, called *Materialized Method Results Structure* (***MMRS*** for short). When method m_i is invoked for a given view object vo_i and this method has been previously set as materialized, then ***MMRS*** is searched in order to get the result of m_i invoked for vo_i. If it is not found then, m_i is computed for vo_i and stored in ***MMRS***. Otherwise, the materialized result of m_i is read instead of executing m_i. When an object used to compute the materialized value of m_i is updated or deleted, then the materialized value becomes invalid. In such a case, appropriate record is removed from ***MMRS***. The removal of the result of method m_j causes that the results of methods that called m_j also become invalid and have to be removed from ***MMRS***. The removal of materialized results from ***MMRS*** is recursively executed up to the root of ***GMC***.

3. Experimental Evaluation

The proposed hierarchical materialization technique has been implemented within so called *View Schema Approach Prototype* (*VSAP*) on top of the *Oracle8i* DBMS, using its object–oriented features. The following environment was used for the experiments: *Oralce9i* running under control of Linux, on a PC with Intel Celeron 333MHz, with 512MB of RAM. The size of a database buffer equalled 16MB.

The experiments were performed for different shapes of *Graph of Method Calls*, as shown in Figure 2. For example, in the first case (Figure 2a) method m_1 called m_{11} and m_{12}. The result of m_1 was computed as the sum of results returned by m_{11} and m_{12}. Similarly, m_{11} called m_{111} and m_{112} by summing up their results. The same computation pattern was used for the rest of methods in this ***GMC***. The experiments were performed for various numbers of root complex objects (from 100 to 5000).

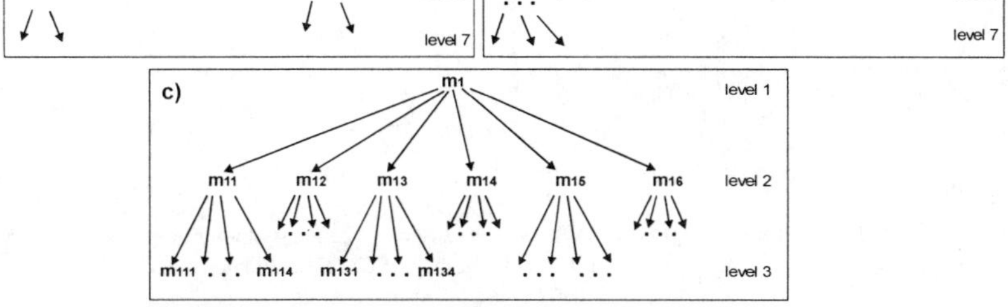

Figure 2. Different shapes of *Graph of Method Calls* used in the experiment

3.1. Storage Space Overhead

The below table summarizes the space overhead for storing the content of ***MMRS*** and ***GMC*** for the shapes of ***GMC*** shown in Figure 2. Methods without input arguments, with 2, and 4 input arguments are taken into account.

Table 1. Space overhead for storing the content of ***MMRS*** and ***GMC***

GMC	Number of arguments	MMRS [kB]	GMC [kB]
a)	0	15 875	14.8
	2	67 469	14.8
	4	285 750	14.8
b)	0	45 500	42.5
	2	193 375	42.5
	4	819 000	42.5
c)	0	3 875	3.5
	2	16 469	3.5
	4	69 750	3.5

3.2. Method Performances

Chart 1a shows the total time overhead for: (1) the execution of method m_l without materialization (*Exe*), (2) the execution of method m_l together with the materialization of its result (*E+M*). Whereas Chart 1b shows the total time overhead for: (3) reading the materialized result of method m_l (*RM*), (4) the invalidation of method m_l (*Inv*), and (5) the rematerialization of a previously invalidated method m_l (*Rem*). These five kinds of time overhead were measured for m_l having 0, 2, and 4 input arguments, for 2000 root complex objects. ***GMC***s had shapes as shown in Figure 2 **a**, **b**, and **c**. The corresponding average times, computed per one root complex object, are presented in Chart 2a and 2b.

In these experiments, the invalidation of *m1* was caused by updating an object used to compute the result of a leaf–method, thus one branch of ***GMC*** was invalidated from the very bottom method to the very top method *m1*.

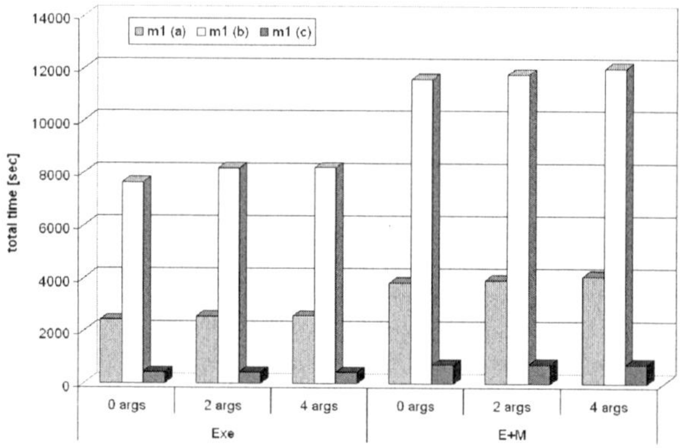

Chart 1a. Total times of processing method m_l having 0, 2, and 4 input arguments, for 2000 root complex objects (one branch of ***GMC*** invalidated); three shapes of ***GMC*** were taken into account

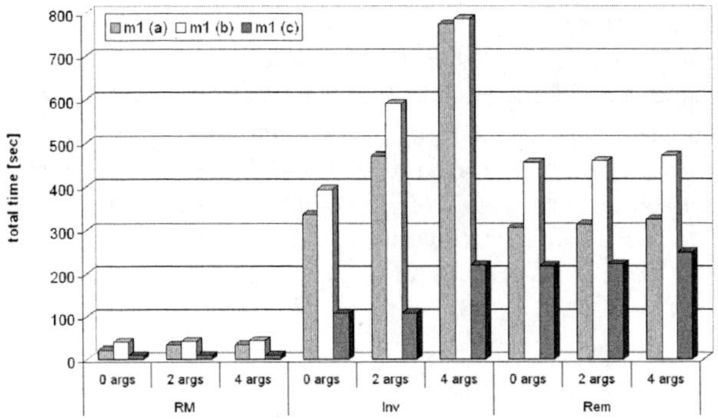

Chart 1b. Total times of processing method m_1 having 0, 2, and 4 input arguments, for 2000 root complex objects (one branch of ***GMC*** invalidated); three shapes of ***GMC*** were taken into account

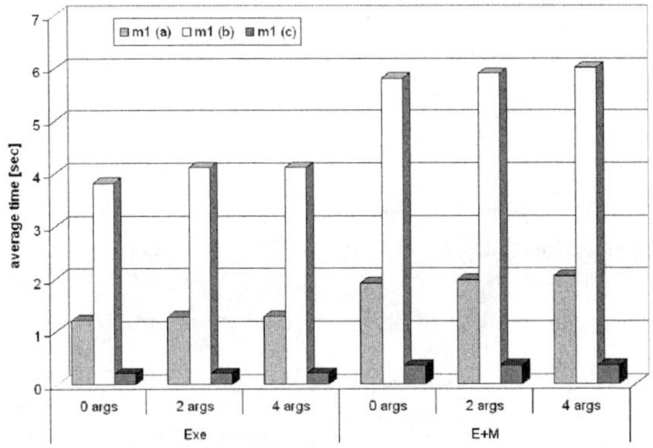

Chart 2a. Average times of processing method m_1 having 0, 2, and 4 input arguments, for 2000 root complex objects (one branch of ***GMC*** invalidated); three shapes of ***GMC*** were taken into account

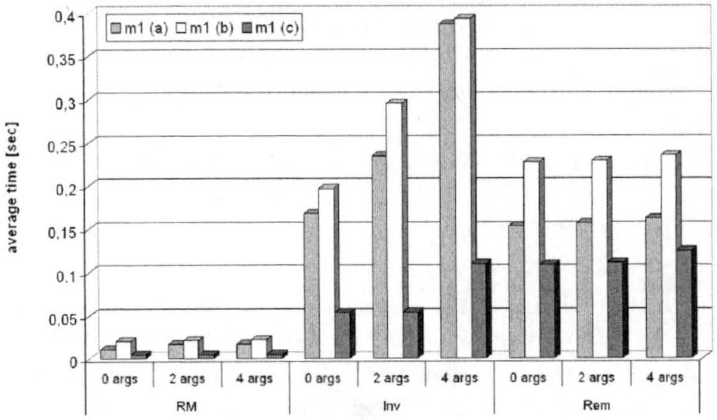

Chart 2b. Average times of processing method m_1 having 0, 2, and 4 input arguments, for 2000 root complex objects (one branch of ***GMC*** invalidated); three shapes of ***GMC*** were taken into account

In order to measure the usefulness of hierarchical materialization we computed the following time coefficient: **tc = (Inv + Rem) / Exe**. This coefficient is different for different ***GMC***s shapes and different numbers of input arguments, as shown in Table 2.

In *case 1*, the value of **tc** equals 0.26, meaning that thanks to the hierarchical materialization technique, method m_1 (the root of ***GMC***) was executed approximately 3.8 times faster than without materialization (column *1/tc*). In *case 2* and *case 3* the execution times were reduced 3.2 and 2.3 times, respectively.

The best performance we gained in *case 4*, *case 5*, and *case 6*, where the execution times were reduced 9.1, 7.7, and 6.7, respectively.

Table 2. Time coefficients for different shapes of ***GMC*** and different numbers of input arguments

		Exe	*Inv*	*Rem*	*tc*	*1/tc*
case 1	m_1 (shape a), 0 param.	1,21	0,17	0,15	0,26	3,8
case 2	m_1 (shape a), 2 param.	1,28	0,23	0,16	0,31	3,2
case 3	m_1 (shape a), 4 param.	1,29	0,39	0,16	0,43	2,3
case 4	m_1 (shape b), 0 param.	3,81	0,20	0,23	0,11	9,1
case 5	m_1 (shape b), 2 param.	4,10	0,30	0,23	0,13	7,7
case 6	m_1 (shape b), 4 param.	4,10	0,39	0,24	0,15	6,7
case 7	m_1 (shape c), 0 param.	0,21	0,05	0,11	0,77	1,3
case 8	m_1 (shape c), 2 param.	0,21	0,05	0,11	0,78	1,3
case 9	m_1 (shape c), 4 param.	0,21	0,11	0,12	1,11	0,9

In *case 7* and *case 8* the execution times were reduced 1.3 times. Whereas, in *case 9* methods' performance deteriorated – was slowed down 0.9 times.

As we can see from the charts and Table 2, input arguments do not introduce much time overhead, provided that the number of input arguments is small and their domains are narrow and discrete.

4. Conclusions

The support for object–oriented views materialization and maintenance with respect to its structure and methods is required when applying such views in object–relational data warehousing systems. Such views are able to: (1) integrate not only data of complex structure but also manage the behavior of data, i.e. methods and (2) transform simple relational data to data of complex structure, and vice versa. In this paper we presented a framework for methods materialization in MOOV which, to the best of our knowledge, has not been previously considered in research. Our *hierarchical* technique of methods materialization was implemented and evaluated by a number of experiments. In this paper we focused on management of methods with input arguments.

From the results that we obtained it is clearly seen that the hierarchical materialization gives good results (1) for ***GMC***s that have more than two levels and where one method calls a few other methods (cf. shape **a** and **b**) and (2) for methods without input arguments or methods having few input arguments each of which has a very narrow discrete domain.

The **tc** coefficient mostly depends (1) on the shape of ***GMC*** and (2) on the number of objects being updated, which in a consequence, impacts the number of methods whose results have to be invalidated and rematerialized.

In current implementation of the prototype system, a database administrator is responsible for choosing a method for materialization. Future work will focus on developing a cost model and a tool that will allow the system to select and visualize the right methods for materialization.

References

[1] Bertino E.: Method precomputation in object–oriented databases. Proceedings of ACM–SIGOIS and IEEE–TC–OA International Conference on Organizational Computing Systems, 1991

[2] Bębel B., Wrembel R.: Hierarchical Materialisation of Methods in Object-Oriented Views: Design, Maintenance, and Experimental Evaluation. Proc. of the DOLAP'01 Conference, Atlanta, USA, November, 2001

[3] Eder J., Frank H., Morzy T., Wrembel R., Zakrzewicz M.: Designing an Object-Relational Database System: Project ORDAWA. Proc. of challenges of ADBIS-DASFAA 2000, Prague, Czech Republic, 2000, pp.223-227.

[4] Huynh T.N., Mangisengi O., Tjoa A.M.: Metadata for Object–Relational Data Warehouse. Proc. of DMDW'2000, Sweden, 2000.

[5] Jhingran A.: Precomputation in a Complex Object Environment. Proc of IEEE Data Engineering Japan, 1991, pp. 652-659

[6] Kemper A., Kilger C., Moerkotte G.: Function Materialization in Object Bases: Design, Realization, and Evaluation. *IEEE Transactions on Knowledge and Data Engineering*, Vol. 6, No. 4, 1994

[7] Wrembel R.: On Materialising Object-Oriented Views. In Barzdins J., Caplinskas A. (eds.): Databases and Information Systems. Kluwer Academic Publishers, 2001, ISBN 0-7923-6823-1, pp. 15-28

[8] Wrembel R.: The Construction and Maintenance of Mateiralised Object–Oriented Views in Data Warehousing Systems. PhD thesis, Poznań University of Technology, Institute of Computing Science, Poznań, Poland, March, 2001

Knowledge-based Software Engineering
T. Welzer et al. (Eds.)
IOS Press, 2002

A Support Method for Widget Replacement to Realize High Usability

Junko Shirogane[1], Kouji Watanabe[1] and Yoshiaki Fukazawa[1]
[1]*Waseda University, Ohkubo 3-4-1, Shinjuku-ku, Tokyo 169-8555, Japan*

Abstract.
In recent years, not only functionality but also usability is required in software. In order to develop highly usable GUI (Graphical User Interface), it is effective that end users evaluate their GUI and the results are reflected on the original GUI. In these cases, it is necessary to replace a widget with another widget, and to reconnect new GUI part with original body part. When widgets are replaced, the operations are usually changed, but the roles of GUI are seldom changed. In this research, we propose a development method for GUI applications with easy operations and also an automatic reconnection method between GUI parts and new body parts in widgets. This reconnection is realized by classifying widgets according to their roles and by replacing methods of widgets with abstract methods categorized by common roles.

1 Introduction

Software has been mainly used by experts of computer systems, but recently, many end users who have little knowledge of computer systems have the opportunity to use software[1]. So, software should be developed with emphases on usability as well as utility in order for end users to easily use software.

It is important for experts of human interface, cognitive psychology and human factors engineering to become members of software development teams as GUI (Graphical User Interface) designers in order to develop usable software. However, the capabilities of good GUI designers are often different from those of good programmers, so GUI designers are required to inform specifications of GUI designs to programmers via papers. So much cost and time is required to inform GUI designs properly.

In order to develop usable GUI, it is also effective for GUI designers and programmers to repeat the process that they show the GUI to end-users, modify GUI according to the results of end-users' evaluation, and show the GUI to end users, and for end users to evaluate the GUI again[2].

GUI is often required to make a change in the operation phase as well as in development for improving usability. In these cases, it is necessary to modify GUI of applications in the operation phase.

Therefore, it is necessary for GUI designers and programmers to consider to change GUI in order to make it usable, and to this end, easy GUI modification is very important for the improvement of usability. In this paper, focusing on easy GUI modification, we propose a method for generating a GUI application and modifying the GUI following the end user's requirement. Application programs are modified automatically in replacing GUI components (widgets) by classifying widgets according to their roles and by replacing methods of widgets with a common role. Our target programming language is Java and widgets used as examples in this paper are GUI parts in Swing package of Java.

2 Features

Our main purpose is easy development of usable GUI applications by realizing easy GUI modification.

In order to develop usable GUI, it is important for GUI not only to be designed by GUI designers but also to reflect the results of evaluation by end users. In this case, widgets in GUI as well as the layouts of GUI are often changed.

For example, there are no guidelines for the appropriate number of items in JComboBox widgets and the appropriate length of strings in JLabel widgets. Therefore, widgets decided by GUI designers are often changed because of the environment of running applications and end users' preference.

Figure 1(a) shows GUI in which a file name in the JComboBox widget is selected and deleted by pushing the "OK" button. Figure 1(b) shows GUI in which a DnDSelect widget is used. In this GUI, the DnDSelect widget displays the given item names with the images of the upper side, fires the action request when the item names are dragged and dropped onto the image of the bottom side, obtains the item names and processes something. In this example, the items of the upper side are files and the item of the bottom side is the dust box. When the selected files are dragged and dropped onto the dust box image, they are deleted. When the number of files is large, (a) is suitable, but when the number of files is small, (b) is suitable. The number of files are not known in design and (a) is used. However, if the number of files are few in the operation, (b) may be required in terms of visibility.

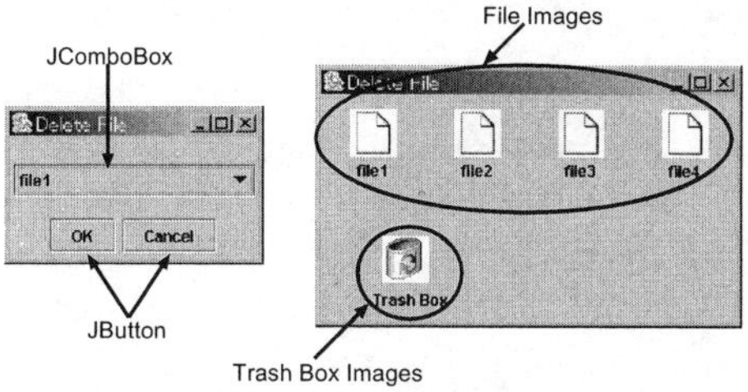

(a) Before Modification (b) After Modification

Figure 1: Example of GUI Modification

When GUI parts are requested to be modified, these GUI parts and body parts of the application must be reconnected. In these cases, it is difficult to find the modification parts from the application with complex GUI. Also, developers must take care to modify the application without bugs. Even for a simple GUI structure, if there are many modification parts, it takes a long time to find and modify these modification parts, and the bug fix needs much additional cost. It is difficult for GUI designers who do not have sufficient programming knowledge to process these, so programmers do the actual modification. However, GUI designers have to inform modification specifications of GUI designs properly to the programmers again, so much cost and time is lost in each replacement of widgets.

In our research, in order to enable easy modification of GUI, we propose a method of GUI modification by replacing widgets while keeping the connections between GUI parts and body parts of the application.

There are various kinds of widgets that have the same roles but different look and feel. By combining these widgets, a greater variety of look and feel can be realized; thus, usable GUI is developed by supporting widget replacement.

In our system, the layout of GUI can be easily defined like RAD (Rapid Application Development) tools. In addition, widgets can be replaced without reconnecting GUI parts and body parts manually. Various ways of task execution can be created by replacing a widget in GUI in order to execute a task with another kind widget. In our research, we define the word "task" as a unit of a sequence of processes in the application. For example, "users select a file and delete" is the task in Figure 1.

3 Guideline for GUI Application Generation

3.1 Roles of Widgets

In this paper, we propose a method for developing GUI applications by analyzing tasks in the roles of widgets, and combining the roles with widgets.

3.1.1 Classification of Widgets

The roles of widgets can be roughly classified as follows:

- Display
- Input (Input by selection)
- Selection
- Action
- Container

"Action" is the role of sending a request for some processes by users' operation and "Container" is the role of mats for putting widgets on. In order to play these roles, widgets have some common functions. For example, in case of "Input (Input by selection)", the input values from users' can be obtained by the "Return the input value(s)" function.

In our research, when widgets having the same roles are replaced, the modification parts of the application program (common functions for setting and obtaining values to play the role) are generated by classifying widgets according to these roles.

3.1.2 Functions for Playing Roles

In order to play the roles as GUI, widgets have many functions. In our research, the targets of replacement are the functions prepared for the above five roles (Display, Input (Input by selection), Selection, Action, Container). Concretely, the target functions are following:

- Display
  - Set the value(s) for displaying
  - Clear the displayed value(s)
  - Receive the displayed value(s)
- Selection
  - Set the value(s) for selection
  - Delete the value(s) for selection
  - Receive the value(s) for selection
  - Receive the selected value(s)
- Input (Input by selection)
  - Receive the input value(s)
  - Clear the input value(s)
  - (Set the value(s) for selection)
- Action
  - Register the object invoked by the action
  - Delete the object invoked by the action from the registration
- Container
  - Add the widget
  - Delete the widget

The methods of widgets for these functions are stored in a list named Widget Replacement List (WRL). In WRL, each widget has method names, the types of the arguments, and the types of return values. If a widget that is not included in the GUI library is used, the widget is classified according to the above roles, and stored in WRL with methods.

3.2 Variables of Widgets

If the signatures (the type and number of arguments and the type of return value) of methods are different from those of the replaced widgets in replacing methods, they are changed to appropriate ones, automatically. In our method, methods are replaced by classifying variables in the widgets.

3.2.1 Single Variable Widgets and Array Variable Widgets

Widgets have variables for playing the roles, and the functions of widgets can be realized by accessing these variables. These variables are roughly classified as single variable and array variable. In our research, the former is called Single Variable Widgets (SVWs), and the latter is Array Variable Widgets (AVWs).

For example, a JLabel widget has a text string for function "Display" and the method for accessing this text string is "void setText(String text)" for "Set the value(s) for displaying" and "String getText()" for "Receive the displayed value(s)". JList widgets can also play the same role as JLabel widgets, but JList widgets have array variables for "Display", unlike JLabel widgets. Their methods are "void setListData(Object[] listData)" for "Set the value(s) for displaying" and "Object getModel().getElementAt(int index)" for "Receive the displayed value(s)". In these methods, some values are set and the accessed variable number is specified.

3.2.2 Method Replacement

In our research, automatic program modification parts in replacing widgets consists of widget generation parts and procedure invocation parts. Widget generation parts can be automatically replaced with the class names of replaced widget.

In the method replacement, it is necessary to change "the number of arguments", "the type of arguments" and "the type of return value" of methods. The number of arguments is automatically replaced, if widgets are replaced between SVWs or between AVWs, because access variables between SVWs or those between AVWs are similar. The types of arguments and return values can be replaced automatically with classes for converting value types in the target programming language.

In replacement between an SVW and an AVW, some SVWs must be replaced with one AVW, or one AVW must be replaced to some SVWs, that is, the number of replaced widgets is different.

In our research, some SVWs are grouped, and the grouped variables are operated in one method. For example, a JRadioButton widget that has a "Selection" role and a JList widget that has an "Input (Input from Selection)" role are replaced. These widgets have the method of "Set the value(s) for selection" and "Receive the selected value(s)" to play the role. The JRadioButton widget is a SVW, so it has the method "void setText(String text)" for "Set the value(s) for selection" and a value itself is set as the argument. Therefore, it is necessary to generate as many widgets and set as many values as selection items. In the case of SVWs, two methods are used for "Receive the selected value(s)", that is, the state of widget is received using "Receive the selected state" method and if the widget is selected, "Receive the value(s) for selection" method is used.

In the case of the JList widget, which is an AVW, "Set the value(s) for selection" method is "void setListData(Object[] listData)". The argument of this method is the array type. Therefore, when AVWs are used for item selection, only one widget is generated and one method can handle those array-type variable. In addition, AVWs have the method corresponding to "Receive the selected value(s)", so the method can return the selected values themselves. In JList widgets, "Object[] getSelectedValues()" is the method.

4 System Architecture

Our system's architecture is shown in Figure 2. The procedures from GUI generation to widget replacement are explained below using selecting and deleting a file as an example.

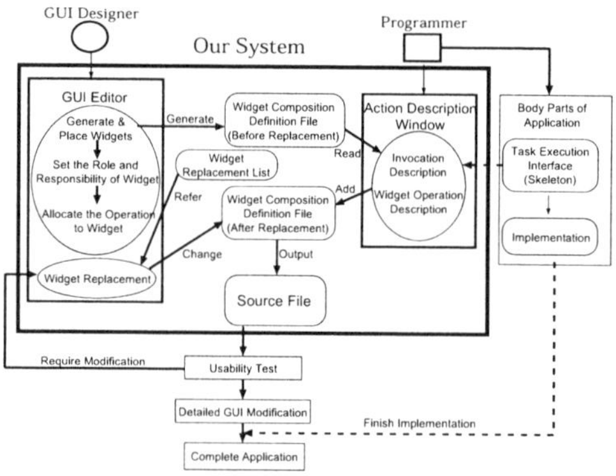

Figure 2: System Architecture

4.1 GUI Generation

First of all, GUI designers who design GUI arrange widgets with reference to the results of task analysis using GUI editor of our system. In this step, GUI designers specify the responsibility of the widget and select one role of the widget from the five roles described in Section 3.1.1. Figure 3 is an example of the window of GUI editor. In Figure 3, the responsibility of the JComboBox widget is "File selection" and the role is "Input (Input from Selection)".

Next, GUI designers connect the action description to the responsibility allocated to the widget to process users' events. In this example, "File selection" is connected to "Delete action".

After that, programmers write the program parts of the actions using our system Figure 4 is a part of program generated by our system. The underlined part of Figure 4 must be filled by the programmers. At this time, the action descriptions selected by GUI designers are used as methods. The arguments and return values are described in a specific format. These descriptions are stored in Widget Composition Definition File (WCDF). Thus, widgets and body parts of the application can be connected without GUI designers' programming. Layout information, for example, its color and size, is included in the WCDF.

Finally, the source code of GUI parts in the application is generated from above the information.

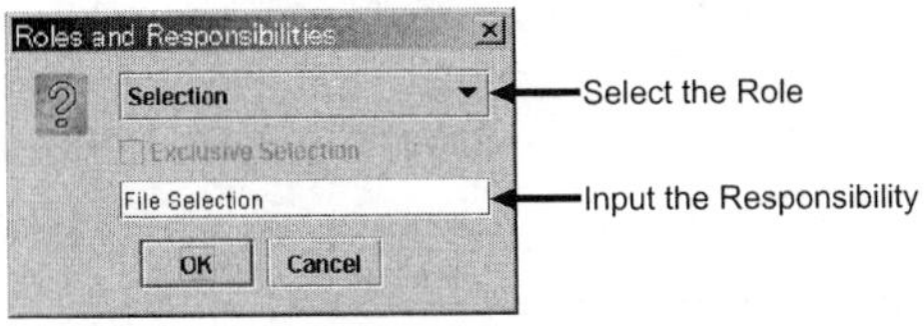

Figure 3: Setting Responsibility and Role

```
String s = new String("");
s = <**(String) File Selection.Receive the selected value**>;
deleteFile(s); // The method for deleting files
```

Figure 4: Action Description

4.2 GUI Modification

GUI designers can replace a widget selected from a set of widgets that have the same role. Figure 5 if an example of file selection. This figure shows that the JComboBox widget is replaced with the DnDSelect widget which has the same role as the JComboBox widget (Figure 1).

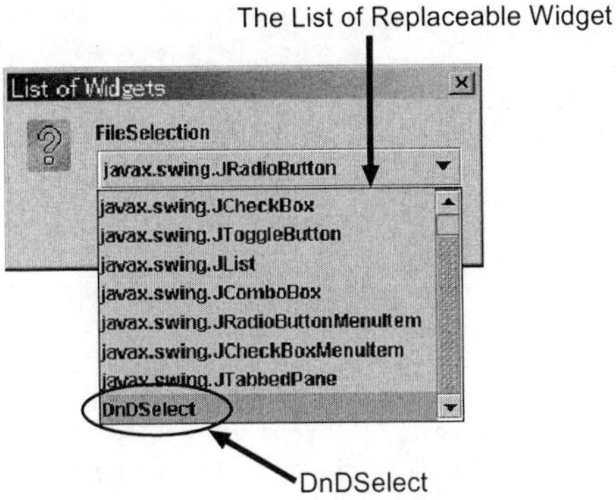

Figure 5: Selection of Target Widget

Our system automatically replaces the methods for the widgets in the WCDF using the WRL. In the example of the WRL in Figure 6, JComboBox widgets and DnDSelect widgets are classified under the same role of "Input (Input from Selection)". JComboBox widgets have "getSelectedItem" for "Receive the input value(s)", and DnDSelect widgets have "getDroppedText" in Figure 6. The types of return values are automatically replaced with the action descriptions by programmers (Figure 4: String). In the DnDSelect widget, the images of files and a dust box are specified by GUI designers, but the selection items are automatically set to the widget.

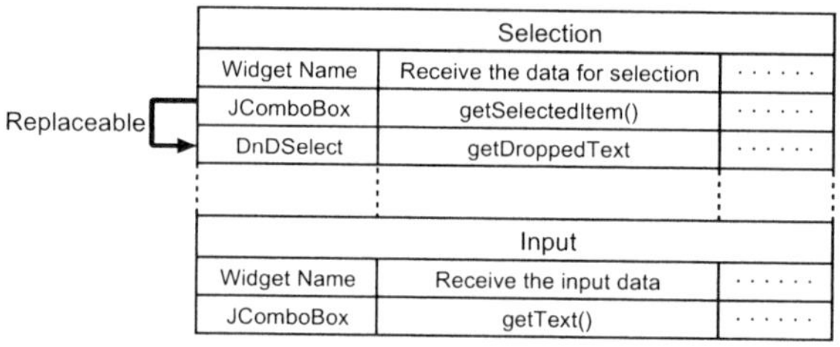

Figure 6: A Part of Widget Replacement List

5 Evaluation

For evaluation, we develop a calendar application using our system, program using by hand and using a RAD tool, and then modify (Figure 5). We have used Forte for Java[3] as the RAD tool. In this application, a memo of each day's schedule can be entered. Before modification, each month is switched using tabs. Monthly memo list can be displayed by double-clicking the tab. After modification, these tabs are replaced with check boxes and when a check box is turned on, the monthly calendar checked in the check boxes is displayed as one window. Monthly memo list is displayed by double-clicking the label of year and month.

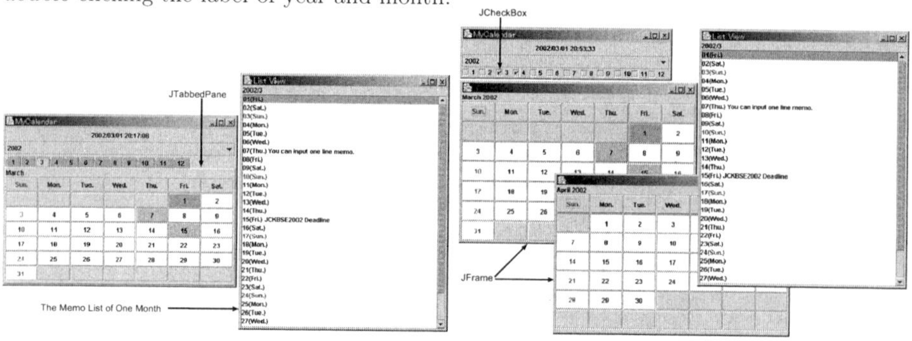

Before Modification After Modification

Figure 7: Calendar Application

The results are shown in Table 1. "Delete" means the number of deleted statements, and "Add" means the number of added statements. "Automatic" means the number of automatic modification statements and "Manual" means the number of manual modification statements in "Delete" and "Add". "Operation" means the number of users' operations, for example, in the case of the RAD tool, we counted "input the displayed string" as one operation, and in the case of our system, we counted "specify the responsibility" as one operation.

Table 1: Comparison of the Modification

	Delete	Add	Automatic	Manual	User Operation
Programming	13	32	/	45	/
RAD tool	18	134	114	38	40
Our system	17	47	54	10	20

According to Table 1, the sum of "Delete" and "Add" is 45 statements in "Programming", and the number of modifications is the smallest. In contrast, in our system, 84% of the modification parts are automatically modified, and its manual modification is least. Now, in our system, it is not possible to replace exclusive selection widgets such as tab with plural selection widgets such as a set of check boxes; thus this is counted as "Manual". In "Operation", the number cannot be compared directly because the grains of operating instructions are different, but the number of "Our system" is about half of the "RAD tool", so it is said that the burden for modification in our system is less than that in RAD tool.

6 Related Works

Various tools, such as VisualAge[4] and JBuilder[5], have been developed and commercialized for application development environment. In these tools, WYSIWYG (What You See Is What You Get) is realized, so developers can visually place widgets and set their attributes, such as size and color. However, it is necessary to have some programming knowledge for using these tools, making it difficult for GUI designers to use these tools.

For GUI generation, there are some proposed methods that model the units of a sequence of processes, called tasks, and generate from these tasks[6] and from collaboration diagrams in UML[7]. However, GUI generation is focused on these tools, and support for widget replacement is not sufficient.

For widget replacement, a method for generating GUI from an application's source code and customizing the generated GUI[8] is proposed. However, it is difficult to replace a widget with another widget that is not included in the library; therefore we think supports for realizing high usability are not sufficient.

7 Conclusions

In this paper, we propose a method for reconnecting GUI parts and body parts of an application in replacing widgets. Replacement not only between single widgets but also between a number of widgets by grouping widgets can be realized.

Our future work is follows:

- Support widgets that are not supported in our current system
- Support operations of widgets that are not supported in our current system

References

[1] X. Ferre, N. Juristo, H. Windl and L. Constantine: Usability Basics for Software Developers, IEEE Software Vol.18, No.19, pp.22-29 (2001).

[2] J. Nielsen: Usability Engineering, Morgan Kaufmann Publishers (1994).

[3] Forte for Java: http://www.sun.co.jp/forte/ffj/

[4] VisualAge: http://www-6.ibm.com/jp/software/ad/vajava/

[5] JBuilder: http://www.borland.co.jp/jbuilder/

[6] M. Ikeda, Y. Takata and H. Seki: *Formal Specification and Implementation Using a Task Flow Diagram in Interactive System Design*, Proc. of The 5th World Multi-Conference on Systemics, Cybernetics and Informatics (SCE2001) (2001)

[7] M. Elkoutbi, I. Khriss and R. K. Keller: *Generating User Interface Prototypes from Scenarios*, IEEE International Symposium on Requirements Engineering (RE'99) (1999).

[8] M. Kitamura and A. Sugimoto: *GhostHouse: A Class Library for Generating Customizable Graphical User Interfaces*, Information Processing Society of Japan(IPSJ) Journal, Vol. 36, No. 4, pp.944-957 (1995). (In Japanese)

Knowledge-based Software Engineering
T. Welzer et al. (Eds.)
IOS Press, 2002

A Domain Ontology Development Environment Using a MRD and Text Corpus

Naomi Nakaya[1] and Masaki Kurematsu[2] and Takahira Yamaguchi[1]

[1] *Faculty of Information, Shizuoka University*
3-5-1 Johoku Hamamatsu Shizuoka 432-8011 Japan
{nakaya, yamaguti}@ks.cs.inf.shizuoka.ac.jp
[2] *Faculty of Software and Information Science, Iwate Prefectural University*
152-52 Takizawasugo Takizawa Iwate 020-0193 Japan
kure@soft.iwate-pu.ac.jp

Abstract. In this paper, we describe how to exploit a machine-readable dictionary (MRD) and domain-specific text corpus in supporting the construction of domain ontologies that specify taxonomic and non-taxonomic relationships among given domain concepts. A) In building taxonomic relationships (hierarchically structure) of domain concepts, some hierarchically structure can be extracted from a MRD with marked sub-trees that may be modified by a domain expert, using matching result analysis and trimmed result analysis. B) In building non-taxonomic relationships (specification templates) of domain concepts, we construct concept specification templates that come from pairs of concepts extracted from text corpus, using WordSpace and an association rule algorithm. A domain expert modifies taxonomic and non-taxonomic relationships later. Through the case study with the Contracts for the International Sale of Goods (CISG), we make sure that our system can work to support the process of constructing domain ontologies with a MRD and text corpus.

1 Introduction

Although ontologies have been very popular in many application areas, we still face the problem of high cost associated with building up them manually. In particular, since domain ontologies have the meaning specific to application domains, human experts have to make huge efforts for constructing them entirely by hand.

In order to reduce the costs, automatic or semi-automatic methods have been proposed using knowledge engineering techniques and natural language processing ones (cf. Ontosaurus [1]). The authors have also developed a domain ontology rapid development environment called DODDLE [2], using a machine-readable dictionary. However, these environments facilitate the construction of only a hierarchically structured set of domain concepts, in other words, taxonomic conceptual relationships.

As domain ontologies have been applied to widespread areas, such as knowledge sharing, knowledge reuse and software agents, we need software environments that support a human expert in constructing domain ontologies with not only taxonomic conceptual relationships but also non-taxonomic ones. In order to develop environments, it seems better to put together two or more techniques such as knowledge engineering, natural language processing, machine learning and data engineering(e.g. [3], [4]).

Here in this paper, we extend DODDLE into DODDLE-II that constructs both taxonomic and non-taxonomic conceptual relationships, exploiting WordNet [5] and domain-specific text corpus (text corpus) with the automatic analysis of lexical co-occurrence statistics and an association rule algorithm[6]. Furthermore, we evaluate how DODDLE-II works in the field of law, the Contracts for the International Sale of Goods(CISG).
constructing domain ontologies.

2 DODDLE-II : A Domain Ontology Rapid Development Environment

Figure 1 shows an overview of DODDLE-II , "a Domain Ontology rapiD Development Environment" that has the following two components: Taxonomic relationship acquisition module using WordNet and Non-taxonomic relationship learning module using text corpus.

A domain expert who is a user of DODDLE-II gives a set of domain terms to the system. A) The taxonomic relationship acquisition module (TRA module) does "spell match" between input domain terms and WordNet. The "spell match" links these terms to WordNet. Thus the initial model from the "spell match" results is a hierarchically structured set of all the nodes on the path from these terms to the root of WordNet. However the initial model has unnecessary internal terms (nodes). They do not contribute to keeping topological relationships among matched nodes, such as parent-child relationship and sibling relationship. So we get a trimmed model by trimming the unnecessary internal nodes from the initial model. In order to refine the trimmed model, we have the following two strategies that we will describe later: Matched result analysis and Trimmed result analysis.
B) The non-taxonomic relationship learning module (NTRL module) extracts the pairs of terms that should be related by some relationship from text corpus, analyzing lexical co-occurrence statistics, based on WordSpace (WS) [7] and an associate rule algorithm(AR). Thus the pairs of terms extracted from text corpus are the candidates for non-taxonomic relationships. NTRL module also extracts candidates for taxonomic relationships from these pairs, analyzing the distance between terms in a document.

We can built concept specification templates by putting together taxonomic and non-taxonomic relationships for the input domain terms. The relationships should be identified in the interaction with a human expert.

3 Taxonomic Relationship Acquisition

After getting the trimmed model, TRA module refines it by interaction with a domain expert, using Matched result analysis and Trimmed result analysis.

First, TRA module divides the trimmed model into a PAB (a PAth including only Best spell-matched nodes) and a STM (a Sub-Tree that includes best spell-matched nodes and other nodes and so can be Moved) based on the distribution of best-matched nodes. A PAB is a path that includes only best-matched nodes that have the senses good for given domain specificity. Because all nodes have already been adjusted to the domain in PABs, PABs can stay in the trimmed model. A STM is such a sub-tree that an internal node is a root and the subordinates are only best-matched nodes. Because internal nodes have not been confirmed to have the senses good for a given domain, a STM can be moved in the trimmed model.

In order to refine the trimmed model, DODDLE-II can use trimmed result analysis. Taking some sibling nodes with the same parent node, there may be many differences about the number of trimmed nodes between them and the parent node. When such a big difference comes up on a sub-tree in the trimmed model, it is be better to change the structure of it.

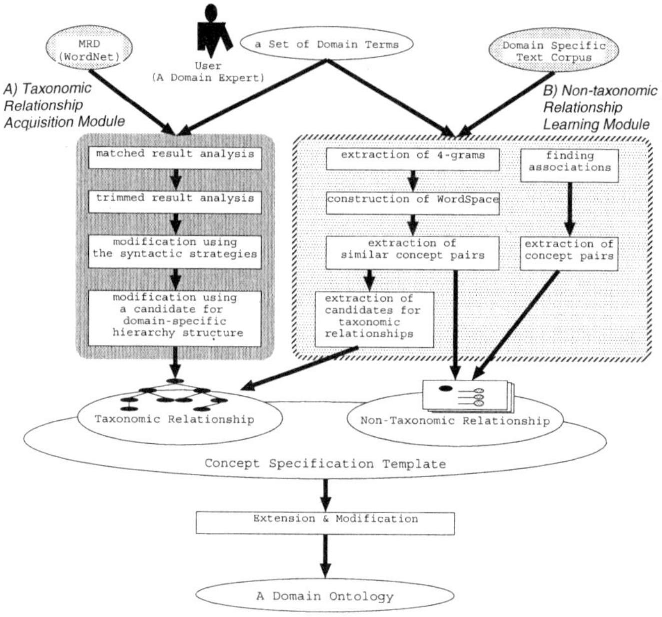

Figure 1: DODDLE-II Overview

DODDLE-II asks a human expert if the sub-tree should be reconstructed or not. Based on the empirical analysis, the sub-trees with two or more differences may be reconstructed.

Finally DODDLE-II completes taxonomic relationships of the input domain terms manually from the user.

4 Non-Taxonomic Relationship Learning

NTRL module almost comes from WS. WS derives lexical co-occurrence information from a large text corpus and is a multi-dimension vector space (a set of vectors). The inner product between two word vectors works as the measure of their semantic relatedness. When two words' inner product is beyond some upper bound, there are possibilities to have some non-taxonomic relationships between them.

NTRL module also use an AR algorithm to find associations between terms in text corpus. When an AR between terms exceeds user-defined thresholds, there are possibilities to have some non-taxonomic relationships between them.

4.1 Construction of WordSpace

WS is constructed as shown in Figure 2.

1. extraction of high-frequency 4-grams Since letter-by-letter co-occurrence information becomes too much and so often irrelevant, we take term-by-term co-occurrence information in four words (4-gram) as the primitive to make up co-occurrence matrix useful to represent context of a text based on experimented results. We take high frequency 4-grams in order to make up WS.

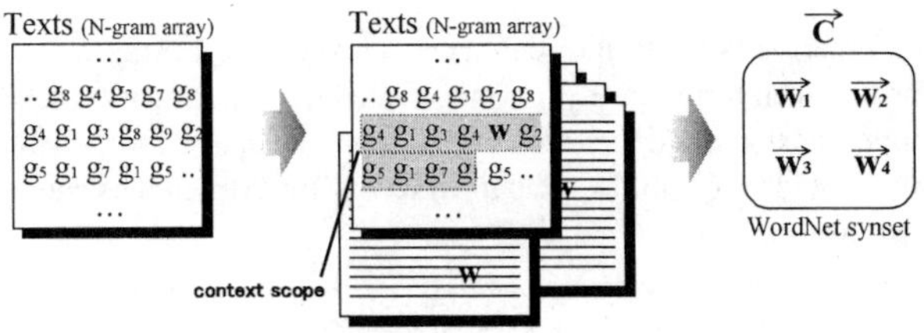

Figure 2: Construction Flow of WS

2. construction of context vectors A *context vector* represents context of a word or phrase in a text. Element $a_{i,j}$ in a context vector $\overrightarrow{w_i}$ is the number of 4-gram g_j which comes up a around appearance place of a word or phrase w_i (called *context scope*). The concept vector counts how many other 4-grams come up in context scope of a word or phrase. The size of context scope is decided by users, depending on the length of sentences included in documents.

3. construction of word vectors A *word vector* $\overrightarrow{W_i}$ is a sum of context vectors $\overrightarrow{w_i}$ at all appearance places of a word or phrase w_i within texts. A set of word vectors is WS.

4. construction of vector representations of all concepts The best matched "synset" of each input terms in WordNet is already specified, and a sum of the word vector contained in these synsets is *concept vector* set to the vector representation of a concept corresponding to a input term. The concept label is the input term. A concept vector $\overrightarrow{C}$ can be expressed with the following formula. Here, $\mathcal{A}(w)$ is all appearance places of a word or phrase w in a text, and $\overrightarrow{w}(i)$ is a context vector at a appearance place i of a word or phrase w.

$$\overrightarrow{C} = \sum_{w \in synset(C)} \left(\sum_{i \in \mathcal{A}(w)} \overrightarrow{w}(i) \right)$$

5. construction of a set of similar concept pairs Vector representations of all concepts are obtained by constructing WS. Similarity between concepts is obtained from inner products in all the combination of these vectors. Then we define certain threshold for this similarity. A concept pair with similarity beyond the threshold is extracted as a similar concept pair.

4.2 Finding Association Rules between Input Terms

The basic AR algorithm is provided with a set of transactions, $T := \{t_i \mid i = 1..n\}$,where each transaction t_i consists of a set of items, $t_i = \{a_{i,j} \mid j = 1..m_i, a_{i,j} \in CS\}$ and each item $a_{i,j}$ is from a set of concepts CS. The algorithm finds ARs $X_k \Rightarrow Y_k : (X_k, Y_k \subset CS, X_k \cap Y_k = \{\})$ such that measures for support and confidence exceed user-defined thresholds. Thereby, support of a rule $X_k \Rightarrow Y_k$ is the percentage of transactions that contain $X_k \cup Y_k$ as a subset and confidence for the rule is defined as the percentage of transactions that Y_k is seen when X_k appears in a transaction.

$$support(X_k \Rightarrow Y_k) = \frac{\mid \{t_i \mid X_k \cup Y_k \subseteq t_i\} \mid}{n}$$

$$confidence(X_k \Rightarrow Y_k) = \frac{\mid \{t_i \mid X_k \cup Y_k \subseteq t_i\} \mid}{\mid \{t_i \mid X_k \subseteq t_i\} \mid}$$

As we regard input terms as items and sentences in text corpus as transactions, DODDLE-II finds associations between terms in text corpus. Based on experimented results, we define the threshold of support as 0.4% and the threshold of confidence as 80%. When an association rules between terms exceeds thresholds, the pair of terms are extracted as candidates for non-taxonomic relationships.

4.3 Constructing and Modifying Concept Specification Templates

A set of similar concept pairs from WS and term pairs from the AR algorithm becomes concept specification templates. Both of the concept pairs, whose meaning is similar (with taxonomic relation), and has something relevant to each other (with non-taxonomic relation), are extracted as concept pairs with above-mentioned methods. However, by using taxonomic information from TRA module with co-occurrence information, DODDLE-II distinguishes the concept pairs which are hierarchically close to each other from the other pairs as TAXONOMY.

A user constructs a domain ontology by considering the relation with each concept pair in the concept specification templates, and deleting unnecessary concept pairs.

4.4 Extracting Taxonomic Relationships from Text Corpus

NTRL module tries to extract pairs of terms which form part of a candidate for domain-specific hierarchy structure. Because we suppose that there are taxonomic relationships in text corpus. In order to do that, we pay attention to the distance between two terms in a document. In this paper, the distance between two terms means the number of words between them. If the distance between two terms is small and the similarity between them is close, we suppose that one term explains the other. If the distance is large and the similarity is close, we suppose that they have taxonomic relationships. According to above-mentioned idea, we calculate the proximally rate between two terms within a certain scope. It is the number of times both terms occur within the scope divided by the number of times only one term occurs within it. We define certain threshold for this proximally rate. Pairs of terms whose proximally rate is within this threshold and the similarity between them is beyond the threshold are extracted as part of a candidate for non-taxonomic relationships. DODDLE-II asks the domain expert if the hierarchy structure from TRA module should be changed into unified one or not.

5 Case Studies for Taxonomic Relationship Acquisition

In order to evaluate how DODDLE is doing in practical fields, case studies have been done in a particular field of law called Contracts for the International Sale of Goods (CISG)[8]. Two lawyers joined the case studies. The details of the case studies are described in [2].

Generally speaking, in constructing legal ontologies, 70 % or more support comes from DODDLE. About half portion of the final legal ontology results in the information extracted from WordNet. Because the two strategies just imply the part where concept drift may come up, the part generated by them has low component rates and about 30 % hit rates. So one out of three indications based on the two strategies work well in order to manage concept drift. Because the two strategies use such syntactical feature as matched and trimmed results, the hit rates are not so bad. In order to manage concept drift smartly, we may need to use more semantic information that is not easy to come up in advance in the strategies.

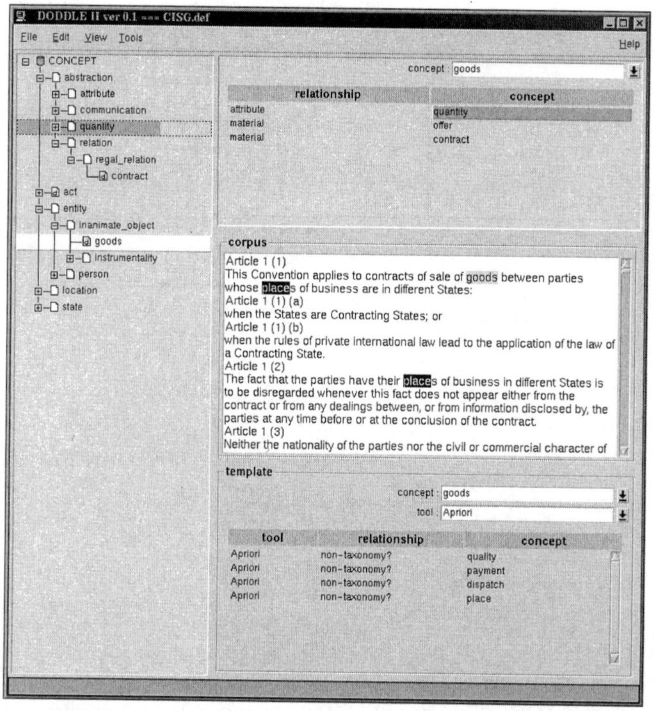

Figure 3: The Ontology Editor

Table 1: Significant 46 Concepts in CISG Part II

acceptance	act	addition	address	assent	circumstance	communication system	conduct
contract	counteroffer	day	delay	delivery	discrepancy	dispatch	effect
envelope	goods	holiday	indication	intention	invitation	letter	modification
offer	offeror	offeree	party	payment	person	place of business	price
proposal	quality	quantity	rejection	reply	residence	revocation	silence
speech act	telephone	telex	time	transmission	withdrawal		

6 Case Studies for Non-Taxonomic Relationship Learning

DODDLE-II is being implemented on Perl/Tk now. Figure 3 shows the ontology editor.

Subsequently, as a case study for non-taxonomic relationship acquisition, we constructed the concept definition for significant 46 concepts of having used on the first case study (Table 1) with editing the concept specification template using DODDLE-II , and verified usefulness. The concept hierarchy, which the lawyer actually constructed using DODDLE in the first case study was used here (Figure 4).

6.1 Construction of WordSpace

High-frequency 4-grams were extracted from CISG (about 10,000 words) and 543 kinds of 4-grams were obtained. The extraction frequency of 4-grams must be adjusted according

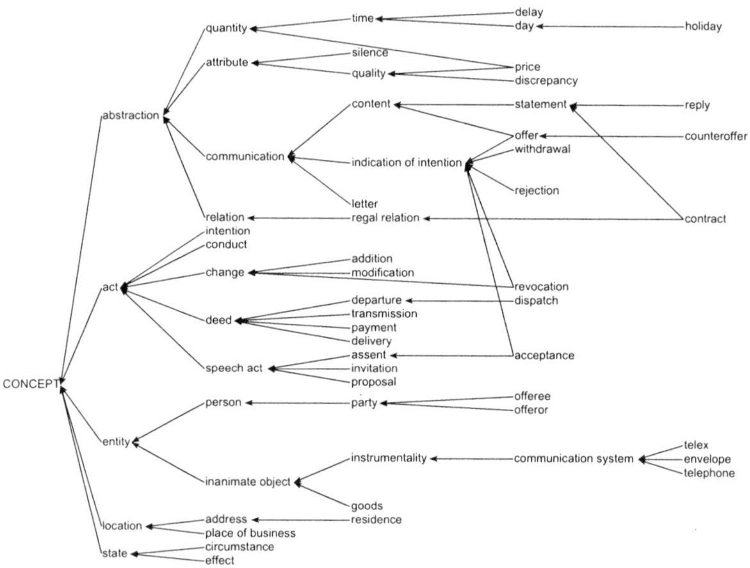

Figure 4: Domain Concept Hierarchy of CISG Part II

to the scale of text corpus. As CISG is the comparatively small-scale text, the extraction frequency was set as 7 times this case. In order to construct a context vector, a sum of 4-gram around appearance place circumference of each of 46 concepts was calculated. One article of CISG consists of about 140 4-grams. In order to construct a context scope from some 4-grams, it consists of putting together 60 4-grams before the 4-gram and 10 4-grams after the 4-gram independently of length of a sentence. For each of 46 concepts, the sum of context vectors in all the appearance places of the concept in CISG was calculated, and the vector representations of the concepts were obtained. The set of these vectors is used as WS to extract concept pairs with context similarity.

Having calculated the similarity from the inner product for the 1035 concept pairs which is all the combination of 46 concepts, and having used threshold as 0.87, 77 concept pairs were extracted.

6.2 Finding Associations between Input Terms

In this case, DODDLE-II extracted 55 pairs of terms from text corpus using the above-mentioned AR algorithm. There are 15 pairs out of them in a set of similar concept pairs extracted using WS.

6.3 Constructing and Modifying Concept Specification Templates

Concept specification templates were constructed from two sets of concept pairs extracted by WS and AR. Table 2 is the list of the extracted similar concepts corresponding to each concept. In Table 2, a concept in bold letters is either an ancestor, descendant or a sibling to the left concept in the concept hierarchy constructed using DODDLE in the first case study. In

Table 2: The Concept Pairs Extracted According to Context Similarity (threshold 0.87)

CONCEPT	CONCEPT LIST IN SIMILAR CONTEXT
acceptance	**communication**, **offer**, **indication**, telex
act	offeror, **assent**, effect, payment, person, quantity, time, goods, **delivery**, **dispatch**, price, contract, delay, withdrawal, offeree, place, quality
assent	offeror, **act**, effect, offer, person, offeree, withdrawal, time, **proposal**
communication	**acceptance**, **offer**, **telex**, conduct, **indication**
conduct	party, telex, communication
contract	effect, act, person, delivery, payment, quantity
delay	delivery, offer, act, payment
delivery	**payment**, quantity, goods, place, **act**, delay, time, contract, person, effect, quality
dispatch	goods, price, **act**, person, quantity, offeror
effect	person, assent, act, offeror, contract, proposal, payment, time, withdrawal, party, delivery
goods	dispatch, quantity, delivery, payment, act, person, price, quality
indication	intention, **acceptance**, **communication**
intention	indication
offer	**acceptance**, assent, **communication**, delay
offeree	withdrawal, **offeror**, assent, act, price
offeror	act, assent, withdrawal, **offeree**, **person**, effect, time, price, dispatch
party	conduct, effect, place, **person**
payment	quantity, **delivery**, place, act, goods, quality, delay, effect, person, contract, time
person	effect, **offeror**, act, proposal, goods, assent, withdrawal, contract, dispatch, payment, delivery, **party**, place, price
place	payment, delivery, time, quantity, party, act, person
price	dispatch, act, offeror, goods, withdrawal, offeree, person
proposal	person, effect, withdrawal, **assent**
quality	quantity, payment, goods, act, delivery
quantity	payment, delivery, goods, act, quality, dispatch, place, contract, **time**
telex	conduct, **communication**, acceptance
time	act, offeror, delivery, place, effect, payment, **quantity**, assent
withdrawal	offeree, offeror, person, price, act, assent, effect, proposal

goods	*non-TAXONOMY*	: **quality**
	non-TAXONOMY	: **payment**
	non-TAXONOMY	: **quantity**

Figure 5: The Concept Specification Templates for "goods"

goods	ATTRIBUTE	: **quality**
	ATTRIBUTE	: **quantity**
	MATERIAL	: **offer**
	MATERIAL	: **contract**

Figure 6: The Concept Definition for "goods" with Editing the Templates

concept specification templates, such a concept is distinguished as TAXONOMY relation. As taxonomic and non-taxonomic relationships may be mixed in the list based on only context similarity, the concept pairs which may be concerned with non-taxonomic relationships are obtained by removing the concept pairs with taxonomic relationships.

Figure 5 shows concept specification templates extracted about the concept "goods". The final concept definition is constructed from consideration of concept pairs in the templates. Figure 6 shows the definition of the concept "goods" constructed from the templates.

6.4 Extracting Taxonomic Relationships from Text Corpus

In this case, we defined the threshold for the proximally rate as 0.78 and the certain scope as the same sentence. DODDLE-II extracted 128 pairs of concepts regarded as having taxonomic relationships from text corpus. 8 pairs out of them have occurred in the concept hierarchy constructed by the user and have not occurred in the trimmed model. That is, they are the same as modifications by the user. It shows that DODDLE-II can extract taxonomic relationships, which are not included in a MRD, from text corpus. But the rate of accepted taxonomic relationships is about 6%(8/128) and is not good. So, we have to improve do that.

Table 3: Evaluation by the User with Legal Knowledge

	# Extracted concept pairs	# Accepted concept pairs	# Rejected concept pairs	Precision	Recall
WS	77	18	59	0.23(18/77)	0.38(18/48)
AR	55	13	42	0.24(13/55)	0.27(13/48)
The join of WS and AR	117	27	90	0.23(27/117)	0.56(27/48)

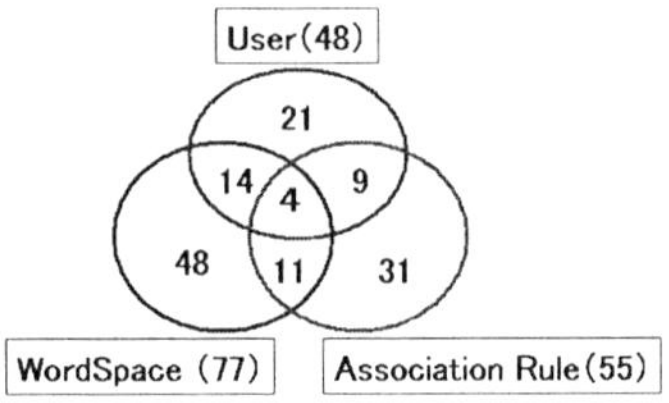

Figure 7: Three Different Sets of Concept Pairs from User, WS and AR

6.5 *Results and Evaluation*

The user evaluated the following two sets of concept pairs: ones extracted by WS and ones extracted by AR. Figure 7 shows three different sets of concept pairs from user, WS and AR. Table 3 shows the details of evaluation by the user, computing precision and recall with the numbers of concept pairs extracted by WS and AR, accepted by the user and rejected by the user.

Looking at the field of Precision in Table 3, there in almost no differences among three kinds of results from WS, AR and the join of WS and AR. However, looking at the field of Recall in Table 3, the recall from the join WS and AR is higher than that from each WS and AR, and then goes over 0.5.

Generating non-taxonomic relationships of concepts is harder than modifying and deleting them. Therefore, taking the join of WS and AR with high recall, it supports the user in constructing non-taxonomic relationships.

7 Related Work

In the research using verb-oriented method, the relation of a verb and nouns modified with it is described, and the concept definition is constructed from these information (e.g. [10]). In [9], taxonomic relationships and Subcategorization Frame of verbs (SF) are extracted from technical texts using a machine learning method. The nouns in two or more kinds of different SF with a same frame-name and slot-name is gathered as one concept, base class. And ontology with only taxonomic relationships is built by carrying out clustering of the base class further. Moreover, in parallel, Restriction of Selection (RS) which is slot-value in SF is also replaced with the concept with which it is satisfied instantiated SF. However, proper evaluation is not yet done. Since SF represents the syntactic relationships between verb and noun, the step for the conversion to non-taxonomic relationships is necessary.

On the other hand, in ontology learning using data-mining method, discovering non-taxonomic relationships using a AR algorithm is proposed by [3] and [4]. They extract concept pairs based on the modification information between terms selected with parsing, and made the concept pairs a transaction. By using heuristics with shallow text processing, the generation of a transaction more reflects the syntax of texts. Moreover, RLA, which is their original learning accuracy of non-taxonomic relationships using the existing taxonomic relations, is proposed. The concept pair extraction method in our paper does not need parsing, and it can also run off context similarity between the terms appeared apart each other in texts or not mediated by the same verb.

8 Conclusions

In this paper, we discussed how to construct a domain ontology using existing MRD and text corpus. In order to acquire taxonomic relationships, two strategies have been proposed: matched result analysis and trimmed result analysis. Furthermore, in order to learn non-taxonomic relationships, concept pairs have been extracted from text corpus with WS and AR. Taking the join of WS and AR, the recall goes over 0.5 and so it works to support the user in constructing non-taxonomic relationships of concepts.

The future work comes as follows: the system integration of taxonomic relationship acquisition module and non-taxonomic relationship learning module and the application to large size domains.

Acknowledgments

We would like to express our thanks to Mr. Takamasa Iwade (a graduate student of Shizuoka university) and Mr.Takuya Miyabe (a student of Shizuoka university) and the members in the Yamaguchi-Lab.

References

[1] Bill Swartout, Ramesh Patil, Kevin Knight and Tom Russ: "Toward Distributed Use of Large-Scale Ontologies", Proc. of the 10th Knowledge Acquisition Workshop (KAW'96), (1996)

[2] Rieko Sekiuchi, Chizuru Aoki, Masaki Kurematsu and Takahira Yamaguchi: "DODDLE : A Domain Ontology Rapid Development Environment", PRICAI98, (1998)

[3] Alexander Maedche, Steffen Staab: "Discovering Conceptual Relations from Text", ECAI2000, 321–325 (2000)

[4] Alexander Maedche, Steffen Staab: "Ontology Learning for the Semantic Web", IEEE Intelligent Systems, 72–79 (2001)

[5] C.Fellbaum ed: "Wordnet", The MIT Press, 1998. see also URL: http://www.cogsci.princeton.edu/~wn/

[6] Rakesh Agrawal, Ramakrishnan Srikant :"Fast algorithms for mining association rules,", Proc. of VLDB Conference, 487–499 (1994)

[7] Marti A. Hearst, Hinrich Schutze: "Customizing a Lexicon to Better Suit a Computational Task", in Corpus Processing for Lexical Acquisition edited by Branimir Boguraev & James Pustejovsky, 77–96

[8] Kazuaki Sono, Masasi Yamate: United Nations convention on Contracts for the International Sale of Goods, Seirin-Shoin(1993)

[9] David Faure, Claire Nédellec, "Knowledge Acquisition of Predicate Argument Structures from Technical Texts Using Machine Learning: The System ASIUM", EKAW'99

[10] Udo Hahn, Klemens Schnattinger : "*Toward Text Knowledge Engineering*", AAAI98, IAAAI-98 proceedings, 524-531 (1998)

Knowledge Modeling and Reasoning

Knowledge-based Software Engineering
T. Welzer et al. (Eds.)
IOS Press, 2002

Role of Case-Based Reasoning in Neurology Decision Support

M. Ivanović*, V. Kurbalija*, Z. Budimac*
Institute of Mathematics and Informatics, Faculty of Science,
Trg D. Obradovića 4, 21 000 Novi Sad, Yugoslavia
e-mail:{mira, kurba, zjb}@im.ns.ac.yu

M. Semnic
Institute of Neurology, Medical School,
H. Veljkova 1-3, 21 000 Novi Sad, Yugoslavia
e-mail: semnicmr@EUnet.yu

ABSTRACT: Case-based Reasoning (CBR) has become a successful technique for knowledge-based systems in different domains including medicine. Medicine is a suitable domain for application of CBR because the knowledge of experts consists of mixture of textbook knowledge and experience, which consists of cases. The possibilities of employing CBR in neurology are analyzed in the paper. A suitable architecture for CBR decision support system in neurology is proposed. System is going to be used in Institute of Neurology Novi Sad.

1. INTRODUCTION

Case-Based Reasoning (CBR) has become successful technique for knowledge-based systems in different domains. This promising technique is based on use of previous experience in form of cases to better understand and solve new problems in particular domain. The main idea is an assumption that, for many particular domains, similar problems usually have similar solutions.

Generally speaking, the CBR systems have not only to provide solutions to problems but also to take care of other tasks occurring when it is used in practice. However, CBR can mean different things depending on the intended use of reasoning:

- Explain current situation according to previously experienced similar situation,
- Critique current situation based on old cases,
- Reason from precedents to understand a current situation,
- Combine old solutions in order to solve a current problem,
- Obtain concensued solution based on previous cases.

* Research is supported by the project: "Development of (intelligent) techniques based on software agents for application in information retrieval and workflows", Ministry of science, Technologies, and Development, Republic of Serbia.

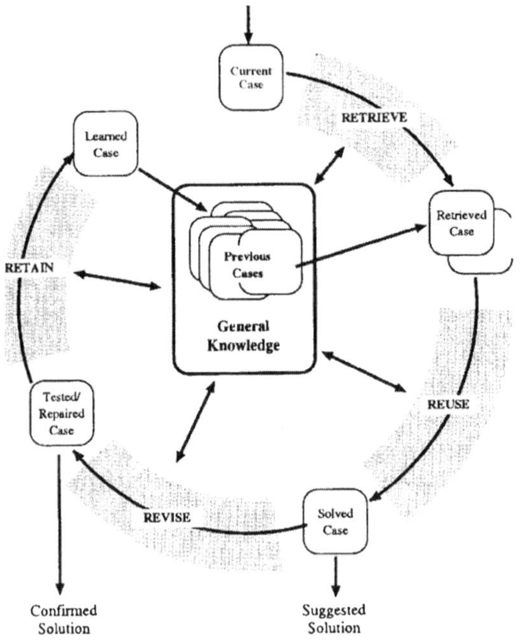

Fig 1. *CBR-cycle* of Aamodt and Plaza (1994)

To summarize, mentioned aspects could be divided into two types: interpretative and problem solving CBR [6]. In interpretative CBR systems the essence is to achieve whether or not a current situation should be treated like previous ones based on similarities or differences among them. In problem solving CBR systems the main task is to propose a solution to a current situation based on the adaptation of solutions to past cases. However in practice, many problems have components of both types of CBR and certainly combination of both methods is employed.

The main phases of case-based reasoning activities are described in the CBR-cycle [1,2] in fig. 1.

In the retrieve phase, the most similar cases to the problem case (current one) are retrieved. In reuse phase some modifications to the retrieved case is done in order to provide better solution to the problem (phase of case adaptation). As the CBR only suggests solutions, there may be a need for a correctness proof or an external validation of expert in particular domain. That is the task of revise phase. In the retain phase the knowledge learned from current case is integrated in the system by modifying some knowledge containers.

Medicine is rather suitable domain for application of CBR because the knowledge of experts consists of mixture of textbook (objective) knowledge and experience (subjective) knowledge, which consists of cases. The problem of updating the changeable subjective knowledge can partly be solved by incrementally incorporating new up-to-date cases [3]. Usually two sorts of knowledge can be clearly separated, and represented in an appropriate manner. Objective knowledge can be represented in forms of rules or functions, while subjective knowledge is contained in cases. So, there are several obvious facts for usage of case-oriented methods in medicine [13]:

1) Reasoning with cases corresponds to the decision making process of physicians.

2) Incorporating current cases obtains automatically updated parts of the knowledge.
3) Two distinguished types of knowledge can be clearly separated.
4) Integration into clinic communication system is easy (cases are routinely stored).

CBR has been mainly applied in medicine for diagnostic and partly for therapeutic tasks. It is often necessary, in diagnosis, to adapt an old case to fit a current problem.

In this paper architecture for CBR decision support system is suggested and its application in neurology domain is analyzed. The rest of the paper is organized as follows. In section 2 some open problems of CBR systems, are outlined. Section 3 is devoted to specification of a particular CBR prototype in neurology. Section 4 concludes the paper.

2. OPEN PROBLEMS OF CBR SYSTEMS

CBR is interesting Artificial Intelligence (AI) technique for application in different domains, but also a learning paradigm which has several advantages [10]:

1) Based on cases stored in memory, instead of deriving new solution from scratch, a CBR system remembers and adapts old ones.

2) CBR reasoner becomes more competent over time, can avoid previous mistakes, and can focus on the most important parts of a problem.

3) CBR approach to learning is most similar to human learning. People take into account and use past experiences to take future decisions.

Apart from these positive aspects, there are still a lot of open problems in building commercial tools. Current commercial tools are mostly oriented towards acquisition and retrieval of cases and its simple adaptation and evaluation. The well-known open problems appearing in CBR systems are mentioned below.

1) Retrieval/selection – the most basic problems are retrieval and selection of cases, since the remaining operations (adaptation and evaluation) will succeed only if the past cases are the relevant ones.

2) Memory organization – good memory organization is extremely important because when the case memory is large retrieval can be very inefficient.

3) Matching – to select the best case it is necessary to be able to match cases. Usually the match cannot be perfect because: - the values of the comparable features are not exactly the same, - there are missing values for some or even many of features.

4) Adaptation/evaluation – a good adaptation of old cases to fit the current case is really important possibility of CBR system. It can reduce significantly the amount of work needed to solve the problem. Evaluation gives to the case-based reasoner feedback about whether or not the current case was solved adequately.

5) Forgetting – another important problem is how to control growth of the case memory. So, it is important to obtain technique for storing and deleting cases.

6) Integration with other techniques – application of CBR in different domains usually requires combination of CBR with other reasoning techniques [12].

2.1. Problems of CBR in medical applications

Some authors [13] think that the main problem of CBR is the adaptation task. It still depends on domain and application characteristics. In medicine, adaptation can be a serious problem, because cases often consist of an extremely large number of features. So some adaptation solutions, typically for medical domains, have been developed:

1) Focusing on retrieval – An idea to avoid adaptation problem is to build retrieval-only systems. Retrieval is used only to find similar cases and present them to the user. Some systems have possibility to point out important differences between current and previous cases. The justification for giving up the adaptation task is that physicians are interested to get information about former similar cases, but wish to reason and bring diagnosis for current patient themselves [11]. A similar approach is to combine CBR with rule-based methods. In some concrete systems if no similar case can be found or if not all adaptation problems can be solved, a separate rule-based component of the system is applied.

2) Generalized cases – in this solution, the main idea is to form abstracted prototypes by generalization from single cases. Though, generalization obtains to structure the case base, to decrease the storage amount by erasing redundant and highly similar cases, additionally it can at least partly help to solve the adaptation problem.

3. A PROPOSITION OF CBR SYSTEM IN NEUROLOGY

Last year a small team at Institute of Mathematics and Informatics, started investigation in the field of CBR methodology. The main proposed task was implementation of CBR system based on [7]. Recently, at Institute of Neurology, appears need to systematize and automatise records of patients has been collecting for ten years. Their basic idea was to store all necessary features for determination of multiple sclerosis disease, and to use previous experiences in diagnosis of current cases.

As it is well known medical diagnosis from surface etiology is difficult since there involves lots of complications. A physician has to carefully investigate a patient's symptoms and testing results, major complaints and pathology examination in order to make a differential diagnosis. It is rather difficult process and it takes years of training and practice for a physician to make correct decisions.

Also it is not easy task to update the medical knowledge incrementally in a traditional medical diagnosis system. Mentioned difficulties can be made easier and more reliable if supplied with a system that contains and provides recommendations from the past diagnosis cases of different morbidity. Since the physician can benefit a lot from prior experiences and cases the CBR approach is rather appropriate for medical domains. So, it seems that unification of these two research directions could be mutually useful.

Multiple sclerosis (MS) is a chronic disease of unknown cause that affects the nervous system (brain, spinal cord and peripheral nerves) in form of multifocal lesions of myelin nerve sheet. It causes damage of vision, muscle strength, sensation, coordination, speech, and bladder control and may affect cognitive functions. MS usually appears in young adulthood (more in females) and Vojvodina is region with high incidence of disease.

Clearly, investigation in this field, which will bring better and more reliable results in diagnosis and maybe some exceptional conclusions of reasons of disease appearence, is extremely important. Based on some mutual requirements and analysis of different medical CBR systems [3, 4, 11, 12, 13] as well, in fig. 2, architecture of CBR system for diagnosis of MS disease is proposed. Proposed architecture has the following main characteristics:

1) Employs CBR technique for retrieval of similar cases with key notifications and evidences between the current and similar cases.
2) Suggests possible diagnosis and gives appropriate explanations of solutions.

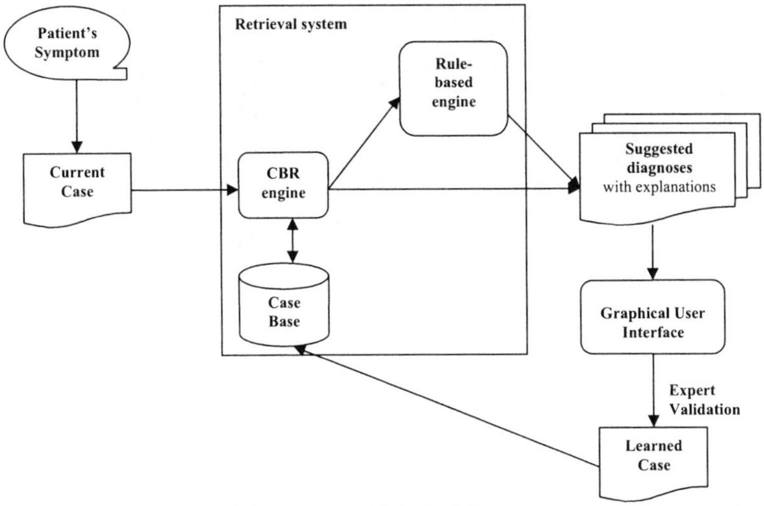

Fig. 2. Proposed architecture of a CBR decision support system in neurology.

To build proposed architecture, a lot of necessary activities have to be analyzed and taken into account:

1) Determination of representation forms for cases and extracting important features.
2) Avoidance of an infinite growth of the case base by clustering cases in prototypes and removing redundant cases.
3) Selection of appropriate retrieval algorithm.
4) System suggests possible diagnoses. But, expert must analyze current patient data and similar prototypes enriched by explanations, in order to achieve final diagnosis.
5) As already mentioned, the main problem of CBR systems in medicine is adaptation task. In the first phase of realization of proposed architecture, expert will be supposed to decide whether current case is different enough to be added in the case base as the new case or even as a new prototype. In future, plans are to automatise as much as possible this process of adaptation and decision. For that, we considered combining CBR with rule-based methods that is rather fruitful mixture in such kind of systems.

By analysing the diagnoses problem of MS disease the appropriate case structure with characteristic features is given in the Table 1. The case has 16 different features representing the most important observations in the diagnoses process of MS disease. List of the features can be extended with some additional ones (it will be done in future versions), if these features are significant for the diagnoses process. The last row in the table represents the correct diagnosis for the corresponding cases.

The cases are stored in the special memory structure - Case Retrieval Net (CRN) [7, 8]. Case Retrieval Nets are memory model that has been developed for efficient retrieval in large case bases. For the efficiency improvement, the cases are grouped into prototypes. All cases of the same prototype are cases with the same diagnoses, so the memorizing of the diagnoses feature of the case is needless because the diagnosis of the case is determined by its prototype.

Table 1. Some MS cases

	Case #1	Case #2	Case #3	Case #4	Case #5
I Natural History and neurological findings					
Course of disease	Relapsing /remitting	Secondary-progressive	Primary-progressive	Relapsing /remitting	Transient retrobulbar neuritis
Duration of the disease (years)	10	15	10	20	3
Motor symptoms	Mild hemiparesis	Paraparesis	Quadriparesis	Mild hemiparesis	-
Spastically	+	+	+	-	-
Cerebella symptoms	Increasing intention tremor	Ataxia	Ataxia of lower limbs, dysmetria, dysarthria	-	-
Sensory symptoms	Paresthesiae dysaesthesiae	Paresthesiae, Trigeminal neuralgia	Paresthesiae	Paresthesiae dysaesthesiae	-
Gait abnormalities	+	+	+	+	-
Bladder dysfunction	Micturition urgency	Retention	Incontinence	Micturition urgency	-
Bowel dysfunction	-	-	+ (mild)	-	-
Visual symptoms	Transient optic neuritis	Diplopia	Permanent loss of visual acuity	-	Isolated retrobulbar neuritis
Cognitive dysfunction	Memory disturbance difficulty in sustaining attention	Memory disturbance	Dementia	Memory disturbance,	-
Psychiatric symptoms	Depression, Drug induced psychosis	Euphoria Pathological laughing and crying	-	Euphoria	-
II Laboratory tests in diagnosis CSF (Cerebrospinal fluid) Oligoclonal IgG bands	+	+	+	-	-
III Visual evoked potentials P100	130/121	171/176	170/165	125/121	137/130
IV Magnetic resonance imaging (TVLL total vol. lesion load) mm^3	170	920	1600	250	0 (optic nerve demil.)
Diagnosis	Definite multiple sclerosis	Definite multiple sclerosis	Definite multiple sclerosis	Probable multiple sclerosis	Possible multiple sclerosis

Table 1 displays results of 16 different features for 5 cases. Fist 3 cases are with the same diagnostics (definite multiple sclerosis) and are to be grouped in the same prototype. Cases 4 and 5 are characteristic for other two possible diagnoses (probable and possible multiple sclerosis). Sign + in appropriate cells designates presence of specified feature, while sign – designates the absence of the feature.

The next problem in medical case-based reasoning systems is avoidance of infinitive growth of case base. Although every case in the diagnoses process is important, it might be redundant for the system, because maybe the system already has the knowledge to propose that diagnoses, or maybe some similar or more general cases already exists in the system. Maintenance of the system will be implemented using *case properties* [5]. For each additional case, system evaluates *correctness, consistency, uniqueness, minimality* and *incoherence,* and makes decision if the case is needed for the system or not. Of course, the neurology expert must firstly decide if the diagnosis is correct. The evaluation of the case properties is the just additional filter, which improves accuracy of the system and reduces the case base growth without losing of correctness.

In this phase of realisation, the problem of forgetting is not realised. We will observe the growth of case base and if the growth will turn to be significant we will develop some forgetting algorithms based on deleting not recently used or least used cases.

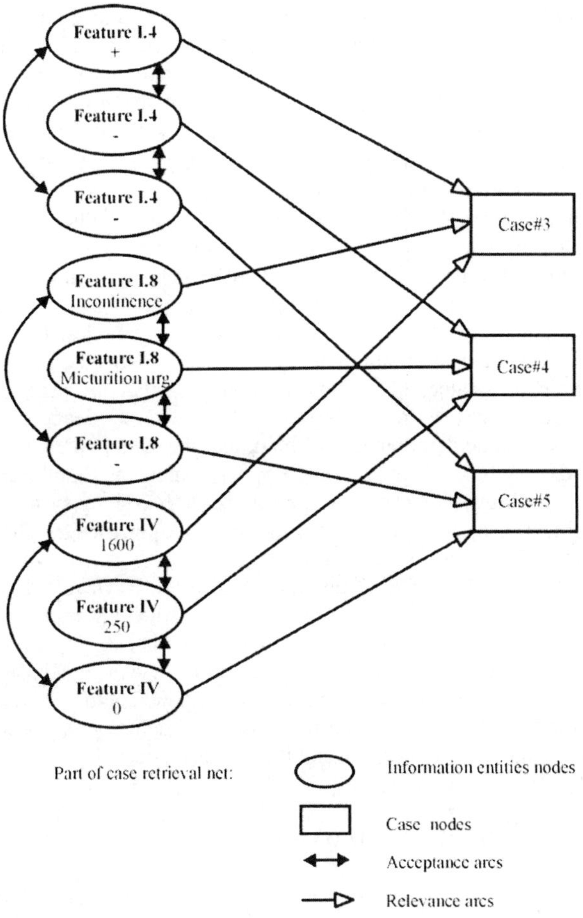

Fig. 3. Example of CRN in the neurology domain.

As mentioned before, cases are organized in the Case Retrieval Net. This net has nodes for each case and nodes for each value of every feature - these values are called *information entities*. There exists an acceptance arc between every two corresponding information entities - information entities of the same feature. Also there exists a relevance arc from information entity to the case, if that information entity is relevant for that case. All the values in the net are weighted with appropriate values.

In Fig. 3 a part of case retrieval net, from this domain, is given. In this figure only 3 features (Spastically - I.4, Bladder dysfunction – I.8, Magnetic resonance imaging – IV) with 3 values for each attribute and for different cases, which makes 9 information entities, are presented. Acceptance arcs are connecting only information entities nodes of the same feature, which means that local acceptance function is defined only between information entities of the same feature. Furthermore, only 3 cases (Case#3, Case#4, Case#5) from this domain are presented in the figure. Relevance arcs represent the influence of information entities on cases. All arcs in the net are weighted by corresponding functions.

At the beginning of the retrieval process, physician has to enter his observations in form of the query, which consists of the values of existing features. For every feature *i* the special numeric value α_i called *importance* is defined. This value contains the information how much is the corresponding feature important for the diagnosis. High values indicate high importance, while lower values indicate lower importance. At the beginning, all importance values have the same default values. Of course, the physician can increase value α_i if he believes that feature *i* has higher importance then some of the others. The physician will decrease the default value of α_i if he considers that the value of the feature *i* is not precise or that this feature is not just so important.

Retrieval process consists of evaluating *acceptance* values for each prototype. Acceptance values are computed by spreading activation process in the net as follows: Information entity nodes are initially activated by α_i. The computation is performed by propagating along the acceptance arcs to further information entity nodes and from all activated information entity nodes over relevance arcs to case nodes. The acceptance value for every prototype is obtained by summing the activations of all cases from that prototype.

If the acceptance values of several prototypes is relatively high then diagnoses of these prototypes is suggested to the physician. However, if acceptance values of all prototypes are below some determined threshold, that means that diagnoses system "never saw something like that before", and that CBR-system cannot suggest the correct diagnoses. In that case physician's query is passed to the rule-based reasoning system, which attempts to solve the problem using some rules from the textbook knowledge. The combination of CBR with rule-based technique is very useful.

System always offers several possible diagnoses. However, the physician must decide which diagnosis is correct. Proposed system just helping him in decision making process. When the physician sets the correct diagnosis, that diagnoses together with the query is passed to the CBR engine in order to learn the new experience. If this case has not any contradictions in relation to all case properties mentioned before the case is included in the case base as the new knowledge. But if just one contradiction has occurred this means that this case is redundant for the system and the case is neglected.

4. CONCLUSIONS AND RELATED WORK

Case-based reasoning technique seems to be suitable for medical knowledge-based systems [1, 7, 10]. Main intention of proposed architecture of CBR system with decision-support elements, was to apply it in a specific medical domain. As Vojvodina is region with high incidence of multi sclerosis disease, research in this field employing promising AI technique, is rather important. Especially, possibility to discover reasons for disease appearance could be significant achievement.

Mutual research is good starting point for employing two emerging fields in achieving useful tool. It could support process of decision making and could help human expert to choose the final diagnosis. Analysis of different CBR medical systems [3, 4, 11, 12, 13] obtains insight in necessary and useful representation techniques, rules, functions and algorithms. Assimilation and application of some well known developed mechanisms like CRN, prototypes, forgetting algorithms, case properties etc. in unique architecture make our approach interesting for realization in neurology domain in Vojvodina.

CRN proved to be a suitable memory organization for decision support applications in medicine domain, because subjective knowledge of medical experts consists of large number of successfully solved problems – cases, and CRN is able to handle case-base of huge size. Prototypes are used for the efficiency improval, and case properties are included for reducing the case base growth.

Now, we are in the beginning phase of implementation of the proposed system. We expect that gathering experience of concrete realization will help us to improve characteristics of the system in future.

References

[1] A. Aamodt, Case-Base Reasoning, Foundation issues, AICOM.

[2] Z. Budimac, V. Kurbalija, Case-Based Reasoning – a Short Overview, Conference of Informatics and IT, Bitola, 2001, (to appear).

[3] L. Gierl, Klassifikationsverfahren in Expertsystemen fur die Medizine, ISBN:0-7734-4054-2, Mellen Univ. Press, Lewiston, 1992.

[4] C.C.Hsu, L.W. Pan, C.S. Ho, Using Inductive Trees to do Case Adaptation in Case-based Reasoning.

[5] Iglezakis, I. (2001), "The Conflict Graph for Maintaining Case-Based Reasoning Systems", *4th International Conference on Case-Based Reasoning (ICCBR 2001),* pp. 263-276, Vancouver, Canada, July/August 2001.

[6] J. Kolodner, An Introduction to Case-based Reasoning, AI Review 6, 3-34, 1992.

[7] Lenz, M., Brtsch-Sporl, B., Burkhard, H., Wess, S. (1998), *Case-Based Reasoning Technology: From Foundation to Applications*, Springer, 1998.

[8] M. Lenz: Case Retrieval Nets Applied to Large Case Bases, draft, Lenz's home-page.

[9] M. Lenz, H.D. Burkhard, S. Bruckner: Applying Case Retrieval Nets to Diagnostic Tasks in Technical Domains, Lenz's home-page.

[10] R. Lopez de Mantaras, E. Plaza, CBR - An Overview, Internet source.

[11]. R and K. Macura, MacRad:Radiology Image Resource with CBR System, In: M. Veloso and A. Aamodt (eds.): Proc of 1st International Conference on CBR, Springer, Berlin, 1995, pp. 43-54.

[12] S. Montani, R. Bellazzi, L. Portinale, Managing Diabetic Patients through a Multi Modal Reasoning Methodology, , Internet source.

[13] R. Schmidt, L. Gierl, Case-based Reasoning for Medical Knowledge-based Systems, Internet source.

Knowledge-based Software Engineering
T. Welzer et al. (Eds.)
IOS Press, 2002

Software Architecture for Intelligent CAD Systems

Toyohiko HIROTA[†], Masa-aki HASHIMOTO[‡]
[†]*Kyushu Sangyo University*
3-1 Matsukadai 2-Chome, Higashi-ku, Fukuoka, 813-8503 Japan
[‡]*Kyushu Institute of Technology*
680-4 Kawazu, Iizuka, 820-8502 Japan

Abstract. This paper proposes software architecture for intelligent CAD systems. Domain-specific specification languages are effective to develop intelligent CAD systems. However, the different domain-specific languages required for individual domains make it difficult to develop various CAD system generators. The proposed software architecture solves this problem by applying a common intermediate language based on the ER model. Moreover, it allows the creation of an integrated CAD system containing multiple domains required by various fields of industry.

1 Introduction

There is a large variety of tools referred to as CAD (Computer Aided Design). The most general and widely used of these are drawing tools used to prepare plans. However, most drawing tools do not directly support design. When such a drawing tool is used to prepare a plan, the user concentrates his attention on the operation of the tool, and it is difficult to focus simultaneously on the plan itself. Therefore, the designer drafts the plan by some other means, and a CAD operator subsequently makes a fair copy of the plan by using a CAD tool. In such a situation, however, information technology is useless to the designer's task.

On the other hand, in many enterprises, tools to design a specific kind of product or part automatically have been developed and used. These tools are informed by the knowledge of the experts, which is formalized to be embedded in the tools. By using such tools, even a novice designer can execute a draft of a plan on an average level. Typically, however, these tools are difficult to maintain after they have been established. It is not easy to modify tools or adapt them to changes in the environment, new technology, or changes in design method. This is because

1. design knowledge is not separated from programming technique, and
2. description of design knowledge is not adequate.

To solve the former problem, we prepare a framework within which design knowledge is described. The second problem is that only programming experts can read the descriptions. Because they are usually not design experts, programming experts cannot grasp the contents of the description. The design knowledge descriptions are likely to be incomprehensible to anyone except the person who wrote them.

One approach by which to avoid the above-mentioned problems involves domain analysis and modeling[1]. Domain analysis and modeling has been adopted as a means for promoting software reuse. It is also effective in putting design knowledge for CAD in order. In this case, the target domain is the field of design, or the design knowledge of the experts in the field. We analyze the domain, and construct a domain model with which we can represent the domain knowledge. For example, a specification language, a diagram, or a table can be a domain model. A domain model should

1. be comprehensible to the designers, and
2. have a proper formal model as its background.

We developed BDL (Building Design Language) specific to the structural design of building. This BDL is not suitable for architectural design, equipment design, and so on. There are two approaches to solving this problem. The first is to extend BDL to specify architectural design or equipment design. In that case, BDL would become a more general specification language. This approach, however, reduces the advantage derived from the specificity of BDL. The second approach is to develop a new language for each domain, in which case one generator is developed for each language. To reduce the work of developing many generators, we adopt an intermediate model. Specifications written with a certain language are translated into the intermediate model, then translated into a programming language. The latter is a translator common to all specification languages. In section 2, we discuss several data models as the intermediate model for the translation.

We aim to develop an integrated CAD system. However, a wide variety of CAD systems is in practical use. Therefore, our CAD systems should be able to exchange CAD data with other existent CAD systems. To implement the data exchange, we must write a conversion program for every combination of CAD systems. The above-mentioned intermediate model is also useful to reduce the work of writing a conversion program.

Our specification languages are nonprocedural: they are superior in terms of minimality, understandability, extensibility, etc., to procedural languages[2]. Subsequently we must add computation methods to the specifications when we generate a CAD system. However, there are several kinds of computation methods. The method is selected based on the component in use. In section 3, we discuss several computation methods for CAD systems.

2 Data model for CAD systems

Though there are many kinds of data models, we focus on the following four, which are suitable for CAD:

1. tree structure model,
2. relational model,
3. ER model, and
4. object model.

2.1 Tree structure model

In Pro/ENGINEER[3], the primary element is a feature, and an object is an assembly of features. A feature consists of a datum and a solid. A datum is a plane, an axis, a point, a coordinate system, or the like, and is used for the reference of model construction. A solid represents a shape of model: that is, a cut, a protuberance, a hole, an angle, a surfacing, or the like. A cut or a protuberance is a 3-dimensional feature that is pressed out, rotated, swept, or blended from a 2-dimensional sectional sketch.

2.2 Relational model

The relational model was proposed by E. F. Codd for database schema[4]. In the relational model, all data is represented as a set of tuples, and each tuple has several attributes. The relationship between two entities is also represented as a tuple: that is, as the combination of primary keys of the entities. IFC (Industry Foundation Classes)[5], the standard data model for CAD in the architectural industry, is described using the EXPRESS language of STEP[6]. The data model applied to EXPRESS language is based on the relational model, and contains the characteristics of the object-oriented data models, which are described in the following:

1. Entity
   An entity corresponds to an object. Therefore, an entity type chiefly describes a class of the IFC. Attributes, class inheritance, and class constraints are defined within the entity type.
2. Attribute
   The attribute values of an entity determine its properties. A type of attribute value can be REAL or BOOLEAN. SET, LIST, ARRAY, and BAG are also types of attribute values. OPTION means that the attribute may have no value.
3. Relationship Entity
   By using only the above-mentioned attributes that refers to entities, an entity can be made to express a relationship between entities.
4. Inheritance
   For example, class 'IfcColumn' inherits its property from its super classes defined in the five levels. Thus, the inheritance hierarchy of the IFC is composed of many levels.
5. Algorithm
   FUNCTION and PROCEDURE statements describe algorithms for calculating attribute values. WHERE statements in entity descriptions define restrictions on the attribute values of their own entities and other entities.

2.3 ER model

The ER model was proposed by P. P. Chen as a unified model for a database[7]. The ER model represents a target domain by entities and relationships. Because the ER model is more straightforward than the r elational model, it is used for the analysis and documentation in designing relational schemas. PSDL[8] is a non-procedural specification language based on the ER model. It is mainly used for business processing, and the PSDL compiler can generate a C program from PSDL specifications.

2.4 Object model

The object model is the most popular model for specifying the static structure of a program[9]. It has many convenient mechanisms by which to abstract concepts. For example, inheritance makes it easy for us to reuse source code, and polymorphism enables us to simplify program control. These mechanisms are useful especially for GUI programs. However, they are not so important for representing data structures. The IFC described in 2.2 adopts the inheritance mechanism, which makes each entity less comprehensive by contrast.

We have been developing a GUI generator for CAD tools[10]. A user has only to construct a class diagram on the screen of our GUI generator, and then the generator can automatically generate a GUI subsystem. Each class in the diagram is a predefined one or a newly defined one for which the user writes the source code. Even when the user defines a new class, the new class typically inherits a certain predefined class, which reduces the work of writing source code.

3 Computation Method for CAD Systems

We classify computation methods from the viewpoint of the sequence of computation:

1. procedure-driven,
2. event-driven,
3. data-driven, and
4. request-driven.

In procedure-driven computation, the computation proceeds according to a predefined procedure. Most programs written in any procedural programming language belong to this type. Other types of programs must be compiled into machine language programs whose type is procedure-driven.

In event-driven computation, an event that occurs randomly initiates a computation that is bound to the event in advance. GUI programs belong in this type. Various events such as pushing a button, selecting an item from a menu, inputting characters in a field, or clicking a mouse initiate a procedure bound to the event, which may read data, update a screen, start a certain computation, and so on.

Data-driven computation is initiated when data necessary to the computation are prepared. An expression to compute necessary data will be computed when every piece of data in the expression has been obtained. When specifying data-driven computations, a 'single assignment' rule is usually used. Therefore, the relation among multiple computations is automatically extracted. For example, an expression to compute variable 'x' must precede other expressions that refer to the variable 'x'. Because the 'single assignment' rule prohibits a loop, some special statements to describe a repetition might be introduced. In JSP (Jackson's Structured Programming)[11], the repetition of computations is derived from the structures of input and output data.

In request-driven computation, an expression to compute data is initiated when the data is requested. The sequence of computation is in the reverse order of that of data-driven computation. A part is displayed on screen, and there are numerous ways in which it can be displayed. Consequently, it is wasteful to prepare all necessary data in advance. The computation should be initiated according to how the part will be displayed. In this case, request-driven computation will omit useless computation.

When a variable is updated, the procedure-driven method and the data-driven method will recalculate the variables dependent on the updated variable. However, in the event-driven method and the request-driven method, there are no means to initiate the recalculation. One of the solutions to this problem is to recalculate all necessary variables when a variable is accessed. However, that wastes processing time. TMS (Truth Maintenance System) manages the dependency among variables to avoid this waste[12]. When a variable is updated, all the variables dependent on the update variable become void. Then the computation method recalculates any voided variable. For example, the CPU time of several editing operations in our CAD was reduced to 0.18 – 0.08 by using TMS[13].

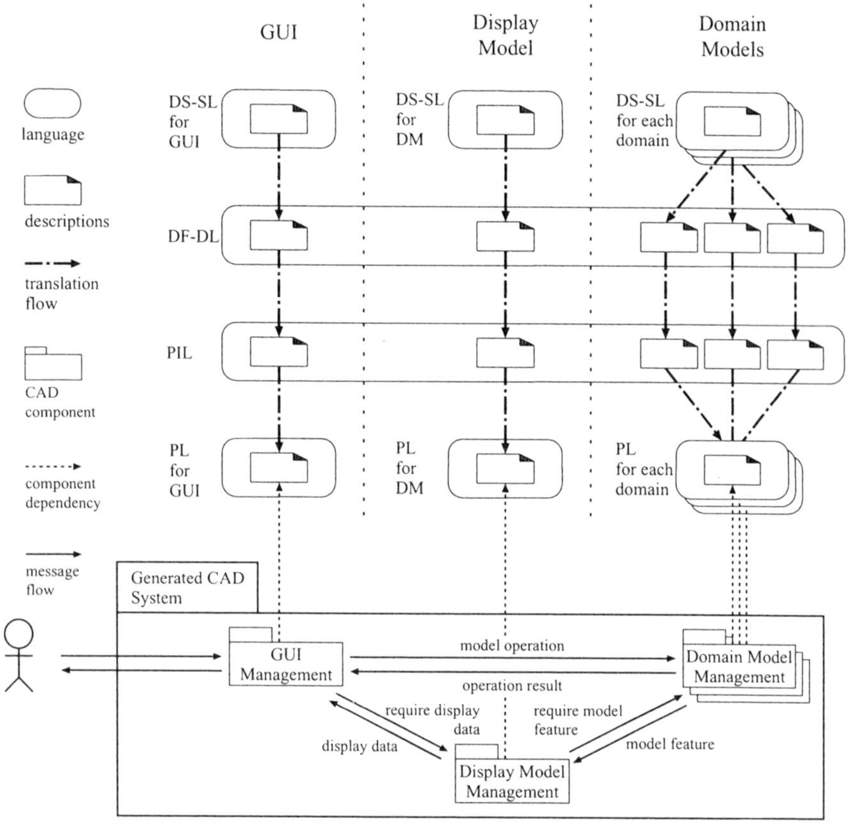

Figure 1: Software architecture of CAD system generation

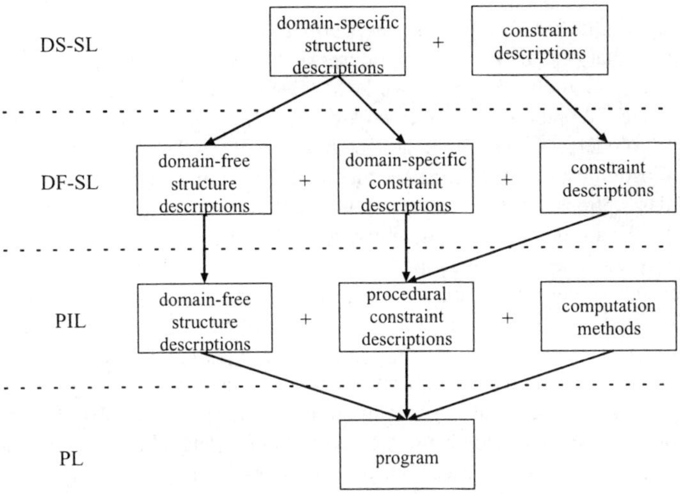

Figure 2: Translation process of specifications

4 Software Architecture for CAD System Generation

Our software architecture determines the components of a system and their translation process from specification languages to programming languages.

4.1 Components of a CAD System

The software architecture is shown in Figure 1. A CAD system can be divided into three primary components based on their respective functions, each of which is expressed as a UML package[14] at the bottom of the figure.

1. Domain model management
   This component manages the product data of the domain by using the various constraints to be satisfied among the data.
2. GUI management
   This component is responsible for supporting an interface for users. It receives operation commands from users and provides methods that allow the users to generate, delete, and modify object data.
3. Display model management
   This component supports a method of displaying object data as defined and modified by the domain model management.

4.2 Translation Process

Specifications of CAD tools are classified into the following:

1. structure descriptions, and
2. constraint descriptions.

Therefore, we translate the specification descriptions in two phases, translation of structure descriptions, and that of constraint descriptions. As discussed in 2, there are many kinds of data models for CAD tools. However, we have selected the ER model as an intermediate model to generate CAD tools, and specified a domain-free specification language (DF-SL) based on the ER model. As we suppose the specifications of CAD tools are written in domain-specific specification languages (DS-SL), structure descriptions in DS-SL are translated into the structure descriptions in DF-SL in the first phase of the translation. In this phase, the constraint descriptions are not substantially translated, but the attributes of the domain specific model are newly added to the constraints.

When translating constraint descriptions to procedures, we must not only translate the constraints but also add computation methods as described in 3. The target language of this translation is not a specific programming language (PL), but a procedural intermediate language (PIL), which is based on an object-oriented programming language. Using the PIL simplifies our work to cover multiple programming languages. Figure 2 summarizes of the above-mentioned translation process. As the translation is applied to each component of the CAD tool, the whole translation process becomes as shown in Figure 1.

4.3 Control Method of CAD Systems

All the components of CAD systems are controlled by the methods appropriate for achieving their imposed functions. These control methods are classified into the following three level groups in our software architecture.

1. Command menu level
   Each design function starts when a designer selects a command menu button in a display window to raise an event. Therefore, the event-driven method is applied to the GUI management component. These highest-level methods refer to the lower level methods.
2. Model-driving level
   The domain model management component should maintain consistency among the product data, which have constraints. Therefore, it should be able to revise the data when a contra-diction is discovered. The TMS (Truth Maintenance System)[12] provides a technique for choosing among actions when a contradiction is discovered in a data set. Employing the TMS can reduce calculation when a change is performed, because it allows recalculation only in the affected range of that change. The display model management component is responsible for expressing how data will be displayed. It must receive data changes immediately from the domain model management. Therefore, the component should also adopt the TMS.
3. Basic level
   Basic level methods provide functions, such as creation and deletion of objects, and the setting of attribute values, which constitutes direct manipulation of the objects in the CAD systems. The methods in this level are automatically embedded to each component.

5 Conclusion

This paper has proposed a software architecture of CAD system generation that allows CAD system development by the domain experts themselves using a domain-specific language.

This software architecture also enables us to build an integrated CAD system that contains multiple domains in a field of industry such as architecture. The resulting integrated CAD systems can introduce an object-oriented database and avoid problems relating to data exchange because they use the homogeneous ER model, which can be restricted to specific domains.

By applying this software architecture, the implementation of a prototype on a UNIX platform was performed. The prototype implementation proved that the software architecture is feasible. However, the problem of execution fficiency must be solved by applying the C++ program code generator, which we are now developing. In future study, we intend to refine the algorithm of procedure generation from the non-procedural DF-SL into PIL.

The worldwide improvement of CALS (Commerce At Light Speed) has been forcing CAD systems to support the entire life cycle of product data. On the other hand, our definition of a 'domain' restricts a field of engineering to a domain with a single abstract structure. Therefore, a CAD system must support multiple domains. For example, an architectural CAD system would support multiple domains such as structure design, equipment installation design, cost estimation, and so on. The specifications of these multiple domains can be integrated by the means of the domain-free specification language.

References

[1] K. Itoh, T. Hirota, S. Kumagai, and H. Yoshida, editors. *Domain Oriented Systems Development: Principles and Approaches*, volume 1 of *Advanced Information Processing Technology*. Gordon and Breach, 1998.

[2] T. Hirota, M. Hashimoto, and I. Nagasawa. A discussion on conceptual model description language specific for an application domain. *IPSJ Journal*, 38(5):1151–1162, 1995.

[3] http://www.ptc.com/products/proe/index.htm.

[4] E. F. Codd. A relational model of data for large shared data banks. *Comm. ACM*, 13(6):377–387, 1970.

[5] International Alliance for Interoperability. Industry foundation classes – release 1.5 model reference documentation final version, 1997.

[6] J. Fowler. *STEP for Data Management, Exchange and Sharing*. Technology Appraisals, 1995.

[7] P. P. Chen. The entity-relationship model: Toward a unified view of data. *ACM Trans. Database Systems*, 1(1):0–36, 1976.

[8] M. Hashimoto and K. Okamoto. A set and mapping-based detection and solution method for structure clash between program input and output data. In *COMPSAC'90*, pages 629–638, 1990.

[9] J. Rumbaugh, M. Blaha, W. Premerlani, F. Eddy, and W. Lorensen. *Object-Oriented Modeling and Design*. Prentice–Hall, 1991.

[10] Y. Miyazaki, K. Katamine, T. Hirota, and M. Hashimoto. A GUI generator for domain specific CASE tools. In *IDPT 1999*, pages 49–56, 1999.

[11] M. A. Jackson. *Principles of Program Design*. Academic Press, 1975.

[12] J. Doyle. A truth maintenance system. *Artificial Intelligence*, 10:231–272, 1979.

[13] T. Hirota, K. Katamine, and M. Hashimoto. Automatic editing operation of building CAD. In *IDPT 1998, Vol.4*, pages 126–133, 1998.

[14] S. Si Alhir. *UML: A Desktop Quick Reference*. O'Reilly, 1998.

Knowledge-based Software Engineering
T. Welzer et al. (Eds.)
IOS Press, 2002

ESTHER – expert system for the diagnostics of drug intoxications

Oleg Larichev[1], Artyom Asanov[1], Yevgeny Naryzhny[1]
Sergey Strahov[2]

[1] *Institute for Systems Analysis, Russian Academy of Sciences, 9, pr. 60 let Octjabrja, 117312, Moscow, Russia*
{oil, art, nev}@isa.ru

[2] *Toxicology Informational Advisory Centre, 3/7 Sukharevskaya sq., p/o 819, Moscow, Russia*

Abstract. Recent years revealed an increase in the number of intoxications in Russia, and according to some estimates drug intoxications constitute as much as 50% of these cases. Therefore problem of urgent diagnostics and emergency care on the pre-admission phase and in hospitals became very important. Taking into account the lack of a specific toxicology experience among general practitioners there was decided to design and develop computer system, which is able to diagnose drug intoxications and provide treatment suggestions.

This paper presents main concepts of an Expert System for Toxicological Help (ESTHER). The most widespread medicines were combined into 25 groups according to the similarity in poisonings diagnostics and treatment. More than 60 clinical signs used by an expert in diagnostics of intoxications were included. The system was deliberately designed to use only clinical signs of poisonings with the view of using it in ambulance cars and hospitals of small towns where accurate laboratory analyses are not available.

The system imitates reasoning of a physician – an expert in toxicology. The ideas of method for knowledge base construction are presented. The architecture of the expert system is discussed in detail as well.

1. Introduction

Drug intoxications constitute a major part of all intoxication cases in Russia (more than 50% according to some estimates). In many cases of severe drug intoxications availability of correct diagnosis and treatment is crucial for patient's life and health. However general practitioners and emergency doctors often have little experience in diagnosing drug intoxications and appropriate treatment.

Therefore, the most important aim of this research was development of an expert system based on the knowledge of experienced physician. The system should be able to recognize drug intoxication case, make assumption about its cause, estimate its severity, explain the diagnosis and provide treatment suggestions. Such system could also be applied as a useful source of advices for young physicians and physicians of different specialisations.

This paper presents main ideas of ESTHER (Expert System for Toxicological Help). Now the system is in the process of certification by Russian Health Ministry officials.

2. Particular features of diagnostics for acute drug poisonings problem

Specific features of diagnostics for drug poisonings problem are as follows:

1. There are a lot of different medicines. They could be allocated into approx. 25 groups on the basis of their influence on human organism. Usually a typical representative for each group can be defined.
2. A set of 5-12 diagnostic signs can be used for the diagnostics of poisonings caused by medicines belonging to one group. The total number of the diagnostic signs is more than 60. They can be divided into several groups: medical examination, patient's complaints, anamnesis, state of central nervous system, cardiovascular system, respiratory system, urinary system, gastrointestinal tract. Each diagnostic sign has a scale of possible values. For example, pulse rate can be described as: tachycardia, normal pulse or bradycardia.
3. In the process of diagnostics a physician creates a holistic image of patient's state on the basis of description in terms of diagnostic signs' values. Generally knowledge about some subset of values is not sufficient for the diagnostics.
4. There are certain groups of drug poisonings described by similar diagnostic signs. For the differentiation among them it is necessary to solve a series of differential diagnostics problems.
5. There are several courses of patient's treatment depending on a type of a drug, severity of patient's state, and a degree of affection on certain systems of human organism.

3. Difficulties in the development of an expert system for the diagnostics of acute medicinal poisoning

From the formal point of view, the diagnostics problem may be presented in the following way. There is a multi-dimensional space of combinations of diagnostic signs' values. With 63 diagnostic signs having in average 3 values on each scale, the total number of such combinations is equal to 3^{63}. It is necessary to allocate these combinations (clinical situations – CS) into different classes of poisonings. Let us note that such classes may intersect. Moreover, it is necessary to distinguish among the degrees of intoxication for each class: mild poisoning or severe poisoning, because this is needed when selecting a treatment course.

Main difficulties in the application of Artificial Intelligence approach for a solution of this problem are:

1. In order to be useful an expert system should closely imitate expert reasoning in the process of diagnostics for all clinical situations. However, direct presentation of all CSs to an expert is impossible due to the large dimension of the problem.
2. One cannot expect receiving expert rules used in diagnosing in the explicit form. It is well known that expert's knowledge is predominantly unconscious.
3. A decision for each CS depends on a combination of diagnostic signs values (holistic image of a possible patient) and cannot be obtained by asking an expert to nominate some coefficients of importance for each diagnostic sign value.
4. At any stage of the expert knowledge elicitation process an expert can make different kinds of errors. It is very desirable to have means that allow discovering errors and eliminating them.

These specific features don't allow (or make it very difficult) using one of the well-known approaches (i.e. [1], [2], [3]) that have many successful applications in other areas. A new approach was to be developed.

4. Methodological approach to the construction of expert knowledge base

Main features of our approach to the construction of expert knowledge base for the drug poisonings diagnostics problem are as follows:

1. 25 knowledge bases imitating expert diagnostics skills are constructed successively for each class of poisonings.
2. For each class of poisonings an expert defines a subset of diagnostic signs and their values needed for the diagnostics. All combinations of the diagnostic signs values define the space of possible patient states.
3. An expert collates values of diagnostic signs by typicality with respect to each class of intoxication.
4. An expert's knowledge is elicited by presenting on a computer screen a description of different CSs in terms of diagnostic signs values. An expert has to assign each CS into one of three classes: strong intoxication with a drug of a corresponding class, mild intoxication, no intoxication by a drug of a corresponding class (different cause of intoxication).
5. In order to save valuable expert efforts, binary relation of domination by typicality is used. If an expert assigns one CS to certain class of intoxication, some other CSs with diagnostic signs values (from the subset used) that are not less typical for this class, can also be allocated into the same

class. Use of this binary relation allows classifying several CSs on the basis of one expert decision. In other words a cone of dominance by typicality is constructed in the space of CSs.

6. Fortunately such cones are intersecting ones. This creates a possibility to check expert's decisions for the absence of contradictions and to find special cases of diagnostic signs interdependence. For each contradictory case the corresponding information is presented to an expert on a computer screen for the detailed analysis.

7. A special algorithm is used when choosing the next CS to be presented to an expert for the classification. The algorithm aims at minimising a number of questions needed for classification of all CSs.

8. For the classes of poisonings that are described with similar sets of diagnostics signs special knowledge bases for differential diagnostics are constructed.

The new approach to the problems of expert knowledge elicitation has been tested previously on different practical tasks [4], [5]. A group of methods based on this approach was developed [5], [6]. The most advanced of them allow obtaining (directly and indirectly) expert classification of 400-600 CSs per hour [6].

After construction the knowledge bases were tested by presenting a number of difficult cases to computer and to an expert. The results demonstrated close imitation of expert reasoning.

5. Formal statement of the problem

Given:

$K = 1, 2, \ldots, N$ – the set of diagnostic signs; n_q – the number of values on the scale of the q-th diagnostic sign ($q \in K$).

L_1, L_2, L_3 – ordered decision classes. L_1 – severe intoxication with some medicine X; L_2 – mild intoxication with medicine X; L_3 – no intoxication with X.

S_q – the set of values on the scale of the q-th diagnostic sign; values on each scale are ordered by typicality for each decision class; the ordering by typicality on the scale of one diagnostic sign does not depend on the values of the other signs.

Cartesian product of the diagnostic signs' scales: $Y = S_1 \otimes S_2 \otimes \ldots \otimes S_N$ creates the set of clinical situations (CS). One CS may be represented as $y^i = (y_1^i, y_2^i, \ldots, y_N^i)$ and $y_q^i \in S_q$.

Needed:

On the basis of information obtained from an expert it is needed to construct the complete (all CSs are classified) and noncontradictory classification.

Let us explain the notion of noncontradictory classification. Having ordered diagnostic signs' scales, it is possible to define anti-reflexive and transitive binary relation P of domination by typicality (for one decision class):

$$P = \{(y^i, y^j) \mid \forall s \in K\ y_s^i \geq y_s^j, \exists s'\ y_{s'}^i > y_{s'}^j\},$$

where $\geq$, $>$ – weak and strong relations of domination by typicality between values on the diagnostic signs' scales.

If $(y^i, y^j) \in P$, then y^i cannot belong to lower class (in the order) than y^j does, and vice versa: y^j cannot belong to higher class than y^i. If this condition is true for any pair $(y^i, y^j) \in P$, then the classification is noncontradictory.

6. Structure of the knowledge base

Knowledge base of ESTHER system consists of 25 knowledge bases for the decision classes (different classes of poisonings) and 40 knowledge bases for differential diagnostics. After expert knowledge has been stored in the knowledge base of the system, it becomes possible for arbitrary CS with any combination of diagnostic signs' values to find out a decision class (or several ones) and severity degree of intoxication.

After the construction of complete and noncontradictory knowledge base, methods of questionnaire theory [7] have been used to produce an optimal decision tree for each class of medicines. Criterion of optimality here is a minimum average number of questions needed to arrive to a conclusion about the existence and severity of poisoning by the drug of this class [8]. Decision tree presents a strategy of putting questions about values of clinical signs with the goal to ascertain the fact of intoxication and state of a patient. Each node of the tree is a question about a value of a diagnostic sign. Depending on the answer the following node is chosen. One of the decision trees embedded into the ESTHER knowledge base is presented on Fig 1.

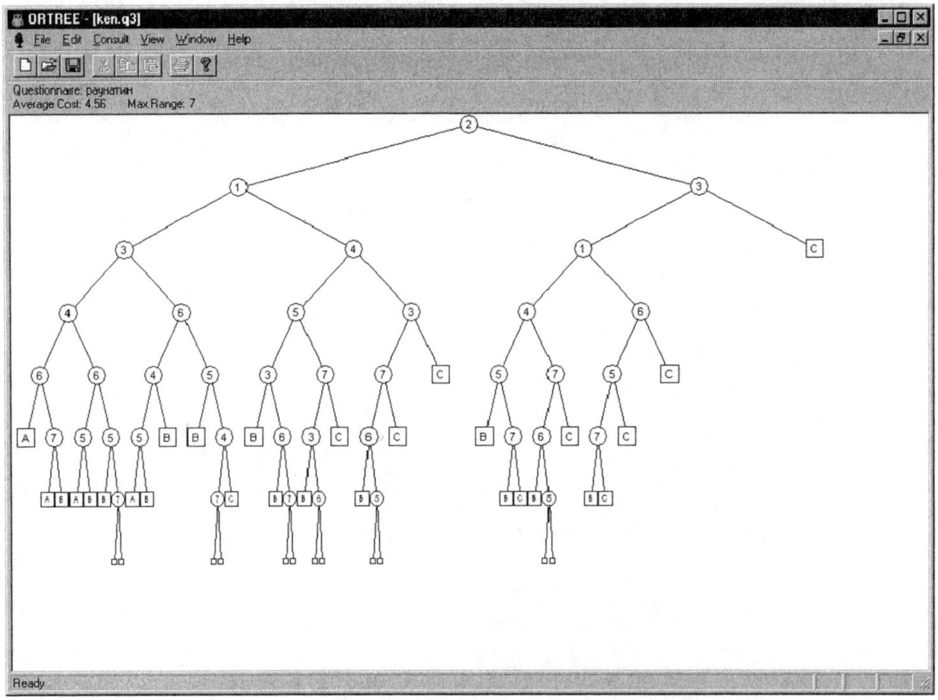

Fig. 1. The constructed optimal decision tree for diagnosing of poisoning by one of the medicines.

In the process of the knowledge base construction, the expert gave information about the most typical values of diagnostic signs for each decision class as well as impossible signs' values. Tables of prohibited values for pairs: "diagnostic sign – decision class" are the important constituent part of the knowledge base. Such tables allow speeding up the diagnostics process.

For the decision classes with similar sets of diagnostic signs the additional knowledge bases have been constructed. The corresponding optimal decision trees allow one to make decision in complex situations when intoxications by several drugs are possible. For such cases ESTHER gives the conclusions like "intoxication by drug A is more probable than one by drug B", "intoxication by drugs A and B is possible". An expert who tested the system noted that these answers increase the quality of system's answers in difficult cases of poisonings.

7. System architecture

Principal modules of ESTHER system and their interactions are represented at the diagram (see Fig. 2).

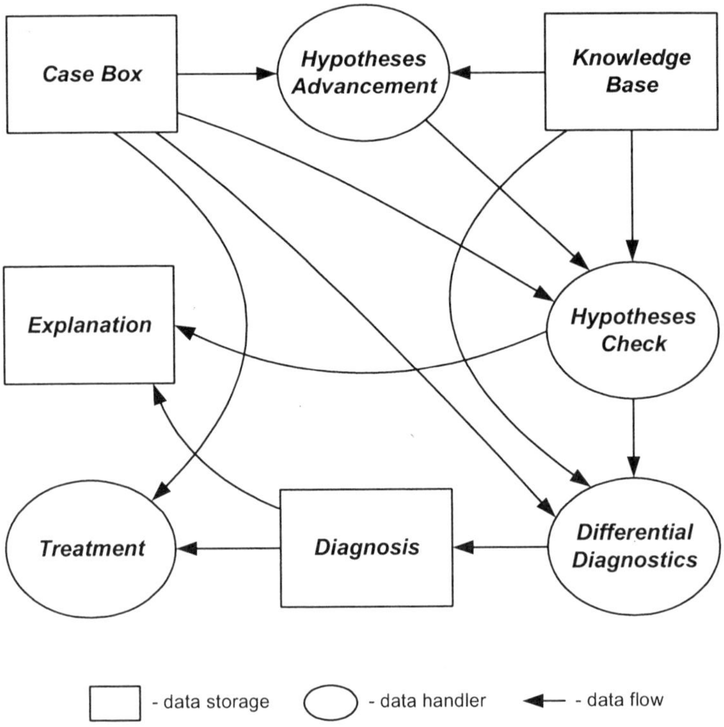

Fig 2. ESTHER principal modules and their interactions

There are two basic modes of a user's work with ESTHER system – data input mode and consultation mode. In the data input mode a user sees a list of clinical signs grouped under the titles: "External examination data", "Anamnesis", "Cardiovascular system", etc. All information about a patient including his/her state, illness history, complaints and so on is stored in the "*Case Box*" module. A user, for example an ambulance physician, successively enters values of clinical signs that are relevant to a particular case. "*Hypotheses Advancement*" module monitors this information and makes suppositions about a possible poisoning cause. If such a supposition arises, it notifies a user and suggests switching to consultation mode for hypotheses checking.

Hypotheses advancement module examines a patient's case with the purpose of discovering typical signs of poisoning by one or another drug. If there are several concurrent hypotheses it selects the one that is supported by the largest number of typical signs' values. When a hypothesis for checking is formed, the hypotheses advancement module either notifies a user about its readiness to switch to consultation mode when system is in the data input mode or transfers the arisen hypothesis to the "*Hypotheses Checking*" module when system is in the consultation mode.

In the consultation mode the system successively checks and puts forward new hypotheses. It takes initiative upon itself and asks the user about values of clinical signs that are needed to confirm or to reject a hypothesis. While checking a hypothesis about a poisoning by some drug, the system uses the constructed optimal decision trees. A pass through the tree is accomplished and at the nodes, where values of clinical signs are still unknown, a user is questioned about values of appropriate signs to reach a conclusion. As a result of this pass one of the following conclusions is drawn: "Serious poisoning by medicine *X*", "Mild poisoning by medicine *X*" or "No poisoning by medicine *X*". The last means that either the poisoning was caused by the medicine other than *X* or there is no drug poisoning at all.

At any time user can break the mode of consultation, switch back to data input mode, add and/or change values of any clinical signs and after that resume the consultation.

While advancing and checking hypotheses the so-called exclusions are used intensively. Exclusion is a rule formulated by the expert in the following form: "Poisoning by the medicine *X* cannot cause the clinical signs' values *a, b, c...*" Our practice revealed that such rules decrease significantly the number of hypotheses to be checked as well as the time necessary to reach a diagnosis.

In general case it may happen as a result of hypotheses checking that several hypotheses about poisonings by different medicines are confirmed. This may be the case if patient actually has taken several medicines as well as when different medicines result in similar clinical pattern. In order to refine the diagnosis the "*Differential Diagnostics*" module is applied. There are special expert rules stored in the knowledge base of the system. They allow distinguishing among medicines similar in clinical patterns in difficult cases. These rules are also stored as optimal decision trees. An oriented graph is constructed in the "*Differential Diagnosis*" module. Nodes of the graph correspond to confirmed hypotheses and arcs correspond to the relations of poisonings' probabilities between different medicines. For example, if differential diagnostics rules state that poisoning by medicine X_1 is more probable than poisoning by medicine X_2, then nodes X_1 and X_2 in the graph are connected by the arc that originates at node X_1 and enters node X_2. After that, the graph is condensed, that is a kernel of undominated nodes is extracted. For each node *X* belonging to the kernel the string "Poisoning by medicine *X* is most probable" is written to the final diagnosis (module "*Diagnosis*"). For the other nodes X' the string "Poisoning by medicine X' is not excluded" is written to the diagnosis. Our discussion with expert revealed that these two wordings are sufficient for practical purposes and there is no need in more precise distinguishing among poisonings' probabilities.

The ESTHER system allows explaining the diagnosis. While passing through a decision tree in the "*Hypotheses Check*" module information about passed tree nodes is stored. That is information about values of clinical signs that were used in diagnosing is recorded. The "*Explanation*" module stores arguments "pro" for each confirmed or rejected hypothesis as well as arguments "contra". The system provides explanations in the following form: "*There is poisoning with medicine X with degree of gravity D* ***because*** *sign S_1 has value s_{11}, sign S_2 has value s_{21} ...* ***in spite of*** *the fact that sign S_3 has value s_{32} etc.*". This allows explaining in a natural way from the user's viewpoint both confirmed and rejected hypotheses. It is important to remark, that physicians use this explanation style as well when explaining their own decisions – usually they enumerate symptoms of poisoning and then say that these symptoms are sufficient for diagnosing.

There is also the module of recommendations on treatment as a constituent part of the ESTHER system ("*Treatment*" on the diagram). It can be used as a reference manual for getting acquainted with basic methods of treatment of poisonings by one or another medicine. Another, more important feature is its ability to give recommendations on the particular given case of poisoning. Using a diagnosis made by other modules of the system and extracting clinical pattern of poisoning from the "*Case Box*" module it is able to recommend treatment with regard to the gravity of poisoning, degree of damage to the systems of human organism. It can also prescribe a symptomatic therapy. Moreover, when prescribing treatment methods and dosage of antidote medicines it is possible to take into account age, weight and illness history of the patient.

Openness of ESTHER system's architecture was an important objective of its designing. Openness principle was followed when designing the knowledge base of the system, inference, explanation and treatment subsystems. Therefore, for example, it is rather simple now to include new groups of medicines that could cause poisonings. This feature is of great importance, because new medicines are emerging continuously.

The system's design provides for separation and encapsulation of a user interface environment shell and the system's knowledge base that was implemented in a specialised high-level scripting language. This guarantees high reusability of the knowledge base handling components and allows easy modification of rules and algorithms included in the system.

8. Conclusion

From our point of view the ability of expert system to behave like a human is the critical factor for its successful application. The developed ESTHER system includes large knowledge base that closely imitates expert knowledge and reasoning in the problem of drug poisonings diagnostics. The system displayed very close coincidence of its answers with diagnoses of a human expert. When confirmed officially this will result in the system certification by Health Ministry authorities.

The system gives to a user a possibility to use active and passive ways of interaction. When ESTHER takes initiative upon itself and starts questioning a user he or she has a good chance of self-education. A user can compare his/her preliminary conclusion with one of the expert – the author of the knowledge base.

It is important to note that the open architecture of ESTHER provides a possibility to add new decision classes (causes of intoxications) and new diagnostic signs for such classes. A revision of individual knowledge bases is also possible for any decision class using knowledge of more experienced (for this class of poisonings) physician.

The expert system for the diagnostics of acute drug poisonings is the example of "knowledge distribution" for large groups of specialists. We believe that appearances of new diseases and new drugs make the problem of "knowledge distribution" for large areas more important.

References

[1] Pople, H.E. The Formation of Composite Hypotheses in Diagnostic Problem Solving: An Exercise in Synthetic Reasoning, The Fifth International Joint Conference on Artificial Intelligence, Boston, MIT, 1977.

[2] Shortliffe, E.H. Computer-based Medical Consultations: MYCIN, New York, American Elsevier, 1976.

[3] Schreiber, A.Th., Wielinga, B.J., Akkermans, J.M., Van de Velde, W. CommonKads: A comprehensive methodology for KBS development. IEEE Expert, 9, 1994.

[4] Larichev, O.I., Mechitov, A.I., Moshkovich, H.M., Furems E.M. The Elicitation of Expert Knowledge, Nauka, Moscow, 1989 (in Russian).

[5] Larichev, O.I., Moshkovich, H.M., Furems, E.M., Mechitov, A.I., Morgoev, V.K.: Knowledge Acquisition for the Construction of the Full and Contradictions Free Knowledge Bases, IEC ProGAMMA, Groningen, The Netherlands, 1991.

[6] O. Larichev, A. Asanov, Y. Naryzhny Effectiveness evaluation of expert classification methods, European Journal of Operational Research, Vol 138/2, pp 260-273, 2002.

[7] Parhomenko, P.P. The Questionnaires Theory: Review, Automatics and Telemechanics, N. 4, Moscow, 1970.(in Russian)

[8] Naryzhnyi, E.V. Construction of the Optimum Questioning Strategy for a Complete Expert Data Base, Automatic Documentation and Mathematical Linguistics, Vol. 30, N. 5, Allerton Press, New York, 1996.

Knowledge-based Software Engineering
T. Welzer et al. (Eds.)
IOS Press, 2002

Modeling Semistructured Data by the Adjacency Model

Jari TÖYLI, Matti LINNA, Merja WANNE
Department of Computer Science
University of Vaasa
P.O.Box 700, FIN-65101 Vaasa, Finland
{jt, mli, mw}@uwasa.fi

Abstract. Semistructured data has been under intensive investigation during the last few years. The main subject of interest has been on the development of new data models and new query languages. The most widely used data model for representing semistructured data is a graph-like or tree-like structure. The problem is to develop a model which could be all-embracing. In order to develop such a model we have introduced a new model called the Adjacency Model (AM). This model is based on three foundational concepts: the adjacency relation system associated with adjacency defining sets (ARST), the unique ARST's and the valid ARST's. Our model is a general model which can be used to represent semistructured data as well as relational data.

1. Introduction

Internet is a huge information source which is not constrained by a fixed structure. This kind of data is commonly called semistructured data. This type of data cannot be modeled by any of the commonly used database models, such as the relational data model or the object data model. If we want to use such data in our business systems, we have to have a way to model it.

During the last few years after intensive investigation, the research community has proposed a new model for representing semistructured data [1, 2]. The new model is a tree-like or graph-like model where the data resides on the edges of the graph [3]. But this new model is not all-embracing and the access time in a naive search can be very long. The Adjacency Model is our proposal for the representation of semistructured data.

The relational model is one of the most widely used model for representing data in business systems. But as the structure of the model is fixed we do not have the possibility to represent this kind of data with it. Neither can we use the object data model as such for the purpose.

The goal of our paper is to show that the Adjacency Model is flexible enough to be used to represent semistructured data. The fact that we can represent semistructured data with the Adjacency Model gives us a solid base for the future work to develop the Adjacency Model to be used also with other types of data.

The rest of the paper is organized as follows. In Section 2 we will briefly present one semistructured data model: the Object Exchange Model. In Section 3 we will introduce the Adjacency Model (mainly based on the concepts introduced by [4,5]) and define the most fundamental concepts. In Section 4 we will give two examples of how semistructured data can be converted into the Adjacency Model. Finally, Section 5 contains some conclusions.

2. Related Works

Semistructured data is data which does not have a fixed structure, but a structure which changes dynamically depending on the application. This causes us a problem when we are modeling the data: we cannot use the models designed for structured data.

This has generated a demand for new and more flexible models which could be used for representing semistructured data. There seems to be a consensus about using a rooted labeled graph for the purpose. Most of the proposed data models are in principle similar, with only minor variations. These variations typically consist of missing data, duplicated fields, or minor changes in the representation. The data can also reside at nodes or edges or at both.

An example to present "schemaless" or "self-describing" data was introduced in the Tsimmis project [6]. The model defined in that project was called Object Exchange Model (OEM), a system for integrating heterogeneous data sources.

The OEM is a graph, where the nodes are the objects, the edges are labeled with attributes, and in which some leaf nodes have an associated atomic value. The graph has a root, i.e. a distinguished object from which all the other objects are accessible. Because of the wide use of OEM as a base model in many projects, it has become the de facto standard for semistructured data model.

In this paper we will address the so-called Adjacency Model. It has a structure quite different from those presented so far but we will show that it can be used to represent semistructured data.

3. The Model

In this section we will define our model, called *Adjacency Model* (AM), for representing semistructured data.

In order to get an exact insight of what an adjacency model is, we will give all the crucial definitions here. In these definitions we are mainly going to use the definitions introduced in [4] and [5].

Definition 1. An *adjacency relation system* (ARS) is a pair (A,R), where $\mathsf{A}=\{A_1,A_2,\cdots,A_n\}$, $n\geq 1$, is a set containing pairwise disjoint finite nonempty sets and $\mathsf{R}=\{R_{ij}\mid i,j\in\{1,2,\cdots,n\}\}$ is a set of relations, where each R_{ij} is a relation on $A_i\times A_j$.

Let (A,R) be an ARS, where $\mathsf{A}=\{A_1,A_2,A_3\}$, $A_1=\{x_1,x_2\}$, $A_2=\{y_1,y_2,y_3\}$, $A_3=\{z_1,z_2\}$, and R consists of the relations

$$R_{11},R_{22},R_{21},R_{23},R_{31}=\phi$$
$$R_{33}=\{(z_1,z_2)\}$$
$$R_{12}=\{(x_1,y_1),(x_1,y_2),(x_2,y_2)\}$$
$$R_{13}=\{(x_2,z_1)\}$$
$$R_{32}=\{(z_1,y_3)\}$$

These relations can be illustrated by the directed graph of Figure 1.

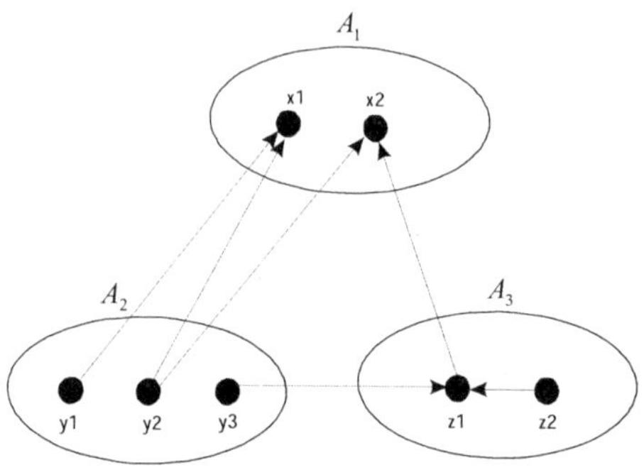

Figure 1: Directed graph illustrating the ARS above.

Definition 2. If $(x,y_1),(x,y_2),\ldots,(x,y_m) \in R_{ij}$ are all the pairs of relation R_{ij} having x as the first component, then each element y_k $(k=1,2,\ldots,m)$ is said to be adjacent to the *element* x. Furthermore, denote by $Ad_j(x)$ the set $\{y_1,y_2,\ldots,y_m\}$.

In the adjacency model, when an element is adjacent to itself, we can ignore the direction of the relation and express the adjacency by a symmetric relation. In many applications the adjacencies are symmetric.

Definition 3. An adjacency relation system (A, R) is said to be *symmetric* if for each pair $x \in A_i$, $y \in A_j$, it holds that $x \in Ad_i(y)$ if and only if $y \in Ad_j(x)$.

The adjacency between two distinct elements can appear, by definition, between the elements of two distinct types (e.g. $x_1 \in Ad_i(y_1)$, $x_1 \in A_i$, $y_1 \in A_j$) or also within the same type (e.g. $y_2 \in Ad_j(y_1)$, $y_1 \in A_j$ and $y_2 \in A_j$). It can also be defined with the help of the so-called adjacency defining set of types when the elements are of different types.

We assume that the elements of each set A_i, $i=1,2,\cdots,n$, represent entities of a certain type T_i. Furthermore, associate with each index pair $i,j \in \{1,2,\cdots,n\}$ a set $K \subseteq \{1,2,\cdots,n\}-\{i,j\}$ of indices and a set of entity types

$$\tilde{T}_{ij} = \{T_k \mid k \in K\}.$$

The set $\tilde{T}_{ij}$ thus gives us the entity types which determine the adjacency between the elements of A_i and A_j.

Definition 4. Elements $x \in A_i$, $y \in A_j$, where $i,j \in \{1,2,\ldots,n\}$ and $x \neq y$, are said to be *adjacent with respect to a set of entity types*

$$\tilde{T}_{ij} = \{T_k \mid k \in K\} \neq \phi$$

if for each $k \in K$ there is an element $z \in A_k$ such that $x \in Ad_k(z)$ and $y \in Ad_k(z)$. The set $\tilde{T}_{ij}$ is called the *adjacency defining set* between the elements of A_i and A_j.

If we assume in Figure 2 that $\tilde{T}_{23} = \{T_1\}$, then y_1 and z_1 are adjacent with respect to $\tilde{T}_{23}$ since $y_1 \in Ad_2(x_1)$ and $z_1 \in Ad_3(x_1)$. $\tilde{T}_{ij}$ may be empty or it may be that $i=j$, which means that we have adjacency between elements of the same type.

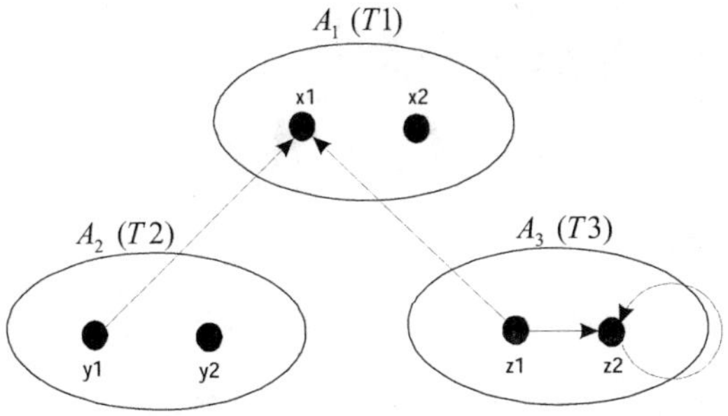

Figure 2: An Adjacency Defining Set.

For an adjacency relation system associated with adjacency defining sets (ARST), we use the notion $(\mathsf{A},\mathsf{R},\tau)$, where τ refers to the set of adjacency defining sets.

Definition 5. Let $(\mathsf{A},\mathsf{R},\tau)$ be an ARST. Elements $x,x' \in A_i$ are said to be *neighbors* if $T_{ii} \neq \phi$ and x,x' are adjacent with respect to $\tilde{T}_{ii}$ or if $\tilde{T}_{ii} = \phi$ and $x \in Ad_i(x')$.

In our model an element can be adjacent to itself (i.e. $i = j$, in the case of relation R_{ii}). This type of adjacency is not considered in [4].

Definition 6. An element $x \in A_i$ is said to be adjacent to itself if $x \in Ad_i(x)$.

An adjacency between two distinct types is considered to be *weak* if it depends only on the definition of relations. If the adjacency is defined with respect to a set of entity types, then the adjacency is *strong*. These two concepts are not considered in [4]. In Figure 1 the adjacency between elements x_1, y_1 is weak and the adjacency between elements y_1, z_1 is strong if $\tilde{T}_{23} = \{T_1\}$. In [4] the concept unique adjacency combines these two concepts.

Definition 7. An ARST $(\mathsf{A},\mathsf{R},\tau)$ is said to be *unique* if for each pair $i, j \in \{1,2,\ldots,n\}$ of integers such that the corresponding adjacency defining set $\tilde{T}_{ij}$ is nonempty and for all elements $x \in A_i$, $y \in A_j$, x and y are adjacent if and only if they are adjacent with respect to $\tilde{T}_{ij}$.

Consider (Figure 3) a set of relations $\mathsf{R} = \{R_{11}, R_{12}, R_{13}, R_{21}, R_{22}, R_{23}, R_{13}, R_{23}, R_{33}\}$, where

$R_{11} = \{(x_1,x_2),(x_2,x_1)\}$,

$R_{12} = \{(x_1,y_2),(y_2,x_1),(x_2,y_2),(y_2,x_2)\}$,

$R_{13} = \{(x_2,z_1),(z_1,x_2),(x_2,z_2),(z_2,x_2)\}$,

$R_{33} = \{(z_1,z_2),(z_2,z_1)\}$,

$R_{21} = R_{22} = R_{23} = R_{31} = R_{32} = \phi$.

and the adjacency defining sets

$\tilde{T}_{11} = \{T_2\}$,

$\tilde{T}_{33} = \{T_1\}$.

$T_{22} = T_{12} = T_{21} = T_{13} = T_{31} = T_{23} = T_{32} = \phi$

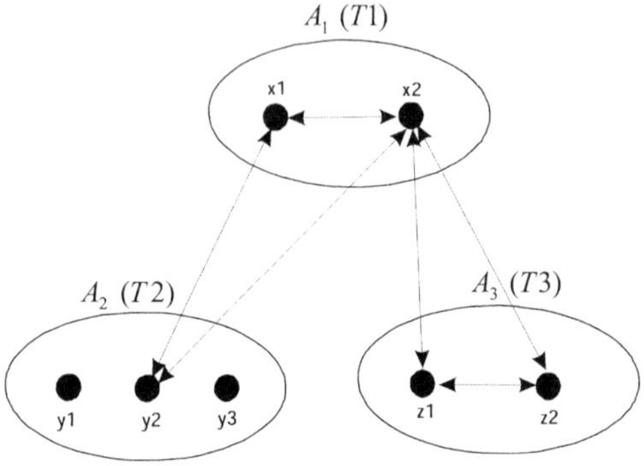

Figure 3: An adjacency defining set.

We can see that elements x_1 and x_2, $x_1, x_2 \in A_i$, are adjacent with each other as well as z_1 and z_2, $z_1, z_2 \in A_j$. The adjacency is defined via the relation R_{11} for x_1 and x_2, and R_{33} for z_1 and z_2, and on the other hand, also with respect to the adjacency defining sets $\tilde{T}_{11}$ and $\tilde{T}_{33}$. If there are no other non-empty adjacency defining sets, the ARST considered is unique.

We can use the notation $T_i \to T_j$ for a relation type to indicate that the relations R_{ij} are defined on $A_i \times A_j$. Furthermore, we can consider sets of relation types

$$\{T_i \to T_j \mid (i,j) \in S\},$$

where $S \subseteq \{1,2,\ldots,n\} \times \{1,2,\ldots,n\}$. This is called a *relation combination* and the relation combination is determined by $S \subseteq \{1,2,\ldots,n\} \times \{1,2,\ldots,n\}$. For an ARST ($\mathsf{A}, \mathsf{R}, \tau$), denote by $\mathsf{R} \mid \mathsf{S}$ the restriction of R on S, i.e.

$$\mathsf{R} \mid \mathsf{S} = \{R_{ij} \in \mathsf{R} \mid (i,j) \in \mathsf{S}\}.$$

Relation combinations have very remarkable importance for the optimization of the queries on semistructured data because they can be used to restrict the search space, and hereby limit the search time used by the query. Here the concept of valid relation combinations plays a key role.

Definition 8. Given the entity types $T_1,\ldots,T_n$, a set $S \subseteq \{1,2,\ldots,n\} \times \{1,2,\ldots,n\}$, and adjacency defining sets τ. A relation combination $\{T_i \to T_j \mid (i,j) \in S\}$ is said to be *valid* if for any unique ARST $(\mathsf{A}, \mathsf{R}, \tau)$ there is no other unique ARST $(\mathsf{A}, \mathsf{R}', \tau)$ such that $\mathsf{R} \mid \mathsf{S} = \mathsf{R}' \mid \mathsf{S}$. Otherwise the relation combination is said to be *non-valid.*

4. Conversion between the Models

In this section we give a short presentation of the conversion process and two examples of it. The conversion process from the semistructured data model into the Adjacency Model proceeds in predefined phases. The main steps are the following:

- pick up the objects of the source model to be modeled as types in the target model
- define the given types as adjacency defining types
- define the adjacencies between the appropriate types and finally

- define the adjacencies which are not considered yet (e.g. the self-loops, adjacencies within the type etc.)

Our first example considers an OEM database (Figure 4) presented by [8]. This graph is represented with the Adjacency Model in Figure 5.

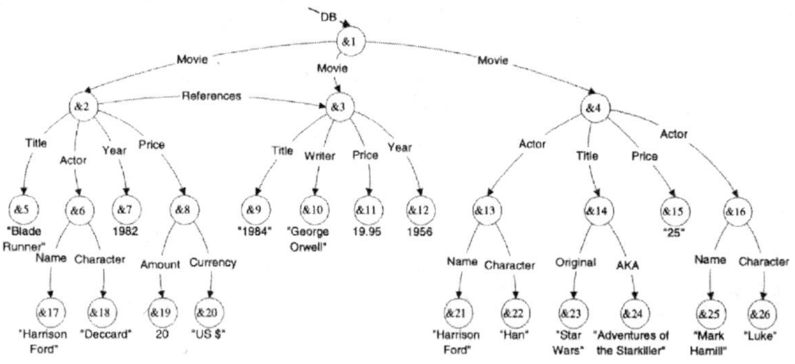

Figure 4. An OEM database.

An OEM (Object Exchange Model) model consists of atomic objects, complex objects and values. In Figure 4 object *&5* is an atomic object, and object *&6* is a complex object. Atomic objects have no outgoing edges and they have also values whereas complex objects have subobjects. Names like *Title* and *Actor* serve as aliases for objects and entry points into the database. *DB* (in this case) is a name that denotes an entrypoint to the system. These are the special characters of an OEM database which is designed for representing semistructured data.

The conversion process can proceed as follows: In Figure 4 we can see that there is a named input edge, which is called *DB*, so we use it as a the entry type. We go through the whole graph and select all distinct edges, and create the corresponding types, like *Movie*, *Actor*, *Title* etc. of them. After that we define the adjacency defining sets of the complex object. These sets are created from those edges (e.g. *Movie*, *Actor*) which end into the nodes (e.g. *&2*, *&6*) that have outgoing edges. Next we create the adjacencies between the elements of the atomic types and the elements of the corresponding adjacency defining types (*Name/Actor*, *Currency/Price* etc.), and finally the adjacencies between the adjacency defining sets.

In Figure 4 we have an edge (i.e. *References*) between two *Movie* objects. This is a very special occurrence, because in the Adjacency Model it is drawn between two elements within the type *Movie*.

Consider next Figure 5. There are thirteen distinct types, some of which are complex and others which are atomic. The complex types are the adjacency defining sets. If we, for instance, take the type *Actor*, we immediately see that some of the elements of the types *Name* and *Character* are adjacent to each other with respect of the type *Actor* ($\tilde{T}_{Name,Character} = \{T_{Actor}\}$). The same holds true e.g. for the elements of the types *Year* and *Title*, which are adjacent with respect to the elements of the type *Movie* ($\tilde{T}_{Actor,Year} = \{T_{Movie}\}$, $\tilde{T}_{Actor,Title} = \{T_{Movie}\}$).

The adjacencies between the elements of the types *Name* and *Actor* (e.g. $\&17 \in Ad_{Name}(\&6)$) are defined by definition of the Adjacency Model, not by an adjacency defining set. This is an example of a *weak adjacency*.

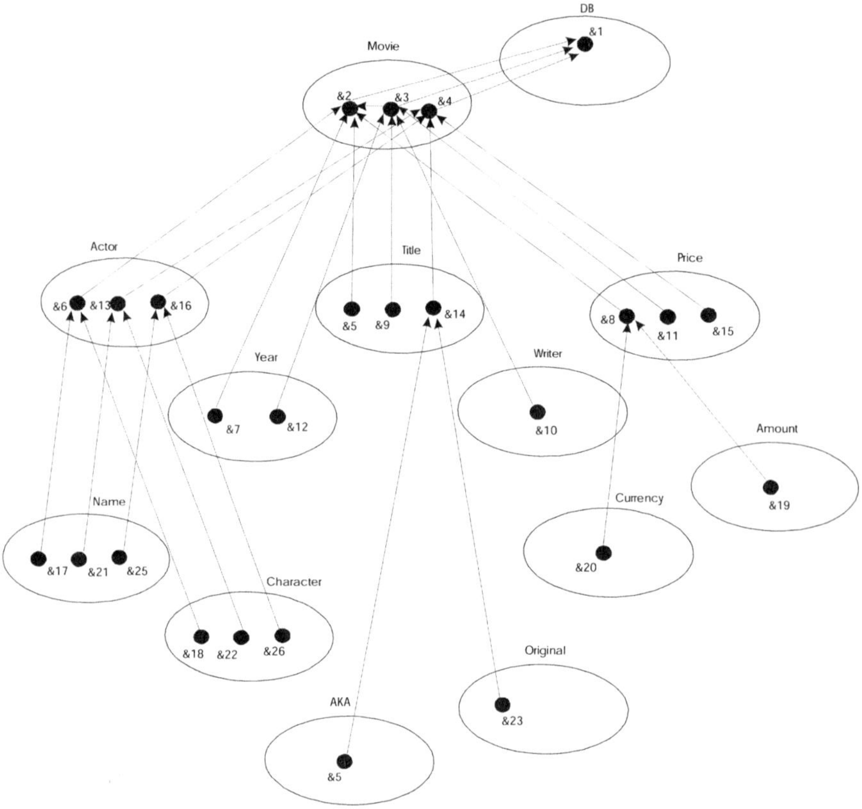

Figure 5. OEM database of Figure 4 modeled by the Adjacency Model.

In Figure 5 the type *Title* as well as the type *Price* has twofolded function, because they have atomic and complex elements within the type. The element *&5* of the type *Title* is atomic (i.e. it has no adjacent elements). On the other hand, the element *&14* has two elements which are adjacent to it (i.e. $\&5 \in Ad_{AKA}(\&14)$ and $\&23 \in Ad_{Original}(\&14)$). This kind of structure is typical of semistructured data, and as we can see there is no problem to represent the both cases.

The edge labeled *References* in Figure 4 is not depicted as a distinct type in the Adjacency Model, because there is a more natural way to represent it. We use only one type to represent an adjacency like this. We just define a relation between the two elements (*&2* and *&3*) of the type *Movie*. In this case we do not have an adjacency defining type and so the adjacency is defined with respect to a weak relation ($\tilde{T}_{ii} = \phi$ and $\&2 \in Ad_{Movie}(\&3)$). It is important to note that with the help of this technique we can reduce the number of distinct types.

Our next example deals with the semistructured data graph of Figure 6. It represents an OEM database, which contains information about the Stanford Database Group [8]. In principle it has the same structure as the OEM database of Figure 4 with atomic and complex objects and values in the leaf nodes, but we can pick up one new feature in the structure. The graph contains a cycle between the nodes &4 and &5 with the edge labels *Member* and *Project*.

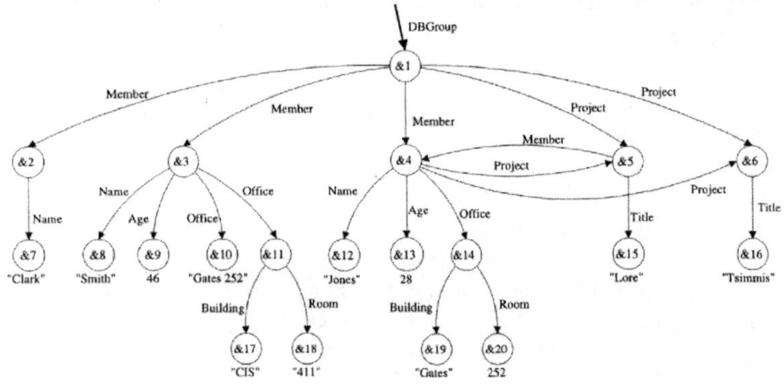

Figure 6. An OEM database with a cycle between nodes &4 and &5 [8].

In the adjacency model (Figure 7) this particular case is presented as an adjacency in both directions. The adjacency can be defined directly by relations $R_{Member,Project}$ and $R_{Project,Member}$ between those types. In this case we, however, have also the possibility to use the adjacency defining type. The adjacency defining type here is the type *DBGroup*, because both of the types *Member* and *Project* are adjacent to the type in question, $\tilde{T}_{Member,Project} = \{T_{DBGroup}\}$.

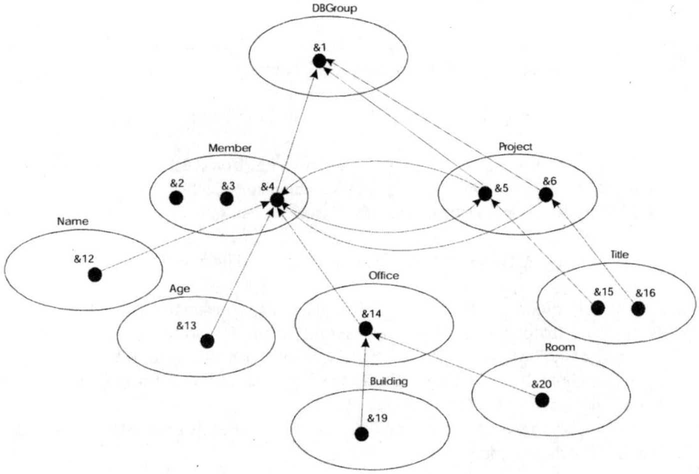

Figure 7. Adjacency into both directions between two elements of two distinct types.

Since $\&5,\&6 \in Ad_{Project}(\&1)$ in Figure 7, the elements &5 and &6 are adjacent with respect to $\tilde{T}_{Project,Project}$. This kind of adjacency is typical in the context of semistructured data when we have a distinct root node (here DBGroup). All edges with the same label (here *Project*) emanating from the root node are adjacent with respect to the same type they represent. The same phenomena can be found between the types Project and Member, where $\&5,\&6 \in Ad_{Project}(\&4)$.

5. Conclusions

As we have seen the Adjacency Model can be used to represent different kinds of semistructured data models found in the literature. Here we have given only two examples. The adjacency model is also appropriate to represent the relational model which shows that the use of the Adjacency Model can also be extended into other areas of interest. However, this work does not include empirical data of some real life applications because we have concentrated on the development of a solid foundation for the model.

One of the benefits of the Adjacency Model compared with other semistructured data models is that the relations between the objects of a graph can in many cases be minimized when using the Adjacency Model, and in the case of a valid relation combination all of the adjacencies can be derived from the relations defined.

There are many extensive subjects (like schema design, query languages etc.) in the area of the Adjacency Model which must be considered more accurate in the future, and the model needs also more evaluation. The next step will be the developing and applying of some fast algorithms of adjacency relation system and to study how they can be applied to semistructured data models.

References

[1] Y. Papakonstantinou, H. Garcia-Molina, and J. Widom. Object Exchange Across Heterogeneous Information Sources. In Proceedings of the International Conference on Data Engineering (ICDE), pp. 251-260, 1995.
[2] Abiteboul, S. 1997. Querying Semi-Structured Data. In Proceedings of International Conference on Database Theory, pp. 1-18.
[3] P. Buneman, S. B. Davidson, and D. Suciu. Programming Constructs for Unstructured Data. In Proceedings of the Workshop on Database Programming Languages, 1995.
[4] M. Wanne. Adjacency Relation Systems. In Acta Wasaensia No. 60. Computer Science 1. Universitas Wasaensis, Vaasa 1998.
[5] M. Wanne, and M. Linna. A General Model for Adjacency. In Fundamenta Informaticae, 38, pp. 39-50, 1999.
[6] S. Chawathe, H. Garcia-Molina, J. Hammer, K. Ireland, Y. Papakonstantinou, J. Ullman, and J. Widom. The TSIMMIS Project: Integration of Heterogeneous Information Sources. In Proceedings of the 100th Anniversary Meeting of the Information Processing Society of Japan, pp. 7-18, 1994.
[7] J. McHugh, J., S. Abiteboul, R. Goldman, D. Quass and J. Widom. Lore: A Database Management System for Semistructured Data. *SIGMOD* Record 26(3), 1997.
[8] J. McHugh, J. Widom, S. Abiteboul, Q. Luo, and A. Rajaraman. Indexing Semistructured Data. Technical Report, the Stanford Database Group, 1998.

Knowledge-based Software Engineering
T. Welzer et al. (Eds.)
IOS Press, 2002

A New Feature Selection Method Based on Dynamic Incremental Extension of Seed Features

Mao Komori, Hidenao Abe, Takahira Yamaguchi
Faculty of Information, Shizuoka University
3-5-1 Johoku Hamamatsu Shizuoka, 432-8011 Japan

Abstract. This paper presents a new feature selection method in data pre-processing of ML/DM(Machine Learning and Data Mining). Our new method starts with a set of seed features that comes up frequently in the results of ML/DM with all the features from a given data set . They can be extended with other features while the incremental extension process can keep higher accuracy of ML/DM than that of the immediate data mining. When the accuracy does not become higher, the above repetition stops and the feature subset at that time is taken as the input dataset of ML/DM schemes. We have compared our new feature selection method with the following popular feature selection methods: filter method and wrapper method. We have done a case study, using fourteen datasets from UCI ML Repository. The case study has shown us that our method gets to or a beyond the level of two popular feature selection methods.

1 Introduction

As ML/DM (Machine Learning and Data Mining) aims to address larger, more complex tasks, it has become increasing important how to deal with the most relevant information in a potentially overwhelming quantity of data. In many cases, the number of features handled by a ML/DM scheme is often excessively large, and the majority of these features are irrelevant or redundant. It is therefore necessary, from a data perspective, to perform pre-processing with the aim of selecting a subset of features. Because of the negative effect of irrelevant features, ML/DM schemes follow the feature selection methods to eliminate irrelevant features. The best way to select relevant features is manually, based on a deep understanding of the domain problem and what the features actually mean. However, as the method by hands takes many costs, we must explore the automatic methods to work to some extent.

This deletion of irrelevant features and reduction in the number of features improves the performance of the ML/DM scheme. As the number of features decreases, the representation of the learning concept becomes easy to understand.

In this paper, we first introduce two popular feature selection methods called the "filter method" and "wrapper method" [1, 2], and then propose a new feature selection method based on the frequency of feature occurrence [3]. Finally we describe how our new method works compared with two popular methods, taking fourteen data sets from UCI ML Repository [4] and a decision tree C4.5 as a learner in order to do this case study.

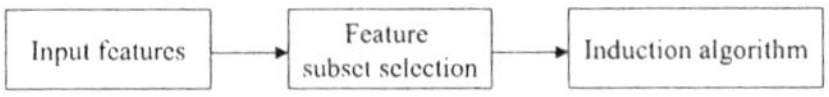

Figure 1: The filter method

2 Feature Selection Method

Given N number of features, the number of feature patterns (subsets) is 2^N. Accordingly, the number of combinations becomes astronomically high as N becomes large, and some way of eliminating irrelevant features in an efficient manner must be found.

When selecting a subset of good features, there are the following popular methods: one method evaluates features based on general data characteristics independent of ML/DM schemes, and the other evaluates feature sets using ML/DM schemes that will ultimately be employed for learning. The former is called the "filter method", because feature sets are subjected to a filtering process to determine the most promising subset before ML/DM schemes begin. The latter is called the "wrapper method" because ML/DM schemes are wrapped into the feature selection procedure.

2.1 Filter Method [5]

The filter method shown in Fig. 1 selects features independent of ML/DM schemes. One scheme categorized as a filter method is Relief-F that allocates relevancy weights to each feature. You could sample instances randomly from a training set and check neighboring records of the same and different classes - "near hits" and "near misses". If a near hit has a different value for a certain feature, the feature appears to be irrelevant and its weight should be decreased. On the other hand, if a near miss has a different value, the feature appears to be relevant and its weight should be increased. After repeating this operation many times, only features with positive weights are chosen.

2.2 Wrapper Method [1, 2]

In the wrapper method shown in Fig. 2, a subset of features is selected using ML/DM schemes in the form of a black box. In short, no knowledge of the scheme other than its simple interface is needed. The feature subset selection scheme conducts a search for a good subset using the ML/DM schemes themselves as part of the function evaluating feature subsets. The wrapper method conducts a search in the space of possible parameters. A search requires a state space, an initial state, a termination condition, and search engine. Searching can be conducted by forward selection beginning with an empty feature set or by backward elimination beginning with a full feature set.

3 Seed Method

While the wrapper method works better than the filter method, the former takes more computational costs. Thus, in order to get to or a beyond the level of the wrapper method with

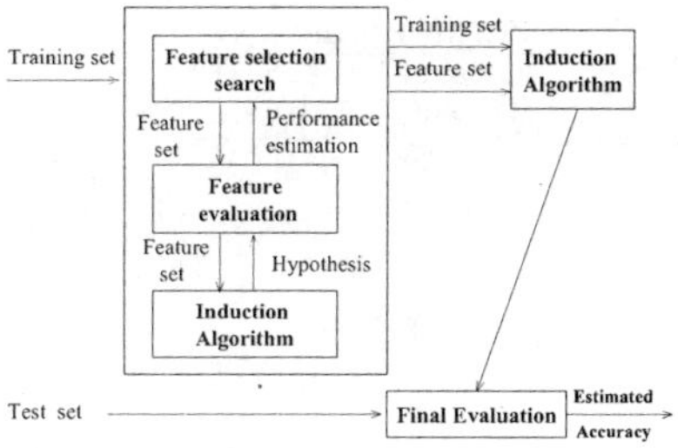

Figure 2: The wrapper method

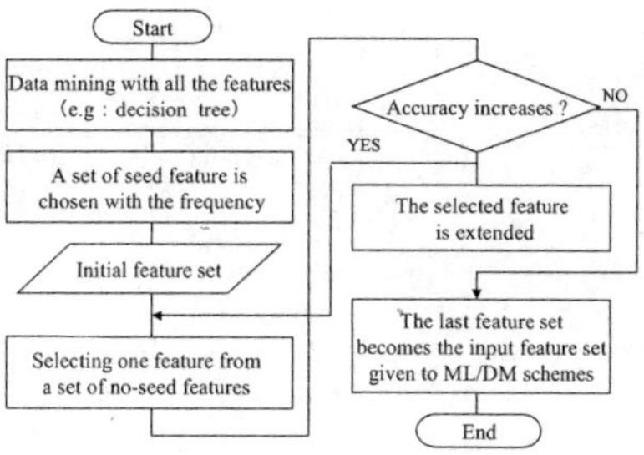

Figure 3: Overview of our seed method

less computational cost, we propose a new method based on dynamic incremental extension of seed features, which is called seed method later as shown in Fig. 3.

At first the seed method executes ML/DM with all features. Then it selects a set of features with the high frequency of occurrence in learned results such as decision tree. It takes this set of features as a set of initial features. They can be extended with other features over and over, while the incremental extension process can keep higher accuracy of ML/DM than that of the immediate ML/DM. When the accuracy does not become higher, the above repetition stops there and the feature subset becomes the input dataset given to ML/DM schemes.

4 Case Studies

This section describes how our seed method works compared with the filter method and the wrapper method. We take fourteen data sets from UCI ML Repository [4] and a decision tree C4.5 as a learner in order to do this case study. Table 1 shows us the details of the data sets; the number of features, the number of classes, the size of training set and the size of test set(CV means ten-fold cross-validation here). Furthermore, we then take the following measurement; accuracy, computational costs and the number of selected features. Furthermore, in the filter method, we use Relief-F scheme described earlier. Additionally in the wrapper method, we use an empty set as the initial state and employ the best first search.

4.1 Accuracy

Table 2 shows us four different kinds of accuracy results from the following feature selection methods: no feature selection method, the filter method, the wrapper method and our seed method. Looking at Table 2, in the case of that the accuracy of some feature selection method gets beyond that of no feature selection method, the sign of plus is attached there. As well, in the case of getting to it, no sign is attached there. Furthermore, in the case of not getting to it, the sign of minus is attached there. Assigning $+1$ to the sign of plus and -1 to the sign of minus, we compute the total value of the three feature selection methods. Thus, our new feature selection method takes the first place among them. Looking at Table 2 in another way, in the case of that some feature selection method gets the highest accuracy, the sign of circle is attached there. Counting up the number of circle, our new feature selection method

Table 1: The details of fourteen data sets from UCI ML Repository

No	Dataset	# Features	# Classes	The size of training set	The size of test set
1	breast-cancer	10	2	699	CV
2	crx	15	2	690	CV
3	Hayes-Roth	5	3	132	28
4	labor-neg	16	2	40	17
5	pima	8	2	768	CV
6	sick	29	2	2800	972
7	audiology	69	24	200	26
8	chess	36	2	3198	CV
9	glass	10	7	214	CV
10	lung-cancer	56	3	33	CV
11	wine	13	3	178	CV
12	monk 1	6	2	124	432
13	monk 2	6	2	124	432
14	monk 3	6	2	124	432

takes the most ones. Furthermore, on the average of accuracy, our seed method takes the first place. Thus we concluded that our new feature selection method works best from the point of accuracy.

4.2 Computational Costs

Table 3 shows us the computational costs taken by three feature selection methods. Comparing the average computational costs, our seed method gets just a little beyond the filter method but the wrapper method gets much beyond our seed method. On one hand, taking large size of data sets such as No.6 "sick" and No.9 "chess", the wrapper method takes so many costs because running learner many times. On the other hand, taking large size of features such as No.4 "labor-neg", No.7 "audiology" and No.10 "lung-cancer", our seed method takes so many costs because of making search space large.

4.3 The Number of Selected Features

Table 4 shows us the number of all the features, the number of the features with no feature selection method and the number of features respectively selected by the three feature selection methods. Comparing the average number of selected features, our seed method is between the filter method with the largest number and the wrapper method with the smallest number. In order to raise the comprehensibility of learned concepts, it is better to reduce the number of selected features. This case study shows us that the wrapper method works best getting the comprehensibility, but it is an issue to make sure why works best.

5 Conclusions

Comparing our seed method with the filter method and the wrapper method from three viewpoints (accuracy, computational costs and the number of selected features), our seed method

Table 2: The accuracy respectively performed by three feature selection methods

No	Dataset	No feature selection method	Filter method	Wrapper method	Seed method
1	breast	95.14%	95.14%	+ 95.71% ○	+ 95.56%
2	crx	85.94%	− 85.65%	+ 86.96% ○	− 85.8%
3	Hayes-Roth	92.86% ○	92.86% ○	− 71.43%	92.86% ○
4	labor-neg	82.35% ○	82.35% ○	− 76.47%	82.35% ○
5	pima	74.08%	74.08%	+ 75.0 % ○	+ 75.0 % ○
6	sick	98.77%	98.77%	98.77%	+ 99.18% ○
7	audiology	84.62%	− 81.62%	+ 92.31% ○	+ 92.31% ○
8	chess	99.53% ○	− 99.47%	− 97.87%	99.53% ○
9	glass	65.89%	65.89%	+ 71.96%	+ 72.90% ○
10	lung-cancer	81.25%	81.25%	+ 84.38% ○	+ 84.38% ○
11	wine	94.94%	94.94%	+ 97.50% ○	+ 97.2 %
12	monk1	75.69%	+ 88.89% ○	+ 88.89% ○	+ 88.89% ○
13	monk2	65.05%	− 62.50%	+ 67.13% ○	+ 67.13% ○
14	monk3	97.22% ○	97.22% ○	97.22% ○	97.22% ○
	Ave	85.24%	85.76%	85.83%	87.88%

takes the first place from the viewpoint of accuracy and the second place from point of computational costs. As future work, we will have more theoretical analysis on our seed method and apply it to different kinds of other data sets.

Table 3: The computational costs respectively taken by three feature selection methods

No	Dataset	Filter method	Wrapper method	Seed method
1	breast	37	26	44
2	crx	43	782	100
3	Hayes-Roth	1	1	4
4	labor-neg	1	16	64
5	pima	29	304	20
6	sick	126	1708	352
7	audiology	2	183	752
8	chess	1753	9060	668
9	glass	4	411	28
10	lung-cancer	1	44	216
11	wine	3	176	68
12	monk1	1	3	20
13	monk2	1	2	12
14	monk3	1	3	16
	Ave	143.07	992.14	168.86

Table 4: The number of features respectively selected by three feature selection methods

No	Dataset	# all the features	# the features with no feature selection	# the features with filter method	# the features with wrapper method	# the features with seed method
1	breast	10	7	10	4	5
2	crx	15	9	14	8	8
3	Hayes-Roth	4	3	3	1	3
4	labor-neg	16	2	13	1	2
5	pima	8	6	8	6	7
6	sick	29	10	25	11	24
7	audiology	69	14	42	9	9
8	chess	36	22	28	12	24
9	glass	10	9	9	5	7
10	lung-cancer	56	2	31	2	2
11	wine	13	3	13	4	6
12	monk1	6	5	3	3	4
13	monk2	6	6	3	0	3
14	monk3	6	2	3	2	2
	Ave	20.29	7.14	14.64	4.86	7.57

References

[1] R. Kohavi, G.H. John : Wrappers for feature subset selection, Artificial Intelligence 97 (1997) 273-324.

[2] A.L. Blum, P. Langley : Selection of relevant features and examples in machine learning, Artificial Intelligence 97 (1997) 245-271.

[3] Mao Komori, Hidenao Abe, Hiromitsu Hatazawa, Yoshiaki Tathibana, Takahira Yamaguchi: A Methodology for Data Pre-processing Based on Feature Selection, The 15th Annual Conference of Japanese Society for Artificial Intelligence (2001) (in Japanese)

[4] C.J. Merz and P.M. Murphy : UCI repository of machine learning databases (1996)

[5] Ian H. Witten, Eibe Frank : Data Mining - Practical Machine Learning Tools and Techniques with Java Implementations - , Morgan Kaufmann Publishers (1999)

Knowledge-based Software Engineering
T. Welzer et al. (Eds.)
IOS Press, 2002

Improving Data Development Process

Izidor Golob, Tatjana Welzer, Boštjan Brumen, Ivan Rozman
University of Maribor, Faculty of Electrical Engineering and Computer Science
Smetanova 17, SI-2000 Maribor, Slovenia.

Abstract. Non integrated data represents a problem which can be seen as a data - information quality problem. After a brief introduction on data and information quality, the process for data development is described. We introduce the framework for the data development process, which understands the concept of the value chain in the enterprise. We argue that it is necessary to re-engineer the processes that create redundant databases into processes that are integrated against a commonly defined database. The result of the research can be used as guidance how to design or re-design processes in order to improve the information quality.

1. Introduction

Data quality represents one of the major problems in organizations' information systems. Ensuring the quality of data in information systems is crucial for decision-support and business-oriented applications. In spite of the fact that decisions are often based on data available, the importance of data quality has been neglected for too long time. One of the main reasons for neglecting the importance of data– (and information-) quality is that organizations treated information as a by-product. Organizations should rather adopt information as the product of a well-defined production process [1].

Another important issue today is data integration. The purpose of data integration is to provide a uniform interface to a multitude of data sources [2]. Many organizations face the problem of integrating data residing in several multiple, redundant, nonintegrated, undocumented, stove-piped sources. However, the management is aware that only consolidated data, free of error, can lead to correct decisions.

To produce high-quality information it is essential to have a quality data definition. The output of a data development process is data definition. The current methodologies for the data development process neglect the existence of many applications in the enterprise and thus produce many disparate, often redundant databases. This leads to poor information quality, however the management needs a rapid access to integrated information of a high quality.

The terms "data" and "information" are both used in different ways in several branches of computer and information science. In this article, we define data as the raw material produced by one or more business processes that create and update it. Information depends on three components: data, definition and presentation.

The fundamental goal of this paper is to develop a framework to be used in a data development process with a goal to raise the quality of the process. The existing methodologies do not pay attention to the concept of a value chain. We define a value chain as an end-to-end set of activities beginning with a request from the customer (an internal or external one) and ending with a benefit to the customer. The methodologies assume that the application, which is subject to the process, is the only one in the environment. We argue there is a need for a methodology that has an value-chain perspective. Instead of having multiple stove-piped databases, efforts must be put to build one, single integrated database.

The notion of "single database" does necessarily mean one physical database structure. It does mean commonly defined data elements.

The rest of the paper is structured as follows: Section 2 briefly reviews the data and information quality and defines a theoretical foundation for this paper. An overview of literature in this field is also given. Section 3 defines the role of data development process in the information production processes context. We further provide a methodology for data development process design and reengineering in this section. Section 4 concludes with a brief summary and outlines several areas for further research.

2. Information Production Processes and Quality

Information production processes are simply the business processes including manufacturing, in which information becomes created, collected, captured or updated [3]. They are performed within information system or its part. An information system is user-interfaced and designed to provide information and information processing capability to support the strategy, operations, management analysis, and decision-making functions in an organization [4]. It may or may not involve the use of computer system.
Information is a finished product of an information production process. We shall further follow the definition of information given by English [3] where information is applied data, depended on data, definition and presentation. The relation between data and information is shown on Figure 1.

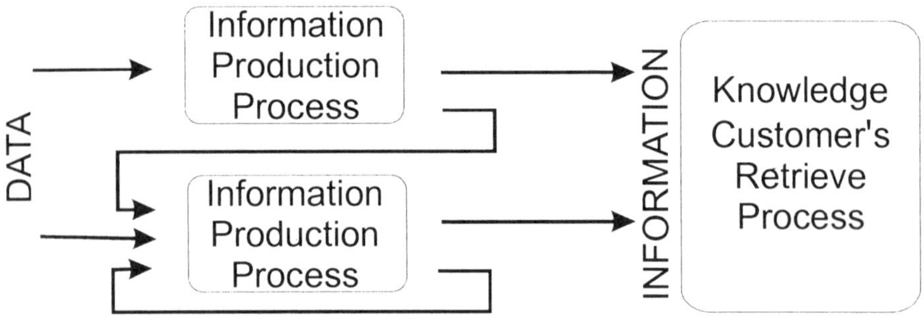

Figure 1: Data, information, information production processes, information customer

Analogously to "data" and "information" terms and based on the survey of literature in [5, 6, 7], we conclude that the standard definition of "data quality" and "information quality" does not exist. The most widely used references describe quality as "fitness for use" [8] or "conformance to requirements". ISO 8402 standard "Quality Management and Quality Assurance Vocabulary" provides the following definition of quality: "The totality of characteristics of an entity that bear on its ability to satisfy stated and implied needs" [7].

There is a lot of research showing the importance of information quality for business and users, such as [9, 10]. In general, it is widely accepted that higher data quality results in better customer service. It is also logical that higher data quality has a positive effect on productivity due to reducing or eliminating unproductive re-work, downtime, redundant data entry, and the costs of data inspection.

3. Data Development Process

Data development process is a process that produces data definition. According to [3], data definition can be seen as (i) information product specification, (ii) as meaning and as (iii) information architecture.

Data definition is to data what a product specification is to a manufactured product. Clearly, it is essential for an enterprise to have a quality information product specification. Without it is impossible to produce consistent high-quality information. It should contain not only names, data types, domains and business rules that govern data, but also data models.

Current methodologies for data development process do not generate common data structures. With such methodologies, each time a new application is introduced to support or automate business processes, a new database is introduced. Such practice results in a number of isolated databases, often redundant. This fails one of the most important issues in today's information systems, which is data integration and has been already discussed. To perform additional data analysis such as data mining or to build a data warehouse, for example, one must integrate data with new integration and cleansing interfaces.

What follows in our paper is a proposal for a framework to be used in a data development process. The main idea is to establish commonly defined data elements in one single integrated database while understanding the concept of the value chain. A useful working definition of the customer is any member of the value chain who either directly or indirectly purchases or influences the purchase of a company's products and services. The end-user is the last member of the value chain to derive or recognize a benefit or value from product, service or offering. To gain a value-chain-wide view of the data, we need to build a data architecture that all the involved customers agree on. The reengineered data development process output now describes common data and individual databases. Common data is shared among processes (applications) in the enterprise. Additionaly, there is no need for additional interfaces, when later one wants to build a data warehouse.

In his research, [11] pointed out that an integration of cross-functions based on a process perspective is expected to increase organizational efficiency. As a logical consequence, we argue that integration of data (and thus removing redundant databases) that are subject to information production processes has a positive impact on information quality. Raising the quality of the data development process as one of the information production processes quality clearly implies higher information quality.

Another clear trend today that supports the need for such a methodology is a trend to accumulate every piece of information available, especially with the advent of data warehouses. Even more, with the rise of Internet as well as intranets the number of available and relevant sources to an organization as well as the quantity of data continues to grow. According to [12], Web-data integration is number one frontier for database theory for the next decade. The conflict with quantity of data is that more data we have to manage, less can we spent on ensuring the data quality. Thus, it is very important to develop processes along with non stove-piped databases that provide a solid, stable but flexible data infrastructure for processes in the enterprise.

3.1. A Framework for Data Development Process

To achieve a substantive improving performance, the information production processes should be first analyzed by certain characteristics from a high-level perspective. These pertain to how different functions are coupled to each other and orchestrated to produce a common process outcome. Data created in one process is required in other downstream processes. Here we look on processes through database lens and propose a framework for data development process improvement.

Enterprises typically have many information production processes. An information production process comprises a set of activities and the interdependencies between them. Each activity is a logical unit of work, performed by either a human or a computer program. Each activation of an information production process generates a process instance, which will achieve a prescribed goal when it terminates successfully. Databases are repositories of data, where data being created, updated or deleted by the processes, is stored and accessed. Data is the glue that connects processes across the enterprise. From this point of view, the fundamental objective for any enterprise integration project is the need to create a global data architecture.

Below a four-phase framework to aid the data development process in effectively building an enterprise-wide data model and data structures is proposed. Phase 1 identifies the data flow among information production processes. Phase 2 is the analysis phase. Phase 3 involves the development or restructuring of the corresponding data models and structure. Phase 4 applies the results of the previous phase and directs new applications to access new data structures rather the legacy databases. Each step is described by description, inputs and outputs.

I. Initial phase of the data development processes

This phase is initiated by identifying the information production processes and the data flow in the enterprise. It is a planning step. We can choose data development or data redevelopment as a fundamental task. In a case of data development, data structures and models are developed. In a case of redesign, the goal is to improve the existing information infrastructure, and goals of the data redevelopment process are defined here.

Having the fundamental task in mind, the following concrete sub-goals are be defined:

- Minimize the unnecessary data redundancy.
- Maximize the interoperatibility among information production processes.
- Design an organizational information architecture that provides an effective linkage between the enterprise-wide user data requirements and the specific applications implemented to satisfy such requirement.
- Standardize the data.

Inputs

- Processes in the enterprise.
- Data used.
- Description of the value chain and its customers.
- Specific business or technical problems.
- Additional user and application requirements.

Outputs

- Detailed description and model of the processes in the enterprise, along with the data being used by the same processes.
- Identification of processes' activities.
- Identification of value chain member – process interrelation.
- Problem identification and resolution aim.
- Specifications.

II. Analysis

In a case where a new application is going to be built, processes' requirements for data are passed as input to this phase. Optionally, in a case of data development process redesign, this step is followed by the identification of potential candidates for redesign.

Based on the identified specifications and other results of the previous phase, the following steps are first performed in this phase:

- Where no existing data structures exist to support the user requirement, new data structures are introduced.
- The entities being used in different parts of a value chain within the enterprise are identified.
- Dependencies (functional dependencies) in the data being collected, created or simply used in a specific process (to eliminate the redundancy at the process level) are determined.
- The mappings from the data in a process to the data, which already reside in the organizational database, are determined.
- Specific business rules that have effect of data values of attributes (e.g.. constraints, completeness rules) are defined.
- Data dependencies among attributes (this would help us generating high-quality user interfaces and thus can ensure a higher level of data quality) are determined.
- Conformity level of data to standardized data is determined.

Inputs

- User and application specifications.
- Description and model of the processes, along with a list of activities that are performed.
- Value chain members and their processes.

Outputs

- Classification of the processes into proposed sub-categories.
- Process/Activity/Data/Chain Member (PADC) diagram.
- Identification of the candidates (processes, activities and/or data) that are subject to the development or restructuring process.

III. (Re)design of the data structures and model

An information infrastructure (this includes data models) must be (re)designed to support the access to common data through the entire chain. A new database that replaces redundant databases is created, containing common, standardized data. Databases belonging to specific applications and separately used by departments, are redesigned in this phase to reflect the new situation.

This phase involves anticipating all the involved parties. Many technical, social, security, quality and political issues must be solved.

The following desirable quality characteristics must be addressed during this phase:

- Data and architectural completeness.
- Data and architectural robustness.
- Data and architectural flexibility.
- Data and architectural comprehensiveness.
- Minimally redundancy.
- Attribute granularity.

- Essentialness of the individual data.
- Definition (business term) clarity.
- Naming and labeling (entity, attribute, abbreviation, acronym) clarity.
- Domain type consistency.
- Naming consistency.
- Business rule completeness and accuracy.
- Data relationship correctness.
- Operational/analytic appropriateness.
- Decision process appropriateness.
- Distributed architecture and design.

Note that some characteristic may be mutual exclusively. A database design cannot be optimized to support both operational and data warehouse activities, for example.

Inputs
- Data specification.
- PADC diagram of existing and proposed system.
- Data, processes or activities to be created or restructured.

Outputs
- New or restructured data and process models.
- Updated PADC diagram.

IV. Applying the results

New applications are instructed to access new data structures rather the legacy databases. Old, redesigned databases are restructured in order to reflect the current data architecture and purged.

The new database and information architecture must be functional. Data must be used by knowledge users, which can provide feedback to refine the architecture and helps raise the organizational self-awareness for the quality.

Input
- Legacy applications and databases.

Outputs
- Updated applications and new databases.
- Feedback on problems.
- Suggestions for improvements.

In reality, a number of cyclical relationships may exist within the phases and steps as refinements and incremental improvements are made to the processes and data structures being used.

4. Conclusion and Further Research

In this paper, we defined a framework for data development process that incorporates the concept of the value chain in the enterprise. The fundamental characteristic of the framework is that it provides a commonly defined database to an enterprise and thus removes unnecessary redundancy at the database level. The framework presented can be seen as a part of an overall methodology for improving the information production process quality.

The framework should be used to coordinate the implementation of new processes and their databases. Where separate databases already exist, the framework should be used as a guidance how to re-engineering the existing processes that create redundant databases into processes, which are integrated against a commonly defined enterprise database.

Further research is required to validate the proposed framework and to further develop metrics to measure the quality of data development process.

References

[1] Wang RY, Lee YW, Pipino LL, Strong DM. Manage Your Information as a Product. Sloan Management Review 1998;39(4).
[2] Friedman M, Levy AY, Millstein T. Navigational plans for data integration. Sixteenth National Conference on Artificial Intelligence (AAAI-99). Orlando, Florida: 1999.
[3] English LP. Improving Data Warehouse and Business Information Quality. Wiley Computer Publishing, 1999.
[4] Yeo KT. Critical Failure Factors in Information System Projects. International Journal of Project Management 2002;20(3).
[5] Xu H. Managing Accounting Information Quality: An Australian Study. International Conference on Information Systems 2000.
[6] Vassiliadis P. Data Warehouse Modeling and Quality Issues. PhD Thesis, 2000.
[7] Abate ML, Diegert KV, Allen HW. A Hierarchical Approach to Improving Data Quality . Data Quality 1998;4(1).
[8] Orr K. Data quality and systems theory. Communications of the ACM 1998;41(2).
[9] Raghunathan S. Impact of Information Quality and Decision-Maker Quality on Decision Quality: a Theoretical Model and Simulation Analysis. Decision Support Systems 1999;26(4).
[10] Chengalur-Smith IN, Ballou DP, Pazer HL. The Impact of Data Quality Information on Decision Making: An Exploratory Analysis . IEEE Transactions on Knowledge and Data Engineering 1999;11(6).
[11] Wu I-L. A Model for Implementing Bpr Based on Strategic Perspectives: an Empirical Study. Information and Management 2002;v 39(n 4).
[12] Vianu V. A Web Odyssey: From Codd to XML Symposium on Principles of Database Systems. 2001.

Position Papers Panel

Knowledge-based Software Engineering
T. Welzer et al. (Eds.)
IOS Press, 2002

A proposal for a swap-type mutation of the genetic algorithm and its application to Job Shop Scheduling problems

Mitsuaki HIGUCHI
Niigata University of International and Information Studies
3-3-1 Mizukino, Niigata 950-2292, Japan

Morio NAGATA
Dept. of Administration Engineering, Faculty of Science and Technology, Keio University
3-14-1 Hiyoshi, Yokohama 223-8522, Japan

Abstract. A good gene sequence in the previous generation may not leave a prototype when crossover and mutation are manipulated using the order expression. That is, crossover and mutation do not always produce an excellent individual. A mutation of character preservation is needed to solve these types of problems. We have proposed a new swap-type mutation and conducted experiments regarding the lowest switching cost for an existing problem in a synthetic resin factory. In this paper, we apply the new genetic manipulation of the swap-type mutation to Job Shop Scheduling problems. The effectiveness of the character preservation operation is examined. Features of this mutation are that it easily leaves desired characteristics and it does not produce lethal genes. We use the swap-type mutation with certain conditions to limit chromosomes of a type whose characteristics are to be preserved into the next generation.

1. Introduction

A scheduling problem often prohibits including the same elements in one schedule. For example, in a synthetic resin factory, a product cannot be manufactured in a factory line twice within a certain period because a switching cost is generated. Therefore, an individual phenotype has to be created as a case of genetic manipulation by a genetic algorithm (GA) for the order expression[1]. However, if crossover and mutation are done using the order expression, a good gene sequence in the previous generation may not leave the prototype.

In our previous research, we proved that crossover and mutation do not always produce excellent individuals. For example, in flight scheduling in which the gene length exceeds 100, the method does not converge on the optimum solution[2] because chromosomes to be adapted are damaged by the crossover and mutation operations. Therefore, genetic manipulation does not always maintain the desired characteristics of the previous generation.

Sub-tour crossover, which has already been proposed[3], may keep good gene sequences from the previous generation in the case of the crossover. We have proposed a new swap-type mutation and conducted experiments regarding the lowest switching cost for an existing problem in a synthetic resin factory.

This paper explains the application of a new genetic manipulation called a swap-type mutation to a Job Shop Scheduling (JSS) problem

2. Relevant research

Research on JSS has been going on since the 1960's. Recently, the simple priority rule method, which is a combination of the AHM method and priority rule, simulated annealing, GA, and other methods have been studied. GA has been reported to be the most promising method[4]. Much research has also been done on the utilization of GA in JSS [5]. Through such research, the property to be protected in the operation of GA has been clarified, and it has come from a feature of JSS[6]. Examples are "The operator produces genotypes such that highly fit building blocks (strings of adjacent genes) can be transferred from parents to a new child;" "The relative gene positions are important;" and 'The operator must produce legal children."

This paper treats scheduling problems in which every product is produced only once within a certain period. For a chromosome in which the mutation is done by a genotype, two identical genes are often generated. In these problems, a lethal gene is produced. According to our research, if crossover and mutation are manipulated using the order expression, the good gene sequence in the previous generation may not leave a prototype[7]. When the gene length is long, this phenomenon is often observed.

Thus, a mutation should be done in the form of a genotype. Furthermore, an operation such as the following will prevent the creation of a lethal gene.

For example, as shown in the study described above, individuals with a chromosome length of 178 did not show any sign of convergence. Even when a good genetic sequence appeared during the process of generation alternation, the previous genetic character of individuals was lost during the next crossover and mutation due to the excessive chromosome length.

There have been many studies on the genetic operations that allow the preservation of genetic character. In addition to the above-mentioned genetic operation (reference 1), there is a crossover method called "distributed GA" by which the population is divided into multiple subpopulations to be crossed over.[8]

However, very few of the attempts that have been made on mutations allow the preservation of the genetic character. The only known method is to exchange adjacent genes.[9] Although this method allows most of the previous generation's character to be preserved, a simple exchange between adjacent loci leaves few possibilities for the drastic mutation of individuals to take place.

3. A swap-type mutation

This study suggests the following operation so that the GA can be applied to the above-mentioned job-shop scheduling (JSS) to induce mutation without changing the genotype while avoiding the generation of lethal genes.

When the number *i* gene (g_i) of an individual, which has a chromosome length of *L*, mutates into a gene identified as $g_{j,}$, which is identical to the number *j* gene, the two g_js in an individual will lead to a lethal gene. However, if the number *j* gene is forcibly mutated into a gene identified as g_i, the alignment of the genetic character will remain in complete sequence except for number *i* and *j* genes.

Let us consider that the length of the gene is 10 and there is a chromosome that has the following genotype: A C E G I B D F H J. It is assumed that the second locus of the chromosome changes from C to H. This is A H D F I B C E G J written in the genotype. The characteristic C E G of the previous generation remains.

Meanwhile, when direct mutation is done as a genotype, the chromosome becomes A H E G I B D F H J after the mutation, and it becomes a lethal gene. Then the ninth locus H changes to C. This is the condition of the second locus before the mutation. Next, the chromosome becomes A H E G I B D F C J. Therefore, not only does it become capable of surviving, but also it preserves E G I B D F as it was within the gene list before the mutation.

A C E G I B D F H J ⇒ A H E G I B D F H J ⇒ A H E G I B D F C J

↑ Mutation — Lethal gene — Forced live gene ↑

Figure 1: Mechanism of a swap-type mutation

The merits of this method are that it not only preserves the genetic character before the mutation but also can mutate, a good property compared with the non-crossed sub-tour crossover when the subset does not agree.

4. Information obtained from the paper presented at JCKBSE2000

The above-mentioned proposal and the information obtained at the JCKBSE2000 are utilized in this paper. The content is summarized as follows:

4.1 The object to which the swap-type mutation applies

Worse results are obtained when the swap-type mutation is applied to all individuals than when the mutation is applied using the order expression because leaving the individual genotype quality with low fitness prevents the generation of good genes. Therefore, in order to retain the necessary genotype quality, the swap-type mutation should be applied only to individuals with good fitness. In practice, in order to aim for the best theoretical fitness, the swap-type mutation is applied only to chromosomes which have results within 5% to 10% from the target value.

4.2 Comparison of the fitness and of the number of generations

Final satisfactory results may be obtained from either our swap-type mutation or mutation by the order expression. Thus, a considerable difference can be seen in the number of generations until they reach the target value. In our present research, the optimum solution was obtained with both methods. Therefore, the significance was examined by comparing the number of generations until the optimum solution was reached.

5. The JSS problem in this study

When the plan is simple and the gene is long, the difference is seen more clearly. We tried a schedule in which overall work time was minimized for work on N pieces composed of two processing procedures by two machines by the sample processing procedure (N jobs, 2 machines, 2 procedures, J-n-2-2).

6. Experiments

The job was done three or four times, as shown in Table 1. We show the experiment with gene length 18. The number of individuals in a generation was from 10 to 100. Crossover was not carried out in this study.

Table 1. Original Problem of J-6-2-2

Production no.	1	2	3	4	5	6	Total
Necessary time for Machine #1	20	8	24	7	15	13	87
Necessary time for Machine #2	15	0	18	13	20	14	80

The probability of the mutation was made to be 1/9 on a gene locus. That is, the opportunity for mutation was an average of two times for each individual, and the minute evolution without crossover was hastened. By changing the initial value of the random number, the results of 100 times were compared. Three experiments were done: mutation by the order expression, swap-type mutation, and combined use.

For the experiment on combined use, three times of a time unit of 94, which is the solution to J-6-2-2, was made the turning point of the fitness. Taking a fitness of approximately 280 as the turning point, good results were obtained. Partial results of the experiment are shown in Table 2. This was the first of 4 experiments.

Table 2. Partial experimental results (Gene length = 18, K: population, B: control point)

Initial	K=10				K=100			
Random No.	B=0	B=275	B=280	B=1000	B=0	B=280	B=290	B=1000
1	85	23	26	58	4	1	3	1
2	3	14	28	65	1	2	4	3
3	15	42	4	50	7	8	45	34
4	14	5	33	72	11	4	4	19

The experiment was started at the initial value of an equal random number, and the population of the zero generation was equalized. The final solutions were similar in both our method and the method using the order expression. Thus, to show the usefulness of our method, we used the victory or defeat of numbers of the achievement generations.

7. Results and Discussion

7.1 Test of statistical hypothesis

Remarkable results were found in the experiment with 10 populations and the J-18-2-2 of one generation (Table 3), which means that the swap-type mutation worked effectively. A fitness of 270 or 275 was considered the control point which leaves the characteristics. We inspected the difference in the average number of generations of 100 cases. The standard deviation was 18.7.

Table 3. Comparison of each method of J-18-2-2 (10 individuals per generation)

Methods	Order expression	Selective application of the swap-type mutation under fitness 270	Selective application of the swap-type mutation under fitness 275	(For reference) Swap-type mutation with no condition
Average number of generations	29.5	20.8	19.9	1831.6
Standard deviation	25.6	18.7	14.7	5254
Victories & defeats for the order expression	-----	59 wins, 30 losses, 11draws	56 wins, 39 losses, 5 draws	17 wins, 81 losses, 2 draws

Because the process of generation in the initial stage changes greatly, the numbers of achievement generations of identical individuals were compared, resulting in 59 wins, 30 losses, and 11 draws. If it is assumed that the percentage of victories is 50%, the hypothesis is rejected at 0.1% in N $(44.5, 4.72^2)$. When we assume that both(order expression and selective application) do not have the difference, the hypothesis is rejected at 3% in $z=8.7/\mathrm{sqrt}(6.55+3.49)=2.75$, which follows the standard normal distribution.

Almost equal results on the control points of 275 were obtained.

7.2 Cases in Which This Genetic Operation Can Be Useful

Such a genetic operation yielded a positive effect in some cases and a negative one in others. The following reason is considered.

In problem J-8-2-2, as shown in Table 1, it is obvious that *product 2*, which can be produced without using *machine 2*, should be produced twice at the end of the cycle in order to yield an optimum solution. We checked how many individuals that produced product 2 twice at the end of the cycle were included among all the generations as a subset (Table 4).

The result indicated that the better the fitness, the higher the probability that individuals included a partial optimum solution. Individuals expected to have high probability of including a partial optimum solution should have their characters preserved, while all others should not have their characters preserved. The results of this study indicated that a character should be preserved if there is approximately a 10% probability of a partial optimum solution being included.

In other words, a swap-type mutation can even be applied to a new problem with an unknown optimum solution, in which case the presence of the partial optimum solution can be estimated from the individual's fitness.

Table4: Content by percentage of partial optimum solution in J-18-2-2

Case Content by percentage	Fitness under 265	Fitness under 270	Fitness under 275	Fitness over 275
Population 100 Generation 10000	100%	29.8%	9.9%	1.4%
Population 10000 Generation 100	100%	22.1%	7.7%	0.9%

8. Conclusion

As described in the previous chapter, our method is effective in the case that the good characteristic is left only in individuals which obtained a result of 110% or 105% for the goal fitness (theoretical value).

In our experiments, the decision about which mutation to choose was decided only by the fitness. However, for an individual which has a gene list which should be partially left, we must contrive to preserve the character even if the fitness is bad. It is considered that increasingly effective genetic manipulation may be possible. If we consider such a contrivance, loss may be avoided in a labyrinth. Good results will be achieved by using two mutations properly and by searching for such an object in the future. The utility of this swap-type mutation can be pursued further.

References

[1] M. Higuchi and M. Nagata: "An application of the genetic algorithm to scheduling problems using the concept of differential penalty." Proceedings of the Second Joint Conference on Knowledge-Based Software Engineering, 1996, pp. 202-205.

[2] M. Higuchi and M. Nagata: "An application of the genetic algorithm to flight scheduling problems." The Institute of electronics, information, and communication engineers, technical report of IEICE, AI95-58, KBSE95-46, 1996, pp. 9-14.

[3] M. Yamamura, T. Ono, and S. Kobayashi: "Character-Preserving Genetic Algorithms for Traveling Salesman Problem." Journal of Japanese Society for Artificial Intelligence, Vol. 17, No. 6, 1992, pp. 117-127 (in Japanese).

[4] J. Kaeschel, T. Teich, G. Goebernik, and B. Meier: Algorithms for the Job Shop Scheduling Problem – A comparison of different methods, http://www/erudit.de/erudit/events/esit99/12553_P.pdf/.

[5] E. Falkenauer and S. Bouffouix: "A genetic algorithm for Job Shop." Proceedings of the 1991 IEEE International Conference on Robotics and Automation, 1991, pp. 824-829

[6] L. Chambers (Ed.): "Practical Handbook of Genetic Algorithms: Applications." Vol. 1, CRC Press, 1995.

[7] M. Kuroda, T. Tanabe, the others. "Production Management." Asakura Shoten, 1989 (in Japanese).

[8] Y. Hanada: "Distributed Genetic Algorithm for Job-shop Scheduling Problems" 42nd Monthly Lecture Meeting, Miki Lab Doshisha Univ. 2001

[9] Yagiura: A dynamic programming method for single machine scheduling, European J. Operational Research, vol.76,pp72.

Knowledge-based Software Engineering
T. Welzer et al. (Eds.)
IOS Press, 2002

A Web-Based VOD Clipping Tool for Efficient Private Review

Nobuhiko Miyahara, Haruhiko Kaiya and Kenji Kaijiri
Faculty of Engineering, Shinshu University, JAPAN.
kaiya@cs.shinshu-u.ac.jp

Abstract. In this paper, we present a web-based tool for learners, to review the parts of the lecture contents that the learners have already attended. Each learner can efficiently review what they want to learn again independent of the scenario in each lecture. We assume that the contents of the lectures are stored in the internet based video streaming systems. The objects are automatically arranged on a screen of this tool, so that each object gets closer to its similar objects.

1 Introduction

Internet contents with video streaming data are increasing, and many kinds of contents become available freely for the internet people. As a matter of course, these kinds of contents are used for the distance learning and/or private study for students and pupils. We simply call these kinds of contents as *streaming contents*.

Now we reconsider the disadvantages of streaming contents in teaching or learning contexts. Even a lecture performed in a real class room is mostly tedium, at least in Japan. The problems are as follows; 1) each student should watch the lecture segments which they have already understood, 2) each student can not review a part of a lecture because lectures will progress independent of each student, 3) each student can not easily refer several parts of a lecture or the other lectures, which are related to a part of the lecture.

Although these problems can be overcomed by streaming technologies, students must directly use primitive functions such as indexing and hyper linking. An integrated tool enables the learners to overcome such problems efficiently. A web-based VOD clipping tool presented in this paper is one of such integrated tools. Our tool gives the following functions for the students; 1)each student can easily clip a part of a lecture, and they can append a label and an annotation to the part, 2)each student can deploy the clipping parts spatially on the screen, 3)each student can view and hear the parts of lectures independent of the lecture scenario.

The rest of this paper is organized as follows. In the next section, we review current technologies for the streaming contents. In section 3, we summarize the requirements of our tool. The design and implementation of our tool are presented in section 4. Section 5 shows the usage of our tool. Finally, we summarize the contribution of our tool and discuss the future works in section 6.

2 Video and audio streaming over the internet for education

Streaming is an on-demand media data transmission technology. Typical streaming systems are Windows media technology and Real Systems. Many systems have been implemented which record real lectures and store them as collaborated streaming data, and several lecture libraries[1, 2] have been realized. The provided functions are primitive, so there are the following problems for educational use: 1)the synchronization must be done manually, 2)the collaboration unit is only WWW pages, 3)VODs have no index.

There are some researches and products about the above problems. WLAP project[1] developed a system for producing, editing, serving Web lectures, but editing functions are provided only for lecturers. We have also developed the VOD authoring system which makes the collaborated VOD semi-automatically using Windows media technology. There also exist some researches about VOD indexing[3, 4]. The objectives of these researches are to make general video databases, and their researches' focus is on automatic indexing and meta data definition. The aim of our research is to make it possible for each student that they make their personal notebook for review. Using our tool, it becomes possible for each student to make personal a lecture video library.

3 Personalized Contexts for Learning

As mentioned in the first section of this paper, we want to let learners free from fixed and uniform scenario for learning such as ordinary lectures, by using the video streaming technology. We first define a minimum unit for learning. We call such kind of unit as a *video object*. A video object should satisfy the following conditions; 1)a video object should have a part of a streaming content. We call such a part as *a video object content*. 2)a learner can understand a video object content without other video objects. 3)a learner can easily find a video object when he wants to view a specific topic. 4)a learner can easily view the neighborhood of a video object content. 5)a learner can decide the significance of a video object content. 6)a learner can categorize his video objects.

Based on these conditions, we have designed a video object with the following attributes; 1)label: The name of this object, 2)URL of streaming, 3)start and end point of this object among the streaming data, 4)annotation, 5)significance: this value is represented as a size of icon for this objects in the current prototype. 6)category: this attribute is represented as a color of icon for this objects in the current prototype.

The target of our tool is lecture videos. Lectures may be classified into some categories. The video object belonging to each category must be collected. We call such a collection of video objects as a *workspace*. Users can define several workspaces and classify each video object into the corresponding workspace. In figure 1, we show an example of the relationships among the streaming contents, video objects, and workspaces. In a workspace, video objects should be deployed along the understanding of a learner. Therefore, a distance between two objects is decided by the degree of these two objects' similarity, which is computed using the understandings of a learner.

4 Design and Implementation

Our tool mainly provides the following two functions to users.

- *Video indexing function*: Users pick up their focused video objects, index, and comment.
- *Indexed Video deploying and browsing function*: Users browse the collected video objects, which are deployed graphically on the screen.

We realized this system based on C/S architecture using IIS and ActiveX control so that users can index and browse lecture videos at any place/time.

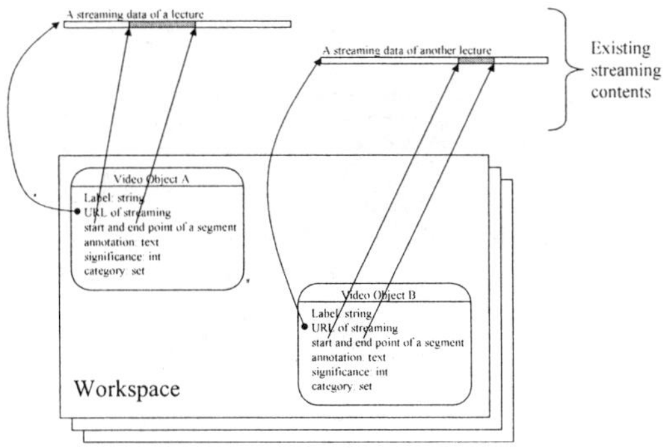

Figure 1: Streaming data, Video Objects and Workspace

Our tool has no automatic indexing function, and users must manually select their focused video object, because indexing should be done depending on each users level of understandings and interesting. Our video library is personal use and only the indexing data is stored personally. VOD is widely used for lectures, so it is very useful that VOD data on any site can be used as library. Our primary design decision is the presentation style of indexed video object. Main functionality of this component is as follows: 1)Visualization of significance and category, 2)Filtering, 3)Automatic deployment of video objects.

5 Usage of our tool

The following is the typical scenario to construct a personal lecture video library:

1. Users select a lecture from the menu.
2. Users scan the video stream, and select the starting and stopping point.
3. Users give the title for this video object.
4. Users give some comments for this video object.

After indexing, video objects are stored in the corresponding workspace. In order to browse video objects, users at first select the workspace, then the set of video objects will be displayed as shown in figure 2. Each video object is displayed as a rectangle with text string which has some color and size, and each video object is connected using similarity link. These color and size can be changed. If the display is so crowded, some filtering may be activated.

6 Example

Here we show a simple example of personal review. Suppose a student has attended two different lectures, one is C programming language and the other is Java programming language. From the lecture of C, the student clips three video objects entitled "C_Pointer", "Primitive_type" and "Array_type", and he annotates each object. From the lecture of Java,

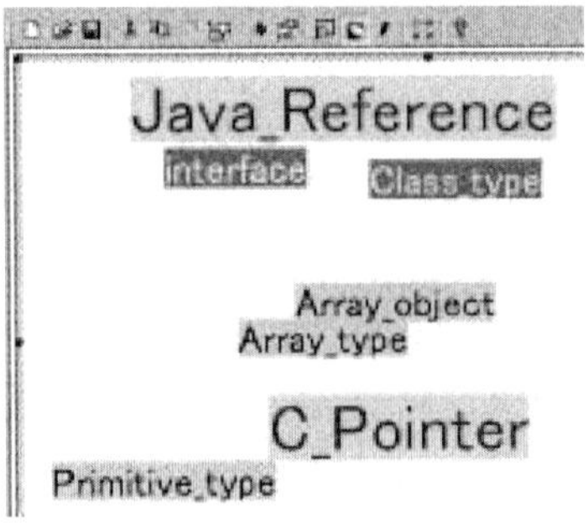

Figure 2: Deployment of Video Objects

he also clips four video objects entitled "Java_Reference", "interface", "Class_type" and "Array_object", and he also annotates each object. Then, our tool automatically deploys these video objects on a window as shown in figure 2.

7 Conclusions and Future works

In this paper, we present a web-based VOD clipping tool for learners to privately review the streaming contents. This tool enables learners to learn lectures freely independent of the predetermined scenario, and to combine related lectures as a private lecture library.

Currently, the deployment of video objects in our tool is decided using only the annotations of each video objects. We want to refine the deployment of video objects for various kinds of learners. Video objects and workspaces of a learner may be shared by the other learners if the learner approves. We should extend the design of video objects for sharing, because video objects are currently intended to be used personally. For better mining of the off-the-shelf video objects and workspaces, additional attributes, for example the reasons why the objects and/or workspaces are collected, are needed in our tool.

References

[1] `http://www..wlap.org/`. WLAP Web Lecture Archive Project.

[2] `http://audio.monash.edu.au/mlo/index.html`. Monash Lectures Online.

[3] S. L. Chan. et. al. Efficient methodology for automatic video-content indexing and retrieval of lecturers for cai systems. In *Edmedia'96*, 1996.

[4] Jane Hunter and etl. A Comparison of Schemas for Video Metadata Representation. In *8th WWW*, 1999.

[5] M. Carrer and etl. An Annotation Engine for Supporting Video Database Population. In *Multimedia Tools and applications 5*, 1997.

[6] David Bargeron and etl. Annotations for Streaming Video on the Web: System Design and Usage Studies. In *8th WWW conf*, 1999.

[7] G. Ahanger and etl. Easy Ed: An Integration of Technologies for Multimedia education. In *WebNet'97*, 1997.

[8] Rune Hjelsvold and etl. Web-based Personalization and Management of Interactive Video. In *10th WWW*, 2001.

Knowledge-based Software Engineering
T. Welzer et al. (Eds.)
IOS Press, 2002

A Text Mining System DIREC: Discovering Relationships between Keywords by Filtering, Extracting and Clustering

MINE, Tsunenori LU, Shimiao AMAMIYA, Makoto
Faculty of Information Science and Electrical Engineering,
Kyushu University
6-1 Kasuga-koen, Kasuga, Fukuoka, Japan, 816-8580
{mine, shimiao, amamiya}@al.is.kyushu-u.ac.jp

Abstract. This paper presents a text mining system DIREC that obtains the relationships between keywords. After gathering Web pages related to a query with search engines and filtering out the pages irrelevant to the query, DIREC extracts pre-specified keywords from the pages left after filtering, and clusters them. Each cluster includes keywords related to each other. The clustered keywords are shown through an Explorer-like graphical user interface. We discuss the experimental results applying the DIREC system to the Research and Education Report Database of the Faculty at Kyushu University.

1 Introduction

The rapid spread of the Internet has brought about a big revolution in information technologies and information environments. The development of the World Wide Web (WWW) especially makes available a lot of knowledge and useful means for accessing electronic information entities. In these circumstances, Web mining or text mining to discover new knowledge from the vast number of Web pages has become more and more attractive. Although a lot of work for obtaining topics or keywords from documents have been performed, there are only few work for finding the inter-relationships between the extracted topics or keywords.

This paper presents a text mining system DIREC(DIscovering Relationships between keywords by filtering, Extracting and Clustering). The DIREC system, first, gathers Web pages related to a query with search engines and filters out the pages irrelevant to the query with support vector machines(SVMs)[5, 1]. Next, it extracts the keywords specified by a user and clusters them. Each cluster embodies the relationships between keywords and between a keyword and other named entities such as persons. It shows the clustered keywords through an Explorer-like graphical user interface. In order to evaluate the performance of the DIREC system, we applied it to the two sets: call for paper(CFP) files of international conferences[3] and the Research and Education Report Database of the Faculty at Kyushu University[4]. The former set is used for evaluating DIREC's following three functions : filtering, extracting and clustering. The later is for evaluating the robustness of the clustering function with a lot of noisy keywords left after morphological analysis and for trying other document set than CFP files. The results confirmed that the DIREC system worked well for obtaining the relationships between topics of conferences, and for discovering the relationships between research keywords.

In what follows, section 2 describes an overview of the DIREC system and section 3 discusses DIREC's clustering performance only for the research keywords due to the limitation of space.

2 The DIREC System

The DIREC system consists of 5 modules: the collecting file module, the filtering file module, the extracting information entity module, the clustering information entity module and the user interface module. This section describes only the clustering information entity module to explain the experimental results shown in section 3. For the other functions, please see [3].

2.1 Clustering Keywords

The clustering procedure consists of the following 3 steps:

1. Calculating the similarity between every pair of keywords.
2. Creating base clusters based on the results of the similarity calculation in the 1st step. (The base cluster will be defined at the next section.)
3. Combining base clusters whose similarity value is over the pre-determined threshold.

2.2 Calculating the Similarity between Keywords

The similarity between keywords is calculated by the proportion of their inclusion in a set of files where each of the keywords appears.

Let T_m be the set of files where keyword m appears, and $|T_m|$ be the number of files included in T_m. $|T_m \cap T_n|$ represents the number of files T_m and T_n have in common.

We set the similarity between two keywords to 1 if one of the following conditions is satisfied and 0 otherwise.

$$|T_m \cap T_n|/|T_m| > TH \quad (1)$$

$$|T_m \cap T_n|/|T_n| > TH \quad (2)$$

The values of TH is decided empirically. Calculating the similarity between every pair of keywords, we make a cluster that includes a keyword and its related keywords, each of whose similarity with the keyword is 1. We call such cluster a **base cluster**.

This method is basically the same as Zamir and Etzioni's method for calculating the similarity between base clusters[6].

3 Discussion of Clustering Results to the Faculty Members' Research Keywords

Research keywords of the faculty were extracted from the Research and Education Report Database of the Faculty at Kyushu University(http://www.ofc.kyushu-u.ac.jp/kyokandb/)[4]. We extracted keywords directly from this database without filtering and extraction phrase. Instead of that, we applied Japanese morphological analyzer 'Chasen'[2] to find keywords matched partially with one another because most of them consist of Japanese compound nouns that had no space delimiter. For example, if the following three keywords: MARUCHI / EJENT (Multi Agent), MARUCHI / EJENT / SHISUTEMU (Multi Agent System), MOBAIRU / EJENT (Mobile Agent) occurred, they should be included in the same cluster because of the common word EJENT(Agent).

After applying morphological analysis to 10972 original research keyword types that came from 1937 faculty members, we obtained 17366 keyword types including original ones. Among them, we empirically selected only the keywords whose number of occurrences in the faculty members' research reports was more than 1 and less than 16 because most of the keywords frequently appeared in the reports were general words. With these keywords, we evaluated both the change of the number of isolated keywords that did not belong to any base clusters and that of the number of clusters created according to the change of the threashold TH_1 and TH_2. Where TH_1 and TH_2 are the threashold value for the proportion of a set of files where each of keywords appears and that of keywords that were shared among base clusters, respectively. From the evaluations, we aimed to confirm whether or not TH in section 2.2, which is here TH_1 , depended on the target documents and to investigate the change of the number of clusters according to TH_2.

Considering the TH_1 through 0.4 to 0.7, the number of clusters of both 0.5 and 0.6 was almost the same, and when TH_1 was 0.7, the number of isolated keywords became more 200 than the case that TH_1 was 0.6. From these results, TH_1 should be more than and equal to 0.5. This result was the same as the clustering topics of international conferences[3]. On the contrary, determining the optimum value of TH_2 seemed to be more difficult. It might be done by making use of the contents of the clusters. Although we only checked cluster 'Artificial Intelligence'[1], the keywords belonging to the cluster almost seemed to match the name of the cluster. Table 1 shows an example of base clusters with keyword **agent**.

4 Conclusion and Future Work

This paper discussed the DIREC system that obtained the relationships between information entities by filtering files, extracting and clustering keywords. We performed experiments with the Research and Education Report Database of the Faculty at Kyushu University. The main objectives of the experiments were to investigate the change of the number of isolated topics that did not belong to any base cluster according to the threshold for the similarity between keywords, and the change of the number of clusters according to the proportion of the common keywords among base clusters. The experimental results showed that the threshold value to the similarity between keywords was almost the same as the case of CFP files[3]. On the contrary, the appropriate threshold for combining base clusters should be investigated furthermore. We are doing further experiments with huge data sets and also investigating how to calculate the similarity between keywords.

[1]We employed the keyword occurring most frequently in a cluster as the name of the cluster

Table 1: An Example of Base Clusters including Keyword 'Agent' when $TH_1 = 6$

Keword	Related Keywords	Faculty Members
Agent	Intelligence, Intelligent, Multi, Parallel Distributed, Discovery Science, Information Retrieval, Autonomous Distributed, Flow, Architecture, Massively Parallel, Knowledge Acquisition, Dialogue System, Control System, Education System, Reinforcement Learning, Inductive Reasoning, Machine Discovery, Machine Learning, Self-teaching Support, Soft Computing	1779, 1374, 377, 276
Machine Learning	Algorithm, Logic, Intelligence, Probability, Graph, Mining, Data Mining, Discovery, Complexity, Reasoning, Complexity Theory, Approximated, Genome Information, **Agent**, Discovery Science, Parallel Algorithm, Distributed Algorithm, Approximated Algorithm, Inductive Reasoning, Machine Discovery, Graph Algorithm	1413, 1374
Autonomous Distributed	Algorithm, Understanding, Intelligence, Intelligent, Robot, Graph, Vision, Distributed, Multi, Real Time, Discription, **Agent**, Parallel Distributed, Flow, Architecture, Parallel Algorithm, Distributed Algorithm, Massively Parallel, Dialogue System, Computational Geometry, Graph Algorithm, Algorithm Engineering	878, 277, 276

In the future, we will implement the DIREC system as a multi-agent system[7].

Acknowledgments

This research was partly supported by a Grant-in-Aid for Scientific Research, Encouragement of Young Scientists(A), No. 13780291 from the Japan Society for the Promotion of Science, and by a Grant for a R&D activities in the information and communications area from the Telecommunication Advancement Organization of Japan.

References

[1] Thorsten Joachims. Svm light: http://svmlight.joachims.org.

[2] Yuji Matsumoto, Akira Kitauchi, Tatsuo Yamashita, Yoshitaka Hirano, Hiroshi Matsuda, Kazuma Takaoka, and Masayuki Asahara. Morphological analysis system chasen version 2.2.8 manual. Technical report, Nara Institute of Science and Technology, 2001.

[3] Tsunenori Mine, Shimiao Lu, and Makoto Amamiya. Discovering relationship between topics of conferences by filtering, extracting and clustering. In *the 3rd International Workshop on Natural Language and Information Systems(NLIS2002)*, to appear, 2002.

[4] Yusuke Nonaka, Sozo Inoue, Katsuhiko Hatano, Tsutomu Harada, Yoshinari Nomura, Mizuho Iwaihara, Tsunenori Mine, and Kazuo Ushijima. Development and operation of a document database for university research and education activities. *Systems and Computers in Japan*, to appear, 2002.

[5] Vladimir N. Vapnik. *Statistical Learning Theory*. JOHN WILEY & SONS, INC., 1998.

[6] Oren Zamir and Oren Etzioni. Web document clustering : A feasiblity demonstration. In *Proceedings of the 21th Intl. ACM SIGIR Conference*, pages 46–54, 1998.

[7] Guoqiang Zhong, Satoshi Amamiya, Kenichi Takahashi, Tsunenori Mine, and Makoto Amamiya. The design and application of kodama system. *IEICE Transactions on Information and Systems*, E85-D(4):637–646, 4 2002.

Knowledge-based Software Engineering
T. Welzer et al. (Eds.)
IOS Press, 2002

Design Creation Support Database System in a Local Industry

Takehiko TANAKA Hiroko TABE Masaru NAKAGAWA
Faculty of Systems Engineering, Wakayama University
930 Sakaedani, Wakayama 640-8510, Japan

Abstract. A database system is described which is available for the upper process of the product design in Japanese lacquer wares and household utensils. The database manages design products, each of which is composed of a 3-D shape and 2-D textures on the shape. Using the database service and the collaboration service that we have been developing, we examine the performance through several experiments and interviews. The results imply that the database service has adequate performance in retrieving data, whereas the collaboration service cannot find improvement in the design quality. The system may be useful not for working out the details of the design, but for making a new design especially by redesign.

1 Introduction

Introducing computer systems into the upper process of the product design in a local industry will bring the benefits such as shortening the design period and accumulating design experience by electronic files. That is why we have been investigating and developing a design-supporting computer system for the local industry of Wakayama, Japan, which produces lacquer wares and household utensils. Our system consists of the *database service* and the *collaboration service*. The database service helps the user not only register the electronic material data and the virtual design products but also retrieve the registered ones. The collaboration service[1] provides the environment where the users in the remote places cooperate on the design of 3-D graphic.

The first half of this paper briefly states the environment and two services of our database system. The last half reports the performance of the developed system from the following viewpoints; (1) the usefulness of the database service, (2) the usefulness of the collaboration service, and (3) the design tests under the realistic situations.

2 Environment

The users of our system are partitioned into *planners*, *designers* and *manufacturers*. The target of our system is supporting the upper process of the product design, where the core work is making a *virtual design product*. Therefore we have been developing our system mainly for designers. Planners and manufacturers usually attend the design collaboration with the collaboration service. A planner plans or reviews a product from the viewpoint of marketability, while a manufacturer criticize a design based on the manufacturing cost.

We have implemented the database service and the collaboration service so that they can behave as Web applications. The client computers and the server computer communicates with each other over Hypertext Transfer Protocol (HTTP).

- A *prototype* is a material object made by rapid-prototyping, based on a virtual design product.
- A *virtual design product* consists of one or more design part.
- A *design part* consists of one or more material.
- A *material* is either one of a (3-D) shape, a texture, or a color.
- Each one of virtual design products, design parts and materials has a Boolean value for publication.

List 1: Data Modeling

3 Data Modeling and Database Service

Our policy of data modeling is listed in List 1. If the system aimed to support the manufacturers, then the design parts would be defined in a recursive way for reuse (for example, see [2]). As for the design parts of the virtual design product, we adopt the concise, non-recursive data modeling, which leads to the smooth, intuitive design. Under the above data model, we constitute several tables in the database management system (DBMS).

The database service provides three ways of retrieving the registered contents; *by keyword*, *by figure* and *by key image*. For realizing the queries by keyword and by figure, when a user attempts to register any data, he or she has to annotate it by specifying keywords and/or choosing a figure from the figure table. VIR DataBlade under the DBMS named Informix Dynamic Server is used for the retrieval by key image.

4 Collaboration Service

Although the main users of the database service is designers, those of the collaboration service is planners, designers and manufacturers. By using the collaboration service the users can distribute the finished or unfinished virtual design products and communicate with each other. This service is effective especially for the repetition of the design modification. Every user has the separate viewpoint of the virtual design product, since our collaboration service provides the synchronization of the file, but not that of the viewpoint. According to the classification in [3], our system is concerned with a real time, different place CSCW (Computer Supported Cooperative Work).

The central functions of the service are uploading and downloading, which we have implemented. We have developed the service[1] which uses a go-it-alone protocol. Now we improve the service so that it may utilize HTTP for uploading and downloading. Meanwhile, existing softwares are borrowed for the mutual communication such as white board, chat (communication with characters) and teleconference.

5 Experiments for Evaluation

5.1 On Database Service

The database server contains about 1,000 records of virtual design products and about 5,000 records of materials. We attempt to test our database service for its usefulness in the sense that the user can obtain some desirable content. The number of the users for the test is 90. We prepare 12 cases and show the corresponding sentences to each user, who uses the database service to find the record matching the case by using any supplied retrieval method. The following data are collected every user and every case; whether or not the user achieves

Table 1: Experiment Results of Database Service

Viewpoint	Result
Achievement	96% are achievable.
Number of operation	100% take not more than 3 times.
Time to finish	43% within 90 seconds.
Subjective evaluation	49% users answer "satisfied."

Table 2: Experiment Results of Collaboration Service

	Lacquer ware	Household utensils	Total
Truly same	0	0	0
Nearly same	4	1	5
Different	0	1	1
Very different	2	4	6
Truly different	1	1	2
Total	7	7	14

the data, the number of retrieval operation, and the time of retrieval. Moreover, subjective evaluations by the questionnaire of the service satisfaction are piled up.

Table 1 shows the results of the test. These results say that the database service is largely effective with regards to the operation.

5.2 On Collaboration Service

We verify whether or not our collaboration service contributes to high-quality design. The number of the users for the test is 32, and they are partitioned into 14 design groups. Each user behaves as a planner, a designer or a manufacturer. Each design group makes a virtual design product, referring to an actual product. After the collaboration is finished, the prototype is made from the virtual design product. The resemblance is evaluated by the collaborators' comparing the prototype with the actual product from the viewpoint of shape and size.

Table 2 shows the results of the test. These results imply that it is difficult to make the completely same object, and that lacquer wares are easier to replicate than household utensils. This difference between lacquer wares and household utensils can be explained by the difference of the variation. As for lacquer wares, there exist fewer sorts of shape because of its tradition. On the other hand, lots of household utensils with unique, practical shapes are proposed every year.

5.3 Design Tests under Realistic Situations

Making the most of the database service and the collaboration service, the users actually make some virtual design products. On three ways of design process, that is a designer-driven design, a planner-driven design, and a redesign, each design group create a virtual design product. The users answer the questions after finishing their collaboration.

The results are shown in Table 3. The columns labeled Planner, Designer and Manufacturer are answered by the planner, the designer and the manufacturer, respectively, while those labeled Operation and Quality are answered by all the users and decided by a majority. These results imply that, for each sort of design process, the most influential person is satisfied. In this sense the collaboration is successful. In any case, however, the operation is good

Table 3: Experiment Results of Realistic Design

	Planner	Designer	Manufacturer	Operation	Quality
designer-driven	yes	no	yes	yes	no
planner-driven	no	yes	no	yes	no
redesign	yes	yes	no	yes	no

Planner: Is this system workable for the planner?
Designer: Is this system workable for the designer?
Manufacturer: Is this system workable for the manufacture?
Operation: Is the operation good?
Quality: Are you satisfied with the quality of the finished virtual design product?

but the quality is discontent.

6 Discussion

Apart from the experiments described in the previous section, we have made several experiments and had interviews with the users[4]. The result of the interviews augments the usefulness and unusefulness of our system.

The experiments report that the database service has adequate performance in retrieving the data, which will contribute to the support for the designers. On the other hand, we have made sure that the collaboration service really supplies an environment for the on-line collaboration, but that the resulting products do not possess as high quality as the collaborators satisfy themselves. Despite of the negative results of our collaboration service, we do not immediately conclude that the on-line collaboration is useless in the design of the local industry. For example, the difficulty in the replication shown in Section 5.2 does not necessarily mean the defect; the collaboration service may help producing new designs, say redesigning.

It is expected that the closer communication in the collaboration produces the better design. Meanwhile, it is difficult in general to determine when the collaboration should be finished. To make these issues clear, we are planning to perform an experiment of the design collaboration with a fixed time limit to draw a comparison with regard to the quality between on-line and off-line collaborations.

References

[1] Tanaka, T., Fukimbara, K., Kawasaki, J., Matsumoto, S., Matsushita, M. and Nakagawa M.: "Support System for Distributed Collaborative 3-D Graphics Design," Proc. 4th Joint Conference on Knowledge-Based Software Engineering, Brno, Czech Republic, pp.31–34, September 2000.

[2] Tatsiopoulos, I. P.: "Object-Oriented Design of Manufacturing Database Helps Simplify Production Management in Small Firms," Lecture Notes in Computer Science, vol.856, pp.204–213, September 1994.

[3] Pfeifer, J., Koo, K. and Yin, P: "Electronic Meetings - CSCW & GDSS," `http://ksi.cpsc.ucalgary.ca/courses/547-95/yin/groupware.html`

[4] Tabe, H.: "Study on the Design Creation Support System in a Specific Local Industry," master's thesis of the Graduate Course, Faculty of Systems Engineering, Wakayama University, February 2002 (in Japanese).

Knowledge-based Software Engineering
T. Welzer et al. (Eds.)
IOS Press, 2002

Dynamic Evaluation of both Students' and Questions' Levels for Generating Appropriate Exercises to Students Automatically

Akira SUGANUMA, Tsunenori MINE, and Takayoshi SHOUDAI
Graduate School of Information Science and Electrical Engineering
Kyushu University, Kasuga 816-8580, Japan
{suga@is, mine@is, shoudai@i}.kyushu-u.ac.jp

Abstract. This paper discusses AEGIS(Automatic Exercise Generator based on the Intelligence of Students) that generates exercises of various difficulty levels according to each student's achievement level, marks his/her answers and returns the marked results to him/her. Guessing the achievement level of each student from his/her trial history, AEGIS selects the most suitable exercise for him/her according to his/her achievement level. It is necessary for AEGIS to evaluate dynamically not only the level but also the difficulty level of the exercises in order that it gives each student a suitable exercise. In this paper, we describe the method to re-estimate them.

1 Introduction

As the Internet has come into wide use, WWW environments provide lots of opportunities to various fields. In the educational domain, many Internet technologies enable us to hold lectures using Web contents as a teaching material and even develop new lecture methods using the technologies. Web data are, therefore, being expanded rapidly as useful materials.

We are devoting ourself to develop a Web-based self-teaching system and to build the tools for helping students understand their subjects [4, 6]. Through our experiences teaching in classes and developing such systems, we recognize the necessity of both a method evaluating students' achievement levels and generating exercises suitable for the students automatically. The well-considered exercises are useful not only to measure the achievement level of the students, but also to improve their performance. Unfortunately, it is not an easy task for any teacher to make exercises with the difficulties suited to their achievement levels. Besides, it is very important to mark their answers to the exercises and return the marked results to them for keeping their learning enthusiasm. These tasks become harder in proportion to the number of the students in a class.

In this paper, we present an automatic student's achievement level evaluator that generates exercises in three question-types from one tagged document, presents them to students and marks their answers automatically. We call the system AEGIS(Automatic Exercise Generator based on the Intelligence of Students)[5]. It is necessary for AEGIS to evaluate dynamically both student's achievement level and the difficulty level of exercise. Although many CAI systems have been proposed[1, 2, 3], our system is different from them in the points of re-usability of pre-existing electronic materials and re-estimation of both the levels.

2 Re-estimation of Achievement Level and Difficulty Level

2.1 Achievement Level of Students

It is very important for AEGIS to estimate an achievement level of each student. AEGIS measures it whenever the student answers a question because such a student level fluctuates constantly. The achievement level of student i at time t is calculated with the following formula:

$$s_{i,t} = \begin{cases} s_{i,t-1} + \dfrac{\sum_{j \in Q}(q_{j,t} - s_{i,t-1})\delta_{i,j}}{\sum_{j \in Q}\delta_{i,j}} & \text{if} \sum_{j \in Q}\delta_{i,j} \neq 0 \\ s_{i,t-1} & \text{otherwise} \end{cases}$$

where Q is a set of questions that he/she answered in the recent 30 trials and $q_{j,t}$ stands for the difficulty level of question j at the time when the achievement level $s_{i,t}$ is calculated. The value, $\delta_{i,j}$, stands for 1 if student i correctly answered question j whose difficulty level is more than his/her achievement level $s_{i,t-1}$ or he/she incorrectly answered question j whose level is less than $s_{i,t-1}$, or 0 otherwise. The achievement level of student i is initialized to 1 when he/she tries a question at first time.

It is quite natural that a student correctly answers the question whose difficulty level is less than his/her achievement level and vice versa. AEGIS, therefore, neglects these trials. AEGIS increases his/her achievement level when he/she can correctly answer the more difficult question and decreases it when he/she cannot correctly answer the easier question.

2.2 Difficulty Level of Hidden Region

The difficulty level of a question is carefully configured because AEGIS uses it to estimate the students' achievement level as described in section 2.1 and refers it to generate a suitable question for a student. Since the teachers set it up with the attribute LEVEL of DEL tag, which is one of tags we defined to embed the information to generate exercises in teaching documents. However, a question evaluated by the teachers as an easy one may not always be answered correctly by lots of students, and vice versa. AEGIS, therefore, utilizes the value of the attribute LEVEL as an initial value of the difficulty level, and re-estimates the level dynamically at regular intervals with the following formula:

$$q_{j,t} = \begin{cases} q_{j,t-1} + \dfrac{\sum_{i \in S}(s_{i,\tau} - q_{j,t-1})\xi_{i,j}}{\sum_{i \in S}\xi_{i,j}} & \text{if} \sum_{i \in S}\xi_{i,j} \neq 0 \\ q_{j,t-1} & \text{otherwise} \end{cases}$$

where S is a set of students who answered the question j between time $(t-1)$ and t, $s_{i,\tau}$ is a student's achievement level at time τ $(t-1 \leq \tau \leq t)$. The value, $\xi_{i,j}$, stands for 1 if students whose achievement level is more than the difficulty level $q_{j,t-1}$ answered it wrongly or students whose level is less than $q_{j,t-1}$ answered it correctly, or 0 otherwise. The initial difficulty level of question j, $q_{j,0}$, is given with the attribute LEVEL of DEL tag by teachers.

Figure 1 illustrates the concept of re-estimating question's difficulty level based on students' achievement level. Point $q_{j,t-1}$ is the difficulty level of question j at time $t-1$. The achievement level of students AEGIS gave question j is distributed in the neighborhood of $q_{j,t-1}$. The distribution seems to be represented by the curve shown in Fig. 1. If a student whose achievement level is less (greater) than $q_{j,t-1}$ answers it correctly (incorrectly), he/she falls into the shaded (dotted) area. Assuming that the difficulty level of the question is overestimated (underestimated) if the area is not empty, AEGIS decreases (increases) the level. An intersection point of the horizontal axis and the line connecting (M_c, N_w) and $(M_w, -N_c)$ finally becomes a new difficulty level of the question, where M_c (M_w) is the mean of the achievement level of students who are contained in the shaded (dotted) area, and N_c (N_w) is the number of the students.

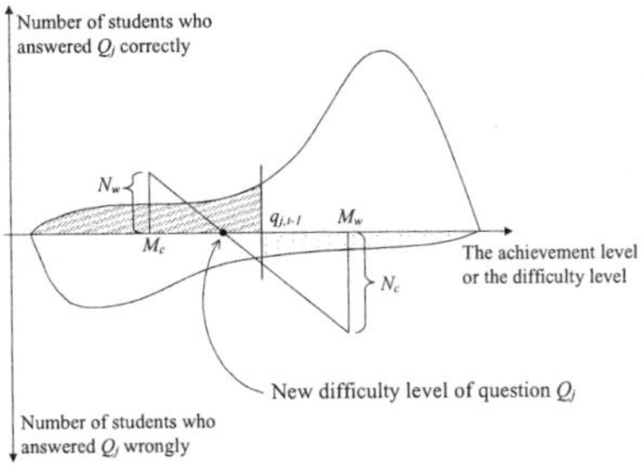

Figure 1: Renewing the difficulty level of a question based on students' achievement level

3 Evaluation with Simulator

AEGIS estimates dynamically both the achievement level and the difficulty level with the equations defined in Section 2. In order to examine their validities, we experimented with a simulator. We assumed that a student correctly (incorrectly) answered questions whose inherent difficulty level($q^{(TRUE)}$) was less (more) than his/her inherent achievement level($s^{(TRUE)}$) and he/she could correctly answer the question with 50% probability if $q^{(TRUE)}$ was equal to $s^{(TRUE)}$. We prepared 100 questions whose inherent difficulty levels were distributed at the equal interval from 0 to 10. Each difficulty level ($q^{(AEGIS)}$) is initialized by $q^{(TRUE)}$. We also prepared 100 students whose inherent levels are distributed between 0 and 10 at the equal intervals. We investigated the following three things:

(1) How does AEGIS estimate the achievement level of a student?

We pulled out the achievement level ($s^{(AEGIS)}$) of three students whose inherent achievement levels are high ($s^{(TRUE)} = 8.0$), middle ($s^{(TRUE)} = 5.0$) and low ($s^{(TRUE)} = 2.0$). Figure 2-(a) shows the variance of $s^{(AEGIS)}$ in a simulation. They were gradually separated each other because they answered questions correctly or incorrectly based on their inherent achievement level. As was expected, each curve of $s^{(AEGIS)}$ in our simulation approximates closely the value of $s^{(TRUE)}$ after about 50 re-estimations.

(2) Can AEGIS provide only questions suitable for a student?

We applied 1,000 questions of various difficulty levels to these students so as to confirm that AEGIS generates good questions suitable for the students' achievement level. Figure 2-(b) shows the distributions of the difficulty levels of questions which each student tried to solve. A student of high (resp. middle, low) achievement level tried a lot of questions of high (resp. middle, low) difficulty level. Let (x, y) be a pair of the mean value x and the standard deviation y of each distribution. (x, y) of each curve is (1.7, 0.82), (4.6, 1.02) and (7.5, 1.19), respectively. This result shows that AEGIS generates questions suitable for the students' achievement level.

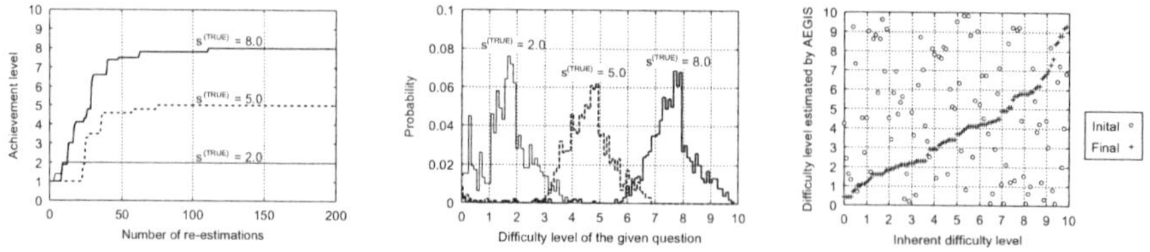

(a) The achievement level (b) The distribution of the given questions (c) The distribution of the difficulty level estimated by AEGIS

Figure 2: Results of the evaluation of AEGIS

(3) How does AEGIS estimate the difficulty level of a question?

We made AEGIS calculate the difficulty level ($q^{(AEGIS)}$) which are initialized by a random number. The distribution of $q^{(AEGIS)}$ is shown in Figure 2-(c). The value of $q^{(AEGIS)}$ of the question whose $q^{(TURE)}$ is high (low) increases (decreases) every re-estimation. The points of $q^{(AEGIS)}$ finally place in order of $q^{(TRUE)}$. We conclude that our method can well estimate the inherent difficulty level of each question.

4 Conclusion and Further work

AEGIS is consequently utilized as not only a system generating exercises but also a tool classifying questions because the re-estimated level keeps close to their real difficulty level. Experimental results with the simulator showed the effectiveness of the algorithm estimating both the achievement level of a student and the difficulty level of a question as were expected. We have a plan to evaluate this system by applying it to the real courses of Computer Literacy, which are taken by more than 2300 students at Kyushu University. We hope it will work fine as an educational tool for every student and help him/her to understand his/her subjects.

This research was partly supported by Kyushu University, the Grant for Special Academic Research P&P, Type C and supported by the Grants-in-Aid for Scientific Research, Priority Areas Research.

References

[1] P. Browning, "TUTORIAL MARKUP LANGUAGE - A CBA SYSTEM," 1998, http://www.soton.ac.uk/ ukgec/workshop/5-cba/minutes.htm#TUTORIAL.

[2] A. Carbone and P. Schendzielorz, "A Web-Based Quiz Generator for Use in Tutorials and Assessment," Global J. of Engng. Educ., vol.I, no.3, 1997, http://www.eng.monash.edu.au/usicee/gjee/vol1no3/paper20.htm.

[3] ClassBuilder GradeBook And Exam Creation Software, http://www.classbuilder.com.

[4] T. Mine, D. Nagano, K. Baba, T. Shoudai, and S. Hirokawa, "On-web visualizing a mechanism of a single chip computer for computer literacy courses," Proc. Int. Conf. on Computers in Education, ICCE'98, vol. 2, pp.496–499, 1998.

[5] T. Mine, A. Suganuma, and T. Shoudai, "The Design and Implementation of Automatic Exercise Generator with Tagged Documents based on the Intelligence of Students: AEGIS," Proc. Int. Conf. on Computers in Education, pp.651-658, 2000.

[6] A. Suganuma, R. Fujimoto, and Y. Tsutsumi, "An WWW-based Supporting System Realizing Cooperative Environment for Classroom Teaching," Proc. World Conf. on the WWW and Internet, pp.830-831, 2000.

Knowledge-based Software Engineering
T. Welzer et al. (Eds.)
IOS Press, 2002

A Method for Efficient Searching at Online Shopping

Tomomi Sanjo
Graduate School of Science and Technology, Keio University
3-14-1 Hiyoshi, Yokohama, 223-8522, Japan
e-mail: sanjo@ae.keio.ac.jp

Morio NAGATA
Faculty of Science and Technology, Keio University
3-14-1 Hiyoshi, Yokohama, 223-8522, Japan
e-mail: nagata@ae.keio.ac.jp

Abstract. Since online shopping has been popularized, it is needed to improve its usability. In order to find out the problems on usability, we observed searching behaviors of some T-shirts at the Web sites. Then, we found that existing search engines on the Web showed too much information for them. This paper proposes an easy search method for goods at online malls. This engine has the following facilities. First, it presents information in a uniform format. Second, the user can find goods by selecting structured keywords. Third, it presents only necessary information by using the user's history of searching. We show the effectives of our proposal with some experiments.

1 Introduction

Since online shopping has become popular recently, some usability problems have been recognized [1]. So we provide 3 facilities to solve problems on difficult searching. We have implemented a search engine including functions to solve it [2]. Using this engine, we have conducted experiments to show the effectiveness of our proposal.

2 Popularization of Online Shopping and its Problems

Online shopping has merits for the users to access to shops everywhere in the world at anytime [3]. Moreover, the companies are able to do one-to-one marketing and the user can obtain suitable information and services at online shopping [4]. Though an essential merit of online shopping is to offer personal services, such services are not provided well [5].

2.1 Purchasing Favorite Goods at Online Malls

It is said that purchasing favorite goods at online malls is difficult. In order to find out its difficulties, we observed purchasing behaviors of some ladies' T-shirts at online malls. There are 70,814 pages related to selling ladies' T-shirts in Japan on June, 2000. The numbers are huge and the same page is displayed many times. We find that it is difficult to find needful information quickly by using existing search engines.

2.2 Problems of Existing Shopping Malls form Purchasing Favorite Goods

There are 3 types of shopping malls. Type 1 mall without searching functions; Type 2 mall with searching functions using free words and rough categories; Type 3 mall with functions using free words and detailed categories.

2.3 Questionnaires to Users

We asked 16 persons to search T-shirts by using above 3 types of shopping malls. Then we distributed questionnaire to them about their usability issues.

3 Three Problems

Our observation and the answers of questionnaires show us the following problems.

(1) Since the display forms of goods in the shops are different from each other.

(2) The user can not find goods by using prepared functions.

(3) Too much needless information for customers is shown in each page.

In order to solve above problems, this paper proposes the following methods [6].

First, to solve problem (1), we classify the goods according to groups in a uniform manner. For problem (2), we provide searching functions in accordance with the purpose of searching goods. We use the key words in a hierarchical structure by the ontology theory[7,8,9]. For problem (3), we use the user's history of keywords and make system to choose appropriate information for the user.

4 An Implementation

4.1 Data Base (DB) of Goods

We collect 50 goods, with 10 heading [names of shops], [comments about the shops], [comments about the goods], [prices of the goods], [sizes], [colors] and so on.

4.2 Key Words

Our system provides useful keywords for searching goods. At first, we extract all words to express the goods from prepared DB. Then, we classify them and generate a hierarchical structure of the keywords (Table 1). We classify these headings to 9 groups [types of fashion], [brands], [designs], [images], [others], [prices], [sizes], [colors] and [materials].

Table 1 A Part of the Hierarchical Structure of Keywords

key words	types of fashion	Asian taste	China
		casual	little T-shirt
		typical	standard
			normal
	brands		
	designs		

Moreover, we grouped some. At that time we use 3 rules to put a word in a group of the typical word. The First rule is grouping by synonyms. The second rule is grouping by colors. The last rule is grouping by images and adjectives. Next we specify a typical word to imagine the goods in a group. Using this word, the customer can search the goods in the group.

4.3 Customizing Functions

4.3.1 Using Search Histories

Our system records words used to search goods for each user. If a particular word is used over 3 times, then this system recognizes the word as one reflecting the user's favorite.

4.3.2 Extracting the User's Favorite with Non-use Keywords

We regard the words which are not used as important information. If a user purchases a goods, then our system refers the key words file. When it finds the words which are not used for purchasing it, ours system records them. If a word recorded over 3 times, we use this word automatically for searching.

4.3.3 Extracting the User's Favorite From a Relation of Keywords

This system also provides the relations of the keywords for distributing user's favorite. The relations are represented as a matrix of the words on tastes (Table 2). Based on this matrix, if a word is used over 3 times, then the related words are used for searching goods.

Table 2 Relations of Tastes

	Asian tasete	casual
Asian tasete		Asian tasete
casual	casual	
typical		
American taste		American taste

5 Experiments

The number of testees is 16. Most of them are beginner of the Internet shopping. Two of them have already enjoyed online shopping. The testees are asked to purchase goods with the specified procedure.

5.1 Effects of Standardized Form

To evaluate the effectiveness of standardized form displaying goods, we ask them to use and compare shopping malls Type 1, 2, 3 in Chapter 2 and our system. The testees are asked to evaluate 5 levels on easiness of understandings information in one page. The result is shown in Table 3.

Table 3 Understandable Infromation

Clearness of infromation (the number of persons)						
levels	1	2	3	4	5	avg of value
existing systems	0	7	5	4	0	2.8
our system	0	1	3	6	6	4.1

The testees answered that the display of our system was easy to be understood.

5.2 Effectiveness of Using Keywords

To evaluate the effectiveness of using hierarchical keyword, we ask the testees to use and compare shopping malls Type 1, 2, 3 and our proposed system, they evaluated by 5 levels of easiness for searching goods. The result is shown in Table 4.

Table 4 Easiness of Searching Goods

Easiness of searching goods (the number of persons)						
levels	1	2	3	4	5	avg of value
existing systems	3	8	3	1	1	2.3
our system	0	0	2	5	9	4.4

This result shows that provided keywords are useful to search goods.

5.3 Easiness of Using

Next, we compared time and numbers of pages finding one of favorite goods by using 3 systems and our system. This result is shown in Table 5(next page). It shows that times and pages of our system are smaller than other systems. In order to show the differences on usability between Type 1, 2, 3 and our system, we have formulated three hypothesizes that there exist no differences between Type 1, 2, 3 and our system respectively on searching time. Using t-test at significant level 10%, we can reject two hypotheses about Type 2, 3 and our system respectively. On the other hand, we can not reject the hypothesis there exists a difference between Type 1 and our system. Since Type 1 has no facilities to support searching, the users abandoned their searching within 5 minutes or so. These results show that usability of our system is better than those of existing systems.

Table 5 Time and Pages (average values)

system	Type1	Type2	Type3	Our System
time (min)	6.6	5.6	6.8	24
s.d.	14.0	20.5	32.1	5.9
page	22.9	22.7	33.4	9.3
s.d.	4.5	4.7	5.1	1.1

5.4 Effectiveness of customization

To evaluate the effectiveness of customization, we ask testees to find 15 goods within database of our system. Next, 15 goods are selected automatically by our system from histories of searching goods. We counted the numbers of favorite goods included automatic selection (Table 6).

Table 6 Numbers of Favorites Goods

	I	II
The number of goods	5.3	6.5

I: The number of goods which are favorite but not included in automatic selection
II: The number of goods which are favorite and included in automatic selection

6 Conclusions

We proposed a system to reflect the user's favorite and to show only needful information. This system uses key words on favorite goods and relations of them. Moreover, it uses the history of each user. These facilities are effective to improve usability of online shopping. However, the following issues are left as future problems. First, we should generate a more precise structure of the keywords. Second, these keywords should be automatically extracted from the sentences written in the natural language.

Reference

[1] OECD/Katuyoshi Mita: Electric Commerce as The Condition of Globalization Market for Customer, CAP, 1999

[2] Tomomi Sanjo, Morio Nagata : A Proposal to Search Items Effectively at Online shopping, 62nd Information Processing Society of Japan, National General Meeting, 2001, 8L-03

[3] Oota Kain : EDI [Electric Commerce] Guide, Marketing Strategy of Electric Commerce, Diamond Harbored · Business, Chu-ou Keizai Sha 1996

[4] Asaoka Tomoo/Ide Kazuaki, Koyama Kenji One to One : Internet Era's Super Marketing, IDL, BNN, 1998

[5] Robert H. Guttman, Alexandor G. Moukas, and Pattie Maes: Agent-mediated Electronic Commerce : A Survey, Proc. of ICIS 1999, 1999, pp. 1-10

[6] Weiguo Fan, Michael D. Gordon: Personalization of search engine services for effective retrieval and knowledge management, Proc. of ICIS 2000, 2000, pp. 20-34

[7] Nakano Mikio, Nasugawa Tetuya, Natural Language Processing for Spread the Field, Information Processing, Vol.40, No.4, 2000, pp. 351～386

[8] Mizoguti Riichiro: Towards Ontology Engineering, The Seventh Pacific Rim International Conference on Artificial Intelligence, Vol. 13, No. 1, 1996, pp. 9～10

[9] Ikeda Mituru :Ontology as the Infrastructure of The Knowledge Ontology, The Seventh Pacific Rim International Conference on Artificial Intelligence, Vol. 13, No. 1, 1996, pp. 11～13

Author Index